Rethinking the
SAT

The Future of Standardized Testing in University Admissions

Rethinking the
SAT

The Future of Standardized Testing in University Admissions

edited by
Rebecca Zwick

ROUTLEDGEFALMER
NEW YORK AND LONDON

Atkinson, Richard C., "Achievement versus Aptitude in College Admissions," *Issues in Science and Technology,* Winter 2001–02, pp. 31–36. Copyright © 2002 by the University of Texas at Dallas, Richardson, Texas. Reprinted with permission.

Geiser, Saul with Roger Studley, "UC and the SAT: Predictive Validity and Differential Impact of the SAT I and SAT II at the University of California," *Educational Assessment,* vol. 8, no. 1, pp. 1–26. Copyright © 2002 by Lawrence Erlbaum Associates, Inc. Reprinted with permission.

Lawrence, Ida M. et al., "A Historical Perspective on the Content of the SAT®," College Board Report No. 2003-3. Copyright © 2003 by College Entrance Examination Board. Adapted with permission. All rights reserved. www.collegeboard.com.

Published in 2004 by
RoutledgeFalmer
29 West 35th Street
New York, NY 10001
www.routledge-ny.com

Published in Great Britain by
RoutledgeFalmer
11 New Fetter Lane
London EC4P 4EE
www.routledge.co.uk

10   9   8   7   6   5   4   3   2   1

Cataloging-in-Publication Data is available from the Library of Congress
ISBN 0-415-948355 (paperback)
ISBN 0-415-948347 (hardcover)

Contents

Preface

Rethinking the SAT: The Future of Standardized Testing in University Admissions took shape during a unique period in the history of college admissions policy. The conference on which it is based was spurred by a February 2001 speech by University of California president Richard C. Atkinson, in which he recommended the elimination of the SAT I (the test we know as "the SAT") as a criterion for admission to the university and advocated an immediate switch to college admissions tests that are tied closely to the high school curriculum.

As *Rethinking the SAT* got off the ground in late 2001, educators, students, policymakers, and journalists around the country were debating the virtues and flaws of the SAT. At the same time, discussions of a more formal kind were taking place between the University of California and the two companies that produce college admissions tests, the College Board and ACT, Inc. In early 2002, the College Board announced that it planned to alter the SAT I; the proposed changes were approved by College Board trustees in June. The new SAT, scheduled to be in place by 2005, will substitute short reading items for the controversial verbal analogy items, incorporate more advanced math content, and add a writing section. These changes are expected to better align the test with the college preparatory courses UC applicants are required to take. Several months later, ACT, Inc. announced that it too would make a change by adding an optional writing section to the ACT during the 2004–2005 school year.

Finally, as *Rethinking the SAT* was being completed, the U.S. Supreme Court ruled on a pair of cases of monumental importance, *Gratz v. Bollinger* and *Grutter v. Bollinger,* which concerned the legality of affirmative action programs in undergraduate and law school admissions at the University of Michigan. This was the first time that the Court had weighed in on affirmative action in university admissions since the *Regents of the University of California v. Bakke* ruling in 1978. While the Court ruled against the undergraduate affirmative action program involved in the *Gratz* case, which awarded bonus points to minority candidates, its decision in *Grutter* strongly endorsed the overall legitimacy of affirmative action policies. According to the majority opinion by Justice Sandra Day O'Connor, "student body diversity is a compelling state interest that can justify the use of race in university admissions."

Rethinking the SAT addresses themes that are at the heart of these significant recent developments: What is the purpose of college admissions testing? What is the history of admissions testing in California and elsewhere? How are admissions test scores related to students' cultural background and academic preparation? How well do these tests predict academic success? Most basically, the book's authors address the question, How should we decide which students get the opportunity to go to the college of their choice?

Since about 65% of four-year institutions admit at least three-quarters of their applicants, a high school student's chances of getting into *some* college are quite good. But most applicants have their sights set on a particular school. At UC Berkeley and UCLA, fewer than one-third of the applicants are accepted; at Harvard, Stanford, and Yale Universities, applicants outnumber available spaces by more than six to one. Clearly, these schools can't simply "pull up some more chairs to the table," a disingenuous metaphor that is sometimes invoked in the admissions context. Instead, the hard truth is that granting one candidate a seat means keeping another one out.

What is the most equitable way to allocate the limited number of slots in prestigious schools? Americans have always been of two minds about this. At the core of our national self-image is a commitment to the idea of providing citizens with equal opportunities for high-quality education. So, if we want all applicants to have equal access to the college of their choice, why not have a "first come, first served" policy, or even a lottery? In fact, the lottery idea has been proposed from time to time and has recently been suggested by Harvard professor Lani Guinier. But even though a lottery admissions policy might seem to exemplify equal opportunity, it would not be popular if it became a reality. Inevitably, some undistinguished and unmotivated students would, by the luck of the draw, win seats in the freshman class away from smart, hardworking kids. And this would be met with outrage because it's also "American" to reward academic excellence, perseverance, and hard work. The lottery seems unfair precisely *because* it doesn't take these into account. Schools, then, are left to seek methods of selecting from among the candidates vying for places. Entrance examinations are one such method.

History of Standardized Testing

Standardized testing had its beginnings in Chinese civil service assessments during the Han dynasty, or possibly even earlier.[1] University admissions tests have a much shorter history, of course, but there is some disagreement about the time and location of the first such test. According to some accounts, admissions testing had its debut in eighteenth-century France. The idea of admitting students to universities based on test scores, rather than privilege, was certainly compatible with the principles of equality that characterized the French Enlightenment. But another account of testing history alludes to an earlier French admissions test—a Sorbonne entrance examination that was required in the thirteenth century. And a College Board publication titled "Why Hispanic Students Need to Take the SAT" claims that admissions testing originated in Spain, noting, "It was in Madrid in 1575 that a scholar . . . proposed that the king establish an examination board to determine university admission." Most historians agree that admissions testing had been instituted in Germany and England by the mid-1800s. It's interesting that in most countries, the use of tests to get *out* of universities preceded the use of tests to get *in*. In the early part of the nineteenth century, when Oxford and Cambridge Universities established stricter examination procedures for graduation, it was still the case that anyone who had the money could get into these prestigious universities.

Standardized admissions testing first took root in the United States during the early part of the twentieth century. In 1900, only about 2% of 17-year-olds—more than three-quarters of them men—went on to receive a college degree. Those applying to college at the turn of the century were faced with a bewildering array of admissions criteria. Course requirements and entrance examinations differed widely across schools. In an attempt to impose order on this chaos, the leaders of 12 top northeastern universities formed a new organization, the College Entrance Examination Board, in 1900. The College Board created a set of examinations that were administered by the member institutions and then shipped back to the Board for painstaking hand scoring. Initially, the Board developed essay tests in nine subject areas, including English, history, Greek and Latin; it later developed a new exam that contained mostly multiple-choice questions—the Scholastic Aptitude Test. This precursor to today's SAT was first administered in 1926 to about 8,000 candidates.

The first SAT consisted of questions similar to those included in the Army Alpha tests, which had been developed by a team of psychologists for use in selecting and assigning military recruits in World War I. These Army tests, in turn, were directly descended from IQ tests, which had made their first U.S. appearance in the early 1900s.

In World War II, as in World War I, tests played a role in screening individuals for military service and assigning them to jobs. During this period, both the College Board and the Iowa Testing Programs, which would later spawn the testing company ACT, Inc., helped the military develop personnel tests. Although the publicity about wartime testing was not always favorable, it produced a surge of interest by educational institutions. World War II also fueled an expansion in the use of standardized testing by creating an urgent need for well-trained individuals who could be recruited into the military; this led to an increased emphasis on college study in the U.S. And the passage of the GI Bill in 1944 sent thousands of returning veterans to college, boosting the popularity of the efficient multiple-choice SAT.

Between the wars, another development took place which was to have a major impact on the testing enterprise—the automatic scoring of tests. Beginning in 1939, the monumental task that had once required many hours of training and tedious clerical work—scoring the SAT—was done by a machine. This change effectively transformed testing from an academic venture to a bona fide industry.

In 1947, Educational Testing Service (ETS) was founded in Princeton, New Jersey, through the merger of the testing activities of the College Board, the Carnegie Foundation for the Advancement of Teaching, and the American Council on Education (all three of which continue to exist as separate organizations). Today, the SAT (now officially called the SAT I: Reasoning Test) is developed and administered by ETS for the College Board, which is the owner of the test. The SAT I is intended to measure "developed verbal and mathematical reasoning abilities related to successful performance in college." (Originally, SAT stood for Scholastic Aptitude Test, which was later changed to Scholastic Assessment Test. Now, SAT is no longer considered to be an acronym, but the actual name of the test.) All the verbal questions and most of the math questions are multiple-choice; each SAT also includes a few math questions that require "student-produced" answers—there are no response choices.

In 1959, a competitor to the SAT in the college admissions test market emerged—the ACT. The American College Testing Program was begun in Iowa City "with no equipment and not even one full-time employee," according to the organization's own description. (Today, the test is simply the ACT, and the company is ACT, Inc. Like SAT, ACT is no longer considered an acronym.)

ACT, Inc. was founded by E. F. Lindquist, a University of Iowa statistician and a man of many talents. Lindquist was the director of the Iowa

Testing Programs, which instituted the first major statewide testing effort for high school students. As an acknowledged expert in standardized testing, he served on ETS's first advisory committee on tests and measurements. Remarkably, he was also the inventor, with Phillip Rulon of Harvard, of the "Iowa scoring machine." Unveiled at a conference sponsored by rival ETS in 1953, this device was the first to use electronic scanning techniques (rather than simply a mechanical approach) to score test answer sheets.

Why start a new college admissions testing program? In Iowa testing circles, the SAT was considered to be geared toward the elite institutions of the east, and its developers were viewed as resistant to change. From the beginning, the ACT was somewhat different from the SAT in terms of underlying philosophy: While the SAT consisted only of verbal and mathematical sections, the ACT was more closely tied to instructional objectives. The original version of the ACT had four sections—English, mathematics, social-studies reading, and natural-sciences reading. It's no coincidence that these subject areas were also included in the Iowa Tests of Educational Development (ITED), which had been used to assess Iowa high schoolers since 1942. In fact, because of scheduling constraints, the first ACT was constructed from the same pool of test items that was being used to assemble new forms of the ITED. In its early years, the ACT was administered primarily in Midwestern states, but it is now used nationwide.

The content of today's ACT is based on an analysis of what is taught in grades 7 through 12 in each of four areas—English, math, reading, and science. Educators are consulted to determine which of these skills they consider necessary for students in college courses. All questions are currently multiple-choice.

Despite decades of contentious debate about standardized admissions testing, about 90% of American colleges and universities require either the ACT or SAT, and both testing programs have recently announced an increase in the number of test takers.

The Genesis of This Book

UC president Richard Atkinson's February 2001 speech reignited ongoing controversies about the use of standardized tests in college admissions. Supporters regard standardized admissions tests as "common yardsticks" for measuring students' academic achievement or potential in a fair and balanced way. But in the eyes of many, these tests restrict educational opportunities for people of color, women, and other groups. And although Atkinson himself made it clear he was not against testing per se, he said he opposed the SAT I partly because it is viewed as being "akin to an IQ test."

The Academic Senate Center for Faculty Outreach and the Committee on Admissions and Enrollment at the University of California, Santa Barbara (UCSB) decided to sponsor a conference, to be held in November 2001, that would allow educators and researchers to engage in a public discussion of these issues. Support for the conference also came from the UC Office of the President and the UCSB Chancellor's Office. The conference coordinating committee was cochaired by Walter W. Yuen, professor of mechanical and environmental engineering and faculty director of the Center for Faculty Outreach, and Michael T. Brown, professor of education and chair of the Committee on Admissions and Enrollment (2000–2002). The other members of the coordinating committee were J. Manuel Casas, Richard P. Durán, Sarah Fenstermaker, Richard Flacks, Alice O'Connor, Denise Segura, and I, representing the Departments of Education, History, and Sociology. The committee members represented a wide variety of views on testing and admissions policy, but all agreed that the conference should address the topic of college admissions very broadly and should not be restricted to a narrow discussion of the pros and cons of the SAT.

Despite its occurrence just two months after the terrorist attacks of September 11, 2001, the conference drew about 350 participants from around the country. The keynote address was given by Richard Atkinson, who was followed by Richard Ferguson, president of ACT, Inc. and Gaston Caperton, president of the College Board. Another featured speaker at the conference was Nicholas Lemann, author of *The Big Test: The Secret History of the American Meritocracy*. In addition to the invited sessions, the conference featured presentations by educators and researchers from universities and testing organizations.

The conference coordinating committee was enthusiastic about the possibility of creating a book based on the conference. As the book's editor, I felt strongly that *Rethinking the SAT* should not be a "proceedings" volume that simply documented the conference presentations. Instead, the book was to be an edited and reviewed compilation of the strongest conference contributions that would be accessible to a wide readership, including college and university officials; high school principals, teachers, and guidance counselors; parents of high school students; legislators and educational policymakers; and members of the press.

The Academic Senate Office of UCSB generously agreed to support the publication of the book. An editorial board was assembled, consisting of UCSB faculty members Michael T. Brown, Joseph I. Castro, Richard P. Durán, Richard Flacks, and Walter W. Yuen. Liz Alix, a staff member in the Department of Education, was hired as editorial assistant. Presenters were asked whether they wanted to participate in the book project; only a few ultimately decided not to do so. The editorial board initially evaluated each potential contribution, recommended which should be included in the book, and suggested revisions. With a few exceptions, such as the featured presentations by Atkinson, Ferguson, Caperton, and Lemann, the contributions were also sent to outside reviewers. I reviewed and edited each contribution and Liz Alix copyedited each paper. We solicited several revisions from most authors in order to allow for the incorporation of reviews and editorial comments, reduce technical content, and achieve comparability with other contributions in length and style.

A special procedure was followed for the addresses by Atkinson, Ferguson, and Caperton. Because we did not have prepared texts that corresponded fully with these presentations, we had the speeches transcribed and sent them to the authors. Atkinson chose to use an earlier version of his talk that had already appeared in published form; Ferguson and Caperton elected to use edited versions of the transcripts.

Instead of including the presentations in the order in which they occurred at the conference, the book has been organized thematically into four sections:

- *Part I, Standardized Tests and American Education: What Is the Past and Future of College Admissions Testing in the United States?* includes the featured addresses by Atkinson, Ferguson, and Caperton, as well as the special presentation by Nicholas Lemann. Also contained here are other chapters about the history, design, and purpose of admissions tests.
- *Part II, College Admissions Testing in California: How Did the California SAT Debate Arise?* is devoted to the SAT debate in California. Its first chapter gives a historical context for the recent debates about the use of admissions testing in California; the second gives a detailed account of the analyses of University of California admissions data conducted by the UC Office of the President.
- *Part III, Race, Class, and Admissions Testing: How Are Test Scores Related to Student Background and Academic Preparation?* addresses the academic preparation and test performance of students from various ethnic and socioeconomic backgrounds, and also features a chapter on SAT coaching.
- *Part IV, The Predictive Value of Admissions Tests: How Well Do Tests Predict Academic Success for Students from a Variety of Backgrounds?* includes research contributions concerning the predictive effectiveness of admissions tests, as well as chapters about alternatives to current admissions procedures. The final paper presents the position of FairTest, a testing watchdog organization.

After these four sections of the book were assembled, experts in higher education and testing were selected to write commentaries that would follow each section. We were very fortunate to recruit as commentators Michael W. Kirst of Stanford University (part I), Eva L. Baker of UCLA (part II), Michael E. Martinez of UC Irvine (part III), and Robert L. Linn of the University of Colorado (part IV).

Note

1. The portion of this preface that describes the history of admissions testing is drawn in part from Chapter 1 of Zwick, R., *Fair Game? The Use of Standardized Admissions Tests in Higher Education.* New York: Routledge Falmer, 2002.

Acknowledgments

I would like to thank the many contributors to this book, especially the conference presenters who tirelessly revised their papers, and the authors of the commentaries that appear at the end of each section of the book. I also greatly appreciate the work of the editorial board members and the additional reviewers: Betsy Jane Becker, Brent Bridgeman, Derek C. Briggs, Wayne J. Camara, Neil J. Dorans, Howard T. Everson, Saul Geiser, Ben Hansen, Janet Helms, Daniel Koretz, David F. Lohman, Michael E. Martinez, Julie Noble, Jesse Rothstein, Amy Elizabeth Schmidt, Jeffrey C. Sklar, Roger E. Studley, Steven C. Velasco, Michael Walker, and John W. Young.

I am most grateful to the University of California Office of the President and the University of California, Santa Barbara for their sponsorship of the conference and the associated book project, and to Claudia Chapman, Marisela Marquez, and Randall Stoskopf of UCSB for their help with the administrative activities needed to bring the project to fruition. I am also thankful to Catherine Bernard of Routledge for her role in making the book a reality.

Special heartfelt thanks go to Liz Alix, the book's editorial assistant, who was responsible for the daily coordination of the project, including contacts with authors, reviewers, editorial board members, transcribers, and publishing staff. But her contributions do not end there: She also skillfully edited every author manuscript, commentary, and preface in this volume. It is no exaggeration to say that the book would not have been completed without her.

Rebecca Zwick
July 2003

List of Contributors

Richard C. Atkinson, President, University of California

Eva L. Baker, Professor, Graduate School of Education and Information Studies, University of California, Los Angeles

Brent Bridgeman, Principal Research Scientist, Educational Testing Service

Derek C. Briggs, Assistant Professor, Quantitative Methods and Policy Analysis, School of Education, University of Colorado, Boulder

Michael T. Brown, Professor, Gevirtz Graduate School of Education, University of California, Santa Barbara

Nancy Burton, Senior Research Scientist, Educational Testing Service

Wayne J. Camara, Vice President, Research and Development, The College Board

Gaston Caperton, President, The College Board

Frederick Cline, Lead Research Data Analyst, Educational Testing Service

Howard T. Everson, Vice President and Chief Research Scientist, The College Board, and Research Professor of Psychology and Education, Teachers College, Columbia University

Richard Ferguson, Chief Executive Officer, ACT, Inc.

Patricia Gándara, Professor, School of Education, University of California, Davis

Saul Geiser, Director, Research and Evaluation, Academic Affairs, University of California, Office of the President

Manuel N. Gómez, Vice Chancellor, Student Affairs, University of California, Irvine

Carol Jackson, Assessment Specialist, School and College Services Division, Educational Testing Service

Michael W. Kirst, Professor, School of Education, Stanford University

Jennifer L. Kobrin, Associate Research Scientist, The College Board

Ida Lawrence, Director, Program Research, Research and Development Division, Educational Testing Service

Nicholas Lemann, Henry R. Luce Professor and Dean, Columbia University Graduate School of Journalism

Robert L. Linn, Distinguished Professor, School of Education, University of Colorado, Boulder

David F. Lohman, Professor, College of Education, University of Iowa

Michael E. Martinez, Associate Professor, Department of Education, University of California, Irvine, and Division of Research, Evaluation, and Communication, The National Science Foundation

Glenn B. Milewski, Assistant Research Scientist, The College Board

Julie Noble, Principal Research Associate, ACT, Inc.

Christina Perez, University Testing Reform Advocate, FairTest

Dorothy A. Perry, Associate Professor and Assistant Dean for Curricular Affairs, School of Dentistry, University of California, San Francisco

Gretchen Rigol, Former Vice President, The College Board

Barbara A. Sawrey, Vice Chair, Department of Chemistry and Biochemistry, University of California, San Diego

Amy Elizabeth Schmidt, Director of Higher Education Research, The College Board

Roger E. Studley, Coordinator, Admissions Research, Student Academic Services, University of California, Office of the President

Tom Van Essen, Executive Director, School and College Services Division, Educational Testing Service

John W. Young, Associate Professor, Graduate School of Education, Rutgers University

Rebecca Zwick, Professor, Gevirtz Graduate School of Education, University of California, Santa Barbara

Editorial Board

Liz Alix, Editorial Assistant

Michael T. Brown, Professor, Gevirtz Graduate School of Education, University of California, Santa Barbara

Joseph I. Castro, Adjunct Associate Professor of Education and Executive Director of Campus Outreach Initiatives, University of California, Santa Barbara

Richard P. Durán, Professor, Gevirtz Graduate School of Education, University of California, Santa Barbara

Richard Flacks, Professor of Sociology, University of California, Santa Barbara

Walter W. Yuen, Professor of Mechanical and Environmental Engineering, University of California, Santa Barbara

Standardized Tests and American Education: What Is the Past and Future of College Admissions Testing in the United States?

This section of the book contains the keynote speech by University of California President Richard C. Atkinson, the featured presentations by the presidents of ACT, Inc. and the College Board, and other chapters about the history, design, and purpose of admissions tests. The section opens with a chapter by Nicholas Lemann, author of *The Big Test: The Secret History of the American Meritocracy* (Farrar, Straus, and Giroux, 1999). Lemann gives a historical context for the recent debates about the SAT. He describes the ways in which the test was shaped by the development of intelligence tests in the early 1900s and by the ideas of James Bryant Conant. As President of Harvard University, Conant sought to use educational testing to admit a more intellectual student body. Although Conant hoped that the use of the SAT would be democratizing, Lemann is convinced that the impact of the SAT has been substantially negative, and he applauds Atkinson's proposal to place a greater emphasis on achievement tests in university admissions.

Lemann's chapter is followed by the contribution from Richard C. Atkinson, which appeared previously in *Issues in Science and Technology*, a publication of the National Academy of Sciences, the National Academy of Engineering, and the University of Texas; Atkinson presented a version of this article, "Achievement versus Aptitude in College Admissions," at the UCSB conference. Atkinson takes a backward look at his February 2001 speech, in which he advocated the elimination of the SAT I as an admissions criterion. He notes that he was surprised by the amount of public reaction—and public misunderstanding—that followed his proposal. He is not, he points out, opposed to standardized testing per se. Instead, his proposal called for the use of tests that measure achievement in specific subject areas. Another of his goals is "to move all UC campuses away from admissions processes employing quantitative formulas and toward a comprehensive evaluation of applicants." Atkinson argues that these changes will increase the fairness of UC admissions policy and will also have a beneficial effect on K–12 education.

In the two subsequent chapters, Richard Ferguson, President of ACT, Inc., and Gaston Caperton, President of the College Board, react to Atkinson's recommendations. Ferguson makes the case that the ACT exam is, and always has been, achievement based, and that it is already substantially in line with Atkinson's proposals. The ACT could be further augmented, Ferguson suggests, to be even better aligned with the college preparatory courses required of UC applicants. He explains the philosophy underlying the ACT, describes the curriculum surveys that are used in its development, and outlines the content of its four components: English, mathematics, reading, and science. Gaston Caperton discusses the history of the College Board and of the SAT. While acknowledging that the SAT has roots in intelligence testing, Caperton argues that comparing the original SAT to the modern SAT is like comparing "what a Chevrolet was 75 years ago and is today." Today's SAT, he says, "measures students' ability to think and reason using words and numbers," skills that are essential in college. Finally, Caperton calls for efforts to improve educational opportunity for all students "long before they sit for the SAT."

The next two contributions, by Manuel N. Gómez and David F. Lohman, are commentaries on the presentations by Atkinson, Ferguson, and Caperton. Gómez makes a strong case for the use of achievement rather than aptitude tests in admissions. He cites UC's own research on the relative predictive value of the SAT I: Reasoning Test and the SAT II: Subject Tests, and also makes note of the finding of Claude Steele and Joshua Aronson that "high-achieving minority students perform very differently on these tests depending on whether they are told the tests are measuring 'intellectual ability' or problem solving 'not intended as diagnostic of ability.'" Gómez is concerned that the SAT does not level the academic bar, as sometimes asserted, and that it has taken on an exaggerated importance in the public mind. A different view is presented by David Lohman, who suggests that "aptitude tests that go beyond prior achievement have an important role to play in admissions decisions, especially for minority students." He presents evidence that scores on "well-constructed measures of developed reasoning abilities" show smaller disparities among ethnic groups than scores on good achievement tests, and argues that tests of reasoning ability can help admissions officers to identify students who do not do well on curriculum tests but can succeed academically if they try hard. According to Lohman, the "problem with the current version of the SAT I may not be that it is an aptitude test, but that it is not enough of an aptitude test."

In the next chapter, Ida Lawrence, Gretchen Rigol, Tom Van Essen, and Carol Jackson discuss the changes in the mathematical and verbal content of the SAT between 1926 and 2002. The 1926 SAT was a stringently timed exam that included seven verbal subtests and two math subtests. Since that time, many rounds of changes have occurred, including a substantial overhaul in 1994 that was based on the advice of a blue-ribbon panel, the Commission on New Possibilities for the Admissions Testing Program. The commission recommended that the content of the test "approximate more closely the skills used in college and high school work." Reading passages grew longer and the associated questions became more analytical. Antonym items were eliminated. Another change was the introduction of some math questions that required students to produce their own solutions rather than select from multiple choices. Also, for the first time, the use of calculators was permitted on the math exams. The authors discuss the SAT changes planned for 2005, which are intended to enhance its curriculum alignment, in light of these previous modifications.

The following chapter, by Howard T. Everson, also discusses changes to the SAT, but in a different context: He proposes a design framework for future college admission tests. The time is right for considering such a framework, Everson argues, because of pressure from educational reformers as well as advances in computing and communications technology and the growing influence of cognitive psychology on assessment. He suggests that the use of more sophisticated cognitive and psychometric models could ultimately "provide descriptions of the students' knowledge or ability structures, as well as the cognitive processes presumed to underlie performance." Test results would therefore be more "diagnostic" in nature and could inform decisions about classroom instruction. Everson ends by describing some promising research efforts that are currently underway in the areas of writing assessment, tests of strategic learning ability, and measures of creative and practical intelligence.

In his commentary on Part I, Michael W. Kirst focuses on the "disconnectedness" of the K–16 education system. He points out that universities typically fail to consider the impact of admissions testing policy on secondary-school students and teachers. Likewise, secondary schools do not take into account the effect of proliferating K–12 assessments on postsecondary institutions. And there is no K–16 accountability system that brings the two disjoint groups of institutions together. Kirst calls for forums that will allow secondary and postsecondary educators and policymakers to deliberate together about assessment issues. He ends by describing some limited but promising programs that are underway in some states to promote linkage between secondary school and university educators.

A History of Admissions Testing

NICHOLAS LEMANN

I worked on my book, *The Big Test: The Secret History of the American Meritocracy,* in relative isolation from 1992 until 1999, when it was published, and even after that I had the feeling that it was almost impossible to conduct the discussion that I had hoped for about the SAT and the issues surrounding it. So it is incredibly gratifying to be able to come to the state where much of the book is set and to find that, thanks to President Atkinson, a debate that should have occurred half a century ago has now been fully joined, and that I get to be a part of it.

I am not a professional educator, and I am also not a statistician or a psychometrician. Plenty of first-rate people in those categories are on the roster for this weekend's conference. I don't think it's useful for me to focus on the specific content of the SAT or its predictive validity relative to other tests. Instead I think that I can contribute best by laying out the history of the big test and the ideas that underlay its growth. I do know more about that than most people here, because the Educational Testing Service, almost a decade ago, kindly granted me access to its extensive historical archive, and I then spent a great deal of time working there. Given the importance of the SAT, it was odd that, outside of a couple of in-house histories produced by ETS and the College Board, the story of how it came to be had never been told in book form. To the millions of people who took the test, it simply existed, like the air we breathe.

But of course nothing simply exists. Not only are tests constructed, like every other social institution; if they are as widely used as the SAT, their use has been constructed also. It is important that we understand how and why that happened—and it's an interesting story, too.

The College Entrance Examination Board was founded 101 years ago. Its purpose, then as now, was to act as an interface between high schools and colleges, which was something both sides wanted, for somewhat different reasons. High schools like to be able to give their students the option of going on to a wide range of institutions of higher education, which is much easier if those institutions have a uniform admissions process. And universities like to ensure that their incoming students are prepared at a uniformly high level, which they can do in part by using admissions tests to influence the high school curriculum. The most notable difference between the College Board then and now was that at its founding, and for fifty years thereafter, it had a small membership mainly confined to northeastern elite boarding and private day schools and to the Ivy League and Seven Sisters colleges into which they fed their graduates. The College Boards, as the board's tests were called, were hand-graded essay exams based on the boarding school curriculum, which each student took over a period of several days.

In 1905 Alfred Binet first administered his famous intelligence test in Paris. Very quickly, here in California, intelligence-test promoters led by Lewis Terman of Stanford University began pushing for the widespread use of an adapted version of Binet's test in American schools. Terman, not Binet, is responsible for the notion that every person has an innate, numerically expressible "intelligence quotient" that a test can discern. His primary interest was in identifying the very highest scorers and then making sure they were given special educational opportunities. One such opportunity was the chance to be among the handful of young Americans who then finished high school and went on to college, with the idea that the society would then get the full benefit of their talents. The idea of identifying and specially training a new, brainy elite was not new to Terman; you can find essentially the same idea in Plato's *Republic,* in Thomas Jefferson's correspondence with John Adams, and in many other places. The idea of using a standardized test to begin this process was not new either. Future Chinese mandarins were being selected by examination more than a thousand years ago, and systems of selection by examination for aspiring government and military officials swept across western Europe in the nineteenth century. What was new was the idea of using IQ tests—as, supposedly, a measure of general intellectual superiority, not mastery of a particular body of material or suitability to a particular task—as the means of selection.

During the First World War, the early psychometricians persuaded the United States Army to let them administer an IQ test to all recruits. This was the first mass administration of an IQ test, and the results were used, in that era when eugenicist ideas were conventional wisdom, to demonstrate the danger that unrestricted immigration posed to the quality of our national intellectual stock. One person who produced such work was Carl Brigham, a young psychologist at Princeton University who also went to work on adapting the Army Alpha Test for use in college admissions. In 1926—by which time, to his immense credit, he had loudly renounced his commitment to eugenics—the College Board experimentally administered Brigham's Scholastic Aptitude Test for the first time.

In 1933 James Bryant Conant became president of Harvard University. Conant, though a Boston-bred Harvard graduate descended from Puritans, rightly considered himself to represent, in class terms, a departure from the Brahmin Harvard presidents before him. He had grown up middle-class in Dorchester, not rich in Back Bay, and he was a true modern academic, a research chemist. Conant saw before him a Harvard College that had become the property of a new American aristocracy, which in turn had been created by the aging, for a generation or two, of the immense industrial fortunes that had materialized in the decades following the Civil War. Harvard was dominated by well-to-do young men from the Northeast, who had attended private schools and who hired servants and private tutors to see to their needs while they went to football games and debutante balls. I want to avoid caricature here—it is wise to remember that the Harvard of that era produced many remarkable figures, from Franklin Delano Roosevelt to T. S. Eliot to Conant himself, and that its sociologically undiverse students were imbued with a respect for open competition—but it is true that Harvard and colleges like it tended to define undergraduate merit primarily in terms of nonacademic, nonquantifiable qualities like "character," which evidently was not usually found in students who went to public high schools.

Conant decided to begin to change Harvard's character not through a frontal assault, but by starting a small pilot program called the Harvard National Scholarships, under which a handful of boys from the Midwest would be chosen on the basis of pure academic promise and brought to Harvard on full four-year scholarships. The problem was how to select them, since they presumably would not be in range, academically or even geographically, of the College Boards. Conant gave two young assistant deans—Wilbur Bender, later Harvard's dean of admissions, and Henry Chauncey, later president of ETS—the task of finding a way of picking the Harvard National Scholars. Bender and Chauncey went around and met all the leading figures in the then-new field of educational testing, and quickly settled on Carl Brigham and his Scholastic Aptitude Test as the answer to their problem. As Chauncey told me the story, when they went to Conant and suggested that the SAT be the means of selection of Harvard National Scholars, Conant wanted to know if it was in any way an achievement test; if it was, no dice. Conant wanted a pure intelligence test, and Chauncey and Bender assured him that the SAT was that.

The Harvard National Scholarship program was a great success, not only in the sense that the scholarship winners did well at Harvard but also, much more important, in the sense that it began a process of redefinition of merit in the Ivy League student body, away from "character" and toward intellectualism. Over time, the process succeeded, and by now elite colleges have changed substantially in the way that Conant wanted them to. In 1938, Conant and Chauncey persuaded all the College Board schools to use the SAT as the main admissions test for scholarship applicants. In 1942, the old College Boards were suspended, "for the duration," and never resumed, so the SAT became the admissions test for all applicants to College Board schools, not just scholarship applicants. Still, the number of takers was quite small, not much over 10,000 a year.

During the war, Henry Chauncey persuaded the army and the navy to use a version of the SAT as a kind of officer candidate test; what was important about that was that it gave Chauncey, a gifted administrator, the chance to demonstrate that he could test more than 300,000 people all over the country on the same day while preserving test security and the accuracy of the scoring. This made it clear that the SAT could be used as a screen for the entire American high school cohort (only during the war did high school become the majority experience for American adolescents), rather than a handful of private-school kids—that it could be the basis for what one College Board official called the "great sorting" of the national population.

When the war ended, Conant and Chauncey, through a series of deft bureaucratic maneuvers backed by the clout and the money of the Carnegie Corporation, set up the Educational Testing Service as what Chauncey privately called "a bread and butter monopoly" in the field of postsecondary educational testing. It's worth noting that what is in effect a national personnel system was set up without any legislative sanction, or press coverage, or public debate—that's why the debate is taking place now, long after the fact.

While all this was going on, Conant was also developing an ambitious, detailed vision for the future not just of Harvard but of American society as a whole. (Remember that during the war years, the busy Conant was mainly occupied with the top-secret Manhattan Project, which developed the atomic bomb–something that would naturally lead one to think in grand terms.) Conant had been a Harvard undergraduate during the heyday of Frederick Jackson Turner, the now deeply out-of-fashion historian of the American frontier, as a leading light of the Harvard faculty. Like Turner, Conant believed that the best and most distinctive feature of American society was the ethic of opportunity for every person to try to rise in the world. The means of realizing this had been the open frontier, but since the late nineteenth century the frontier had been closed. Now the country was threatened by the twin dangers of right-wing industrial plutocracy on the one hand, and immigrant-borne socialism on the other. Our only chance of salvation lay in finding a new way to do what the frontier had done, and the best means at hand, Conant thought, was the public school system.

Here we come to the point about Conant's thinking that I want to emphasize most forcefully. Although he always used a lusty, and no doubt sincere, rhetoric of democracy and classlessness—his best known wartime article was called "Wanted: American Radicals"—he was actually, throughout his long career, preoccupied mainly with elite selection. To put it in a slightly different way, he believed passionately in operating an open, national, democratic contest for slots in a new elite—in the manner of an updated, scientized version of the Cinderella story, with the SAT as the glass slipper—and he tended to conflate this project with the overall triumph of democratic values. As early as the late 1930s, he was complaining that too many young Americans were going to college. After the war, he was probably the number-one opponent of the G.I. Bill and the number-one proponent of the comprehensive high school in which only a small, aptitude-tested group would get a demanding academic education.

Conant did wrestle occasionally—especially in a fascinating unpublished fragment of a book manuscript, called "What We Are Fighting to Defend"— with the question of why creating a democratically selected elite would necessarily have a democratizing effect on the country as a whole. (And later, in California, Conant's friend Clark Kerr wrestled with the same question.) Conant usually answered with three predictions, none of which has come true: first, that membership in the new elite would be a one-generation affair, with those chosen coming mainly from obscure backgrounds and their children returning to such backgrounds; second, that members of the new elite would mainly devote themselves to public service, rather than using the opportunities they had been given to pursue lucrative private careers; and third, that they would be admired and respected as national leaders by the general populace. He did not envision elite college admission as a contest for rich rewards that prosperous parents would try to rig in favor of their children. As was the case with Lewis Terman fifty years earlier, Conant's social idea was not actually all that new or all that American—I think he had in mind creating the kind of national technocrat-administrator class that exists in France and Germany—but he added to it the new elements of selection by aptitude testing, as Terman had, and, the invocation of the sacred American democratic tradition. He especially liked quoting, somewhat selectively, it must be said, Thomas Jefferson as a kind of patron saint of his ideas.

Practically the first thing ETS did, even before it had been officially chartered, was open a branch office in Berkeley, California. That was the symbolic beginning of a period in which the membership of the College Board grew exponentially and in which the SAT became a national test, and one required by public universities as well as private ones. This is a development worth dwelling on for a moment. What we now know about American higher education, especially public higher education, in the decades following the Second World War is that it became a mass system, the first in the history of the world to be based on at least the hope that college could be universal. Logically, this goal and the SAT don't necessarily go together. After the war, a commission on higher education appointed by President Harry Truman issued a clarion call for the expansion of public universities, but didn't even think to mention the need for admissions testing; conversely, as I mentioned, the founders of ETS, at just the same moment, were quite opposed to our sending many more young people on to college. So how did the two principles, expansion and the SAT, get joined together?

ETS began with seed money from the Carnegie Foundation, but it did not get an ongoing operating subsidy; it was expected to find a way to become self-sustaining financially. The money flow into ETS, then as now, went like this: if a college decided to require the SAT, then each applicant would have to pay ETS a fee upon taking the test. It is a classic third-party-payer system. Therefore ETS had a powerful incentive to persuade more and more universities to require the SAT, and imposing the requirement was cost-free to the universities. At public universities, the main force pushing for use of the SAT was faculties—specifically, their steady move toward the German-style tenured research model of professorship. Historically, most public universities had served in-state populations, had been minimally selective, had relied upon high school transcripts as the main credential for admission, and had had very low four-year graduation rates. All of that forced college professors into a role that was uncomfortably close to that of high school teachers. As faculties became more ambitious, they began to see admission by SAT as a way of nationalizing, academicizing, and reducing student bodies, which would free them to concentrate on their research. So there was a strong fit between ETS's ambitions and faculties' ambitions that wound up linking the SAT to the growth of public universities. By the time Henry Chauncey retired as ETS's president, in 1970, there were more than two million individual SAT administrations a year.

It was two full decades after the establishment of the ETS office in Berkeley that the University of California finally agreed to require the SAT of all its applicants, thus instantly becoming ETS's biggest customer and making the SAT system truly national. At the original, Ivy League, private school end of the SAT system, the institutions of higher education were already elite;

the drama was one of altering the composition of the elite. At the western, public end of the system, universities were relatively open and relatively closely matched curricularly to public high schools; the drama was making at least some of them, elite, and untying them from the high schools. So the East Coast master narrative of the old prep-school establishment, with its Jewish quotas and all-male schools and quasi-hereditary admissions and so on, giving way to the new meritocrats, is far less applicable here in California.

No significant accomplishment ever fails to have unintended consequences, so I don't want to sound facile in noting that there have been a few of them here. In the present context, the main one to note is that a test adopted for the purpose of choosing a handful of scholarship students for Harvard wound up becoming a kind of national educational standard for millions of high school students. If the SAT had only been used for Conant's original project in 1933, I still wouldn't agree with him that one can find an intelligence test that picks up only innate academic ability, not family background or the quality of education. But now that the SAT's use is so much wider, it makes for an interesting exercise to ask ourselves this question: if there were no existing tests and we were given the project of choosing one to stand as the main interface between high school and college, what would that test ideally look like? In other words, for the purpose the SAT now serves, would you, absent the weight of custom and history, employ the SAT?

Actually, you might. But if you did, you would, in your decision, be implicitly making certain assumptions that it's useful to state explicitly. As all of you know, the technical discussion of the value of the SAT tends to be conducted in terms of predictive validity: how much does the SAT add to the transcript's ability to predict an applicant's college grades, especially in the short run? The nontechnical discussion tends, in its way, to be just as narrow, or even more narrow: it is very heavily preoccupied with the question of the apportionment of a small, scarce, precious resource, admissions slots at highly selective elite universities. As I said at the outset, I am not the person at this conference best equipped to discuss predictive validity, and you'll get other chances to discuss it in detail. So let me just say that the data seem to show that other tests, notably the SAT II achievement tests but also the ACT and, at some schools, the Advanced Placement Exams, can be substituted for the SAT I without causing a significant erosion in predictive validity.

By the terms of the nontechnical discussion, the argument for the SAT is essentially Conant's from 70 years ago: it helps you find extraordinarily talented students whom you'd otherwise miss because they haven't had the chance to go to good schools (or even, as true SAT believers sometimes argue to me, because even though they have gone to good schools, they haven't studied hard). The College Board's Amy Schmidt kindly sent me some statistics she had put together on "discrepant SAT" results, which give us some sense of this high-aptitude, low-achievement population. The main point is that there aren't many of them. About three thousand students a year get above a 630 on the verbal portion of the SAT I and below a 550 on the SAT II writing test; only about five hundred students a year get above a 650 on the math portion of the SAT I and below a 540 on the SAT II Math IC test. We are being pretty narrow if we make serving that small group the overriding factor in choosing our main national college admissions test. If Conant's biggest worry was that someone of truly extraordinary talent, a future Albert Einstein or Werner von Braun, might, in America, spend a lifetime behind a plow, I would say the risk of that today is zero, with or without the SAT, because our education system is so much more nationalized and so replete with standardized tests and talent-identifying programs. Still, the structural assumption behind a present-day argument for the SAT as against the alternatives is that the project of trying to pick just the right students for highly selective universities should be the driving force in the selection of our big test.

I find it frustrating that so much of the discussion of the SAT is either explicitly or implicitly based on this assumption. The overwhelming majority of SAT takers will not be going to a highly selective university. What is the effect of our use of that test, as opposed to other tests, on them? On the whole, it's not healthy. With achievement tests, especially if those tests are aligned with the high school curriculum, the way to get a good score is to study the course material in school. Advanced Placement courses are a good example: the classes themselves are the test prep. With the SAT, the signaling is not nearly as benign. Although the word *aptitude* has been removed from the name of the test and most people don't know about the SAT's specific historical roots in intelligence testing, it's well enough enshrined in the high school version of urban legend that the SAT is a measure of how innately smart you are that scores become internalized as a measure of life-long worth, or lack thereof. That's why nobody ever forgets them. On the other hand, although the test was adopted because it was supposed to factor out high school quality, it is widely received as a measure of high school quality. That's why suburban communities' real-estate values can fluctuate with their high schools' average SAT scores, and why reports of rises and falls in the national average scores invariably lead to op-ed celebrations or condemnations of our educational system. For high schools, it's very difficult to improve average scores, and for students, it's very difficult to improve individual scores, without resorting to pure test prep—that is, instructional courses in test-taking tricks, which often are very expensive, begin at an early age, and are delivered with a message of cynicism about how the world works. The solution to the problem of low achievement test scores is, to a much greater extent, more studying by the student and better instruction by the school. When a school has persistently low average SAT scores, the standard response is to shrug fatalistically. When a school has persistently low average achievement test scores, the standard response, increasingly as the educational standards movement sweeps across the country, is to demand improvement and provide the resources and technical assistance to make it possible.

Conant did believe in improving public elementary and secondary education, but two factors held him back from proposing the kind of standards regime toward which we are now moving. First, public education was still too new and too decentralized—it would have seemed an insuperable project to him in the 1930s to institute meaningful national educational standards. Second, and more important, the truth is that Conant just didn't think most people had enough intellectual ability to benefit from an academic high school curriculum, let alone a college education. It was the extraordinarily talented few who were always his main concern; he was not nearly as preoccupied with the untapped potential of the average-scoring many. So although he always used the language of American exceptionalism, I think the standards movement is more genuinely in the unique American tradition—the essence of which is seeing potential in everyone—than the advent of the SAT meritocracy was.

I haven't mentioned affirmative action thus far, though I discuss it extensively in my book. It is another of the unintended consequences of the SAT— unintended in the sense that issues of race and ethnicity appear nowhere in the discussions surrounding the founding of the system. Here in California, the issue of affirmative action put the SAT into play and led to an overall reexamination that has now produced President Atkinson's proposal. As I read the data, if the University of California switches from the SAT I to the SAT II, the change will be substantially affirmative action-neutral; the idea of switching is not a Trojan horse really meant to solve the affirmative action problem, as several conservative writers have speculated in print. The question President Atkinson has raised is a separate and, to my mind, more important one: In picking a test that serves as the basic interface between high school and college, should we consider the overall interests of everyone that choice affects, or only the interests of the highly selective colleges? I suspect that the Atkinson proposal, when put into effect, will have much more impact on high schools than on universities. That is the furthest thing from a strike against it. It is entirely appropriate for the state's public university system to consider the interests of the state's public high school system. In a larger cost-benefit analysis, the university stands to lose not at all, or at most very marginally, in its ability to select students, and high school students stand to gain a great deal.

As I go around speaking about the SAT, I sometimes get accused of wanting to "shoot the messenger." Strictly speaking this isn't true, in the sense that I do not favor abolishing standardized tests, I respect the SAT as a highly professional instrument, and I do not want college admissions to be conducted on the basis of heredity or ethnic patronage. But the phrase does capture something: tests don't exist in a social vacuum. The way they are used embodies ideas about how society should work. I think the main idea behind the enshrinement of the SAT as our big test is that the project of educational elite selection is so overwhelmingly important that if we get it right, everything else in our society will fall into place. And it's true—*that* is a messenger I want to shoot. I propose that, especially since we have been so successful already at setting up an improved elite selection system, we now rely on quite a different main idea: that if we can guarantee a really good public education for every young American, everything else in our society, including elite selection, will fall into place. Starting with that idea leads surely in the direction of our replacing aptitude tests with achievement tests, and I heartily applaud President Atkinson for trying to do so.

Achievement versus Aptitude in College Admissions

RICHARD C. ATKINSON

Every year, more than a million high school students stake their futures on the nation's most widely used admissions test, the SAT I. Long viewed as the gold standard for ensuring student quality, the SAT I has also been considered a great equalizer in U.S. higher education. Unlike achievement tests such as the SAT II, which assess mastery of specific subjects, the SAT I is an aptitude test that focuses on measuring verbal and mathematical abilities independent of specific courses or high school curricula. It is therefore a valuable tool, the argument goes, for correcting the effects of grade inflation and the wildly varying quality of U.S. high schools. And it presumably offers a way of identifying talented students who otherwise might not meet traditional admissions criteria, especially high-potential students in low-performing high schools.

In February 2001, at the annual meeting of the American Council on Education (ACE), I delivered an address questioning the conventional wisdom about the SAT I and announced that I had asked the Academic Senate of the University of California (UC) to consider eliminating it as a requirement for admission to UC. I was unprepared for the intense public reaction to my remarks. The day before I was scheduled to deliver them, I went to the lobby of my hotel to get a copy of the *Washington Post*. I was astounded to find myself and excerpts from the speech on the front page; an early version had been leaked to the press. To my further astonishment, an even more detailed story appeared on the front page of the *New York Times.*

And that was only the beginning. In the months since my address, I have heard from hundreds of college and university presidents, CEOs, alumni, superintendents, principals, teachers, parents, students, and many others from all walks of life. Television programs, newspaper editorials, and magazine articles have presented arguments pro and con. I was most struck by the *Time* magazine article that had a picture of President Bush and me side by side. The headline read, "What do these two men have in common?" Those who have speculated that the answer is that we had the same SAT scores are wrong. I did not take the SAT. I was an undergraduate at the University of Chicago, and at that time the university was adamantly opposed to the concept of aptitude tests and used achievement tests in its admissions process. *Time* was simply observing that we share an interest in testing.

It came as no surprise that my proposal to take a hard look at the role and purpose of the SAT I and standardized tests in general attracted the attention of educators, admissions officers, and testing experts. I have been impressed and pleased by the many researchers, professors, and psychometricians who have shared with me their findings and experience regarding the SAT. But I was also surprised at the number of letters I received from people who had no professional connection with higher education. I heard from a young woman—an honors graduate of UC Berkeley with an advanced degree from Princeton—who had been questioned about her 10-year-old SAT scores in a job interview; an attorney who, despite decades of success, still remembers the sting of a less-than-brilliant SAT score; an engineer who excelled on the SAT but found it bore no relation to the demands of college and his profession; a science student who scored poorly on the SAT and was not admitted to his college of choice but was elected to the National Academy of Sciences in later years. Clearly, the SAT strikes a deep chord in the national psyche.

The second surprise in the months after my speech was the degree of confusion about what I proposed and why I proposed it. For example, some people assumed I wanted to eliminate the SAT I as an end run around Proposition 209, the 1996 California law banning affirmative action. That was not my purpose; my opposition to the SAT I predates Proposition 209 by many years. And as I said in my ACE speech, I do not anticipate that ending the SAT I requirement by itself would appreciably change the ethnic or racial composition of the student body admitted to UC.

Others assumed that because I am against the SAT I, I am against standardized tests in general. I am not; quite the opposite is true. Grading practices vary across teachers and high schools, and standardized tests provide a measure of a student's achievements that is independent of grades.

But we need to be exceedingly careful about the standardized tests we choose.

So much for what I did not propose. Let me turn briefly to what I did propose. I requested the Academic Senate of UC to consider two further changes in addition to making the SAT I optional. The first is to use an expanded set of SAT II tests or other curriculum-based tests that measure achievement in specific subject areas until more appropriate tests are developed. The second is to move all UC campuses away from admissions processes employing quantitative formulas and toward a comprehensive evaluation of applicants.

In a democratic society, I argued, admitting students to a college or university should be based on three principles. First, students should be judged on the basis of their actual achievements, not on ill-defined notions of aptitude. Second, standardized tests should have a demonstrable relationship to the specific subjects taught in high school, so that students can use the tests to assess their mastery of those subjects. Third, U.S. universities should employ admissions processes that look at individual applicants in their full complexity and take special pains to ensure that standardized tests are used properly in admissions decisions. I'd like to discuss each in turn.

Aptitude versus Achievement

Aptitude tests such as the SAT I have a historical tie to the concept of innate mental abilities and the belief that such abilities can be defined and meaningfully measured. Neither notion has been supported by modern research. Few scientists who have considered these matters seriously would argue that aptitude tests such as the SAT I provide a true measure of intellectual abilities.

Nonetheless, the SAT I is widely regarded as a test of basic mental ability that can give us a picture of students' academic promise. Those who support it do so in the belief that it helps guarantee that the students admitted to college will be highly qualified. The SAT I's claim to be the "gold standard of quality" derives from its purported ability to predict how students will perform in their first year of college.

Nearly 40 years ago, UC faculty serving on the Academic Senate's Board of Admissions and Relations with Schools (BOARS) gathered on the Santa Barbara campus to consider the merits of the SAT and achievement tests. At that point, UC had only run experiments with both kinds of tests. In the actual process of admissions, UC used standardized tests in admissions decisions for only a small percentage of students who did not qualify on the basis of their grades in selected courses. BOARS wanted answers to a couple of critical questions: What is the predictive power—what researchers call the "predictive validity"—of the SAT for academic success at UC? How might it improve the process of admissions?

To answer these questions, BOARS launched a study that compared the SAT and achievement tests as predictors of student performance. The results were mixed. In the view of the board, the achievement tests proved a more useful predictor of student success than did the SAT, both in combination with grades and as a single indicator. But the benefits of both tests appeared marginal at the time. As a result, both the SAT and achievement tests remained largely an alternative method for attaining UC eligibility. In 1968, UC began requiring the SAT I and three SAT II achievement tests, although applicants' scores were not considered in the admissions process. Rather, the SAT I and SAT II tests remained largely a way of admitting promising students whose grades fell below the UC standard and an analytical tool to study the success patterns of students admitted strictly by their grades in UC-required courses.

This policy lasted until the late 1970s. As historian John Douglass has noted in a number of studies on the history of UC admissions, not until 1979 did the university adopt the SAT as a substantial and formal part of the regular admissions process. That year, BOARS established UC's current Eligibility Index: a sliding scale combining grade point average (GPA) in required courses with SAT scores to determine UC eligibility. Even then, GPA remained the dominant factor in this determination. UC established the Eligibility Index largely as a way of reducing its eligibility pool in light of a series of studies that showed UC accepting students well beyond its mandated top 12.5 percent of statewide graduates. The decision to include SAT scores in the Eligibility Index was based not on an analysis of the SAT's predictive power but on its ability to serve as a screen that would reduce the pool of eligible students.

Fortunately, today we do have an analysis of the SAT's value in admissions decisions. Because our students have been taking the SAT I and the SAT II for more than three decades, UC is perhaps the only university in the country that has a database large enough to compare the predictive power of the SAT I with that of the achievement-based SAT II tests. UC researchers Saul Geiser and Roger Studley have analyzed the records of almost 78,000 freshmen who entered UC over the past four years. They concluded that the SAT II is, in fact, a better predictor of college grades than the SAT I. The UC data show that high school grades plus the SAT II account for about 21 percent of the explained variance in first-year college grades. When the SAT I is added to high school grades and the SAT II, the explained variance increases from 21 percent to 21.1 percent, a trivial increment.

Our data indicate that the predictive validity of the SAT II is much less affected by differences in socioeconomic background than is the SAT I.

After controlling for family income and parents' education, the predictive power of the SAT II is undiminished, whereas the relationship between SAT I scores and UC freshman grades virtually disappears. These findings suggest that the SAT II is not only a better predictor but also a fairer test for use in college admissions, because its predictive validity is much less sensitive than is the SAT I to differences in students' socioeconomic background. Contrary to the notion that aptitude tests are superior to achievement tests in identifying high-potential students in low-performing schools, our data show the opposite: The SAT II achievement tests predict success at UC better than the SAT I for students from all schools in California, including the most disadvantaged.

UC data yield another significant result. Of the various tests that make up the SAT I aptitude and the SAT II achievement tests, the best single predictor of student performance turned out to be the SAT II writing test. This test is the only one of the group that requires students to write something in addition to answering multiple-choice items. Given the importance of writing ability at the college level, it should not be surprising that a test of actual writing skills correlates strongly with freshman grades.

When I gave my speech to ACE, this comprehensive analysis of the UC data comparing the two tests was not available. My arguments against the SAT I were based not on predictive validity but on pedagogical and philosophical convictions about achievement, merit, and opportunity in a democratic society. In my judgment, those considerations remain the most telling arguments against the SAT I. But these findings about the predictive validity of the SAT I versus the SAT II are stunning.

Curriculum-Based Tests

If we do not use aptitude tests such as the SAT I, how can we get an accurate picture of students' abilities that is independent of high school grades? In my view, the choice is clear: We should use standardized tests that have a demonstrable relationship to the specific subjects taught in high schools. This would benefit students, because much time is currently wasted inside and outside the classroom prepping students for the SAT I; the time could be better spent learning history or geometry. And it would benefit schools, because achievement-based tests tied to the curriculum are much more attuned to current efforts to improve the desperate situation of the nation's K-12 schools.

One of the clear lessons of U.S. history is that colleges and universities, through their admissions requirements, strongly influence what is taught in the K-12 schools. To qualify for admission to UC, high-school students must attain specified grades in a set of college-preparatory classes that includes mathematics, English, foreign languages, laboratory sciences, social sciences, and the arts. These requirements let schools and students alike know that we expect UC applicants to have taken academically challenging courses that involve substantial reading and writing, problem-solving and laboratory work, and analytical thinking, as well as the acquisition of factual information. These required courses shape the high-school curriculum in direct and powerful ways, and so do the standardized admissions tests that are also part of qualifying for UC.

Because of its influence on K-12 education, UC has a responsibility to articulate a clear rationale for its test requirements. In my ACE address in February, I suggested what that rationale might contain: 1) The academic competencies to be tested should be clearly defined; in other words, testing should be directly related to the required college preparatory curriculum. 2) Students from any comprehensive high school in California should be able to score well if they master the curriculum. 3) Students should be able, on reviewing their test scores, to understand where they did well or fell short and what they must do to earn higher scores in the future. 4) Test scores should help admissions officers evaluate the applicant's readiness for college-level work. The Board of Admissions and Relations with Schools is in the process of developing principles to govern the selection and use of standardized tests. These principles will be an extremely important contribution to the national debate about testing.

Universities in every state influence what high schools teach and what students learn. We can use this influence to reinforce current national efforts to improve the performance of U.S. public schools. These reform efforts are based on three principal tenets: Curriculum standards should be clearly defined, students should be held to those standards, and standardized tests should be used to assess whether the standards have been met.

The SAT I sends a confusing message to students, teachers, and schools. It says that students will be tested on material that is unrelated to what they study in their classes. It says that the grades they achieve can be devalued by a test that is not part of their school curriculum. Most important, the SAT I scores only tell a student that he or she scored higher or lower than his or her classmates. They provide neither students nor schools with a basis for self-assessment or improvement.

Appropriate Role of Standardized Tests

Finally, I have argued that U.S. universities should employ admissions processes that look at individual applicants broadly and take special pains to ensure that standardized tests are used properly in admissions decisions. Let me explain this statement in terms of UC.

UC's admissions policies and practices have been in the spotlight of public attention in recent years as California's diverse population has expanded and demand for higher education has skyrocketed. Many of UC's 10 campuses receive far more applicants than they can accept. Thus, the approach we use to admit students must be demonstrably inclusive and fair.

To do this, we must assess students in their full complexity. This means considering not only grades and test scores but also what students have made of their opportunities to learn, the obstacles they have overcome, and the special talents they possess. To move the university in this direction, I have made four admissions proposals in recent years:

Eligibility in the Local Context (ELC), or the Four Percent Plan, grants UC eligibility to students in the top 4 percent of their high school graduating class who also have completed UC's required college preparatory courses. Almost 97 percent of California public high schools participated in ELC in its first year, and many of these had in the past sent few or no students to UC.

Under the Dual Admissions Program approved by the regents in July 2001, students who fall below the top 4 percent but within the top 12.5 percent of their high school graduating class would be admitted simultaneously to a community college and to UC, with the proviso that they must fulfill their freshman and sophomore requirements at a community college (with a solid GPA) before transferring to a UC campus. State budget difficulties have delayed implementation of the Dual Admissions Program, but we hope to launch it next year.

For some years, UC policy has defined two tiers for admission. In the first tier, 50 to 75 percent of students are admitted by a formula that places principal weight on grades and test scores; in the second tier, students are assessed on a range of supplemental criteria (for example, difficulty of the courses taken, evidence of leadership, or persistence in the face of obstacles) in addition to quantitative measures. Selective private and public universities have long used this type of comprehensive review of a student's full record in making admissions decisions. Given the intense competition for places at UC, I have urged that we follow their lead. The regents recently approved the comprehensive review proposal, and it will be effective for students admitted in fall 2002.

Finally, for the reasons I have discussed above, I have proposed that UC make the SAT I optional and move toward curriculum-based achievement tests. The Academic Senate is currently considering this issue, and its review will likely be finished in spring 2002, after which the proposal will go to the Board of Regents.

The purpose of these changes is to see that UC casts its net widely to identify merit in all its forms. The trend toward broader assessment of student talent and potential has focused attention on the validity of standardized tests and how they are used in the admissions process. All UC campuses have taken steps in recent years to ensure that test scores are used properly in such reviews; that is, that they help us select students who are highly qualified for UC's challenging academic environment. It is not enough, however, to make sure that test scores are simply one of several criteria considered; we must also make sure that the tests we require reflect UC's mission and purpose, which is to educate the state's most talented students and make educational opportunity available to young people from every background.

Achievement tests are fairer to students because they measure accomplishment rather than ill-defined notions of aptitude; they can be used to improve performance; they are less vulnerable to charges of cultural or socioeconomic bias; and they are more appropriate for schools, because they set clear curricular guidelines and clarify what is important for students to learn. Most important, they tell students that a college education is within the reach of anyone with the talent and determination to succeed.

For all of these reasons, the movement away from aptitude tests toward achievement tests is an appropriate step for U.S. students, schools, and universities. Our goal in setting admissions requirements should be to reward excellence in all its forms and to minimize, to the greatest extent possible, the barriers students face in realizing their potential. We intend to honor both the ideal of merit and the ideal of broad educational opportunity. These twin ideals are deeply woven into the fabric of higher education in this country. It is no exaggeration to say that they are the defining characteristics of the U.S. system of higher education.

The irony of the SAT I is that it began as an effort to move higher education closer to egalitarian values. Yet its roots are in a very different tradition: the IQ testing that took place during the First World War, when two million men were tested and assigned an IQ based on the results. The framers of these tests assumed that intelligence was a unitary inherited attribute, that it was not subject to change over a lifetime, and that it could be measured and individuals could be ranked and assigned their place in society accordingly. Although the SAT I is more sophisticated from a psychometric standpoint, it evolved from the same questionable assumptions about human talent and potential.

The tests we use to judge our students influence many lives, sometimes profoundly. We need a national discussion on standardized testing, informed by principle and disciplined by empirical evidence. We will never devise the perfect test: a test that accurately assesses students irrespective of parental education and income, the quality of local schools, and the kind of community students live in. But we can do better. We can do much better.

References

Atkinson, R. C. (2001). "Standardized tests and access to American universities," 2001 Robert Atwell Distinguished Lecture, 83rd Annual Meeting of the American Council on Education, Washington, D.C., February 18, 2001. Online at http://www.ucop.edu/pres/prespeeches. html.

Douglass, J. A. (1997). *Setting the conditions of admissions: The role of university of California faculty in policymaking.* Study commissioned by the University of California Academic Senate, February 1997. Online at http://ishi.lib.berkeley.edu/cshe/jdouglass/publications.html.

Douglass, J. A. (2001). "Anatomy of conflict: The making and unmaking of affirmative action at the University of California," in D. Skrentny (Ed.), *Color Lines: Affirmative Action, Immigration and Civil Rights Options for America.* Chicago: University of Chicago Press.

Geiser, S. and Studley, R. (2001). *UC and the SAT: Predictive validity and differential impact of the SAT I and SAT II at the University of California.* University of California Office of the President, October 29, 2001. Online at http://www.ucop.edu/pres/welcome.html.

Standardized Tests
and American Education

RICHARD FERGUSON

I find it most interesting to be asked to contribute to a conference on rethinking the SAT. Actually, I've been thinking about the SAT for many years—going all the way back to when I took it in high school. I would have taken the ACT Assessment®, but ACT wasn't founded until a year after I graduated!

I appreciate the invitation President Richard Atkinson extended to ACT and others to entertain ways in which we might be helpful to UC and to the State of California as they look to the prospect of enhancing admissions testing. Clearly the process of admitting students to college is a very important task, perhaps one of the most important each institution faces. It has a huge impact on students, on the institutions, on the well-being of the state—even on the health of the nation. So there is no topic more deserving of the scrutiny and the attention it is receiving now. And we at ACT certainly are delighted to be a part of the dialogue.

You won't be surprised if I suggest to you that the ACT Assessment is an achievement test. Its roots are in that particular orientation. We believe that the ACT directly addresses the very concerns that have been so well described, defined, and discussed here in recent months—that students should be examined on the basis of achievement, not aptitude; that standardized tests should be clearly linked to specific subjects taught in high school; that in the admission process, schools should look at students as complete individuals and use test results appropriately in making decisions. These are some of the very basic principles that we have been concerned with since ACT's founding more than 40 years ago.

After having reviewed the University of California standards, including the requirements for college preparatory courses (the A–G requirements), we acknowledge that the ACT is not the total answer. However, I believe it would be an eminently doable task to augment the ACT in ways that would make it a very effective tool for addressing many of the concerns you have identified.

The tests in the ACT Assessment are achievement oriented and curriculum based. This means that their content is based solely on the academic knowledge and skills typically taught in high school college-preparatory programs and required for success in the first year of college. The ACT measures achievement in the core curriculum areas critical to academic performance and success. For this reason, ACT Assessment scores are extremely effective for making not only college admissions decisions but also course placement decisions.

The four tests in the ACT Assessment cover English, mathematics, reading, and science. Here's a short overview of each of the tests, since I know some members of the audience are not as familiar with the ACT as they are with the SAT.

- *English* measures understanding of the conventions of standard written English and of rhetorical skills. Spelling, vocabulary, and rote recall of rules of grammar are not tested. The test consists of five prose passages, each of which is accompanied by a sequence of multiple-choice questions. Different passage types are used to provide a variety of rhetorical situations. Passages are chosen not only for their appropriateness in assessing writing skills but also to reflect student interests and experiences.
- *Mathematics* is designed to assess the math skills students have typically acquired in courses taken up to the beginning of grade twelve. The questions require students to use reasoning skills to solve practical problems in mathematics. Knowledge of basic formulas and computational skills are assumed as background for problems, but complex formulas and extensive computation are not required. The material covered on the test emphasizes the major content areas that are prerequisites to successful performance in entry-level courses in college math.
- *Reading* measures reading comprehension. Questions ask students to derive meaning by referring to what is explicitly stated and reasoning to determine implicit meanings. The test includes four prose passages representative of the levels and kinds of text commonly

found in college freshman courses. Notes at the beginning of each passage identify its type (e.g., prose fiction), name the author, and may include brief information that helps in understanding the passage.

- *Science* measures interpretation, analysis, evaluation, reasoning, and problem-solving skills required in the natural sciences. The test presents seven sets of scientific information, each followed by a set of multiple-choice questions. The scientific information is conveyed in one of three formats: data representation, research summaries, and conflicting viewpoints.

The content and skills measured by the ACT Assessment are determined by our nation's school and college faculty. Every three years, we conduct a national curriculum study, the only project of its kind in the nation. We examine what is being taught in our nation's schools and what students should know and be able to do in order to be ready for college-level work. A nationally representative sample of teachers in grades 7 to 12 plus college faculty who teach entry-level courses in English, mathematics, and science participate in this project. The study group includes California educators. The specifications for the ACT Assessment are based directly and substantially on the results of these curriculum studies.

Because the four tests in the ACT Assessment are based on school curricula, the scores not only provide normative information (that is, how well a student performed on the test relative to other students), but also tell students what they are likely to know and be able to do based on their performance. These statements, called Standards for Transition®, describe the skills and knowledge associated with various score ranges for each of the four tests. Students can compare their performance to that of other students and can refer to the Standards for Transition to identify their own areas of strength and weakness.

Across the country, high schools, colleges, and state education agencies are also using the Standards for Transition. High schools are using the Standards to place students in courses, evaluate their course offerings, plan instructional interventions, evaluate student progress, and prepare their students to meet college expectations. Colleges and state higher education agencies are using these standards to effectively articulate their academic expectations for entering students, set appropriate scores for placing students in entry-level courses, and identify students who have the skills necessary to enter a particular institution and succeed in the courses it offers.

I would like to focus briefly on a couple of notions that we think are important to the UC institutions and to postsecondary institutions in the state and across the nation. We recognize that many factors contributed to the decision the UC regents recently made for the comprehensive review of student application materials. This admissions process is consistent with our perspective that there are many different variables one can entertain in any particular system of admission. We believe that the ACT does address significant academic skills that are pertinent and important to these considerations. Later in this conference, one of my colleagues will speak directly to the validity of the ACT. I won't touch on that now, but I will observe that a major benefit of the ACT is that not only does it focus on achievement, but it is also a very effective predictor. The claim that an achievement test would not be an effective predictor of how students will perform in college is simply inaccurate.

I won't go into great detail about all the different uses now being made of the ACT, both nationally as well as here in California. But admissions selection is certainly one of the most prevalent. We know that's a critical issue for the UC system and we believe the ACT addresses it very well. Course placement is an issue we also address effectively in different settings. Support for student advising—particularly providing information to students that enables them to prepare themselves early and well for college—is a hallmark of what we have been doing at ACT.

We acknowledge that in California and, in fact, in states around the nation, many students—particularly those in urban and rural schools—are disadvantaged in some way with respect to the adequacy of their educational experience. We believe very strongly that achievement differences, including those that we observe today, can be addressed, minimized, and ultimately eliminated if all the right forces are brought to bear. We believe that educational and career guidance is an important element in helping all interested parties—be they students, parents, counselors, or teachers—become aware of what needs to happen if students are to make successful transitions to postsecondary education and work.

Colleges and universities care deeply about whether the students they admit will persist to graduation and they are also concerned about the many factors that can jeopardize student success. ACT has long believed that it is good practice to consider several sources of information besides test scores in making admission decisions. For this reason, the ACT Assessment provides information about a number of noncognitive characteristics, such as out-of-class activities and accomplishments, leadership, career interests, education and career plans, and expressed need for help. Such information can be used to identify students who are likely to persist in college, and to address areas of interest and need that students themselves perceive. Many colleges also use this information for course placement, scholarship selection, career counseling, academic advising, institutional research, recruitment, and enrollment management.

Obviously, rigorous courses are a very significant issue. As many of you know, for years we have reported the fact that only about two-thirds of all students applying for postsecondary education actually have taken the core courses—four years of English and three of math, social studies, and science. To this day, that is the case. Again, a well-constructed assessment and admissions program can inform good decisions by students, parents, teachers, and counselors. We believe that if we really are serious about ensuring that all students have maximum opportunity for admission to college, a lot of steps have to be taken much earlier on in the process.

ACT has had a long-standing commitment to fairness in testing. We recognize that societal inequities affect the quality of education in every state and across the country. Not all schools receive equal economic resources; not all schools provide equal quality education; and not all students get the instructional support they need to be equally well prepared to enter college. Our goal in developing the ACT Assessment—and all of our tests— is to make sure that no additional inequities are introduced into the test design, development, administration or scoring processes that might create an unfair advantage or disadvantage for one student or group over another.

All the concerns we have been discussing motivated us to create the ACT Educational Planning and Assessment System—EPAS®. This integrated system begins at grade 8 with a program called EXPLORE®, includes a program at grade 10 called PLAN®, and concludes with the ACT Assessment at eleventh or twelfth grade. We believe the system drives opportunity for students who might not otherwise see their skills and abilities developed, and might not otherwise perceive the opportunities that are there for them.

We chose the names for the programs in EPAS very thoughtfully. Our belief is that the eighth grade is a key time. Young people ought to be exploring, ought to be getting information and insight about career paths they might consider taking. At this age it is much too early to decide on what they may be, but students ought to be exploring and learning. So our system includes both interest and academic assessments which help students begin to focus, to recognize that if they aspire to be an engineer or a teacher, decisions they make now, decisions their parents, counselors, and others make, will affect their ability to realize their dreams later on. Bad decisions—not taking the right courses, not learning the skills that they need—will work against them in that regard.

At the 10th-grade, in the PLAN program, the message is that it is time to begin getting more serious, to start making plans for life after high school, and to choose courses with those plans in mind. At this age, so many young people simply stop taking math courses, stop taking science courses—often making such choices uninformed about the personal consequences of these decisions.

The programs in EPAS are linked in a system that includes the assessments, interpretive information, student planning materials, and instructional support. Information is also provided through a program evaluation dimension for schools and for individual teachers. At the classroom level, math teachers, science teachers, and English teachers all have very specific feedback that speaks to the skills the students have or do not have and then facilitates changes they may need to make in their instructional strategies.

Our aim with the Educational Planning and Assessment System is simply to help students and schools set and achieve standards for learning. It will not come as any great surprise to you that we have compared ACT content and the standards that are reflected in EPAS to the California standards and requirements, and have found that there is huge overlap. That does not surprise us either, because we regularly speak to teachers, to professors, and to others who tell us what is important, what should be covered by our achievement measures. Our shared aim, then, is to ensure readiness for postsecondary education and to monitor student progress over time toward that goal.

We have put all the EPAS programs on the same score scale—for those of you who are not familiar with the ACT, our score scale is 1 to 36. Of 8th-graders who complete the EXPLORE math test and score 11, we know that, had they taken the much more difficult ACT Assessment that day, they very likely would have scored an 11 on it as well. The message to students is that, depending on what you do in the next three or four years, you can move up from the 11 you'd have scored had you taken the ACT math test today. You can actually improve on that score. We have enormous amounts of data now that indicate—depending on patterns of course-taking between grade 8 and grade 12—how you might perform on the ACT assessment as a 12th-grader. The challenge is getting the message to all young people—be they disadvantaged or advantaged, majority or minority, or just currently unmotivated to take the right path, the more difficult one—that there are future consequences to the choices they make now. The good news is that they can affect what the outcomes will be by making smart choices now.

In many respects, what we at ACT are saying is that we tend to view college admissions as a process, not a point in time. Though an admissions office makes a decision about an applicant on a given day, the reality is that the whole admissions process began much earlier. We believe that early awareness and intervention offer the best assurance that all students will be prepared for the transitions they make after high school, whether to further education or to work. We believe that junior high or middle school is not too soon to begin the career and educational exploration process. The programs in EPAS guide students through a systematic process of career exploration, high school course planning, and assessment of academic progress, to help ensure that they are prepared for college work. EXPLORE, targeted at 8th-and 9th-grade students, begins this longitudinal process. PLAN, for 10th-grade students, provides a midpoint review in high school. And the ACT Assessment provides students in grades 11 and 12 a comprehensive picture of their readiness for college.

Longitudinal monitoring of career plans, high school coursework plans, and academic progress can help identify students who need help along the way in career planning, academic achievement, or identifying courses they need to take to be ready for college. If students are to enter college ready to learn and to persist to graduation, they must begin to plan and prepare when they are in middle school. Our belief is that the more well-timed, appropriate, and useful information everyone has, the more solid, reliable advice they're getting, the more likely it is they will be able to choose from among a whole range of those good options we want for all of our children in all our schools.

At ACT, we have developed a chart describing the skills and knowledge associated with different ACT test score ranges. For example, for students who score in the range of 10 to 14 on the math test, the chart shows the specific skills they would have the capability to perform. Providing that information to teachers along with the scores—and we do that at the 8th grade, the 10th grade, and again at the 12th grade—gives them a huge array of information they and curriculum specialists can actually address. We think this is important to higher education in general. We are really focusing on the success of individual students, and we think that achievement testing, as is represented by the ACT, provides a very effective tool for doing that.

Let me just make a couple of concluding comments. We have matched the ACT to the K through 12 standards at the secondary level and prepared an extensive report that shows very high overlap with those standards. We have done the same thing with respect to the postsecondary institution requirements and the A–G requirements. So we know there is a good fit there. But we also recognize that your interests, as we have heard them expressed over time, suggest a desire for a broader assessment. The need for a writing assessment was something we also heard very clearly this morning.

Though we believe that our achievement tests cover an important core of skills of a general character, we also recognize that particular needs will vary by system. I would simply observe that from our perspective, we believe that it is quite possible to augment the ACT to address those larger needs that the system, the BOARS committee, [Board on Admissions and Relations with Schools], and others are identifying. We welcome the opportunity for collaboration in that regard in the future and have many ideas about ways in which it could be managed. We believe that can be accomplished in a manner that strengthens the predictiveness of our assessment. And it can be completed in a reasonable time frame, if there is clear definition of what the interests are.

ACT's record confirms that we can effectively address the very significant concerns we all have about underrepresented students and the need to prepare them to make effective transitions from high school into the UC system. We believe this can be achieved in a process that honors the interests the faculty have expressed through the work of the BOARS committee and others.

We hope that, as you are considering the challenges you are facing, you will look very closely at the ACT Assessment. It is an achievement testing program that has a long history of very successful use in widely diverse settings throughout the nation. Even more important, it offers many of the attributes that you have so carefully and thoughtfully identified as important to the future of the admissions process in the State of California.

Doing What Is Important
in Education

GASTON CAPERTON

Like many of you, I was powerfully affected by the events of September 11, 2001, and so was the entire country. For me, at least, those things that were important prior to 9/11 are even more important; the less important stuff is now even less important. I was struck by a powerful collective sense that we ought not waste time. We should be straightforward in our conversations with one another and direct and meaningful in what we do. We should believe in what we say and what we care about. Those are good and strong and powerful feelings for us to have.

Then there is what I call "fade away." I was not in New York City on September 11, but when I returned to the city two days later I promised myself that I would no longer waste time on the unimportant. Then "fade away" occurs, and a month or two passes and you find yourself caught up again in the unimportant. So I am particularly grateful to come here to talk with you about something important: the issues surrounding the use of the SAT at the University of California and elsewhere.

A little more than two years ago I was at my desk at Columbia University when I got a phone call from a search firm asking if I would be interested in interviewing to be the president of the College Board. At first I was not at all interested in being the president of a testing company. But after learning more about what the College Board is and what it does, I became very interested. And today I'm deeply proud and deeply blessed to preside over the College Board and all its good works.

Like me, many people really know little about the College Board. It is a hundred-year old organization that was created by some of the giants in education. Today it has 4,200 members—colleges, universities, and schools all across the nation. I work for a board of trustees. They are college presidents, school superintendents, guidance counselors, financial aid officers, professors, teachers—people like you and me. They are from all over the country. They are diverse and they are deeply committed to the issue of equity. The mission of the College Board is to prepare, inspire, and connect kids to college and opportunity with a focus on equity and excellence.

I am proud to have with me today eight people from the College Board. Each is a professional; each is dedicated to the mission and values of the College Board. They care and they are at this conference today to share with all of you their expertise and deep understanding of the role of testing in the college admissions process.

The issues before us today are the result of four very good things. The first is that nearly everyone in the world wants to come to America. It is truly the land of opportunity, and California exemplifies that. Earlier, Dr. Atkinson presented statistics on the changing demographics here in California. These demographics are changing because people from all over want to be here. The second is that the University of California is one of the greatest institutions of higher education, not only in this country but in the world. It is a marvelous opportunity to chase the American dream. So everybody wants to come to one of the schools at the University of California . . . another good thing. The third good thing is that the University of California has more well-prepared students than ever applying for admission. That, too, is good news. And finally, the fourth is that the University of California cares deeply about equity and diversity.

Dr. Atkinson has talked about the steps he has taken to address these issues. He has recommended, for example, that the SAT I not be used in the admission process but that, instead, the university require students to submit five SAT II achievement tests when they apply. This represents an important shift in admissions testing by an institution that is an important and influential member of the College Board. So when the president of the University of California speaks up, the College Board listens. And we have listened. But let me share with you today what others in this country think about the SAT I and the SAT II and their role in college admissions.

Some History

The origin of the SAT I goes back about 75 years when the College Board sought to create a test that would be useful for assessing students from all manner of secondary schools—and home schooling, back then—to determine their readiness for college. It is true that much of the SAT I's earlier framework evolved from what we knew then about aptitude and intelligence. But what we knew then and what we know today about the psychology of learning and achievement are as different as what a Chevrolet was 75 years ago and is today. Both have four tires and a steering wheel, but they are very different technologically and socially. Today's SAT I is a highly evolved measure of students' developed analytical skills and abilities. Simply put, it measures students' ability to think and reason using words and numbers. These skills and abilities, we have come to learn, are essential to the process of education, to doing well in college.

The SAT II tests, by contrast, are a battery of 22 one-hour tests that measure the knowledge and skills students have learned in academic courses in high school. They are the very best achievement tests this country has to offer, and I can understand why Dr. Atkinson supports their extended use in the admissions process. However, it is important to note that the 60 most highly selective colleges and universities in the U.S. continue to do what the University of California has done—that is, they continue to use the combination of the SAT I and the SAT II tests to admit students to their campuses. They do so because they want to have as much information about a student as possible when making this important decision and they believe these two very different tests give them the kind of information they need to make the very best decision they can make.

There are a lot of people in California who will help decide how the University should modify its admissions process, and I know that they will make a wise decision. Moreover, I can assure them that we will support their decision and work in whatever ways we can to make that decision a good one for the University. Indeed, my colleagues and I are here today to provide data, materials, expertise and insight to ensure that the decision-making process is well informed. We're here to discuss, to learn, and to listen. We feel we have the best tests in the world, but we believe they can be improved and we are here to listen and learn how to make them better serve your needs.

A Candid Conversation

Earlier, I said I was here to have a candid conversation about the SAT. The question, however, is not about tests but about making a difference—about doing what is important. For me, it is not about tests. It is not even about whether our youngsters can or will learn when they come to the University of California. Of course they can; of course they will learn. For me, it all has to do with an unequal education system, not only in your state, but in this country. We are dealing with identifiable groups of students who come to school less ready to learn than others. They have been provided less qualified teachers. They have been given poor facilities and, worst of all, usually they have been subjected to very low expectations at home, in their schools, and in their communities.

Let me share a personal example. My sister is five years older than me, and she made nothing but A's in school. Today she serves on the local school board. She has served on the state school board in North Carolina and now she serves on the University board of trustees. She was a straight-A student—Phi Beta Kappa, everybody's dream student. Along comes her younger brother—me—and in the fourth grade, after struggling to learn to read, my parents and I learned that I am dyslexic. Now, I ask, do you think my parents had to spend more time and more money and more heartaches on my education or my sister's? You see, the students who are going to provide the diversity that this institution wants and needs are like me. They need a lot more, not a lot less. That's the problem we're dealing with and that's what we at the College Board care deeply about today.

Today's College Board

Today at the College Board half the organization works with colleges in the admissions and testing process. The other half works to make our middle schools and secondary schools the best they can be. Indeed, we are adding new programs to enable us to work more effectively on issues of student preparation, and we are seeing some success. These programs are in statewide efforts in Florida and Maryland. More recently, the University of Michigan asked if we would join them and use our program in Detroit, one of the toughest places in the country, to improve their schools. My hope, my deep hope, is that some day we will gather together to see how we can combine our resources to make that kind of impact here in California. I believe that is how we make a difference, how we do what is important. Discussions of the SAT are important, but even more important are discussions of how we can pull together to improve educational opportunity for all students long before they sit for the SAT.

Remarks on President Atkinson's Proposal on Admissions Tests

MANUEL N. GÓMEZ

Aptitude, achievement, assessment—you would think, given the robust history of standardized testing in America, that we would have been able to agree on what these different terms mean and measure by now. Are they so full of meaning that we simply haven't been able to ferret out all relevant connotations and denotations, or have they been traded so frequently in the educational marketplace that their significance has faded or blurred, like the dye on a dollar bill? Perhaps a bit of both.

According to testing expert Claude Steele, whose research on stereotype threat has energized the debate over the fairness of standardized testing, the U.S. is "the only nation in the world that uses aptitude tests in higher education admissions rather than tests that measure achievement—how much a person has learned in earlier schooling, which are typically better predictors of success in higher education than aptitude tests" (Steele, 1999). Comprehensive research undertaken by the University of California supports this distinction. For our admissions cohorts, the SAT II is a consistently stronger predictor of college grades than either the SAT I or high school grade point average, even when we control for socioeconomic status and ethnicity. In fact, the SAT II seems to be an even stronger predictor of UC grade point average at the most selective campuses. In his own research at Stanford University and the University of Michigan, Steele has found that the SAT generally measures only 18% of the factors that contribute to freshman grades, with the predictive validity of the SAT diminishing in each subsequent year. He also points out that a difference in scores from person to person or group to group by as much as 300 points "actually represents a very small difference in skills critical to grade performance" (Steele, 1999).

I articulate these points knowing that they will probably only serve to bolster the SAT critics and incense SAT supporters who can point to their own validity studies to support continued use of the SAT I in admissions decisions. William Bowen and Derek Bok, for example, support the use of the SAT in college admissions, having found in their research that it did have some predictive value for academic persistence beyond the baccalaureate. However, even they caution that using the SAT as a predictor is more effective for white students than black students, and that a significant number of students in the cohort they studied went on to graduate school despite SAT scores of less than 1,000. In both studies—UC's and Bowen and Bok's (1998)—it is important to keep in mind that we are looking at an already high-achieving cohort of students. This, I believe, is a crucial point, particularly given Claude Steele and Joshua Aronson's findings that high-achieving minority students perform very differently on these tests depending on whether they are told the tests are measuring "intellectual ability" or problem solving "not intended as diagnostic of ability" (1998, p. 405). Whether or not you agree with the theory of stereotype threat, it is significant that a student's perception of the test's meaning can significantly alter performance.

Given this, I go back to my initial point about the correct label for the A in SAT. Does the fact that A no longer stands for anything mean that the test itself is invalid, or that it measures nothing? One of the architects of the SAT, Carl Brigham, said himself that the test measures "schooling, family background, familiarity with English, and everything else, relevant and irrelevant" (Lemann, 1999, p. 34). I agree that the test can give us a good deal of information. What I think we need to be looking at more closely, however, is exactly what kind of information the test does give us.

Some critics of UC president Richard Atkinson's proposal to replace the SAT I with the SAT II in admissions decisions seem to think that President Atkinson has taken a unilateral stand against standardized testing, a perception that is clearly untrue. One such critic, Virginia Postrel, has argued that "Public institutions have a greater duty to avoid arbitrarily indulging the tastes of their admissions officers. Deemphasizing tests that put everyone on the same rating scale makes arbitrariness more likely" (2001, p. M-5). I agree with Ms. Postrel that public institutions possess a social imperative to be as fair as possible. But our historical assertion that the SAT I levels the academic bar is unconvincing to me. A standard is only as good as the measures that hold it up. But even more disturbing to me is the exaggerated importance the SAT has taken on in the public mind in recent years, reflecting a perception of merit that eclipses the many other factors which determine a student's ultimate educational success. What are we really afraid of? I have to admit that I remain somewhat puzzled by the so-called quality or merit argument, especially given the fact that we admit only the top 12.5% of California students. *All* students within this range have earned a UC education. Does anyone actually believe that in the absence of the SAT I, UC admissions processes will become arbitrary? I don't think so. But I *do* think that we need to look seriously at our investment in a standardized test which, to this day, remains unable to define its own standard.

References

Bowen, W. G., & Bok, D. (1998). *The shape of the river: Long-term consequences of considering race in college and university admissions.* Princeton, NJ: Princeton University Press.

Lemann, N. (1999). *The big test: The secret history of the American meritocracy.* New York: Farrar, Straus and Giroux, 1999.

Postrel, V. (2001). Dropping the SATs is an excuse to drop standards. *Los Angeles Times,* February 25.

Steele, C. M. (1999). Expert report of Claude M. Steele. *Gratz, et al. v. Bollinger, et al.,* No. 97-75231 (E. D. Mich.). *Grutter, et al. v. Bollinger, et al.,* No. 97-75928 (E. D. Mich.).

Steele, C. M., & Aronson, J. (1998). Stereotype threat and the test performance of academically successful African Americans. In C. Jencks & M. Phillips (Eds.), *The black-white test score gap.* Washington, DC: Brookings Institution.

Aptitude for College:
The Importance of Reasoning Tests
for Minority Admissions

DAVID F. LOHMAN

College admissions tests are expected to serve multiple and often contradictory purposes. Because of this fact, an admissions test that serves one purpose well may serve other purposes poorly. The two most important purposes of admissions tests are (1) to report on students' academic development to date and (2) to predict the likelihood of their success in college. Each of these goals is hard to accomplish with one test; achieving both with the same test may be impossible. Because of this, I argue that aptitude tests that go beyond prior achievement have an important role to play in admissions decisions, especially for minority students.

Before embarking on a discussion of aptitude testing, it is helpful to consider briefly a few of the difficulties that attend the seemingly simple goal of reporting on the level of academic knowledge and skill that students have acquired during their previous schooling. Achievement tests that are closely aligned to the common curriculum are most useful for this purpose. Such tests can help focus the efforts of both teachers and students on the knowledge and skills that will be used to make admissions decisions. This is generally viewed as a good thing unless, as seems often to be the case with high-stakes tests, the test unduly narrows the curriculum. Furthermore, high school students—especially those in different regions of the country—experience different curricula, so a test that represents the common curriculum must focus on students' general educational development. Such tests often contain relatively little specific content or conceptual knowledge. Science tests, for example, typically include tasks that require examinees to show that they can set up experiments or engage in other forms of scientific reasoning, but they generally do not sample what students might know about the periodic table or the function of the respiratory system. Again, some view this as a good thing. They believe that science should be about process, not content. Others think that ignoring content knowledge distorts the measurement of what students have learned, especially poor children who attend schools that emphasize learning content and basic skills more than problem solving and critical thinking. Finally, some argue that achievement tests should present tasks that mimic authentic performances, such as conducting science experiments, writing essays on topics of personal interest, or reasoning mathematically about ill-structured problems. Others argue that this is not always possible or desirable. In short, the seemingly simple goal of reporting on what students know and can do is not as straightforward as it might seem.

The second purpose of admissions tests is to look forward and predict the likelihood of a student's success in some yet-to-be-experienced environment. This aspect of admissions testing is less clearly represented in the current debate. The key concept here is aptitude, specifically aptitude for academic learning in different university programs. Dr. Richard Atkinson is right when he complains about "ill-defined notions of aptitude." But the concept of aptitude—whether well or poorly defined—is central to this discussion.

Aptitude

Students arrive at the university with characteristics developed through life experiences to date. These include their knowledge and skills in different academic domains, their ability to think about fresh problems, their motivation and persistence, their attitudes and values, their anxiety levels, and so on. The university experience may be conceptualized as a series of situations that sometimes demand, sometimes evoke, or sometimes merely afford the use of these characteristics. Of the many characteristics that influence a person's behavior, only a small set aid goal attainment in a particular situation. These are called aptitudes. Specifically, aptitude refers to *the degree of readiness to learn and to perform well in a particular situation or fixed domain* (Corno, et al., 2002). Thus, of the many characteristics that individuals bring to a situation, the few that assist them in performing well in that situation function as aptitudes. Examples include the ability to take good notes, to manage one's time, to use previously acquired knowledge appropriately, to make good inferences and generalizations, and to manage one's emotions. Aptitudes for learning thus go beyond cognitive abilities. Aspects of personality and motivation commonly function as aptitudes as well.

However, the same situation can evoke quite different ways of responding in different individuals. As a result, different measures of aptitude may be required to predict the performance of students who follow different routes to academic success. Because of this fact, a good selection system must cast a broad, not narrow, net. It must also look carefully at the demands and opportunities of different university environments, since defining the situation is part of defining the aptitude.

An example may help clarify how the same situation can evoke predictably different ways of responding. Students who come from different segments of our society often find the same college environment to be more or less consistent with their prior school experiences. For some, the situation will be familiar and will allow the use of practiced ways of responding. For others, however, the same situation will require more personal adaptation and novel problem solving. One of the factors that moderate such relationships is social class. Educational reformers are once again rediscovering the extent to which reforms that emphasize independent thinking in mathematics, for example, are often better received by middle- and upper middle-class students than by lower-class students (e.g. Lubienski, 2000). If the goal is to find lower-class students who are likely to succeed in college and beyond, then one must sample more than the curriculum that committees of middle-class educational reformers prefer and that middle-class students are likely to have experienced. Put differently, one must have a view of aptitude that embraces more than past achievement of the "common" curriculum.

One possibility is to use test tasks that sample abilities students have developed through their everyday experiences. Given the diversity of such experiences, one must find a way to sample quickly the sophistication of the students' reasoning in a broad range of contexts. Those who study reasoning abilities have investigated many different ways of constructing items to do this. Analogies repeatedly emerge as one of the most efficient item types. Although the format is ancient, research on how people solve such problems is extensive and recent. Dr. Atkinson rightly argues that verbal analogy items should not be the object of instruction, and that some analogy items seem primarily to test vocabulary knowledge. But eliminating such items will not necessarily produce a better test. The analogy format allows one to sample the efficacy of both past and present verbal reasoning processes across a much broader range of domains than could ever be represented in a necessarily smaller sample of reading passages. And even though good analogy items require more than vocabulary knowledge, word knowledge is not as irrelevant as it might seem to be. Indeed, well-constructed vocabulary tests are among the best measures of verbal reasoning. This is because students learn most new words by inferring their meanings from the contexts in which the words are embedded, and then remembering and revising their understandings as they encounter the words anew. Achieving precise understandings of relatively common but abstract words is thus an excellent measure of the efficacy of past reasoning processes in many hundreds or thousands of contexts. On the other hand, knowledge of infrequent or specialized words, while sometimes useful as a measure of prior achievement, estimates reasoning poorly and thus should be avoided on an aptitude test that aims to measure reasoning rather than domain knowledge.

However, public debates about testing policies rarely deal in such subtleties (Cronbach, 1975). Appearances matter more than substance, so if analogy items appear inauthentic or problematic, they will be (indeed, now have been) eliminated. The sad part of this story is that, as explained later on, those who are most enthusiastic about this change are likely to benefit least from it. For its part, ETS has not always built analogy items in ways that would allow reasonable defense of the reasoning construct they are intended to measure. Indeed, it is possible to build good analogy items for 12th graders using words that most 7th graders know.[1]

A Revisionist History of the SAT

The untold story of the SAT is really about how the concept of aptitude was at first embraced, then simply assumed, then became an embarrassment, and, most recently, abandoned. The problem with a word such as *aptitude* is that everyone thinks that they know what the word means, so they are not inclined to check their understandings against more careful expositions. This is a common problem in psychology. Many key psychological constructs—such as learning, motivation, or intelligence—have deeply entrenched everyday meanings. Because of this, some psychologists have invented new terms for psychological constructs (e.g. Cattell, 1965) or have tried to abandon value-laden terms in favor of less value-laden terms. Christopher Jencks (1998) believes that the only way to eliminate this sort of "labeling bias" in ability tests is to relabel the test. This was the solution initially proposed by those who attempted (unsuccessfully, as it turned out) to change the middle name of the SAT from *aptitude* to *assessment.* Unfortunately, there is no value-free synonym for *aptitude.*

The root of the problem is that Carl Brigham adopted the word *aptitude* in his test without a good theory of what aptitude might be. Brigham's background was in intelligence testing, so he (and many others) assumed that the intelligence tested by his test was the most important scholastic aptitude. Clearly, testing aptitude was also Alfred Binet's original intent. He sought to devise a series of tests that would identify those who were unlikely to benefit from formal schooling and who would instead need special training. Harvard's President James Bryant Conant also wanted to measure aptitude, but for the opposite purpose. His goal was to find students who were likely to succeed at Harvard but who had not attended one of the handful of private schools from which Harvard selected most of its students. Why not use an achievement test instead? As Nicholas Lemann observed, "What Conant didn't like about achievement tests was that they favored rich boys whose parents could buy them top-flight instruction" (1999, p. 38). Those who would rely solely on achievement tests to forecast college success still need to worry about this issue.

The history of the SAT might have been quite different had its founder been Walter Bingham instead of Carl Brigham. Whereas Brigham's background was in intelligence testing, Bingham's expertise was in what we would call industrial psychology. Bingham's *Aptitudes and aptitude testing* (1937) is still worth reading, especially in conjunction with some of the more tortured treatises on the aptitude-achievement distinction of later theorists who had greater competence in multivariate statistics than psychology. Industrial psychologists—from Clark Hull to Richard Snow—have always had more success in thinking about what aptitude might be than many of their counterparts in education. Predicting how well applicants are likely to succeed in a job for which they have little or no prior training is as commonplace in industry as it is uncommon in education. But it is when the mismatch between prior experience and future job demands is greatest that we must think most clearly about why some succeed while others fail. Put differently, educators are easily lulled into thinking that they understand *why* some succeed when at best they understand *who* has succeeded in the past. As long as both the system and the participants remain the same, those who succeeded in the past will indeed be the most likely to succeed in the future. But change either the individual or the system and the prediction fails.

The goal of aptitude testing, then, is to make predictions about the individual's likelihood of success and satisfaction in some yet to be experienced situation on the basis of present behavior. Bingham (1937) spoke of aptitude as readiness to learn some knowledge, skill, or set of responses. This "readiness to acquire proficiency" also included affective factors such as interest or motivation. Bingham also emphasized that aptitude does not refer to native endowment but rather to present characteristics that are indicative of future accomplishment.

> Whether [a person] was born that way, or acquired certain enduring characteristics in his early infancy, or matured under circumstances which have radically altered his original capacities is . . . of little practical moment. . . . And so, when

appraising his aptitude, whether for leadership, for selling, for research, or for artistic design, we must take [the person] as he is—not as he might have been. (p. 17)

Unfortunately, this view of aptitude was less intuitively appealing than one that emphasized the contributions of biology. Early studies of the mental abilities of twins seemed to support beliefs that intelligence and other scholastic aptitude tests really did measure something innate (see, e.g., Lohman, 1997, for one explanation). The developers of the SAT had a more nuanced understanding, generally acknowledging that the abilities measured by the SAT were not innate and developed over time. Further, these abilities were said to be "influenced by experience both in and out of school." (Donlon & Burton, 1984, p. 125). But without a clear theory of what aptitude might be, such caveats were easily ignored.

In the educational literature, some of the best early thinking about aptitude can be found in John B. Carroll's writings about foreign language aptitude. Once again, this case is closer to the task faced by industrial psychologists than by those who would predict the ability to read critically in college from similar reading abilities displayed in high school. In devising tasks for his foreign language aptitude test, Carroll could not assume prior proficiency in the foreign language. Therefore he sought to create test tasks that had a "process structure similar to, or even identical with, the process structures exemplified in the actual learning tasks, even though the contents might be different" (Carroll, 1974, p. 294). One cannot accomplish this goal unless one first has a reasonably good understanding of the processing demands of tasks in the target domain. Prior to the advent of cognitive psychology, understanding cognitive processes was largely a matter of having good intuitions. But we now know quite a bit about the cognitive demands of different instructional environments, and of the characteristics of persons that are necessary for and therefore predictive of success in those environments (Corno et al., 2002). In other words, we are in a much better position to build aptitude tests today than Carl Brigham was back in the 1920s when he assembled the first edition of the SAT.

Aptitude testing, then, is not about measuring innate capacities—whatever these might be. Rather, it begins with a careful examination of the demands and affordances of the target environment and then attempts to determine the personal characteristics that facilitate or impede performance in those environments. The affordances of an environment are what it offers or makes likely or makes useful. Placing chairs in a circle affords discussion; placing them in rows affords attending to someone at the front of the room. Thus, the first task in developing a good aptitude test is careful study of the target domain, especially of its demands and affordances.

We need much more of this work at the university level. The second task is to identify those characteristics that predispose individuals to succeed in the environment. Prior knowledge and skill are often the best predictors of success in academic environments. But these are not the only personal characteristics that matter. The ability to reason well in the symbol systems used to communicate new knowledge is particularly important for those who cannot rely as readily on well-developed systems of knowledge in the domain. Likewise, the ability to persist in one's efforts to attain a difficult goal is also critical for those who start the race several steps behind. This means that although achievement tests may better direct the efforts of students in secondary school, and report on the extent to which they have achieved the common curriculum, tests that measure reasoning abilities and other aptitudes for success in college can help admissions officers find students who are likely to succeed in spite of less than stellar performance on the achievement test. This leads to the next point.

Fluid-Crystallized Ability Continuum

When discussing a selection system, it is helpful to keep track of the commonalities and differences among the measures that are used. One way is to track the extent to which different tests estimate students' abilities to solve familiar problems using practiced routines versus their abilities to solve unfamiliar problems using general reasoning abilities. Figure 1 shows such a continuum.

Assessments differ in the extent to which they are tied to context and situation. For example, course grades are based on tests, projects, and other assignments that are tightly bound to the particular learning context.

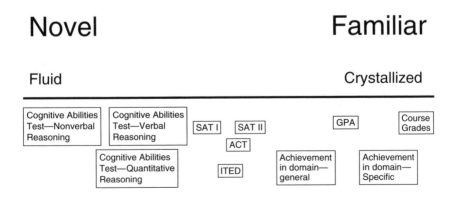

Figure 1. Fluid-Crystallized Ability Continuum.

Some psychologists refer to the knowledge and skill measured by such assessments as *crystallized* abilities. Averages of grades across courses are less tied to any one context. Achievement tests that aim to measure students' understanding of a common curriculum require more transfer. When there is no common curriculum or when we choose tasks that are deliberately novel for our assessments, then we move tasks even farther to the left.

In other words, as we move from right to left on this continuum, we move from measures that are embedded in the curriculum to measures that have no obvious connection to the curriculum. The latter are sometimes called *fluid* reasoning abilities. To the extent that assessments are meant to inform students what they should know, tests near the right are clearly more useful. But to the extent that we want measures that have added value beyond high school grades, then we need to measure abilities at different points along this continuum. This is because assessments that are nearer each other will generally be more highly correlated: students identified as likely to succeed in college by one test will tend to be the same students identified by the other test. In this regard, you will notice that although I have placed SAT I to the left of SAT II general tests and the ACT, I have not placed them very far apart.

One way to think about the current debate is in terms of where along this sort of continuum college entrance tests should lie. Some favor moving toward the right. They do this in part because they want measures more closely aligned with the curriculum. Some do this because they treat freshman grade point averages (GPAs) as the gold standard and seem not to realize that grades are only one of many possible measures of success in learning. Many also want to get as far as they can from measures of reasoning abilities that remind them of IQ tests. Disdain for item types such as analogies is grounded in a legitimate concern that such item types should not be the object of instruction, in a legitimate concern for the extent to which knowledge is indeed situated, but also in a failure to appreciate what we have learned about the measurement of human cognitive abilities in the past twenty years. This leads to the next point.

The Importance of Fluid Reasoning Abilities in a Selection System

It is commonly believed that tests of general reasoning abilities that use the sort of items once used on IQ tests are inherently biased against minorities. Some of these tests and some of the items on them were bad by any standard. But we have learned a thing or two since 1920 about how people think and about how to measure thinking. In fact, scores on well-constructed measures of developed reasoning abilities actually show *smaller* differences between white and minority students than do scores on good achievement tests. And this is one of the main reasons why tests that measure reasoning abilities using nonacademic tasks can be helpful in the admissions process. They can assist in identifying students who do not do particularly well on the more curriculum-based tests, but who are likely to succeed if they work hard.

Figure 2 shows data for 11th-grade students who participated in the joint 2000 national standardization of the Iowa Tests of Educational Development (ITED) and the Cognitive Abilities Test (CogAT). The ITED is a general achievement test for high school students. Parts of the test are very similar to the ACT assessment; parts are similar to the SAT. It shows high correlations with both. The ITED score used here is the core total, without math computation. This total score includes tests for critical reading of literary materials, social studies, and science; reading vocabulary; correctness and appropriateness of expression; and mathematical concepts, problems, and interpretations. The CogAT measures reasoning abilities in three domains or symbol systems: verbal, quantitative, and figural (or nonverbal). The Nonverbal Battery is least tied to the curriculum. The item formats are well-established. They include sentence completions, series completions, classification problems, matrix problems, and yes, even verbal and figural analogies. Although these item formats are old, the construction of items was informed by thirty years of research in cognitive psychology on how people solve such problems and how test items can be constructed better to measure reasoning abilities (see, e.g., Lohman, 2000).

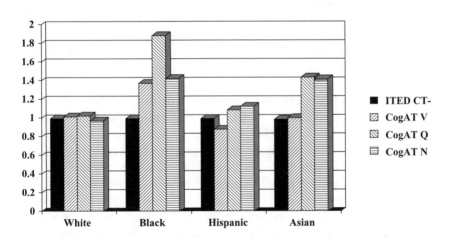

Figure 2. Ratio of the number of students in each ethnic group scoring above the 70th percentile on each test to the number scoring above the 70th percentile on the ITED. By definition, the ratio is fixed at 1.0 for the ITED (black bar). Ratios for the Verbal (V), Quantitative (Q), and Nonverbal (N) batteries of the CogAT are shown in the three hash-marked bars.

The question is, What is the percentage of minority students who score above the 70th percentile on the ITED and each of the three batteries of the CogAT? Grade 11 was chosen because the data are generally more dependable than at grade 12, although here it makes little difference. The 70th percentile was chosen to insure a sufficient sample size for all four groups. Similar patterns are observed at higher cut points. Each column in figure 2 scores shows the increment (or decrement) in the percentage of students who would be selected using a particular CogAT score versus the percentage who would be selected using the ITED achievement test. Thus, the first bar in each set is fixed at 1.0. Look first at the data for white students. It makes little difference which test is used. Now look at the data for black students. All three reasoning tests—but especially the CogAT Quantitative Battery—show increases over the achievement test in the percentage of black students who would be selected. For Hispanic students, the Verbal Battery shows a drop. Making nuanced judgments about the meanings of words in the English language is not a strength. However, quantitative and especially nonverbal reasoning scores are higher. Finally, for Asian Americans, the Quantitative and Nonverbal batteries are once again more likely to identify able students. Those who are concerned about the number of minority students admitted should be concerned about the kind of tests that are administered. The recent report by Bridgeman, Burton, and Cline (2001) comparing the percentage of minority students admitted under SAT I and SAT II did not find this difference. This reinforces my assertion that these tests are actually closer to each other than some would expect. Indeed, the problem with the current version of the SAT I may not be that it is an aptitude test, but that it is not enough of an aptitude test. Over the years it has become more and more achievement-like. The pressure to eliminate discrete item types (such as analogies and sentence completions) and include more "authentic" tasks promises to make the SAT even more like an achievement test. This means that there is a growing need for an alternative measure of students' abilities that is not so strongly tied to the goals of the common curriculum. Such a test could be offered as an optional but separate battery. It could provide important information for admissions committees when they are confronted with applications from poor and minority students who have not scored sufficiently well on the achievement-oriented tests, especially those who show evidence of persistence and a desire to succeed in school.[2]

It is important to understand that the differences between the CogAT and the ITED shown in figure 2 are not due to bias in the achievement test. Much of the discussion about origin of social class differences in mental test scores (e.g., Eells, 1951) and the reaction of conservative psychometricians to it (e.g., that of Arthur Jensen [1980], who was a student of Kenneth Eells) is based implicitly or explicitly on the assumption that a good test of mental ability should somehow be able to see through the veneer of culture and education to the "real" or "innate" differences that lie below the surface. That students who have had a superior education are better able to understand and critically examine the sort of abstract educational ideas presented on the ITED is no more surprising than the fact that those who have had better training in, say, basketball can participate at higher levels in that sport. Good measures of school learning must emphasize those aspects of the curriculum that educators value most. Nevertheless, good measures of reasoning abilities can be built in order to reduce the direct influences of schooling.

A related confusion is the expectation that measures of fluid reasoning abilities should better predict criteria such as course grades than do achievement test scores or grades in previous courses. In chemistry there is a saying, "like dissolves like." In psychometrics of prediction, the parallel dictum is "like best predicts like." When freshman GPA is the criterion, then, other things being equal, high school GPA will generally be the best predictor, measures of achievement the next best predictor, and measures of fluid reasoning the weakest predictor. If common exams at the end of the first year of college were the criterion, then similar measures of past achievement would probably be the best predictor. And if the ability to solve unfamiliar problems inside or outside of one's field of study were the criterion, then measures of fluid reasoning in the same symbol system might top the list of predictors.

There is an extensive literature on the characteristics of persons and tasks that predict school learning. Correlations between college entrance tests and freshman GPA are a small and exceedingly unimportant part of that literature. Indeed, I am astonished that such studies show anything given the diversity of grading criteria and course content across instructors, domains, and schools (see Young, 1990, for one effort to accommodate some of these factors). In their summary of the predictive validity of the SAT, Willingham, Lewis, Morgan, and Ramist (1990) conclude that "a simple analysis of the relationship between [freshman GPA] and scores on pre-admission predictors conceals almost as much as it reveals" (p. 84). Most notably, when the criteria are grades in particular courses rather than GPA, the SAT is a consistently better predictor than high school GPA. In large measure, this is due to the diversity of grading standards across courses that enter into the first-year GPA. Further, grades in large undergraduate classes are commonly determined by performance on objective tests. This means that the course grade may be simply a rough surrogate for two or three course-specific achievement tests. But there are many other ways to measure success in learning, and correlations among these measures typically show considerable divergence. Therefore, decisions about which students to admit should make a serious effort to gather and find the predictors of measures of academic success other than GPA. Continuing to accumulate information on the predictors of first-year GPA may help track local variation in this rather modest relationship, but little else. Looking at a diversity of learning outcomes within large classes can show the value of other measures. However, finding measures that best predict success in a given system can have the paradoxical effect of identifying students likely to succeed in a system that might be in dire need of repair. Indeed, one of the more important uses of measures of fluid and crystallized abilities in research on academic learning has been to identify instructional methods that *reduce* the relationship between learning success and reasoning abilities or prior achievement. Systematic declines in the predictive validity of both the SAT and high school GPA from 1970 to 1988 at some institutions may reflect such adaptations in instructional methods.

An Analogy to Physical Skills

One should not infer that fluid reasoning abilities are innate and that crystallized achievements are developed. Both fluid and crystallized abilities are developed. The primary difference lies in the extent to which abilities are developed through explicit, focused training and practice or are instead the more indirect outcomes of such experiences. But this is difficult to understand because our intuitive theories of abilities constantly get in the way. The best way I have found to understand the difference between ability (as aptitude) and achievement (as outcome) is by analogy to physical skills. Let me return to the continuum of transfer shown in figure 1. This time, however, the domain is physical skills rather than cognitive abilities (see figure 3).

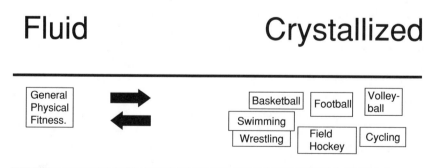

Figure 3. Physical fitness as aptitude for learning physical skills and as an outcome of participation in such activities.

Crystallized abilities are like knowledge and skill in playing different sports. These skills are developed through years of practice and training. Athletes show different levels of competence across sports just as students show different levels of competence in various school subjects. But athletes also differ in their levels of physical fitness. Physical fitness is aptitude for acquiring skill in most sports. Athletes who have higher levels of physical fitness or conditioning will generally have an easier time learning new skills and will perform those that they do learn at a higher level. But physical fitness is also an *outcome* of participation in physically demanding activities. Further, some sports—such as swimming—are more physically demanding than other sports and result in higher increments in physical conditioning for those who participate in them. In a similar manner, reasoning abilities are both an input to as well as an outcome of good schooling (see Snow, 1996; Martinez, 2000). Indeed, expecting a measure of reasoning abilities to be independent of education, experience, and culture is like expecting a measure of physical fitness to be uninfluenced by the sports and physical activities in which a person has participated.[3]

The task of selecting students for university training is akin to selecting students who are likely to succeed in college-level athletics. The best predictor of students' abilities to play football or basketball in college is their demonstrated abilities to play those same sports in high school. In like manner, the best indicator of their abilities to get good grades in college is their abilities to get good grades in similar courses in high school. When athletes come from small schools, however, evaluating athletic skill is difficult unless coaches can arrange a common competition such as a summer basketball tournament. Similarly, achievement tests in particular domains can provide a common yardstick across schools. Suppose, however, that when we have assembled our football team we are short of wide receivers, or on our basketball team of someone to play center. The question, then, becomes one of finding people who are likely to succeed even though their athletic performance thus far has not been stellar. What we look for are athletes who have the requisite physical skills (such as strength, speed, or agility) and at least a moderate level of skill in the sport. Our intention would be not simply to put these athletes on our team but first to provide them with extra training. Similarly, if students were admitted because they had shown high levels of general reasoning ability but had lower grades and achievement test scores, then we would want them to know that we thought they had the ability to succeed but that they would need to work harder than other students to do so.[4] This is exactly what happened to many students from small high schools who were admitted to competitive universities because tests like the earlier versions of the SAT gave them the opportunity to do so.

Conclusions

The allocation of opportunity in society inevitably involves tradeoffs. Decisions that best accomplish one goal may impede the attainment of another, equally cherished outcome. Mental tests have long been recognized as providing one important source of information for college admissions. But tests that best serve the function of measuring prior accomplishment may not be the best measures of future promise. The late Lee Cronbach observed that strange ironies attend the history of mental testing (1975). Ability tests were once viewed as the liberators of talent for those not privileged by wealth and social status. Then we discovered that they were not as blind to culture or privilege as their advocates had assumed and that they did not measure innate potential in anyone. So they were replaced in many quarters by tests deemed to be fairer because they measure school learning. The irony, though, is that good measures of school learning can show an even larger advantage for the advantaged than measures of reasoning abilities, but only when the reasoning tests are not strongly tied to school learning too. Reasoning tests thus have a place at the admissions table. It is not at the head of the table, as some once thought; rather, such tests provide a way to supplement grades and other measures of past achievement. This is especially important for those who through choice or circumstance have not participated fully in the academic system, or for anyone who is embarking on a course of study that will require new ways of thinking and responding not captured in measures of past achievement. In other words, prior achievement is often an important aptitude for future learning. But it is never the only aptitude, and sometimes not even the most important aptitude.

Notes

1. For example, consider the verbal analogy items on the 12th grade level of the Cognitive Abilities Test (Lohman & Hagen, 2001). The typical correct answer is a word that can be used correctly in a sentence by about 75% of 7th graders. The average vocabulary level of all other words in the analogy items is grade 5. Nevertheless, the analogy items are quite difficult. The typical 12th-grade student answers only about half of the items correctly.
2. For various reasons, I do not think that the test should be as removed from the curriculum as the analytic subtest that was recently eliminated from the GRE. Academic learning depends most heavily on students' abilities to reason with words and with quantitative concepts. But one can measure these abilities in ways that reduce the impact of formal schooling (see note 1).
3. This analogy also acknowledges the importance of biological factors, but makes clear the absurdity of the all-too-common inference that an unbiased ability test (or unbiased test of physical fitness) should somehow not be influenced by experience.
4. Note that just as a high level of physical fitness cannot overcome a complete lack of training in a sport, so will high scores on a more fluid reasoning test typically not overcome a lack of knowledge and skill in the domain. This is why I emphasize the importance of students having attained at least a *moderate* level of knowledge and skill in the domain.

References

Bingham, W. V. (1937). *Aptitudes and aptitude testing*. New York: Harper & Brothers.

Bridgeman, B., Burton, N., & Cline, F. (2001). *Substituting SAT II: Subject tests for SAT I: Reasoning test: Impact on admitted class composition and quality*. College Board Research Report No. 2001-3. New York: College Entrance Examination Board.

Carroll, J. B. (1974). The aptitude-achievement distinction: The case of foreign language aptitude and proficiency. In D. R. Green (Ed.), *The aptitude-achievement distinction* (pp. 286–303). Monterey, CA: CTB/McGraw-Hill.

Cattell, R. B. (1965). *The scientific analysis of personality*. Baltimore: Penguin Books.

Corno, L., Cronbach, L. J., Kupermintz, H., Lohman, D. F., Mandinach, E. B., Porteus, A. W., & Talbert, J. E. (2002). *Remaking the concept of aptitude: Extending the legacy of Richard E. Snow*. Mahwah, NJ: Erlbaum.

Cronbach, L. J. (1975). Five decades of public controversy over mental testing. *American Psychologist, 30*, 1–14.

Donlon, T. F. & Burton, N. W. (1984). The construct and content validity of the SAT. In T. F. Donlon (Ed.), *The College Board technical handbook for the Scholastic Aptitude Test and Achievement Tests*. New York: College Entrance Examination Board.

Eells, K. (1951). *Intelligence and cultural differences*. Chicago: University of Chicago Press.

Jencks, C. (1998). Racial bias in testing. In C. Jencks & M. Phillips (eds.) *The black-white test score gap* (pp. 55–85). Washington, DC: Brookings Institution Press.

Jensen, A. R. (1980). *Bias in mental testing*. New York: Free Press.

Lemann, N. (1999). *The big test: The secret history of the American meritocracy*. NY: Farrar, Straus and Giroux.

Lohman, D. F. (1997). Lessons from the history of intelligence testing. *International Journal of Educational Research, 27*, 1–20.

Lohman, D. F. (2000). Complex information processing and intelligence. In R. J. Sternberg (Ed.), *Handbook of intelligence*, (2d ed. pp. 285–340). Cambridge, MA: Cambridge University Press.

Lubienski, S. T. (2000). A clash of social class cultures? Students experiences in a discussion-intensive seventh-grade mathematics classroom. *Elementary School Journal, 100*, 377–403.

Martinez, M. E. (2000). *Education as the cultivation of intelligence*. Mahwah, NJ: Erlbaum.

Snow, R. E. (1996). Aptitude development and education. *Psychology, Public Policy, & Law, 2*, 536–60.

Willingham, W. W., Lewis, C., Morgan, R., & Ramist, L. (1990). *Predicting college grades: An analysis of institutional trends over two decades*. Princeton, NJ: Educational Testing Service.

Young, J. W. (1990). Adjusting cumulative GPA using item response theory. *Journal of Educational Measurement, 27*, 175–86.

A Historical Perspective on the Content of the SAT

IDA LAWRENCE
GRETCHEN RIGOL
TOM VAN ESSEN
CAROL JACKSON

The recent debate over admission test requirements at the University of California sparked a national discussion about what is measured by the various tests—in particular, what is measured by the SAT, the popular name for the College Board's SAT I: Reasoning Test. The public's interest in the SAT was reflected in the media attention that greeted a June 2002 announcement that the College Board's trustees had voted to develop a new SAT (the first administration of which is set for March 2005).

Frequently downplayed in the news stories was the fact that the SAT has been reconfigured several times over the years. Some of the modifications have involved changes in the types of questions used to measure verbal and mathematical skills. Other modifications focused on liberalizing time limits to ensure that speed of responding to questions has minimal effect on performance. There were other changes in the administration of the test, such as allowing students to use calculators on the math sections. Still other revisions have stemmed from a concern that certain types of questions might be more susceptible to coaching.

Since 1970, test developers have also worked to ensure that test content is balanced and appropriate for persons with widely different cultural and educational backgrounds. The steepest increases in test volume since 1973 have been among students of Asian and Hispanic/Latino descent; the proportion of African American test takers has also increased.

Each redesign has been intended to make the test more useful to students, teachers, high school counselors, and college admission staff. As a result, today's test items are less like the "puzzle-solving" questions in the early SATs and more like problems students encounter regularly in school course work: problems that measure reasoning and thinking skills needed for success in college and in life.

This article presents an overview of changes in the verbal and mathematical content of the SAT since it was first administered in 1926. At the end, we will briefly discuss the latest planned changes to the test.

Early Versions of the SAT (1926–1930)

The 1926 version of the SAT bears little resemblance to the current test. It contained nine subtests: seven with verbal content (definitions, classification, artificial language, antonyms, analogies, logical inference, and paragraph reading) and two with mathematical content (number series and arithmetical problems). The time limits were quite stringent: 315 questions were administered in 97 minutes. Early versions of the SAT were quite "speeded"—as late as 1943, students were told that they should not expect to finish. Even so, many of the early modifications to the test were aimed at providing more liberal time limits. In 1928, the test was reduced to seven subtests administered in 115 minutes, and in 1929, to six subtests.

In addition to seeking appropriate time limits, developers of these early versions of the SAT were also concerned with the possibility that the test would influence educational practices in negative ways. On the basis of empirical research that looked at the effects of practice on the various question types, antonyms and analogies were used, because research indicated they were less responsive to practice than were some of the other question types (Coffman, 1962).

Beginning in 1930, the SAT was split into two sections, one portion designed to measure "verbal aptitude" and the other to measure "mathematical aptitude." Reporting separate verbal and mathematical scores allowed admission staff to weight the scores differently depending on the type of college and the nature of the college curriculum.

Changes to the Verbal Portion of the SAT Since 1930

Verbal tests administered between 1930 and 1935 contained only antonyms, double definitions (completing sentences by inserting two words from a list of choices), and paragraph reading. In 1936, analogies were again added. Verbal tests administered between 1936 and 1946 included various combinations of item types: antonyms, analogies, double definitions, and paragraph reading. The amount of time to complete these tests ranged between 80 and 115 minutes, depending on the year the test was taken.

The antonym question type in use between 1926 and 1951 was called the "six-choice antonym." Test takers were given a group of four words and told to select the two that were "opposite in meaning" (according to the directions given in 1934) or "most nearly opposite" (according to the 1943 directions). These were called "six-choice" questions because there were six possible pairs of numbers from which to choose: (1, 2), (1, 3), (1, 4), (2, 3), (2, 4), and (3, 4). Here is an example of medium difficulty from 1934:

gregarious$_1$ solitary$_2$ elderly$_3$ blowy$_4$ (Answer: 1, 2)

Here is a difficult example from 1943:

1-divulged   2-esoteric   3-eucharistic   4-refined   (Answer: 1, 2)

In the 1934 edition of the test, test takers were asked to do 100 of these questions in 25 minutes. They were given no advice about guessing strategies, and the instructions had a quality of inscrutable moralism: "Work steadily but do not press too hard for speed. Accuracy counts as well as speed. Do not penalize yourself by careless mistakes."

In 1943, test takers were given an additional five minutes to complete 100 questions, but this seeming generosity was compensated for by a set of instructions that seem bizarre by today's standards: "Work steadily and as quickly as is consistent with accuracy. The time allowed for each subtest has been fixed so that very few test takers can finish it. Do not worry if you cannot finish all the questions in each subtest before time is called." However, those directions were consistent with that era's experimental literature on using instructions to control the trade-off between speed and accuracy (e.g., Howell & Kreidler, 1964).

In 1952, the antonym format was changed to the more familiar five-choice question. Here is an example from 1960:

VIRTUE: (A) regret   (B) hatred   (C) penalty   (D) denial
(E) depravity   (Answer: E)

The five-choice question is a more direct measure of vocabulary knowledge than the six-choice question, which is more like a puzzle. There are two basic ways to solve the six-choice antonym. The first is to read the four words, grasp them as a whole, and determine which two are opposites. This approach requires the ability to keep a large chunk of material in the clipboard of short-term memory while manipulating it and comparing it to the resources of vocabulary knowledge that one brings to the testing situation. The other approach is to apply a simple algorithm to the problem: "Is the first word the opposite of the second word? If not, is the first word the opposite of the third word? If not, is the first word . . . " and so forth until all six choices have been evaluated.

Most test takers probably used some combination of the two methods, first trying the holistic approach, and if that didn't work, using the more systematic approach. The latter approach probably took longer than the former; given the tight time constraints of the test at this time (18 seconds an item!), test takers who relied solely on the systematic approach were at a disadvantage.

Note that in one of the examples above (1-divulged 2-esoteric 3-eucharistic 4-refined), the vocabulary is quite specialized by the standards of today's test. The word *eucharistic* would never be used today, because it is a piece of specialized vocabulary that is more familiar to some Christians than to much of the general population. Even the sense of *divulged* as the opposite of *esoteric* is obscure, with *divulged* taking the sense of "revealed" or "given out," while *esoteric* has the sense of "secret" or "designed for, or appropriate to, an inner circle of advanced or privileged disciples."

The double-definition question type was a precursor of the sentence-completion question that served as a complement to antonyms by focusing on vocabulary knowledge from another angle. This question type was used from 1928 to 1941. Here is an example of medium difficulty from 1934:

A _____ is a venerable leader ruling by _____ right.
mayor$_1$ patriarch$_2$ minister$_3$ general$_4$
paternal$_1$ military$_2$ ceremonial$_3$ electoral$_4$ (Answer: 2, 1)

This is a fairly straightforward measure of vocabulary knowledge, although it too contains some elements of "puzzle solving," as the test taker is required to choose among the 16 possible answer choices. In 1934, test takers were given 50 of these questions to answer in 20 minutes.

A question type called paragraph reading was featured on the test from 1926 through 1945. These questions presented test takers with one or two sentences of 30–70 words and asked them to identify the word in the paragraph that needed to be changed because it spoiled the "sense or meaning of the paragraph as a whole." From 1926 through 1938, test takers were asked to cross out the inappropriate word, and from 1939 through 1946, they were asked to choose from one of 7 to 15 (depending on the year) numbered words.

Here is an easy example from 1943:

Everybody$_1$ in college who knew$_2$ them at all was convinced$_3$ to see what would come$_4$ of a friendship$_6$ between two persons so opposite$_7$ in tastes, and appearances.

(Answer: 3)

The task here is less like a reasoning task than a proofreading task, and the only real source of difficulty is the similarity in sounds between the words *convinced* and *curious*. A careless test taker might be unable to see *convinced* as the problem because she simply corrected it to *curious*.

Here is a difficult (in more senses than one) example from the same year:

At last William bade his knights draw off$_1$ for a space$_2$, and bade the archers only continue the combat. He feared$_3$ that the English, who had no$_4$ bowmen on their side, would find the rain of arrows so unsupportable$_5$ that they would at last break their line and charge$_6$, to drive off their tormentors$_7$.

(Answer: 3)

This question tests reading skills, but it also tests informal logic and reasoning. The key to the difficulty is that as the test taker reads the beginning of the second sentence, he or she probably assumes that William is English—it is only when the reader figures out that the English have no bowmen that he realizes that William must be *fighting* the English. Here the issue of outside knowledge comes in. Readers who are familiar with English history know that a William who used archers successfully was William the Conqueror in his battles against the English. This knowledge imparts a terrific advantage, especially given the time pressure. It also helps if the test taker knows enough about military matters to accept the idea that a military leader might want the opposing forces to charge.

The paragraph-reading question was dropped after 1945. The verbal test that appeared in 1946 contained antonyms, analogies, sentence completions, and reading comprehension. With the exception of antonyms, this configuration is similar to that of today's SAT and represents a real break with the test that existed before. Changes were made in the interest of making the test more relevant to the process of reading: the test is still a verbal reasoning test, but the balance has shifted somewhat from *reasoning* to *verbal* skills.

Critics of the SAT often point to its heritage in the intelligence tests of the early years of the last century and condemn the test on account of its pedigree, but it is worth noting that by 1946 those question types that were most firmly rooted in the traditions of intelligence testing had fallen by the wayside, replaced by questions that were more closely allied to English and language arts. According to a 1960 ETS document, "the double definition is a relatively restricted form; the sentence completion permits one the use of a much broader range of material. In the sentence completion item the candidate is asked to do a kind of thing which he does naturally when reading: to make use of the element of redundancy inherent in much verbal communication to obtain meaning from something less than the complete communication" (Loret, 1960, p. 4). The change to reading comprehension items was made for a similar reason: "The paragraph reading item probably tends to be esoteric, coachable, and relatively inefficient, while the straightforward reading comprehension is commonplace, probably non-coachable, and reasonably efficient in that a number of questions are drawn from each passage" (Loret, 1960, pp. 4–5).

This shift in emphasis is seen most clearly by comparing the paragraph-reading questions discussed above with the reading-comprehension questions that replaced them. By the 1950s, about half of the testing time in the verbal section was devoted to reading. At this time the passages ranged between 120 words and 500 words. Here is a short reading comprehension passage that appeared in the descriptive booklet made available to students in 1957:

> Talking with a young man about success and a career, Doctor Samuel Johnson advised the youth "to know something about everything and everything about something." The advice was good—in Doctor Johnson's day, when London was like an isolated village and it took a week to get the news from Paris, Rome, or Berlin. Today, if a man were to take all knowledge for his province and try to know something about everything, the allotment of time would give one minute to each subject, and soon the youth would flit from topic to topic as a butterfly from flower to flower and life would be as evanescent as the butterfly that lives for the present honey and moment. Today commercial, literary, or inventive success means concentration.

The questions that followed were mostly what the descriptive booklet described as "plain sense" questions. Here is an easy- to medium-difficult example:

> According to the passage, if we tried now to follow Doctor Johnson's advice, we would
>
> (A) lead a more worthwhile life
> (B) have a slower-paced, more peaceful, and more productive life
> (C) fail in our attempts
> (D) hasten the progress of civilization
> (E) perceive a deeper reality

(Answer: C)

Although this question can be answered without making any complicated inferences, it does ask the test taker to make a connection between the text and her own life.

Here is a question in which test takers were asked to evaluate and pass judgment on the passage:

> In which one of the following comparisons made by the author is the parallelism of the elements least satisfactory?
>
> (A) Topics and flowers
> (B) The youth and the butterfly
> (C) London and an isolated village
> (D) Knowledge and province
> (E) Life and the butterfly
>
> (Answer: E)

Here the test writers were essentially asking test takers to identify a serious flaw in the logic and composition of the passage. According to the rationale provided in the descriptive book, "the comparison" made in (E) "is a little shaky. What the author really means is that human life would be like the life of a butterfly—aimless and evanescent—not that human life would be like the butterfly itself. The least satisfactory comparison, then, is E." This question attempts to measure a higher-order critical-thinking skill.

Verbal tests administered between 1946 and 1957 were quite speeded: they typically contained between 107 and 170 questions and testing time ranged between 90 and 100 minutes. With each subsequent revision to the verbal test, an attempt was made to make the test less speeded. To accommodate different testing times and types of questions, and still administer a sufficient number of questions to maintain test reliability, the mix of discrete and passage-based questions was strategically altered.

Table 1 shows how the format and content of the verbal portion of the test changed between 1958 and today. Between 1958 and 1994, changes were relatively minor, involving some shifts in format and testing time, but little change in test content. More substantial content changes to the verbal test were introduced in the spring of 1994 (see Curley & May, 1991):

- Increased emphasis on critical reading and reasoning skills
- Reading material that is accessible and engaging
- Passages ranging in length from 400 to 850 words
- Use of double passages with two points of view on the same subject
- Introductory and contextual information for the reading passages
- Reading questions that emphasize analytical and evaluative skills
- Passage-based questions testing vocabulary in context
- Discrete questions measuring verbal reasoning and vocabulary in context

Table 1: Numbers of Questions of Each Type in the Verbal Test

	1958–1973/74	1973/74–1978/79	1978/79–1994/95	1994/95–CURRENT
Antonyms	18	25	25	
Analogies	19	20	20	19
Sentence Completions	18	15	15	19
Reading Comprehension	35	25	25	
	(7 passages)	(5 passages)	(6 passages)	
Critical Reading				40
				(4 passages)
Total Verbal Questions	90	85	85	78
Total Testing Time	75 minutes	60 minutes	60 minutes	75 minutes

Antonyms were removed, the rationale being that antonym questions present words without a context and encourage rote memorization. Another important change was an increase in the percentage of questions associated with passage-based reading material. For SATs administered between 1974 and 1994, the frequency of passage-based reading questions was at 29%. To send a signal to schools about the importance of reading, in 1994, passage-based reading questions were increased to 50%. This added reading necessitated an increase in testing time and a decrease in the total number of questions. In comparison to earlier versions of the SAT, reading material in the revised test was chosen to be more like the kind of text students would be expected to encounter in college courses (see Lawrence, Rigol, Van Essen, & Jackson, 2002, for an example of the new type of critical reading material).

The 1994 redesign of the SAT took seriously the idea that changes in the test should have a positive influence on education and that a major task of students in college is to read critically. This modification responded to a 1990 recommendation of the Commission on New Possibilities for the Admissions Testing Program to "approximate more closely the skills used in college and high school work" (Commission on New Possibilities for the Admissions Testing Program, 1990, p. 5).

Changes to the Mathematical Portion of the SAT Since 1930

The SATs given in 1928 and 1929 and between 1936 and 1941 did not contain any mathematics questions. The math section of the SAT administered between 1930 and 1935 contained only free-response questions, and students were given 100 questions to solve in 80 minutes.

The directions from a 1934 math subtest stated, "Write the answer to these questions as quickly as you can. In solving the problems on geometry, use the information given and your own judgment on the geometrical properties of the figures to which you are referred." Here are two questions from that test:

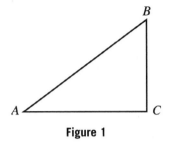

Figure 1

1. In Figure 1, if $AC = 4$, $BC = 3$, $AB =$

   (Answer: $AB = 5$)

2. If $\dfrac{b}{2} + \dfrac{b}{5} = 14$, $b =$

   (Answer: $b = 20$)

These questions are straightforward but are not as precise as those written today. In the first question, students were expected to assume that the measure of $\angle C$ was $90°$ because the angle looked like a right angle. The only way to find AB was to use the Pythagorean theorem assuming that $\triangle ABC$ was a right triangle. The primary challenge of these early tests was mental quickness: how many questions could the student answer correctly in a brief period of time? (Braswell, 1978)

Beginning in 1942, math content on the SAT was tested through the traditional multiple-choice question followed by five choices. The following item is from a 1943 test:

If $4b + 2c = 4$, $8b - 2c = 4$, $6b - 3c = $ (?)
(a) -2 (b) 2 (c) 3 (d) 6 (e) 10

The solution to this problem involves solving simultaneous equations, finding values for b and c, and then substituting these values into the expression $6b - 3c$.

In 1959 a new math question type (data sufficiency) was introduced. Then in 1974 the data sufficiency questions were replaced with quantitative comparisons, after studies showed that those types of questions had strong predictive validity and could be answered quickly.

Both the data sufficiency and quantitative comparison questions have answer choices that are the same for all questions. However, the data sufficiency answer choices are much more involved, as the following two examples illustrate.

Data Sufficiency Item

Directions: Each of the questions below is followed by two statements, labeled (1) and (2), in which certain data are given. In these questions you do not actually have to compute an answer, but rather you have to decide whether the data given in the statements are *sufficient* for answering the question. Using the data given in the statements *plus* your knowledge of mathematics and everyday facts (such as the number of days in July), you are to blacken the space on the answer sheet under

A   if statement (1) ALONE is sufficient but statement (2) alone is not sufficient to answer the question asked,
B   if statement (2) ALONE is sufficient but statement (1) alone is not sufficient to answer the question asked,
C   if BOTH statements (1) and (2) TOGETHER are sufficient to answer the question asked, but NEITHER statement ALONE is sufficient,
D   if EACH statement is sufficient by itself to answer the question asked,
E   if statements (1) and (2) TOGETHER are NOT sufficient to answer the question asked and additional data specific to the problem are needed.

Example:

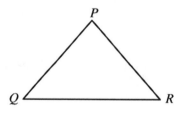

Can the size of angle *P* be determined?

(1) $PQ = PR$
(2)   Angle $Q = 40°$

Explanation:

Since $PQ = PR$ from statement (1), $\triangle PQR$ is isosceles. Therefore $\angle Q = \angle R$.

Since $\angle Q = 40°$ from statement (2), $\angle R = 40°$. It is known that $\angle P + \angle Q + \angle R = 180°$. Angle *P* can be found by substituting the values of $\angle Q$ and $\angle R$ in this equation. Since the problem can be solved and both statements (1) and (2) are needed, the answer is C.

Quantitative Comparison Item

Directions: Each of the following questions consists of two quantities, one in Column A and one in Column B. You are to compare the two quantities and on the answer sheet blacken space

A if the quantity in Column A is greater;
B if the quantity in Column B is greater;
C if the two quantities are equal;
D if the relationship cannot be determined from the information given.

Notes:
1. In certain questions, information concerning one or both of the quantities to be compared is centered above the two columns.
2. A symbol that appears in both columns represents the same thing in Column A as it does in Column B.
3. Letters such as x, n, and k stand for real numbers

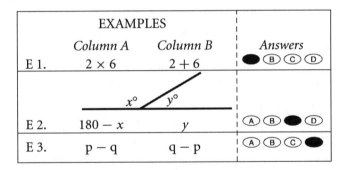

Example:

Column A

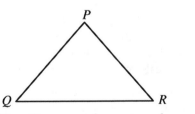

Column B

Note: Figure not drawn to scale.
$$PQ = PR$$

| The measure of $\angle Q$ | | The measure of $\angle P$ |

Explanation:

Since $PQ = PR$, the measure of $\angle Q$ equals the measure of $\angle R$. They could both equal 40°, in which case the measure of $\angle P$ would equal 100°. The measure of $\angle Q$ and the measure of $\angle R$ could both equal 80°, in which case the measure of $\angle P$ would equal $20°$. In one case, the measure of $\angle Q$ would be less than the measure of $\angle P$ ($40° < 100°$). In the other case, the measure of $\angle Q$ would be greater than the measure of $\angle P$ ($80° > 20°$). Therefore, the answer to this question is (D) since a relationship cannot be determined from the information given.

Note that both questions test similar math content, but the quantitative comparison question takes much less time to solve and is less dependent on verbal skills than is the data sufficiency question. Quantitative comparison questions have been found to be generally more appropriate for disadvantaged students than data sufficiency items (Braswell, 1978).

Two major changes to the math section of the SAT took place in 1994: the inclusion of some questions that require test takers to produce their own solutions rather than select multiple-choice alternatives and a policy permitting the use of calculators.

The 1994 changes were made for a variety of reasons (Braswell, 1991); three very important ones were to:

- Strengthen the relationship between the test and current mathematics curriculum
- Move away from an exclusively multiple-choice test
- Reduce the impact of speed on test performance.

An important impetus for change was that the National Council of Teachers of Mathematics (NCTM) had suggested increased attention in the mathematics curriculum to the use of real-world problems; probability and statistics; problem solving, reasoning, and analyzing; application of learning to new contexts; and solving problems that were not multiple-choice (including problems that had more than one answer). This group also strongly encouraged permitting the use of calculators on the test.

The 1994 changes were responsive to NCTM suggestions. Since then there has been a concerted effort to avoid contrived word problems and to include real-world problems that may be more interesting and have meaning to students. Here is a real-world problem from a recent test:

An aerobics instructor burns 3,000 calories per day for 4 days. How many calories must she burn during the next day so that the average (arithmetic mean) number of calories burned for the 5 days is 3,500 calories per day?

(A) 6,000
(B) 5,500
(C) 5,000
(D) 4,500
(E) 4,000

(Answer: B)

The specifications changed in 1994 to require probability, elementary statistics, and counting problems on each test. Concepts of median and mode were also introduced.

$$20, 30, 50, 70, 80, 80, 90$$

Seven students played a game and their scores from least to greatest are given above. Which of the following is true of the scores?

    I.   The average (arithmetic mean) is greater than 70.
   II. The median is greater than 70.
  III. The mode is greater than 70.

  (A) None
  (B) III only
  (C) I and II only
  (D) II and III only
  (E) I, II, and III

(Answer: B)

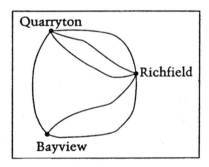

The figure above shows all roads between Quarryton, Richfield, and Bayview. Martina is traveling from Quarryton to Bayview *and back*. How many different ways could she make the round-trip, going through Richfield exactly once on a round-trip and not traveling any section of road more than once on a round-trip?

  (A) 5
  (B) 6
  (C) 10
  (D) 12
  (E) 16

(Answer: D)

Student-Produced Response Questions

Student-produced response (SPR) questions were also added to the test in 1994 in response to the NCTM Standards.

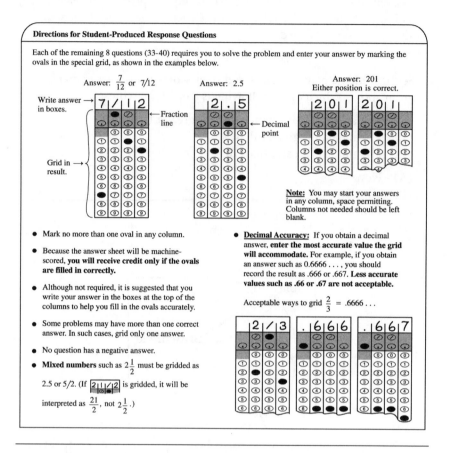

The SPR format has many advantages:

- It eliminates guessing and back-door approaches that depend on answer choices.
- The grid used to record the answer accommodates different forms of the correct answer (fraction versus decimal).
- It allows questions that have more than one correct answer.

Student-produced response questions test reasoning skills that could not be tested as effectively in a multiple-choice format, as illustrated by the following example.

What is the greatest 3-digit integer that is a multiple of 10?

(Answer: 990)

There is reasoning involved in determining that 990 is the answer to this question. This would be a trivial problem if answer choices were given.

The SPR format also allows for questions with more than one answer. The following problem is an example of a question with a set of discrete answers.

The sum of k and $k + 1$ is greater than 9 but less than 17. If k is an integer, what is one possible value of k?

Solving the inequality $9 < k + (k + 1) < 17$ yields $4 < k < 8$. Since k is an integer, the answer to this question could be 5, 6, or 7. Students may grid any of these three integers as an answer.

Another type of SPR question has correct answers in a range. The answer to the following question involving the slope of a line is any number between 0 and 1. Students may grid any number in the interval between 0 and 1 that the grid can accommodate—1/2, .001, .98, and so on. Slope was another topic added to the SAT in 1994 because of its increased importance in the curriculum.

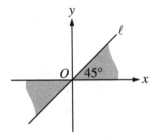

Line m (not shown) passes through O in the figure above. If m is distinct from ℓ and the x-axis, and lies in the shaded region, what is a possible slope for m?

The introduction of calculator use on the math portion of the test reflected changes in the use of calculators in mathematics instruction. The following quantitative comparison question was used in the SAT before calculator use was permitted, but it is no longer appropriate for the test. (Directions for quantitative comparison questions appear earlier in this article; basically, test takers must decide which is greater, the quantity in Column A or Column B; they can also decide that the two quantities are equal or say that there is not enough information to answer the question.)

Column A	*Column B*
$3 \times 352 \times 8$	$4 \times 352 \times 6$

Explanation:

Since 352 appears in the product in both Column A and Column B, it is only necessary to compare 3×8 with 4×6. These products are equal, so the answer to this problem is (C).

This question tested reasoning when calculator use was not permitted, but it only tests button pushing when calculators are allowed. A more appropriate question for a current SAT would be:

Column A	*Column B*

$$0 < x < 1 < y < z$$

$2xy$	$2yz$

This question invites a comparison of two products, and since both products contain $2y$, and $y > 0$, it is only necessary to compare x with z. Since $x < z$, the correct answer is (B), as the quantity in column B is greater than the quantity in column A.

The math portion of today's SAT can be described as a measure of the ability to use mathematical concepts and skills in order to engage in problem solving. It asks that students go beyond applying rules and formulas to think through problems they have not solved before. This emphasis on problem solving in mathematics mirrors the higher academic standards that are in effect in virtually every state. The NCTM and other bodies have long argued that mathematics education should not merely inculcate students with knowledge of facts and algorithms but should aim to create flexible thinkers who are comfortable handling nonroutine problems.

Table 2 shows how the format and content of the math portion of the test has changed between 1942 and today.

Table 2: Numbers of Questions of Each Type in the Mathematics Test

	1942–1959/60	1959/60–1974/75	1974/75–1994/95	1994/95–CURRENT
5-Choice Multiple Choice	48	42	40	35
Data Sufficiency	12	18		
Quantitative Comparison			20	15
Student-Produced Response				10
Total Mathematical Items	60	60	60	60
Total Testing Time	75 minutes	75 minutes	60 minutes	75 minutes

Changes Planned for the 2005 SAT

This article has shown the various ways in which the SAT has evolved since its introduction in 1926. As we have shown, more recent changes have been heavily influenced by a desire to reflect contemporary secondary-school curricula and reinforce sound educational standards and practices.

The pending redesign of the SAT will enhance its alignment with current high school curricula and emphasize skills needed for success in college, which include reading, writing, and mathematics. To highlight the importance of reading, the "verbal reasoning" section of the test will be renamed the "critical reading" section. Analogies, which are not covered in most high school English classes, will be replaced by more questions on both short and long reading passages from a variety of fields, including science and the humanities.

Current SAT test takers are assumed to have had at least a year of high school algebra and geometry, but the math section of the new test will include items from more advanced courses such as second-year algebra; quantitative comparisons, which are not part of classroom instruction, will be eliminated. Concepts tested may include functions, fractional and negative exponents, absolute value, rational equations and inequalities, radical equations, and geometric notation.

The biggest change to the SAT will be the addition of a writing test with multiple-choice questions on grammar and usage and a student essay. Questions will require students to identify sentence errors, improve sentences, and improve paragraphs; for the essay, students will be asked to take a position on an issue and support it with reasons and evidence from their reading, experience, or observation.

The writing test will measure basic writing skills, not creative writing ability. It will be about 50 minutes long (the essay portion will be approximately 25 minutes), and the length of the reading and math tests will be adjusted so that the entire new SAT will require about three hours and 35 minutes to administer, rather than the current three hours.

Many of the motivations that led to previous modifications in the SAT continue to be relevant as we prepare to revise the test once again, but the basic and most important challenge is always to ensure that the SAT is fair for all students and that it effectively meets the needs of college admission offices.

Note

The authors would like to thank Barbara Hames at Educational Testing Service (ETS) for her assistance with rewriting and editing several versions of this paper, and Amy Darlington at ETS for identifying archival materials.

References

Braswell, J. (1978, March). The College Board Scholastic Aptitude Test: An overview of the mathematical portion. *Mathematics Teacher*, vol. 71, 168–180.

Braswell, J. (1991). Overview of changes in the SAT mathematics test in 1994. Paper presented at the annual meeting of the National Council on Measurement in Education, April 5, 1991, Chicago.

Coffman, W. E. (1962). The Scholastic Aptitude Test 1926–1962. Paper presented to the Committee of Examiners on Aptitude Testing.

Commission on New Possibilities for the Admissions Testing Program (1990). *Beyond prediction.* New York: College Entrance Examination Board.

Curley, W. E., & May, G. (1991). Content rationale for the new SAT-verbal. Paper presented at the annual meeting of the National Council on Measurement in Education, April 5, 1991, Chicago.

Howell, W. C., & Kreidler, D. L. (1964). Instructional sets and subjective criterion levels in a complex information-processing task, *Journal of Experimental Psychology* 68(6): 612–614.

Lawrence, I. M., Rigol, G. W., Van Essen, T., & Jackson, C. A. (2003). *A historical perspective on the content of the SAT.* Research Report No. 2003–3. (ETS Research Report RR-03-10.) New York: College Entrance Examination Board.

Loret, P. G. (1960). *A history of the content of the Scholastic Aptitude Test.* Princeton, NJ: Educational Testing Service.

Innovation and Change in the SAT:
A Design Framework for Future
College Admission Tests

HOWARD T. EVERSON

Try all things, and hold fast to that which is good.
St. Paul to the Thessalonians, A.D. 50

Introduction

Science teaches that measurement is central to understanding the world around us. As our knowledge of the world develops, our ways of knowing and measuring change accordingly. The history of science provides many illustrative examples. England's Henry I, for example, circa A.D. 1100, established the yard, and all the measurement implied today by the term *yardstick*. As he figured it, a yard was the distance from the tip of his nose to the very end of his outstretched thumb. Six hundred years later, the French introduced a more standard measure of distance, the meter, which was based on calculations of the circumference of the earth measured on a line running north-south through Paris and divided by 40,000,000. Today the meter—the scientific standard of length—is measured by the distance light travels in a vacuum in $^1/_{299,792,458}$ of a second. Clearly as we understand more about nature, the precision of our measurements improves.

Like other forms of measurement, the SAT—the common yardstick for measuring students' academic preparation for college—will be refined and improved upon as we learn more about the psychology of human abilities and how to measure them with precision. This chapter outlines what some of those improvements might be. Speculating about the future is always risky, particularly when it comes to the SAT. The obvious caveat is that these ideas are relatively new and, at best, represent hunches and speculations grounded in research. Nevertheless, I will attempt to sketch a framework for guiding the innovations we are likely to see in the next generation of college admission tests.

There are at least three reasons why the time is right to think about the future of the SAT. The first is the mounting pressure from educational reformers who are developing content, performance, and assessment standards for high school graduation. When, for example, in 2001, the president of the University of California, Richard C. Atkinson, proposed dropping the SAT as a requirement for admission to the University of California, he called for a closer alignment between college admission tests and the high school curriculum. Atkinson's comments fueled the debate about what college admission tests ought to measure. His remarks raised questions such as: Are admission tests used only to predict grades in the first year of college? Should college admission tests provide all students with the opportunity to demonstrate their varied academic talents and abilities? Should they signal what colleges and universities want in applicants, thereby driving curriculum at the secondary school level? These questions go the very heart of the issue of what college admission tests like the SAT should measure and why. These are questions of purpose, rationale, and validity.

Similarly, advances in computing and communications technology will influence the content and form of college admission tests in the future. The computer's potential for presenting test items and tasks using simulations and multimedia will move large-scale testing beyond the constraints of multiple-choice formats, providing design advantages over traditional forms of paper and pencil tests. Coupled with software systems that track and monitor examinee performance during testing, it is not difficult to imagine more informative adaptive testing systems that, in the future, provide richer and more dynamic forms of assessment (Bennett, 1993, 1998). We see, too, with the recent growth of telecommunications networks, the possibility of using the Internet to deliver tests, thereby providing students and their families with greater access to admission tests and more convenient testing opportunities (Bennett, 1994, 1998).

Third, and perhaps most important, is the influence of cognitive and educational psychology on testing and assessment. Many scholars and theorists working in the area of human learning and intelligence have outlined ways in which educational assessment will benefit and change as the result of research (see, for example, National Research Council, 2000; Snow & Lohman, 1989). Richer analyses of existing tests will, no doubt, improve our understanding of what they measure and why. Moreover, like other areas of scientific inquiry, research in these areas is likely to lead to the use of new and different measures, as well as improved precision of measurement in existing areas.

To remain relevant in the future, succeeding generations of the SAT, as in the past, must incorporate advances in psychology, measurement science, and technology. Change and innovation in college admission tests will progress very slowly if driven solely by the swirl of politics and the atheoretical positions of foes of standardized testing. Modifying the SAT to meet future needs calls for a test-design framework built on the principles of cognitive theory, modern measurement science, and a commitment to technology-based design and delivery systems that promote innovation without sacrificing access and equity. This background theme of a principled design framework is intended to move the SAT from its current task-based focus to an assessment system better positioned to incorporate advances in measurement.

Before exploring these ideas in detail, it may be instructive to trace briefly the evolution of the SAT over the past 75 or so years. This perspective aids our understanding of the educational and social role of the SAT and places college admission testing in a broader cultural context. Then, with this as background, a design framework for the future SAT is proposed and recent research into new constructs is reviewed. The chapter closes with an outline of a generative research agenda designed to support and advance the proposed framework for innovation.

The Evolution of the SAT

From time to time throughout the 20th century, the College Board introduced changes to the SAT. Indeed, today the College Board has an active research program to explore adding to the SAT measures of writing and strategic learning ability, as well as of broader intellectual competencies such as practical and creative thinking, reasoning, and problem solving. This research is described later in this chapter. For now it is instructive to begin by tracing briefly the evolution of the SAT since its inception in 1926. As noted earlier, this historical view of the SAT serves to place college admission testing within the broad cultural context of American higher education.[1]

The central role of the College Board, from its beginning in 1900, has been to promote the transition from high school to college by creating a system of assessments and other services to facilitate college going across the United States. In 1901, for example, 973 students took College Board entrance examinations in nine academic subjects—English, French, German, Latin, Greek, history, mathematics, chemistry, and physics. By 1910, the number of students taking the College Board tests had grown nearly fourfold, with 3,731 students taking the subject matter examinations. Unlike today, the admission tests administered in the early part of the 20th century were created within a college preparatory curriculum framework. These were demanding tests that required candidates to submit lengthy essays as part of the examination process. Clearly, the content and measurement practices were not reflective of the needs of psychometric specialists, but rather were driven more by the demands and expectations of faculty from a small number of highly selective colleges and universities that jealously guarded the postsecondary admission process early in the century.

Following the success of the U.S. Army's large scale testing program in World War I, the College Board admission tests had, by 1925, come under the influence of the intelligence testing movement associated with Robert Yerkes, Henry Moore, and Carl Brigham. Recognizing this trend in psychological and educational measurement, the board adopted the intelligence testing framework proposed by a commission chaired by Carl Brigham and introduced the Scholastic Aptitude Test (SAT) as the uniform college admission test. This shift signaled a clear change in the test's framework, moving decidedly away from the curriculum-based achievement measures characteristic of earlier College Board examinations. The first SAT, administered on June 23, 1926, to 8,040 candidates, included nine subtests: seven with verbal content—definitions, classification, artificial language, antonyms, verbal analogies, logical inference, and paragraph reading; and two with mathematical content—arithmetical problems and number series. Like the current SAT, the scores were reported on a scale with a mean of 500 and standard deviation of 100.

Three short years later, in 1929, again under the direction of Carl Brigham, the SAT was modified to have two separate sections, measuring verbal and mathematical aptitudes with scores reported for each section and with differential weights depending on the college(s) receiving the examinees' scores. In 1937, the board's Achievement Tests (today referred to as the SAT II tests) were introduced, and those scores were also reported on a scale with a mean of 500 and standard deviation of 100, like the scale used on the original SAT. Test score reports went only to the colleges; students and parents were not privy to the SAT scores.

At around the same time, the College Board introduced technology into the SAT with the advent of machine-scored answer sheets, allowing the test to be made up entirely by efficient and inexpensive multiple-choice question-and-answer formats. A short time later, in June 1941, the scores on every form of the SAT were equated directly to scores on preceding forms to allow for trend analyses. Thus, we see a test design framework emerging that included merging the sciences of intelligence testing and psychometrics with early data storage and computing technologies. By the end of World War II, the framework for the SAT reflected the prevailing notions of the centrality of verbal and mathematical aptitudes, coupled with the use of multiple-choice formats and norm-referenced scoring to ensure comparability from year-to-year (Coffman, 1962).

After nearly four decades characterized by continuity and little change, the SAT was modified again in the early 1990s. These changes were in response to calls for reform in education more generally. Perhaps the most important change was a shift away from the long-held belief that aptitudes for college success were fixed or immutable, with a move to an assessment framework that included the measurement of verbal and mathematical abilities that develop over time—both in and outside of school. It remains unclear, however, to many working on the frontiers of cognitive psychology and psychometrics how these abilities change, and what conditions foster their development. Nonetheless, this minor change was a nod in the direction of those who argued that schooling ought to matter when it comes to performance on the SAT.

The verbal section, for example, included measures of critical reading, vocabulary in context, and analogical reasoning. Similarly, the mathematics section stressed the application of mathematical concepts and quantitative comparisons, and permitted examinees to use calculators when taking the test. The tests were renamed (and renormed) and the acronym SAT I was introduced, while direct references to the Scholastic Aptitude Test were abandoned. The Board's admission testing program now included the SAT I Reasoning Test and the SAT II Subject Tests.

Moving from early notions of intelligence and aptitude testing, the SAT evolved over the course of the 20th century to include a greater emphasis on developed abilities, while at the same time responding to educational reforms. Looking back, we see that as our knowledge of learning and educational measurement increased, the SAT was modified accordingly. Throughout its history, changes in the SAT were discrete, one-shot events. Looking ahead, we anticipate advances in measurement, psychology, and technology will continue, and the SAT will be expected to adopt a framework that will permit it to keep pace by introducing innovation through a continuous improvement design process.

A Design Framework for the SAT

As noted above, maintaining the SAT's relevance in the college admission process depends largely on the framework that guides innovation in the future. The background theme, again, is that explicating the test design framework for the SAT makes continuous improvement sustainable and provides opportunities to introduce a new generation of college admission tests without the disruption that often accompanies sweeping technological change.[2] The need for a design framework is motivated by progress in four areas related to testing and assessment—cognitive psychology, learning theory applied to academic disciplines, psychometric modeling, and information technology (Almond, Steinberg, & Mislevy, 2002). We ensure improved measurement now and in the future by designing and developing tests that conform to the principles that we refer to as evidence-centered assessment design. These principles guide the decisions that will be made based on test results, and then work backward to develop the necessary tasks, delivery mechanisms, scoring procedures, and feedback mechanisms (Almond et al., 2002). A design framework, for example, provides test developers with a common language for discussing the knowledge, skills, and abilities measured by the SAT, and why they are essential to success in college and beyond. These discussions, one could argue, help create consensus about the role and value of the SAT, sharpen the focus on its measurement goals and, along the way, demystify what the SAT measures and why it measures those constructs and not others. Thus, as our understanding of what the SAT measures is increased, test scores have more meaning and a richer body of information is available to schools, colleges, and universities. Higher education policies and the role of standardized testing benefit from improved measurement as well. And, perhaps more important, we are better positioned to evaluate students' abilities and potentialities, and to make changes to the SAT in the future.

Networks of Assessments

As computing technology has transformed itself—and the worlds of business, science, and education change along with it—computer uses have moved from numerical calculators to data processing machines to interacting networks of intelligent information retrieval, control, and delivery systems. In this world of networks and information webs, it is easy to imagine a future where the best schools, teachers, and courses are available to all students (Bennett, 1998; Everson, 1998; Penzias, 1995; Stewart and Everson, 1994). This scenario suggests that tests and assessments designed with a single, narrow focus—such as summative forms of assessment—may be unnecessary in the future.

In some sense the future is already here. Distance learning opportunities are more widely available. Computer-based adaptive tests—that is, assessments in which the examinee is presented with different test questions or tasks matched to her ability or skill levels—are in widespread use with the College Board's Accuplacer tests as well as with the Graduate Record Examination (GRE), the Graduate Management Admission Test (GMAT), the Test of English as a Foreign Language (TOEFL), and others. In these instances and others, computers construct the tests, present the items adaptively, score the responses, and generate reports and analyses. The potential of computer-based testing can be pushed further, and more intelligent forms of assessment are possible, even likely (Bennett, 2001; 2002). Nearly a decade ago Randy Bennett (1993) framed the future of intelligent assessment this way:

> Intelligent assessment is conceived of as an integration of three research lines, each dealing with cognitive performance from a different perspective: constructed-response testing, artificial intelligence, and model-based measurement.... These tasks will be scored by automated routines that emulate the behavior of an expert, providing a rating on a partial credit scale for summative purposes as well as a qualitative description designed to impart instructionally useful information. The driving mechanisms underlying these tasks and their scoring are cognitively grounded measurement models that may dictate what the characteristics of items should be, which items from a large pool should be administered, how item responses should be combined to make more general inferences, and how uncertainty should be handled (p. 99).

This convergence of computer-based testing with advanced networks makes possible new forms of college admission tests, which may include, for example, more complex items and tasks, seamless branching across content areas and domains, and modular components. This merging of theory and technology also makes likely the introduction of new test delivery systems, remote scoring of constructed responses, and more powerful means for summarizing and communicating test performance. These advances in information technologies, no doubt, will provide platforms for the next generation of the college admission tests. If Bennett (1998) is right, new technology will be the prime mover of innovation in educational testing. Bennett makes a strong argument for a future-oriented design framework for the SAT that accommodates technological advances, improved measurement, and breakthroughs in the learning sciences.

Model-Based Measurement

The SAT, and tests like it, have been based on classical measurement principles.[3] The dominant goal of this psychometric approach to measurement was to estimate an examinee's relative position on a scale that measures a latent variable—for example, an aptitude for verbal or mathematical reasoning. This classical test model was developed largely to permit inferences about how much knowledge, aptitude, or ability an individual possesses in a normative sense. In the case of the SAT the cognitive abilities the test assesses are verbal and mathematical reasoning. In general, this measurement model has proved useful for inferences related to selection and classification. This classic psychometric approach is much less helpful for making instructional decisions or for diagnosing learning or achievement deficiencies—an oft-stated measurement goal of many new assessments (Nichols, Chipman, & Brennan, 1995).

With the emergence of the cognitive perspective in the learning sciences, the emphasis shifts from measures of how much a student has learned, or where he ranks on a continuum of achievement, to a focus on the importance of how knowledge is organized, and how students reorganize that knowledge to represent and solve problems. Educational measurement now needs to tell us more about what students know. Indeed, this theoretical shift underscores the need for measurement models that distinguish learners in terms of their knowledge states, cognitive process abilities, and strategies for solving problems (National Research Council, 2001).

In response to the challenge articulated by the National Research Council's Committee on the Foundations of Assessment (NRC, 2001), a number of new and promising psychometric approaches with a decidedly cognitive flavor are in development. These include, for example, latent trait models, statistical pattern classification methods, and causal probabilistic networks. While these measurement models may rank students along a proficiency scale, their intent is to build on detailed task analyses and cognitively rich representations of how knowledge is structured by learning in school to produce assessments that inform instruction in ways that are diagnostic as well as prescriptive (Nichols, Chipman, and Brennan, 1995).

Many of these newer models attempt to provide descriptions of the students' knowledge or ability structures, as well as the cognitive processes presumed to underlie performance on single test items or tasks, or sets of tasks. Thus, if successfully developed and adapted, they hold promise not only for tests like the SAT, but also for dynamically linking assessment and instruction (Everson, 1995).

New test items and tasks will be needed to capture the complexity of reasoning, problem solving, and strategic thinking that is emerging from the learning sciences. It is not likely that traditional item characteristics, such as item difficulty or person ability, will be of much use for assessments that are theory based. As Susan Embretson (1996) suggests, "applying cognitive principles to the design of test items requires analyzing how item stimulus content influences the cognitive processes, strategies, and knowledge structures that are involved in item solving" (p. 29). Test items and tasks that go beyond the four- or five-option multiple-choice format will be required. Innovations in technology and theory will enable the development of a variety of constructed-response formats and simulations to support the evaluation of a broader range of abilities. As any young school kid can tell you, it is not difficult to imagine that computer-based simulations that capitalize on multimedia have a good deal of potential for future assessments.

Together, these relatively new psychometric models all take the important step of attempting to integrate cognitive psychology and model-based measurement. Indeed, they are seen as intelligent forms of assessment (Bennett, 1993), and as efforts that synthesize methods and techniques from three vital research areas, artificial intelligence and expert systems, modern psychometrics, and cognitive psychology—that is, smart tests. To be useful in a theory-based test design framework a number of issues will have to be resolved. More work, for example, is needed on the painstaking task analyses that foreshadow cognitive model development in various academic domains like mathematical problem solving or language learning. As measurement science and computer technologies advance so too does our ability to gather and incorporate evidence from other cognitively rich constructs—such as metacognitive abilities, problem solving strategies, prior knowledge, and response mode preferences. These various forms and combinations of evidence could be incorporated into a design framework for assessment in the SAT.

New Measures

Students' developed abilities in, for example, verbal reasoning, reading comprehension, writing, and mathematical problem solving may be assessed in the future with test items and tasks that are based on stronger theoretical foundations. Achievement tests reflect what students know and can do in specific subject areas. Assessments of cognitive abilities, on the other hand, are not the same as subject-matter achievements. They are often more general, and together with measures of achievement, may provide more comprehensive diagnoses of academic potential. This view of educational achievement stresses not only knowledge as the product of learning but also knowledge as a means to more advanced levels of learning. Indeed, the potential exists for an SAT that provides cognitive profiles of developed abilities not only in the traditional verbal and mathematical domains but also in the subject-specific domains, such as writing and reading comprehension, which provide direct connections to classroom learning.[4] By incorporating this view of learning in its framework, the SAT's relevance to educational reform is strengthened.

Beyond Verbal and Mathematical Reasoning

In this section I outline a representative set of constructs that holds promise for improving our ability to predict success in higher education and, therefore, adds value to the SAT. The constructs currently in the research and development pipeline fall into three broad categories: (1) the more or less traditional achievement areas, such as writing; (2) measures of strategic learning ability; and (3) theory-based measures of intellective competence, such as practical and creative intelligences. Collectively, these research efforts are aimed at improving the precision of the SAT as a measure of developed abilities. Here is a snapshot of some of those efforts.

Writing Ability

"Writing is thinking on paper," notes William Zinsser in his short but wonderful book *Writing to Learn* (Zinsser, 1988). Striking a similar note, the National Writing Project introduced its 2001 annual report by declaring, "Writing is pivotal to learning and to success in and beyond school." That writing is central to success in college is not in dispute. The issue for the SAT is how best to assess the construct of writing ability. As researchers working in this domain are quick to point out, narrating a story, revising a memo, or reporting on current events all come under the general heading of writing, and all differ with respect to the knowledge, skills, and abilities they draw upon (Breland, Bridgeman, & Fowles, 1999). Thus, designers of the SAT are left with the question of whether writing is a unitary construct and, if not, how best to assess it.

The College Board has long been concerned about how to assess writing skills with efforts going back more than 40 years (Breland et al., 1999). Early efforts to assess writing using a single essay written on an assigned topic had score reliability estimates that were unacceptably low. The board's Admission Testing Program introduced an indirect measure of writing in Test of Standard Written English (the TSWE) in 1974. The TSWE was designed to correlate with more direct measures of writing, such as essays, and the scores were used for placement into college English courses. Mounting concerns over writing, coupled with research by F. I. Godshalk, Frances Swineford, and William Coffman (1966), led the board to introduce a 20-minute essay to the test in December 1977. Today, the SAT II Writing Test is a one-hour test that consists of 60 multiple-choice questions and a 20-minute essay. The multiple-choice questions address common writing problems such as consistency of expression, logical construction, clarity and precision of language, and sentence structure. The 20-minute essay is written in response to an assigned topic and read by two readers using holistic scoring methods. The multiple-choice section score is combined with the essay rating, and students' scores are reported on a 200 to 800 scale. In 2002, over 200,000 students took the SAT II Writing Test, and their average score was 600. With test volumes at these levels, and average performance improving over time, optimism for adding writing to the SAT I is warranted.

Indeed, test development proposals are under consideration now for introducing a writing section to the SAT I in the spring of 2005, modeled after the writing assessment currently used in SAT II. Again, the board's concerns about students' ability to write and its longstanding commitment to improve the measurement of those academic skills and abilities central to success in college led to the decision to add both direct and indirect measures of writing to the SAT I. If, indeed, writing is thinking on paper, as Zinsser suggests, and if writing is central to learning in school and in college, then adding a measure of writing to the SAT I fits within the design framework of college admission tests and the construct (i.e., writing ability) should add to both the predictive and consequential validity of the test. The essay, undoubtedly, is a sample of the kind of writing required in college that, in turn, ought to produce stronger correlations between the SAT writing score and college grades. Hence, we expect increased predictive validity for the SAT I. In addition, the essay signals the importance of writing in the college admission process. Thus, we expect the consequence will be an added emphasis on the teaching and learning of writing skills.

Strategic Learning Skills

Research on the border between cognitive psychology and educational measurement is yielding promising methods for assessing students' understanding of their ability to learn. Recent work in the general area of self-regulated learning and problem solving (Tobias and Everson, 2002; Weinstein, 1995; Zimmerman and Schunk, 2001), for example, adds to the evidence suggesting that successful students are strategic learners. According to this view, strategic learners are able to take responsibility for their own learning by setting realistic learning goals and using knowledge about themselves as learners as part of their approach to learning. Strategic learners, apparently, use a variety of cognitive processes—for example, the metacognitive skills and abilities of planning, monitoring and modifying their learning strategies, to achieve their educational objectives.

There is an emerging body of research that suggests self-regulated learners are more efficient and effective learners (Tobias & Everson, 2002; Zimmerman & Schunk, 2001). This research makes clear, for example, that students who have developed the abilities to analyze, plan, execute, and evaluate academic tasks outperform their less capable counterparts in a variety of academic settings—giving them a decided advantage in the classroom.

Given the importance of self-regulated learning and study strategies, a number of self-report type measures have been developed to assess individual differences in strategic learning and study skills. The Learning and Study Strategies Inventory, the LASSI (Weinstein, Schulte, & Palmer, 1987), is perhaps the most widely used instrument. The LASSI is a self-report instrument consisting of 76 items organized into ten subscales measuring students' attitudes toward learning, motivation for academic achievement, time management skills, test anxiety, ability to concentrate, information processing, the ability to select main ideas in text, the use of study aids, frequency of self testing, and the use of test strategies. The LASSI requires students to estimate the degree to which a statement is indicative of their learning experiences by making a selection from 1 (Not at all like me) to 5 (Very much like me). Test scores are reported by subscale and feedback to students usually comes from teachers and guidance counselors. The LASSI has been adapted for use in both high school and college settings.

Curious about the construct of learning strategies and how they might predict students' academic achievement, we conducted research to estimate the association between students' LASSI scores and measures of academic achievement—that is, on college admission test scores (the preliminary SAT) and high school grade point average.

We sampled 1,645 students from 11 U.S. high schools and collected their LASSI scores, their high school grade point averages, and their Preliminary SAT/National Merit Scholarship Qualifying Test (PSAT/NMSQT) test scores. The students were either 10th and 11th graders at the time of testing, and about 45% of them were girls.[5]

We conducted a series of regression analyses of the type used typically to predict students' grade point averages (GPA) using their PSAT/NMSQT verbal and math scores and their LASSI scores. Generally we were interested in estimating how much the LASSI scores improved our ability to predict students' GPAs, once the effects of their pre-SAT scores were controlled statistically. Surprisingly, we found that the LASSI—as a measure of strategic learning ability—improved our predictions of academic achievement by 11% overall. Earlier work (Goff & Ackerman, 1992; Ackerman & Heggestad, 1997; and Dennis, Sternberg, & Beatty, 2000), suggests that measures of individuals' typical cognitive performance—such as self-reports like the LASSI—may be used along with maximal-performance cognitive-skills measures (e.g., the PSAT/NMSQT or the SAT I) to increase validity of admission and selection decisions. The results of our study using the LASSI are promising, and tend to support the positions reached by the earlier researchers. Thus, I suspect that we will continue to work to improve the measurement qualities of self-reports like the LASSI and better assess the feasibility of using such measures as part of the SAT in the future.

Multiple Intelligences

In collaboration with Robert Sternberg and his colleagues at the Yale University Center for the Psychology of Abilities, Competencies, and Expertise (the PACE Center), the College Board is developing new measures based on more advanced understanding of the psychology of human abilities and how they develop. Our hope is to better identify a broader range of student abilities and thereby prepare a more diverse population of students for success in college. Because abilities beyond conventional verbal and mathematical reasoning abilities are required for success in and out of college, including a broader spectrum of abilities should help refine the metrics of the SAT. Research suggests, for example, that other abilities, including creative and practical intellective competencies, are also important to school and life success. The theory animating these new forms of assessment is rooted in Sternberg's (1985, 1988) triarchic theory of human intelligence.

Sternberg's triarchic theory suggests that intelligent individuals are ones who figure out their strengths and weaknesses and find ways of capitalizing on their strengths while at the same time compensating for and remediating their weaknesses. In particular, they demonstrate a balance of analytical, creative, and practical abilities to achieve success in life. *Analytical intelligence* is characterized as the aspect of intelligence assessed typically by the reasoning component of traditional tests of literacy, numeracy, and problem solving—seen clearly in tests like the SAT, for example. *Creative intelligence*, by contrast, is the aspect of intelligence that accounts for the generation of novel ideas or solutions to problems and is measured by tasks requiring creative thinking. And finally, *practical intelligence* is often thought of as the everyday aspect of intelligence—used when one makes everyday decisions or solves everyday problems

Crucial to practical intelligence is *tacit knowledge*—the knowledge base one needs to acquire to adapt to, shape, and select environments. Though key to practical intelligence, tacit knowledge is not taught directly or specifically. Often this knowledge is not even talked about, let alone taught formally. An example of tacit knowledge is knowing what to say to a teacher or professor when you disagree with her—when to voice the disagreement, and how to express it without belligerence or offensiveness. This is the knowledge one needs to function practically and effectively in an environment. It often ranges from extremely domain-specific knowledge (e.g., how to program a computer) to relatively domain-general information (e.g., how to organize one's time).

It is important to note, too, that the three types of abilities are used in different ways. Analytic abilities are used to analyze, judge, evaluate, compare, contrast, and critique. Creative abilities, on the other hand, are used to create, invent, discover, and imagine, while practical abilities, the ones all too often overlooked in educational testing, are used to implement, put into practice, and act.

In collaboration with the College Board, researchers at the PACE Center have developed prototype tests to measure these abilities, as well as achievements—creative work, leadership roles, and the like—based on these abilities. These new measures are currently in the early stage of research and development and are undergoing pilot testing in a series of preliminary field studies initiated in the spring and summer of 2001 with students from ten colleges and universities around the country. These prototypes, and the data generated from the initial field studies, will remain in the R&D pipeline for at least two more years undergoing further testing and refinement before they can be introduced as part of the admission testing battery sponsored by the College Board.

Other Noncognitive Measures

In addition to our work on learning and study strategies, and our work with Yale University's PACE Center, our R&D efforts also focus on noncognitive measures as well. For example, initial work is underway to develop a biographical inventory of past experiences and/or accomplishments, and a situational judgment inventory that, together, may add to the prediction of college success. In general, this work borrows from current theories of job performance and looks at the domain of college performance through this lens (Oswald, Schmitt, Ramsay, Kim, & Gillespie, in press). More specifically, if the domain of college success skills is broader than the traditional measures of academic achievement, then we may find evidence for the value of noncognitive predictors such as social skills, interests, and personality in predicting college performance (see Oswald et al., in press). Though these measures are in the very early stages of development, the data gathered thus far suggest that they may be useful for predicting first year grade point averages, as well as students' self-assessments of their academic ability, while having relatively low correlations with SAT scores and other more traditional measures of academic ability. These noncognitive measures, generally, may provide college admission committees and others with information that goes beyond what we can measure using the SAT—leadership qualities, a gauge of a student's academic self-esteem, and a measure of how well a student would handle the everyday problems of college life. Their potential for preparing and connecting students to college, and ensuring their success in college, is promising.

Conclusion

This is an exciting time for the SAT. Change and innovation are in the air. The R&D programs presented in this chapter, I believe, have promise for creating a strong theoretical foundation for the next generation of the SATs. The design framework outlined here suggests a shifting view of testing and assessment, and depicts a future for large-scale assessment that addresses the many, often competing, demands and driving forces in education and society.

Clearly, an ambitious program of research will be required to make the next generation of the SAT useful not only for selection and prediction, but also for placement and diagnosis, as the design framework implies. The board, no doubt, will continue its research in a number of promising areas, including (1) developing new measurement constructs that go beyond verbal and mathematical reasoning—for example, critical reading, problem solving, and metacognition; (2) designing new item types and response formats; (3) developing psychometric models for multidimensional scales and cognitive diagnosis; and (4) communicating examinee performances in ways that inform teaching and learning.

Reform and innovation appear to be everywhere in education— particularly when it comes to large-scale assessment. Portfolios, standards-based assessment design, performance assessments, and computer-adaptive test methods are just some of what we see when we look across the land-scape. Technological innovation, as was noted earlier, will transform not only how we test but what we test. Networks of closely aligned tests are easily imagined. It is clear, too, that rapidly advancing scientific areas like the brain sciences, artificial intelligence, and the psychology of learning will influence testing by reshaping the conceptual basis of teaching and learning. The challenge for organizations like the College Board and the Educational Testing Service is to learn from these innovations, and to incorporate what is new and helpful while, at the same time, following St. Paul's caution to hold fast to the things that are good.

Notes

An earlier version of this paper was presented at the conference entitled Rethinking the SAT in University Admissions, held at the University of California, Santa Barbara, November 16– 17, 2001. The research reported in this paper was supported by the College Board. Requests for copies of this paper should be sent to Dr. Howard T. Everson, c/o the College Board, 45 Columbus Ave, New York, NY, 10023.

1. For a more detailed description of the changes to the SAT from 1926–2001, see Lawrence, Rigol, Van Essen and Jackson, 2002, an abbreviated version of which appears in this volume.
2. For a more detailed presentation of the notion of a principled design framework see Everson, 2000.
3. A more detailed discussion of the measurement models presented here can be found in Everson, 1998.
4. See Commission on New Possibilities for the Admissions Testing Program, 1990.
5. For a complete description of the LASSI and how we studied its structure and its predictive validity, see Everson, Weinstein, and Laitusis, 2000.

References

Ackerman, P. L., & Heggestad, E. D., (1997). Intelligence, personality, and interests: Evidence of overlapping traits. *Psychological Bulletin, 121,* 219–45.

Almond, R. G., Steinberg, L. S., & Mislevy, R. J. (2002). Enhancing the design and delivery of assessment systems: A four process architecture. *Journal of Technology, Learning, and Assessment, 1(1)*, Available online at http://www.jtla.org.

Bennett, R. E. (1993). Toward intelligent assessment: An integration of constructed-response testing, artificial intelligence, and model-based measurement. In N. Frederiksen, R. J. Mislevy, & I. Bejar (Eds.), *Test theory for a new generation of tests*. Hillsdale, NJ: Erlbaum.

Bennett, R. E. (1994, October). The role of technology in creating assessments that increase participation in post-compulsory education. Paper presented at the annual meeting of the International Association for Educational Measurement, Montreal, Canada.

Bennett, R. E. (1998). Reinventing assessment: Speculations on the future of large-scale educational testing. Princeton, NJ: Policy Information Center, Educational Testing Service. Available online at http://www.ets.org/research/pic/bennett.html.

Bennett, R. E. (2001). How the Internet will help large-scale assessment reinvent itself. *Education Policy Analysis Archives, 9(5)*. Available online at http://epaa.asu./epaa/v9n5.html.

Bennett, R. E. (2002). Inexorable and inevitable: The continuing story of technology and assessment. *Journal of Technology, Learning, and Assessment, 1(1)*, Available online at http://www.jtla.org.

Breland, H. M., Bridgeman, B., & Fowles, M. E. (1999). *Writing assessment in admission to higher education: Review and framework*. College Board Report No. 99–3. New York: College Board.

Coffman, W. E. (1962). The scholastic aptitude test, 1926–1962. Paper presented to the Committee of Examiners on Aptitude Testing, Princeton, NJ: Educational Testing Service.

Commission on New Possibilities for the Admission Testing Program. (1990). *Beyond prediction*. New York: College Entrance Examination Board.

Dennis, M. J., Sternberg, R. J., & Beatty, P. (2000). The construction of 'User-Friendly' tests of cognitive functioning: A synthesis of maximal- and typical-performance measurement philosophies. *Intelligence, 28(3)*, 193–211.

Embretson, S. E. (1996). Cognitive design principles and the successful performer: A study on spatial ability. *Journal of Educational Measurement, 33(1)*, 29–39.

Everson, H. T. (1995). Modeling the student in intelligent tutoring systems: The promise of a new psychometrics. *Instructional Science, 23*, 433–52.

Everson, H. T. (1998). A theory-based framework for future college admission test. In S. Messick (Ed.), *Assessment in higher education: Issues of access, quality, student development and public policy*. Hillsdale, NJ: Erlbaum.

Everson, H. (2000). A principled design framework for admission tests: An affirmative research agenda. *Psychology, Public Policy, and Law, 6 (1)*, 112–20.

Everson, H., Weinstein, C. E., & Laitusis, V. (2000). Strategic learning abilities as predictors of academic achievement. Paper presented at the annual meeting of the American Educational Research Association, New Orleans.

Godshalk, F. I., Swineford, F., & Coffman, W. E. (1966). *The measurement of writing ability*. New York: College Entrance Examination Board.

Goff, M., & Ackerman, P. L. (1992). Personality-intelligence relations: Assessment of typical intellectual engagement. *Journal of Educational Psychology, 84*, 537–52.

Gordon, E. W. (2002). Affirmative development: Looking beyond racial inequality. *College Board Review, 195*.

Lawrence, I., Rigol, G. W., Van Essen, T., & Jackson, C. A. (2002). A historical perspective on the SAT 1926–2001. College Board Report No. 2002–7. New York: College Board.

National Research Council, Committee on the Foundations of Assessment, J. Pellegrino, N. Chudowsky, & R. Glaser, (Eds.). (2001). Knowing what students know: The science and design of educational assessment. Washington, DC: National Academy Press.

National Writing Project (2001). *Annual Report 2001*. Berkeley: University of California.

Nichols, P. D., Chipman, S., & Brennan, R. (Eds.) (1995). *Cognitively diagnostic assessment*. Hillsdale, NJ: Erlbaum.

Oswald, F. L., Schmitt, N., Ramsay, L. J., Kim, B. H., & Gillespie, M. A. (in press). *Noncognitive predictors of college student success*. New York: College Board.

Penzias, A. (1995). *Harmony: Business, technology, and life after paperwork*. New York: Harper Collins.

Snow, R. E., & Lohman, D. F. (1989). Implications of cognitive psychology for educational measurement. In R. L. Linn (Ed.), *Educational Measurement*, 3d ed., (pp. 263–332). New York: Macmillan.

Sternberg, R. J. (1985). *Beyond IQ: A triarchic theory of human abilities.* New York: Cambridge University Press.

Sternberg, R. J. (1988). *The triarchic mind: A new theory of intelligence.* New York: Viking.

Sternberg, R. J. (1997). *Successful intelligence.* New York: Plume.

Stewart, D. M., & Everson, H. T. (1994). Educational assessment and national standards: The equity imperative. In M. Nettles (Ed.), *Equity and assessment* (pp. 263–72). Boston: Kluwer Academic Press.

Tobias, S., & Everson, H. T. (2002). Knowing what you know, and what you don't know. College Board Report (2002–4). New York: College Board.

Weinstein, C. E. (1995). Innate ability versus acquired ability: A student dilemma. *Innovation Abstracts, 18(3)*. Austin, TX: National Institute for Staff and Organizational Development.

Weinstein, C. E., Schulte, A. C., & Palmer, D. R. (1987). Learning and Study Strategies Inventory (LASSI). Clearwater, FL: H & H.

Zimmerman, B. J., and Schunk, D. H. (2001). *Self-regulated learning and academic achievement.* Mahwah, NJ: Erlbuam.

Zinsser, W. (1988). *Writing to learn.* New York: Harper & Row.

Commentary on Part I: Admissions Testing in a Disconnected K–16 System

MICHAEL W. KIRST

Admissions literature focuses upon what is most beneficial to postsecondary education without contemplating the impact of admissions tests upon secondary schools, K–12 students, and teachers. Admissions tests send powerful and clear signals to all K–12 groups about what knowledge is most worth knowing and how it should be taught. There is often no sense of a tradeoff between more data for higher education admissions and the required secondary teaching and testing time. Should secondary students spend time cramming for SAT I analogies, if these are not part of the K–12 curriculum or state education standards? The heavy weight that University of California gives to SAT II writing will encourage more high school composition. However, SAT II writing prompts feature a personal or reflective essay, while many high school exams focus upon analysis, reporting, and argument. As UC president Richard Atkinson correctly states in his paper, "One of the clear lessons of U.S. history is that colleges and universities, through their admissions requirements, strongly influence what is taught in the K–12 schools."

Probably the biggest issue is the proliferation of tests in grades 9 through 11 that occurs because of the postsecondary assessments for admission, and the new statewide tests created by the K–12 standards movement. For example, California tests all students in grades 9 through 11 with a crosscutting mathematics and language arts assessment, and has state-mandated end-of-course exams in most academic subjects, such as biology, U.S. history, and English literature. As of 2003, none of these K–12 tests are used as an admissions factor by the University of California or California State University. The California State University placement exam includes more advanced mathematics than SAT I. During the Spring of the 11th grade, there is a particularly onerous amount of testing for UC applicants that includes the SAT I, SAT II, Advanced Placement tests, and at least six state K–12 tests that have no admissions or placement stakes for students.

Education standards and tests are set in different K–12 and postsecondary orbits that only intersect for students in Advanced Placement courses (Venezia, Kirst, & Antonio, 2003). How else could 49 states (all but Iowa) set K–12 standards and assessments without talking with higher education institutions and state boards for higher education? The huge disjuncture between K–12 and postsecondary school standards results in a lack of K–16 understanding, collaborative design, and knowledge about the assessments used by each education level. Higher education is concerned with the upward trajectory of pupils—for example, admissions tests' purported ability to predict student performance in the first year of college. Secondary education is concerned with high school graduation and the attainment of annual state and federal growth goals for K–12 state assessments. Secondary educators rarely discuss or consider the impact upon postsecondary education that new and expanding assessment policies might create. Moreover, there is no K–16 accountability system that might cause the two levels to work together on common assessment goals or reduce postsecondary remediation.[1]

Historical Evolution

This chasm between the levels of education in standards and assessments is deeply rooted in U.S. education history (Clark, 1985; Timpane, 1998). The origin of the disjuncture between lower and higher education in the United States stems, in part, from the way the United States created mass education systems for both K–12 and higher education. In Europe, by contrast, the higher grades of secondary education were designed for an elite group who would be going on to universities. European universities have long played a major role in determining the content of the secondary-school curriculum and both the content and format of secondary-school examinations. For example, professors at British universities like Oxford and Durham grade the A-levels taken by students during their last year of secondary education, and these essay exams figure crucially in a student's chances for university admission.

Over time, the chasm between lower and higher education in the United States has grown greater than that in many other industrialized nations, but at one time U.S. colleges and universities did play an important role in the high schools (Kirst & Venezia, 2001). In 1900, for example, the College Board set uniform standards for each academic subject and issued a syllabus to help students prepare for college entrance subject-matter examinations. Prior to that, each college had its own entrance requirements and examinations. Soon after, the University of California began to accredit high schools to make sure that their curriculums were adequate for university preparation.

In the postwar years, however, the notion of seamless K–16 academic standards vanished. "Aptitude" tests like the SAT replaced subject-matter standards for college admission, and secondary schools added elective courses in nonacademic areas, including vocational education and life skills classes. Today, K–12 faculty and college faculty may belong to the same discipline-based professional organizations, but they rarely meet with one another to plan curriculum or integrate assessments. K–12 policymakers and higher education policymakers cross paths even less often.

Universities provide some good arguments to explain why they pay little attention to K–12 standards or assessments. First, the universities emphasize that they are not involved in the creation or refinement of the K–12 standards. Second, the universities observe that both politics and technical problems effect frequent changes in state K–12 standards. Third, they note that the K–12 assessments have not been evaluated to see how well they predict freshman grades (although such evaluations are not difficult to conduct). The result is a K–16 babble of education standards that leads to unclear signals for students (particularly those from low-socioeconomic-status families), high remediation rates, and much misdirected energy by students caught between conflicting standards.

Placement Tests

For 80% of students who do not go to selective four-year schools, a crucial standard is an institutionally administered placement exam that is not very well aligned with the ACT or SAT I. Yet placement exams are essential for channeling students into noncredit postsecondary remedial courses. The Education Trust and Rand Corporation reviewed the similarities and dissimilarities between secondary school exams, admissions tests, and placement tests (Education Trust, 1999; Le & Hamilton, 2002). The Education Trust mathematics results are presented below.

Table 1: Distribution of Topics on Standardized Math Tests

				PERCENTAGE OF QUESTIONS DEVOTED TO		
	ALGEBRA 1	GEOMETRY	DATA, PROBABILITY, STATISTICS	NUMBER THEORY, ARITHMETIC, COMBINATORICS, LOGIC	ALGEBRA 2	TRIGONOMETRY/ PRECALCULUS
Privately Developed High School Assessment Tests						
TerraNova	14	29	23	21	0	0
Stanford 9 m/c*	29	25	25	21	0	0
State High School Assessment Tests						
Kentucky (CATS)**	9	33	17	18	20	0
Massachusetts (MCAS 10)†	23	28	13	18	13	5
New York	29	26	9	26	9	3
Texas (TAAS)‡	12	23	3	53	0	0
College Admissions Exams						
SAT I	47	23	3	23	3	0
ACT	25	27	5	18	12	8
Privately Developed College Placement Tests						
Compass	14	23	0	19	25	15
Accuplacer (algebra)	25	0	0	0	75	0
Accuplacer (calculus)	16	0	0	0	63	21

Source: Education Trust, 1999, p. 27.
*Stanford Achievement Test, 9th edition, multiple-choice
**Kentucky Commonwealth Accountability Testing System
†Massachusetts Comprehensive Assessment System
‡Texas Assessment of Academic Skills

Note that the content priorities of tests are all over the place, and the admissions tests require different mathematics than the placement tests. If the mathematics admissions tests predict freshman grades, why are they so different from the mathematics placement tests? Moreover, many K–12 state end-of-course tests in biology and chemistry have a different concept than the ACT science test.[2] Why should the ACT admission tests for science and social studies be so different from the end-of-course test concept in many states? Gaston Caperton claims the SAT II tests are the "very best achievement tests this country has to offer" (in this volume, p. 35). I wonder why he thinks SAT II is so much better than the end-of-course K–12 tests devised by the New York Regents or the states of Maine, Virginia, and Maryland. For example, some of these states' K–12 assessments have longer and different writing samples than SAT II, a domain that Atkinson says is so important for postsecondary success. According to Caperton, 60 institutions require SAT II for admissions, while millions take state-administered end-of-course tests at grades 10–12 that are not used for postsecondary admissions or placement. This is probably a legacy of the aptitude orientation of past admissions policies that Nicholas Lemann stresses in his contribution to this volume.

The Senior Year Problem

The papers in this volume by Ida Lawrence, Gretchen Rigol, Tom Van Essen, and Carol Jackson and by Howard Everson provide useful histories of postsecondary assessments, but the background they provide needs to be supplemented by a historical sketch of the K–16 disjuncture. For example, one unfortunate result of this historical evolution is the high school senior year (Kirst, 2001). The American educational system does little to discourage high school seniors from focusing on matters other than academic work. Rather than using the senior year to complete their secondary education and continue to prepare for postsecondary education, many seniors take less demanding courses and pay less attention to them. Some students use this time for goofing off; others earn money for college or complete nonpaid internships.

For the 70% of students who go on to postsecondary education directly after high school, the primary academic tasks for senior year are, in their view, to graduate on time and to enter college, possibly an open enrollment community college. The first of these tasks may be accomplished by taking the easiest courses that meet the school's graduation requirements. The second of these tasks does not require much effort after the first semester of senior year. Few college admissions decisions rely on senior-year grades, and colleges rarely withdraw an admissions offer to a prospect whose grades drop sharply.

The students' view is, of course, shortsighted. But it is hard for students to see beyond the twin goals of high school graduation and college admission. And in their minds, these goals are not very different. They do not realize that meeting their high school graduation requirements does not mean that they are prepared for college. From this perspective, senior slump appears to be the rational response of high school seniors who have met their gradua- tion requirements. Indeed, neither secondary nor postsecondary education claims the academic content of the senior year as a basis for further edu- cation. The lack of effort in the senior year for students not going to the most selective institutions can land them in remediation or cause them to earn poor freshman grades. For example, not taking math in the senior year is a high risk factor for inadequate first-year postsecondary math perfor- mance. By contrast, the United Kingdom and European university entrance exams are at the end of the last year of high school, and are integrated with secondary assessments.

Where to Go from Here

Lemann poses the following issue (p. 13) that should frame the future policy directions:

> The question President Atkinson has raised is a separate and, to my mind, more important one: in picking a test that serves as the basic interface between high school and college, should we consider the overall interests of everyone that choice affects, or only the interests of the highly selective colleges? I suspect that the Atkinson proposal, when put into effect, will have much more impact on high schools than on universities. That is the furthest thing from a strike against it. It is entirely appropriate for the state's public university system to consider the interests of the state's public high school system. In a larger cost-benefit analysis, the university stands to lose not at all, or at most very marginally, in its ability to select students, and high school students stand to gain a great deal.

My colleagues and I have written extensively about how to devise specific policies to implement Lemann's intent (Venezia, Kirst, & Antonio, 2003). But nothing will happen if the two levels of education do not have forums to deliberate and make mutual assessment policy. This will not be easy given the different professional structures and traditions whereby K–12 leaders and faculty meet mostly with themselves, and not higher education. The striking lack of an official role for higher education institutions in devising K–12 standards must not be perpetuated. If the K–16 leaders do not form a more inclusive and effective community, then elected politicians will step into the breach. Educators may not like the results of this political interven- tion. The disjunctures between K–12 and higher education will be hard to mend in the absence of a K–16 institutional entity whose mission is K–16 alignment and reform. Currently, there are few opportunities for K–12 educators to discuss, much less resolve, questions about academic standards with college and university faculty or policymakers. Very few states have any policy mechanism for specific decisions concerning K–16 standards and assessment, and higher education coordinating bodies do not include K–16 standards alignment within their purview. The disciplinary and professional associations have the potential to serve as a locus for such discussion, but these are organized into separate K–12 and postsecondary units.

Promising Initiatives

Some promising practices are emerging—a project called Standards for Success (S4S) has asked first-year university teachers in English and mathematics about the key knowledge and skills that first-year students need.[3] Several college presidents have endorsed these S4S standards. Moreover, the results have been compared to state K–12 standards and assessments with strong implications concerning possible revisions in these standards. Five states are part of the American diploma project that has examined the content and skills in the major K–16 assessments, including placement tests. These five states are discussing how to better relate their assessments including placement. Georgia has a P–16 statewide council that is working on linking subject matter academic standards for secondary school to the first two years of postsecondary education.

Some potential new policies could utilize the K–12 assessments as a significant admissions factor or substitute the university assessment as the 11th grade instrument for state K–11 testing. California may be a leader in the first approach and Illinois has implemented the second. California K–16 policymakers and test designers met to consider revised grade 11 statewide tests as a component of University of California comprehensive admissions. California State University will use the K–12 test for its placement decisions and drop its own placement test. Illinois gives the ACT to all 11th grade students as a supplement to its own K–12 standards-based test. This Illinois approach sends clearer academic signals about postsecondary standards to secondary students.

Notes

1. For the design of a P–16 accountability system, see Venezia, 2002.
2. Most of the reading tests at K–12 and higher education measure reading proficiency solely with multiple-choice items. College admissions tests are more likely than either college placement or state high school tests to assess inference skills. College placement tests are more likely to assess recall skills than are state tests or college admissions exams. Few commercially-available placement tests require students to produce a writing sample. In contrast, the majority of state high school tests require a writing sample. See Le & Hamilton, 2002.
3. See the Standards for Success website at s4s.org.

References

Clark, B. (1985). *The school and the university.* Berkeley and Los Angeles: University of California Press.

The Education Trust (1999). Ticket to nowhere: The gap between leaving high school and entering college and high-performance jobs. *Thinking K–16, 3(2),* 16–31.

Kirst, M. (2001). *Overcoming the high school senior slump: New education policies.* San Jose, CA: National Center for Public Policy and Higher Education.

Kirst, M. & Venezia, A. (2001, September). Bridging the great divide between secondary schools and postsecondary education. *Phi Delta Kappan,* 92–97.

Le, V. & Hamilton, L. (2002). Alignment Among Secondary and Postsecondary Assessments in Five Case Study States, Santa Monica: Rand Corporation, MR-1530.0.

Timpane, P. M. (1998). *Higher education and the schools.* Denver: State Higher Education Executive Officers.

Venezia, A. (2002). *A student-centered P–16 accountability model.* Denver: Education Commission of the states.

Venezia, A., Kirst, M. W., & Antonio, A. (2003). *Betraying the college dream: how disconnected K–12 and postsecondary education systems undermine student aspirations.* Stanford, CA: Stanford Institute for Higher Education Research.

College Admissions Testing in California: How Did the California SAT Debate Arise?

Part II is devoted to the SAT debate in California, which was sparked by University of California President Richard C. Atkinson's speech in February 2001, during which he advocated eliminating the SAT I: Reasoning Test as a criterion for UC admission. The first paper, by Dorothy A. Perry, Michael T. Brown, and Barbara A. Sawrey of the UC-wide Board on Admissions and Relations with Schools (BOARS), gives a historical context for the recent debates about the use of admissions testing in California. The authors note that, in "the minds of the American populace, degrees from elite colleges and universities like UC are among the best means of entry into esteemed, powerful, lucrative, and interesting social roles...." Perry, Brown, and Sawrey trace the development of UC admissions policy beginning with the admissions principles embedded in the university charter in 1868—that admissions decisions "be broadly representative of sectarian and political orientations, geographical residence, and sex."

In the wake of Atkinson's 2001 speech, BOARS discovered that despite the existence of an evolving set of admissions principles, UC had never had any formal guidelines for the use of admissions tests. What is the purpose of these tests within the framework of UC admissions policy, and what properties should they possess? BOARS then began a year of work that culminated in the development of a policy document that endorsed the use of admissions tests at UC "to assess academic preparation and achievement of UC applicants" and listed the desired properties of these tests.

As part of this reconsideration of UC admissions policy, BOARS commissioned an analysis of UC admissions data, to be carried out by researchers at the UC Office of the President. The result was an October 2001 report, *UC and the SAT: Predictive Validity and Differential Impact of the SAT I and SAT II at the University of California,* by Saul Geiser with Roger Studley. The findings of this study were presented by Saul Geiser at the UCSB conference. The chapter by Geiser and Studley in this section, which is based on the original report, is reprinted from the journal *Educational Assessment.*

The study examined the value of SAT I: Reasoning Test scores, SAT II: Subject Test scores, and high school grades in predicting freshman grade point average at the University of California and also investigated the role of economic factors in predicting grades. The study concluded that the SAT II was superior to the SAT I in predicting freshman grades. According to Geiser and Studley, the SAT II is also a fairer test for use in college admissions because it is less sensitive than the SAT I to differences in socioeconomic and other background factors. They also found that eliminating the SAT I and relying more heavily on the SAT II in admissions would have little impact on the ethnic composition at UC campuses. The Geiser-Studley study results were invoked frequently in policy discussions about the role of the SAT at the University of California.

In her commentary on this section, Eva L. Baker describes the "underlying conflicts between the goals and the reality of changing University of California admissions practices." In doing so, she draws upon the contrasts between the British and American systems of university admissions to point out the inherent difficulties in attempting to simultaneously optimize the selection of qualified individuals for university study and improve student learning at the secondary-school level. She stresses the importance of collecting data on the effects of any modification of the UC admissions system. For example, would a greater reliance on achievement-based examinations yield a more capable entering class? Would fewer students fail on university placement exams? Would students progress more rapidly through their academic programs? She concludes by urging UC faculty and administrators to "recognize that the time will come for even more change, with the continuing goals of making our educational system stronger, fairer, and more effective."

Rethinking the Use of Undergraduate Admissions Tests: The Case of the University of California

DOROTHY A. PERRY
MICHAEL T. BROWN
BARBARA A. SAWREY[1]

Introduction

Who should be admitted into our nation's elite colleges and universities, such as the University of California (UC), and how should these determinations be made? These questions are much easier to pose than to answer. Moreover, the answers create an extraordinary high-stakes competition encompassing college-bound students, the State of California, and the nation. A UC education is highly prized because of its quality. In the minds of the American populace, degrees from elite colleges and universities like UC are among the best means of entry into esteemed, powerful, lucrative, and interesting social roles, including occupations (Beatty, Greenwood, & Linn, 1999). That education symbolizes a pathway to opportunity. It represents a dream that, with hard work and persistence, coupled with the knowledge and skill developed at the University, anyone can ascend to economic and social success, regardless of social standing and resources.

The desire to advance oneself through education is a dream of great promise and power to families and students because of its attainability. A

University of California education is considered among the most affordable and democratically available of any higher education in the world (Douglass, 1997).

In fact, democratic access has been a hallmark of the University of California since its inception. The Organic Act of 1868, passed by the California legislature, provided the charter for the state's land-grant university and explicitly required that UC admissions decisions be broadly representative of sectarian and political orientations, geographical residence, and sex. In 1974, the California legislature called on each segment of public higher education in California (the California Community Colleges, the California State College and University system, and the University of California system) to approximate the sociodemographic composition of the state's high school graduates. The Regents of the University of California approved a policy to this effect in 1988 and reaffirmed it in 2001, stating that "the University shall seek out and enroll, on each of its campuses, a student body that demonstrates high academic achievement or exceptional personal talent, and that encompasses the broad diversity of backgrounds characteristic of California."[2] Subsequently, UC President Richard C. Atkinson (2001), in an address at the American Council on Education, announced his request that UC faculty consider dropping the SAT I and other "aptitude" tests in favor of tests that measure mastery of subject matter expected to be taught and learned in a college preparatory curriculum. That request generated both a faculty and public debate about appropriate admissions tests.

The UC Context

The Board of Admissions and Relations with Schools (BOARS), the UC Academic Senate committee responsible for recommending admissions policies and practices to the Senate, searched UC archives for the history of faculty thought on the question of admissions testing and made an important discovery: UC faculty adopted a policy to use admissions tests, specifically the SAT tests, to help manage the growing demand for admission into the system, but never formally articulated principles to guide that use. Inquiries into a number of similarly selective universities across the country uncovered an absence of explicit principles guiding the selection and use of admissions tests. That absence suggested a need for a defined set of principles concerning the purposes of admissions tests and the properties that they should possess.

It is important to note that the National Research Council sponsored a report that strongly recommended that college and university officials charged with admissions should review the role of tests in admissions and craft policies for their use (Beatty et al., 1999). To date, however, no model exists to guide an approach to this very complex and sensitive public policy area.

All colleges and universities grapple with the questions of whom to admit and how. To the extent that admission into higher education institutions is characterized as "competitive," meaning that more qualified applicants apply than can be accepted, the issues of fairness, egalitarianism, and effectiveness of decisions become increasingly significant. Officials of institutions that are competitively situated like the University of California system might find the approach of UC faculty to rethinking admissions testing useful.

As part of its general responsibility to set undergraduate admissions policy, BOARS is charged with determining how examinations will be used in the establishment of eligibility and admission to the University.[3] The California Master Plan for Higher Education requires that the university identify and offer admission to the top 12.5% of high school graduates in the state. In keeping with that responsibility, BOARS recommended the addition of admissions test scores to the university's eligibility requirements almost 40 years ago. Before and since, the use of admissions tests has been reconsidered on several occasions and the specific role that test scores play has been adjusted. However, the broad policy questions surrounding the appropriate use of admissions tests at the university have never been adequately studied.

This report describes an intensive review of the university's use of admissions tests that BOARS began in February 2001. The immediate impetus for this work was the February 15, 2001 letter from President Atkinson requesting that the faculty reconsider UC's current testing policy.[4] However, the question of the appropriateness of admissions tests has come up frequently in public discussion of the university's admission processes and was the subject of substantial discussion at the University of California Freshman Admissions Policy Conference held in Oakland, on December 7, 2000. In order to provide UC faculty with the latest research and thinking on admissions testing, a national conference was hosted by the University of California at Santa Barbara on November 16–17, 2001, titled Rethinking the SAT: The Future of Standardized Testing in University Admissions.

Organization of the Chapter

What follows is a presentation of BOARS' analysis on the question of the appropriateness of admissions testing, organized in a manner consistent with BOARS' process of deliberations. BOARS' approach to that reassessment could serve as a useful model to other colleges and universities, in that BOARS:

- articulated the goals to be obtained by the reassessment
- reviewed how standardized admissions tests are currently used
- studied the history of standardized testing in admissions with a particular focus on the history of UC's incorporation of standardized testing in admissions

- reviewed the empirical justifications for using standardized admissions tests and commissioned a series of studies designed to evaluate support for these justifications using UC data
- considered important policy issues in using admissions tests
- formulated and recommended policy-guiding principles for the selection and use of admissions tests

That decision-making process and its resulting recommendations has led to a UC partnership with ACT, Inc., and the College Board to create tests that UC faculty might approve as meeting BOARS' principles. BOARS members consider this work to be scientifically and pedagogically sound and of potential interest to a national audience. At the present time, the test development work continues and BOARS is optimistic that the principles will be realized.

Goals of BOARS' Reassessment of UC's Use of Admissions Tests

In reconsidering the use of admissions tests by UC, BOARS sought to:

- understand the historical and philosophical background of UC's use of admissions tests, including the principles that led to the original decision to include test scores in the determination of eligibility and selection and that should guide their future use[5]
- examine carefully the empirical justifications for the use of admissions tests, including their ability to predict undergraduate performance at UC
- consider carefully the policy implications of the university's admissions test requirement—in particular its relationship to the college preparatory work students undertake in high school—and identify desirable policy goals for UC's use of particular tests to fulfill that requirement
- evaluate the degree to which existing test options meet the needs of the University's faculty and students
- draw conclusions and make recommendations regarding the future use of admissions tests for the purposes of both eligibility and selection at specific UC campuses that will lay the groundwork for a broader faculty dialog on these issues

In the coming decade, the University of California, among other schools, faces a substantial increase in student demand for places at all of its campuses. As the period of increased demand unfolds, it seems particularly important to assure ourselves and the public that the means used to determine which students will be offered the opportunity of a UC education are as educationally sound as possible and fully consistent with fundamental principles of openness and fairness.

Current Use of Tests at UC

The University of California currently requires applicants to present the following test scores to determine eligibility and for use by the campuses in their selection processes:

1. One of two tests of language arts and mathematics:
   a) *ACT.* The ACT assessment is a three-and-a-half hour test created by ACT, Inc., and described as a curriculum-based achievement test designed to assess students' critical reasoning and higher order thinking skills in four core content areas: English, mathematics, reading, and science (ACT, Inc., 2000, p. 11.) Students taking the ACT receive subscores in the four disciplines covered as well as a combined total score.

   or

   b) *SAT I.* The SAT I: Reasoning Test is a three-hour test of "critical reading and problem solving" ability that is developed and administered by the Educational Testing Service and owned by the College Board (The College Board, 2001, p. 4). Students taking the SAT I receive two scores, one in verbal reasoning and one in math reasoning.

   At present, roughly 25% of UC applicants submit both ACT and SAT I scores. Approximately 73% submit only SAT I test scores and about 2% submit only ACT scores. Composite scores on the ACT and SAT I are highly correlated with one another and concordance tables enable the University and others to convert scores on one test to approximately equivalent scores on the other (Dorans, 2000), allowing either test to be used in the UC Eligibility Index, described below.

2. *SAT II Subject Tests.* Three achievement test scores are required, one in writing, a second in math (level 1 or level 2), and a third area of the student's choice. The SAT IIs, formerly known as the College Entrance Examination Board Achievement Tests, are designed and administered by the Educational Testing Service and owned by the College Board. Each SAT II is a one-hour multiple-choice achievement-type test designed to assess mastery of high-school level work in one of 21 different fields, including the natural and social sciences, languages, literature, writing, and two different levels of mathematics.[6]

UC uses scores from these tests in several ways. First, all students are required to present a combination of high school grade point average, or GPA (calculated on required UC-approved college preparatory courses) and test scores that meets the minimum requirements of the "Eligibility Index," a weighted scale that combines test scores with the GPA earned in UC required courses so that high test scores can balance out lower grades and vice versa. The Eligibility Index is used to identify the top 12.5% of high school graduates. The test score portion is calculated by totaling each student's three SAT II scores, multiplying this total by two, and adding the total SAT I combined Math and Verbal score (or ACT equivalent). At present, UC eligibility is sufficient for admission to three campuses in the UC system that admit undergraduate students, while the other six employ additional selection guidelines and criteria that include use of admissions test scores. Each campus has designed a selection system that evaluates admissions applications consistent with faculty-approved university-wide guidelines.[7]

Finally, SAT II scores in particular fields are used for placement purposes in various campus departments and fields of study. BOARS' recommendations focus on the first two purposes, eligibility and selection; use of test scores at individual campuses is determined locally by faculty members, providing that it is consistent with university-wide guidelines.

A Brief History of Standardized Admissions Tests

BOARS' review of the history of standardized admissions tests revealed useful information. The admissions tests used today by the University of California (and most selective colleges and universities in the United States) trace their heritage from two distinct lines: (1) written examinations required historically for entrance into private colleges; and (2) aptitude tests that grew out of changing social needs and notions of intelligence in the late 1800s that were designed to provide a means of sorting large numbers of people into appropriate occupational or intellectual categories and, therefore, contributing to the efficient organization of democratic society.

Through the nineteenth century, college entrance examinations had traditionally been oral tests administered by traveling examiners and restricted generally to the eastern seaboard. After the turn of the century, the tests underwent a transformation to written examinations administered on a regional basis and capable of reaching a much broader audience. The College Board, then named the College Entrance Examination Board, was formed in 1900 as one of those regional agencies serving the private colleges of the Northeast and their "feeder" college preparatory secondary schools, also generally private. The important purposes of the College Board were to help regulate the diverse admissions requirements of various colleges and universities and to help standardize college preparation in the high schools. Throughout the first three decades of the twentieth century, the "college boards" were week-long essay examinations of the curriculum provided in elite boarding schools (Lemann, 1999, p. 28).

Examinations began to change with the introduction of the SAT (at that time an abbreviation for Scholastic Aptitude Test; the SAT was later renamed Scholastic Assessment Test in 1993 and, one year later, became the SAT I: Reasoning Test or, simply, the SAT I [Zwick, 2002]), which was first administered by the College Board in 1926. The original Scholastic Aptitude Test drew upon intelligence tests that were developed in the late 1800s and early 1900s, versions of which were administered on a large scale to army recruits during World War I. In the early 1930s it attracted the attention of then president of Harvard University, James Bryant Conant, who was searching for a means to identify highly talented young men from obscure educational backgrounds who nonetheless would succeed at Harvard. Notably, by that time, the creator of the SAT, Carl Brigham, had begun to express deep reservations about the notion of testing innate abilities and had come to advocate achievement tests over aptitude tests (Lemann, 1999, p. 33). Conant believed, however, that tests of achievement would always favor those who had the financial resources to attend the best preparatory schools and saw in the SAT a tool for restructuring society by counterbalancing the benefits of inherited privilege in favor of innate talent.

In 1930, the Scholastic Aptitude Test was divided into verbal and mathematical portions (Lawrence, Rigol, Van Essen, & Jackson, 2002, p. 2). Also during the 1930s, the College Board developed a series of hour-long multiple-choice achievement tests (the antecedents of today's SAT II) to replace the essay examinations. By the late 1930s the combination of the SAT (verbal and mathematics portions) and the achievement tests was administered at hundreds of test sites around the country, although the written essay examinations were also still in wide use. It was not until World War II that the traditional written examinations were abandoned. In 1947, with strong support from Conant, the Educational Testing Service (ETS) was formed as a central testing agency for the entire nation, and the College Board turned its test development activities over to ETS. Even though by the 1950s items "most firmly rooted in the traditions of intelligence testing" had been replaced (Lawrence et al., 2002, p. 3), and despite later changes that were reportedly designed to ensure that test content was consistent with school-based learning (Lawrence et al., 2002, p. 3), the SAT continues to the present day to suffer wide and intense criticism as a test of "ill-defined notions of aptitude" (cf. Atkinson, 2001) or native intelligence.

It is important to note that some educators were concerned both about the monopolistic dominance of ETS in creating college admissions tests and the perceived shortcomings of tests of general cognitive ability. Most notably, University of Iowa professor E. F. Lindquist, a well-known psychometrician and the developer of the Iowa Tests of Educational Development, formed a rival testing company, American College Testing (ACT, Inc.) as an alternative to ETS and the College Board–sponsored SAT. Lindquist was a believer in expanding the numbers of Americans attending college, and created the ACT test as an achievement-type admissions test designed to provide diagnostic information that would enable students to prepare themselves for college and aid colleges in both placement and admissions (Lindquist, 1958). The ACT quickly gained popularity among public universities in the Midwest and the southern United States, while the SAT (currently called the SAT I) continued to be seen as the test of choice in the Northeast and for more elite private institutions. Today, the ACT is widely accepted by both public and private institutions throughout the United States as an alternative to the SAT I.

The Adoption of Admissions Tests by the University of California

In the mid-1950s, BOARS first began serious consideration of the use of standardized tests in establishing admissions requirements for the University of California.[8] Up until the 1920s, UC could accommodate most students who applied, and they were admitted based upon graduation from UC-accredited high schools, performance on a set of examinations, or recommendation from the high school principal. By the 1930s, students were required to complete a specific set of high school courses and grades in these courses were considered in determining admission. During this period the Academic Senate considered—and rejected—the use of standardized admissions tests.[9]

By the 1950s, the University began confronting serious problems associated with rapid growth. The G. I. Bill had increased enrollments significantly and the baby boom generation had already entered the school system, and would soon be on the way to college. A 1955 statewide planning study suggested that the university experiment with the use of "aptitude and achievement" tests. In 1957, BOARS agreed to conduct a series of experiments with the SAT, designed to assess whether (1) the test improved prediction of freshman grades; (2) it could be used to assess grade inflation; and (3) it could be used to help manage enrollment growth. With the support of ETS, the SAT was administered to all freshmen entering UC in the fall of 1960. UC faculty, upon reviewing the results of the study, again rejected the use of standardized admissions tests because: (1) they wanted to maintain immediate control over admissions; and (2) data showed that grades in required and UC-approved courses were stronger and more consistent predictors of scholastic success in college than test scores. A subsequent study showed that achievement tests were better correlated with freshman GPAs than the SAT, but the difference was not enough to convince UC faculty of the value of adopting them as an admissions test requirement.[10]

By the mid-1960s, however, the position of faculty had shifted. Eligibility studies conducted in 1965 and 1966 estimated that the university was significantly out of compliance with the California Master Plan for Higher Education in that it was drawing students from more than the top 12.5% of graduating high school students, thus affecting the other California college and university systems. Adopting an admissions test requirement was seen as a "relatively easy" means of adjusting the size of the pool of students eligible for admission into UC.

In 1968, the UC Academic Assembly accepted BOARS' recommendation that the university require the SAT and three College Board Achievement Tests (precursors to the SAT II Subject Tests); the requirement took effect soon after. BOARS' recommendation was based on the expectation that admissions tests would: (1) help identify areas of applicant strengths and weaknesses; (2) identify instructional strengths and weaknesses of applicants' schools; (3) improve the ability to identify students likely to succeed at the university; and (4) provide some ability to adjust for differences in high school grading practices. It should also be noted that UC faculty agreed to no longer accredit California high schools, something it had done to standardize the quality of university preparation since 1871. As a result of the change, students with GPAs between 3.0 and 3.1 were required to present a total score on the SAT and the three achievement tests of 2,500. Students with GPAs above 3.1 were automatically eligible. Test scores were required, but were irrelevant for determining eligibility.

Over the past 35 years, BOARS has adjusted the testing requirement several times. In 1977, the option of taking the ACT in lieu of the SAT was added to the testing policy.[11] The 1977 Eligibility Index was calculated with only the total SAT/ACT score and the GPA, but the scores on the College Board Achievement Tests were still required. In 1992, the index was adjusted again to address renewed concerns that the UC eligibility pool had grown beyond the top 12.5% of high school graduates. And in 1996, the index was revised to incorporate rescaling of the SAT (which had been renamed "SAT I: Reasoning Test") and achievement tests (which had been named "SAT II: Subject Tests"; Zwick, 2002). In 1999, the Eligibility Index was extended across the full breadth of the GPA range; thus, high school grades in required and approved courses alone could not ensure eligibility for admission. Most significantly, the SAT II exam scores were incorporated in the Eligibility Index for the first time and figured prominently, as the combination of the three SAT II test scores were now weighted twice as heavily as the SAT I composite score.

Empirical Justifications for the Use of Admissions Tests
BOARS' review of the history of admissions testing at UC, its discussions with testing experts (including colleagues within the UC community and beyond, as well as representatives of the major testing agencies), and general

observation of the public conversation over admissions tests revealed a number of different but related assumptions regarding the value of tests in making admissions decisions:

- admissions tests are a valid measure of student preparation and/or promise that have been proven to add to an institution's ability to predict student success beyond the predictive information that high school grades alone provide
- admissions tests provide a standardized measure of preparation that is independent of the variability among grading patterns inevitably present when reviewing the records of students from thousands of high schools across the country
- admissions tests can identify as-yet-undeveloped talent (viz., aptitude) in students who, for a variety of reasons, may not have worked to their full potential in high school, but who will nonetheless excel in college

Each of these theories about the value of admissions tests has contributed to some degree to their adoption by UC and by other institutions of higher learning across the country. For many both inside and outside the academy, some of these assumptions are deeply ingrained and have the status of unassailable fact. Prior to developing a set of principles and recommendations regarding the use of tests, however, BOARS decided it should undertake additional study to determine to what extent these theories about the value of tests—particularly the predictive value of the tests and the relative value of aptitude tests versus achievement tests—were actually borne out in the available data about student performance *at UC*.

BOARS commissioned a study in 1997 that was conducted by staff of the Office of the President of the University of California and designed to assess the predictive value of SAT I and SAT II scores. The SAT I was selected for study rather than the ACT because nearly all UC applicants take the SATs, while only a small self-selected group take ACT. The study, which examined the first-year grades of the class entering UC in the fall of 1996, concluded that a composite of the SAT II math and writing scores that were required of all applicants was more predictive of freshman performance than the SAT I composite, which since 1977 had been the only test score utilized in computing the Eligibility Index. The study suggested that the superior performance of SAT II tests in predicting freshman grades might be "due to the somewhat different nature of the SAT II exams, which are curriculum driven ... in contrast to the SAT I which [is a] general reasoning test" (Kowarsky, Clatfelter, & Widaman, 1998, p. 6). This study also found that the third SAT II exam score, which is a subject test selected by each applicant, yielded a small but statistically significant additional predictive value above those of the other four exams.[12] On the basis of that study, UC's Eligibility Index was changed to add the SAT II scores and weight them more heavily than the SAT I.

Early in 2001, BOARS commissioned a larger study that was conducted by the UC Office of the President to explore further the value of admissions test scores in predicting success at UC. The conclusions presented in this chapter were gleaned from this study, which involved regression analyses of the records of a pool of 77,893 students who applied and were admitted to UC as freshmen from fall 1996 through fall 1999 (Geiser & Studley, 2001A; see also Geiser & Studley, this volume).[13] Students' high school grades (as expressed in the UC-calculated weighted GPA[14]) and SAT I and SAT II scores were compared to freshman GPA to determine the relative value of admissions test scores in predicting first-year performance.[15] In addition, correlations between the various test scores and socioeconomic and demographic information were examined. Finally, BOARS members evaluated campus-specific studies (e.g., Brown, Velasco, and Castillo, 2001) that had relevance to BOARS' research questions.

Predictive Validity

The primary conclusions of the BOARS-commissioned study on the usefulness of admissions test scores in identifying successful students are:

- Overall, high school GPA in UC-required and approved courses was the best predictor of freshman-year grades and a variety of other quantitative criteria of performance at the University of California. In a standard regression formula where the outcome variable, freshman-year GPA was regressed on a combination of high school GPA, the total SAT I score, and the total SAT II score, the standardized regression coefficient (beta weight) for high school GPA was .27 for the four-year sample, as opposed to .07 for the SAT I and .23 for the SAT II (Geiser & Studley, 2001A; also this volume). Virtually all of the existing literature on the relative value of grades and admissions test scores in predicting first-year performance confirms the finding that high school GPA is the best predictor. Data on UC students has shown this since 1960 and it was a factor in the hesitancy of the Academic Assembly to adopt BOARS' original 1958 recommendation to employ admissions tests. Recent UC data (e.g., Brown, Castillo, & Velasco, 2001) also indicated that other UC performance criteria, such as five- and six-year graduation rates, freshman retention rates, and freshman probation rates, were best predicted by high school grades in required and approved courses, with the SAT II Writing Test making an identifiable contribution.

However, the SAT I and other SAT II test scores were statistically irrelevant.

- Test scores contributed a statistically significant increment of prediction when added to a regression analysis combining grades and test scores. When the effects of different combinations of predictor variables were studied in the full sample of almost 78,000 collected over four years, adding scores from the SAT I and SAT II to high school GPA in the prediction equation increased the amount of variance in freshman-year GPA explained to 22.3 %, from 15.4% for the GPA alone. Notably, the combination of high school GPA and the SAT II composite explained 22.2% of the variance, only slightly less (.1%) than with all three variables.
- The SAT II appeared overall to be a better predictor of freshman grades at UC than the SAT I. In a series of regression equations that examined various individual predictors, a composite of the three SAT II scores performed slightly better than either the SAT I or high school GPA in two of the years studied and for the full four-year pool. For the entire sample, the three-test SAT II composite explained 16% of the variance in freshman grades, compared to 15.4% for high school GPA and 13.3% for the SAT I combined math and verbal scores (Geiser & Studley, 2001A; also this volume).

These analyses were conducted on various subpopulations of the pool to determine whether the findings were consistent across campuses, and academic disciplines. The findings were remarkably consistent.

Identifying Students with High Potential

One strength that admissions tests are commonly thought to have over high school grades—and that aptitude-type tests are commonly presumed to have over achievement-type tests—is an ability to identify students with high aptitude who have not yet demonstrated their potential. The theory has at least two main variants that were evaluated empirically with UC data. The first is that students with high aptitude who come from economically or socially disadvantaged backgrounds and attend schools with fewer resources or less rigorous curricula will score relatively low on achievement tests, as opposed to aptitude tests, because they are held back by the poor education they have received. The second is that, regardless of the type of school attended, some very talented students simply do not perform to their potential in high school (perhaps because they have not been sufficiently challenged or engaged), nor, consequently, do they perform well on achievement-type tests (tests linked to quality of schooling), but they will score well on aptitude tests. In either case, those students are commonly thought to be "late bloomers" or "diamonds in the rough" who would excel when placed in the rich and challenging intellectual environment of university life. The data indicated that this was not the case.

An analysis of freshman performance data disaggregated by the type of high school (from "low" to "high" performing, as measured by California's Academic Performance Index (API), which considered a number of factors related to student achievement) indicated that, for all levels of schools measured by the API, the SAT II remained the stronger predictor for UC students relative to the SAT I. The predictive ability of the SAT I improved for schools at the lower end of the API, but it remained significantly less predictive than the SAT II (Geiser & Studley, 2001A; also this volume). Similar patterns emerged when data were disaggregated and analyzed according to students' high school GPA. The SAT II was the stronger predictor of freshman grades across all quintiles of high school GPA despite the increasing predictive power of the SAT I for students with lower GPAs.[16]

Though supported by little evidence, the "diamond-in-the-rough" hypothesis holds credence for many who believe that students who score poorly on achievement tests and perform poorly in high school might, nevertheless, have strong academic aptitude. They believe that such aptitude could be indicated by high SAT I scores and that the students would thrive later in the challenging environment of a competitive college or university. However, existing research shows that achievement tests and reasoning tests were at best equivalent predictors of college performance and that reasoning tests were not necessarily less sensitive to curriculum and instruction than achievement tests (Geiser & Studley, 2001B). Nonetheless, BOARS sought to determine if there was any empirical evidence to support the hypothesis with respect to UC students. One research approach was to study data regarding discrepant scores—cases where students' scores differed substantially on SAT I and SAT II tests. Significantly, those cases were quite rare. Out of a sample of nearly 78,000 students, a total of 3,607 students (4.63% of the total) were found to have SAT I and SAT II total scores that differed from one another by more than one standard deviation. Of these, 1,859 received significantly higher scores on the SAT I and 1,748 received significantly higher scores on the SAT II. When the threshold for considering scores discrepant was increased to 1.5 standard deviations, the number of students dropped to 343—0.44% of the total. That is, in 199 out of 200 cases, the information provided by the two different types of tests was very similar.

In addition, the characteristics of the discrepant score group with higher SAT I scores were inconsistent with the view that such individuals come from disadvantaged backgrounds and would thrive at UC if given the opportunity. Analyses revealed that, on average, the group of UC students who scored relatively higher on the SAT I than on the SAT II came from families with higher incomes, performed less well in high school, performed less well after arriving at UC, were more likely to be white, and were less likely to be under-represented minorities than either the similar-score group or the group with higher SAT II scores. Surprisingly, the discrepant score group with higher SAT II scores were more likely to come from families with lower incomes, performed better at UC, and were a more racially/ethnically diverse group relative to the group with higher SAT I scores or the similar-score group.

Finally, it could also be argued that a "diamond in the rough" was simply a student with high grades and high test scores but who comes from an academically weak high school—one that doesn't have many rigorous or challenging classes. Recall, however, that the high school GPA, no matter what the general performance of students in the high school (i.e., the API level of the school), was the best predictor of the freshman GPA earned at UC. Recall as well that the SAT II was the superior predictor of freshman success at all API levels of schools, albeit less so at the bottom end of the scale. Consider, in addition, that SAT II and SAT I scores were highly correlated, so that students coming from weak educational backgrounds and earning good grades were just as easily identified by the SAT II scores as by SAT I scores. Notably, one of the study's findings was that the entire battery of high school grades and test scores became somewhat less useful in predicting the performances of students from lower performing schools. All of the findings suggest that admission decisions regarding high performing students from low performing schools might best consider the overall context of the students' achievements.

When all was considered, in the opinion of BOARS there was no evidence to corroborate any of the theories that the SAT I Reasoning Test had special value in identifying students who had not performed well in high school or on achievement tests but in fact possessed academic aptitude that would reveal itself at the University.

Relationship to Socioeconomic and Demographic Characteristics
It is well known that admissions tests of all types—along with high school grades and other indicators of academic achievement—are strongly correlated with family income. This does not appear to reflect bias in the tests, but rather the inescapable fact that schools in California—like those anywhere—vary widely in available resources, and students from poor families are more likely to attend schools with fewer resources. The members of BOARS were concerned about the "disparate impact" admissions tests might have on students from socioeconomically disadvantaged circumstances, because one of UC's goals is to effectively identify worthy students from all backgrounds.

Therefore, BOARS reviewed data disaggregated by student socio-economic factors. In those analyses, two measures of socioeconomic status—family income and parental education—were included to assess their conditioning effects on the predictive validity of the SAT I and SAT II. Including those variables along with SAT II scores and high school GPA in the analysis increased the predicted variance in freshman GPA from 22.2% to 22.8%. When the SAT I was then added as a predictor, the predicted variance did not increase beyond 22.8%, indicating that once socioeconomic variables are included, SAT I scores do not add to the prediction of freshman grades. The findings suggested that SAT I scores contributed no additional power to predict UC freshman GPA that was not already accounted for by high school GPA, SAT II scores, and socioeconomic status.

BOARS also reviewed data considering differences in performance on SAT I Reasoning and SAT II Achievement tests for students of different races and ethnic groups. As is the case with family income, certain patterns emerged in scores on all tests: white and Asian-American students tended to have higher scores, on average, than African-American, American Indian, and Chicano/Latino students. However, the analysis revealed few differences within groups for performance on the SAT I versus the SAT II math and writing tests, and none of those differences were significant.[17]

Therefore, BOARS found no evidence that the SAT I Reasoning Test performed better than the SAT II achievement tests in predicting performances for students from more challenged socioeconomic circumstances or different demographic groups.

Conclusions Regarding Empirical Justifications

In BOARS' view, extant research and analyses of UC data support the use of achievement tests as at least equivalent predictors to tests of "aptitude" or "general reasoning ability." However, the empirical evidence does not appear so compelling that it should drive a decision to prefer one type of test to another. Rather, it appears that UC faculty and others charged with setting admissions policy should carefully consider the educational policy implications of selected tests and base their conclusions and future actions on educational policy grounds.

Policy Issues Associated with UC's Admissions Test Requirement

Admission to the University of California is a highly sought-after public resource. Access to that resource should be based on sound principles and an understanding of the educational and social implications of different choices.

BOARS' review of the history of the development of admissions tests and of their use at the University of California pointed clearly to the fact that the original decision to adopt the testing requirement and create the Eligibility

Index was driven only in part by policy goals. Pragmatic needs to reduce the size of the eligibility pool and to rank-order applicants to selective campuses in a simple, efficient way played substantial roles. In BOARS' current view, pragmatic reasons—while important—are insufficient justification for the adoption of a test requirement or the selection of a specific test battery. And while the additional predictive validity that admissions tests provide was convincing in terms of the value of admissions tests in general, the relative statistical properties of the admissions tests currently in use by the university were not sufficient to support the continued use of these tests without modification, or to drive a decision regarding the specific design of a future test battery.

On what, then, should the university base decisions regarding its use of admissions tests? In BOARS' lengthy discussions of the role of admissions tests and the desirability or lack thereof of particular kinds of tests, the following interrelated policy issues emerged that BOARS concluded should be carefully considered when making decisions about UC's admissions test requirement:

- *The relative merits of tests that measure achievement versus those that purport to measure aptitude.* BOARS is strongly persuaded that achievement-type tests offer the University a number of advantages over aptitude-type tests. The original justification for the use of admissions test scores in determining eligibility rested largely on their role as "objective" measures that could be applied to the whole applicant pool and, therefore, provide information that was independent of high school grades, which are subject to inconsistency across schools and teachers. BOARS assumes that the university seeks to measure mastery of the college-preparatory curriculum that the university requires for eligibility, that using scores from appropriate admissions tests as a complement to high school grades increases our ability to achieve this goal, and that achievement exams are more suited to measuring that mastery than exams designed to measure general reasoning ability. Moreover, achievement tests have the potential for feedback, providing information that students and their families can use to prepare for college and that schools can use to evaluate and improve their own programs, part of UC faculty's original reasoning for adopting standardized admissions tests as an admissions requirement. Focusing on achievement tests rather than aptitude tests also avoids the historical association of aptitude tests with intelligence tests.
- *The messages that the test requirement sends to students and their families.* Clearly, an important aspect of any admissions test is the nature of the message it sends to students. The university's

traditional eligibility requirements—that is, the combination of college-preparatory coursework and scholarship (GPA) requirements—send a clear message: the best way to prepare for postsecondary education is to take a rigorous and comprehensive college-preparatory curriculum and to excel in this work. The message is reinforced by the university's comprehensive admissions review policy that emphasizes the importance of taking a challenging curriculum and excelling across a broad range of areas. In the view of BOARS, achievement tests reinforce that message. Students who take challenging courses, work hard, and master the subjects will see their effort pay off not only in good grades but also in high scores on tests that measure mastery of the work they have undertaken in high school. That message is consistent with, and underscores, current efforts to improve the quality and rigor of K–12 education in the state.

- *The degree to which admissions tests should be related to the curriculum UC applicants are expected to study in high school.* BOARS is mindful of the influence that colleges and universities have in determining what is taught in high schools. The university's own historical role well into the 1960s as the accreditor of high school curricula in California speaks to this influence. UC's requirements for coursework in history and social science, English, mathematics, laboratory science, foreign language, and the arts help shape the curricula California's schools offer. In BOARS' view, it follows that the university's testing policy should be more consistent with the coursework requirements. In that regard, it is noteworthy that while UC applicants are required to complete coursework in six curricular areas, they are currently expected to submit admissions test scores in only three: English/language arts, mathematics, and a third area that they may choose.

- *The burden that our test requirements place on students and schools.* At present, applicants to the University of California are required to take four examinations that require a minimum of six hours and from two to four separate testing sessions. Although this requirement has not changed in the almost 40 years that have passed since UC adopted its admissions testing policy, the context in which the requirement is seen has changed. Educators, students, and families frequently decry the proliferation of tests that have accompanied the growth of the standards and accountability movements in education. Not only do students spend more time taking tests, but increased competition for spaces in the university and the proliferation of test preparation services put additional pressure on them to spend even more time preparing for admissions tests. In addition, each test charges a fee (although major testing agencies offer fee waivers for low-income students) and the cumulative total of these fees—not to mention the cost of test preparation programs—can be daunting to many families. Moreover, UC data showed that some of the tests currently being required were redundant. For example, the SAT I provided test scores in language skills and math and two of the required SAT II Subject Tests were in math and writing. In addition, the SAT II writing test was more predictive of success at UC than the SAT I Verbal Reasoning Test and the total SAT I test score did not add significantly to predicting UC success after high school grades in approved and required courses and the total SAT II score had been considered. One of BOARS' goals in considering options for revising the admissions test policy was to avoid increasing the burden, in terms of time or money, that UC's requirements place on potential applicants.

In the view of BOARS, consideration of such issues underscored the need for a sound set of principles and a description of desirable admissions test properties to guide the development of a new admissions test requirement for the University of California.

Recommended Principles

1. BOARS endorses the continued use of admissions tests. In the view of BOARS, admissions tests offer important benefits to the university by providing information about student mastery of key areas of the college preparatory curriculum that adds to and complements the information provided by the high school GPA.

   Given the important role that admissions tests play in determining access to UC, it is critical that their use be governed by clear principles. The purposes and the properties required of tests used by the University must be clearly articulated and understood. BOARS has recommended to the faculty of the University of California the adoption of the following policy regarding the purposes and properties of admissions tests for use by the University of California.

2. Admissions tests will be used at the University of California
   • to assess academic preparation and achievement of UC applicants
   • to predict success at UC beyond that predicted by high school GPA
   • to aid in establishing UC eligibility
   • to aid in selecting students for admission at individual UC campuses

3. The desired properties of admissions tests to be used for these purposes include the following:
   - An admissions test should be a reliable measurement that provides uniform assessment and should be fair across demographic groups.
   - An admissions test should measure levels of mastery of content in UC-approved high school preparatory coursework and should provide information to students, parents, and educators, enabling them to identify academic strengths and weaknesses.
   - An admissions test should be demonstrably useful in predicting student success at UC and provide information beyond that which is contained in other parts of the application. (It is recognized that predictors of success are currently limited, and generally only include first-year college GPA and graduation rate. As this field advances, better predictors should be identified and used in validating admissions tests.)
   - An admissions test should be useful in a way that justifies its social and monetary costs.
4. BOARS also has recommended that, as a matter of principle, the faculty regularly review UC's admissions testing policy and practices to ensure that tests are being used in a way that is consistent with these principles and desired properties of admissions tests.

Epilogue

BOARS has undertaken to propose a policy based on agreed-upon properties of testing, and upon the purposes for which admissions tests are created, rather than simply working within the constraints of existing tests. We consider this an opportunity to work with testing agencies and interested parties to move toward admissions tests that more precisely fit the needs of the University of California. Since the principles were articulated, BOARS has been working closely with ACT, Inc., the College Board, and ETS representatives in discussing future directions in testing. Both ACT, Inc. and the College Board have announced major revisions to their national tests, the tests of English and mathematics knowledge and skills that UC has used for many years. ACT, Inc. has asserted that their test is currently developed to content standards based upon the learning and teaching expectations of college and university professors, teachers, and curriculum specialists, lacking only writing assessment to supplement the English subtest of the exam. ACT, Inc. is planning to provide a writing assessment that will be available as an option for students needing to submit such scores.[18] The College Board has announced changes to the SAT I that include: (1) elimination of verbal analogies items;

(2) elimination of quantitative comparison items; (3) expanding the coverage of the mathematics reasoning test to include third year high school mathematics; (4) adding critical reading passages to assess reading comprehension; and (5) adding a writing assessment.[19] It is anticipated that both revised tests will provide achievement testing in English skills, including a writing sample, and mathematics skills at the level of expected competence for entering freshman students. If so, the use of such tests would also provide the opportunity for UC to utilize additional subject-matter achievement tests in order to evaluate applicants across the broader range of the college-preparatory curriculum. BOARS expects to evaluate the degree to which the proposed changes to the national admissions tests aligns with its principles and refer its recommendations to the Academic Assembly of the University of California.

Notes

This chapter excerpts major portions of the University of California's Academic Senate Board of Admissions and Relations with Schools' report *The use of admissions tests by the University of California* to the Academic Senate (submitted January 30, 2002).

1. Dorothy A. Perry served as chair of the University of California Board of Admissions and Relations with Schools from 1999 to 2002, Michael T. Brown currently serves as vice-chair, and Barbara A. Sawrey serves as chair.
2. University of California Board of Regents, Policy on undergraduate admission, approved May 20, 1988. University of California Board of Regents, Policy on future admissions, employment and contracting: Resolution rescinding SP-1 and SP-2, approved May 16, 2001.
3. Standing Order of The Regents 105.2 delegates to the Academic Senate authority for "determin[ing] the conditions of admission" (April 18, 1969). Academic Senate Bylaw 145.B.3 includes among the duties of BOARS "determin[ing] the basis of the examinations used to satisfy admissions requirements" (Amended May 26, 1982; available at http://www.ucop.edu/senate/manual/blpart2.html#bl145).
4. Richard C. Atkinson to Michael Cowan, February 15, 2001.
5. The term *eligibility* refers to qualification for admission into the University of California, but not necessarily into a particular campus of the university. Students who are identified as eligible for admission must have successfully completed UC-required and approved course-work and have submitted all application materials, including required test scores. Eligible students make up a total of 12.5% of high school graduates in the state and can apply to multiple UC campuses, with a guarantee of admission to at least one campus within the system. The term *selection* is defined as admission to one or more of the ten individual UC campuses, which is extremely competitive at most of the campuses. The ten UC campuses are: UC Berkeley, UC Davis, UC Irvine, UCLA, UC Merced, UC Riverside, UC San Diego, UC San Francisco, UC Santa Barbara, and UC Santa Cruz.
6. In addition, the SAT II writing exam includes a writing sample and several of the language tests have optional listening sections.
7. *Guidelines for implementation of university-wide policy on undergraduate admissions*. Oakland: University of California Office of the President, 2001.
8. BOARS is indebted to John Douglass, senior research fellow at the Center for Studies in Higher Education at UC Berkeley, for the comprehensive and thoughtful analysis of the historical record provided in *Setting the Conditions of Undergraduate Admissions: The Role of University Faculty in Policy Making* (University of California Academic Senate, 1977). We have drawn extensively from Douglass's work for this section of our paper, which he graciously agreed to review for accuracy.

9. John Douglass, personal communication, January 23, 2002.
10. Douglass, personal communication, January 23, 2002.
11. In accepting BOARS' recommendation, The Regents noted their approval of "offer[ing] applicants an additional option . . . The choice of whether to submit SAT or ACT scores will be up to the applicant."
12. Prior to recommending any changes in 1999, BOARS commissioned simulation studies designed to ensure that changing the relative weights of the various scores would not adversely affect the representation of any racial/ethnic group in the eligibility pool. No adverse effects were found.
13. Students who enrolled at UC Santa Cruz were excluded from some analyses because the campus did not assign letter grades and therefore could not compute a numeric GPA. In addition, only two years of UC Riverside data were included in the original analysis, due to anomalies in the data. Riverside data for the missing years have since been obtained and reanalyzed to confirm the robustness of the findings.
14. UC calculates the high school GPA using only courses that meet the "A–G" requirements, which is a required course pattern of a minimum of 15 year-long high school courses, and adding one grade point for as many as eight UC-approved honors, advanced placement, or college-level course; thus an A in an approved honors course counts for five points rather than four, and many students submit GPAs above 4.0.
15. It should be noted here that historically the measure of "student success" most commonly used in validity studies of admissions tests—and the one on which the College Board and Educational Testing Service base statistical studies of SAT I and SAT II scores—has been the first-year college GPA. This is because intervening variables (including differing academic programs pursued by individual students and the intellectual and personal development students experience during their college years) serve to weaken substantially the predictive relationship between precollege factors like high school GPA and test scores and eventual college GPA. Predictive validity studies justify use of freshman-year GPA by citing its correlation with GPA at graduation. Nonetheless, faculty and admissions officers involved in determining eligibility and selection criteria and processes point out that maximizing freshman-year GPA is at best a relatively minor goal of the admissions evaluation process. While highly cognizant of the weaknesses involved in using freshman GPA, BOARS could not identify an alternative and therefore followed the generally accepted practice of using freshman-year GPA as the outcome variable indicating success in college.
16. Saul Geiser, presentation to BOARS, December 18, 2001.
17. It is important to note that in an independent reanalysis of the UC data, Rebecca Zwick and Jeffrey Sklar have corroborated most of Geiser and Studley's findings although they conclude that the SAT I was a better predictor for Latino students and that the SAT I was not especially sensitive to socioeconomic factors. The Zwick-Sklar report is titled "Analysis of University of California Admissions Data from the UC Office of the President," dated March 29, 2002, and is available from Professor Zwick at the Gevirtz Graduate School of Education at the University of California at Santa Barbara. See also Zwick, this volume and Zwick, Brown, & Sklar (2003).
18. ACT, Inc. announcement (http://www.act.org/news/releases/2002/08-27-02.html)
19. College Board announcement (http://www.collegeboard.com/press/article/0,1443,11147,00.html)

References

ACT, Inc. (2001). *College admissions assessment: Debunking myths and misrepresentations.* Iowa City, IA: ACT, Inc.

Atkinson, R. C. (2001). Standardized Tests and Access to American Universities. The 2001 Robert H. Atwell Distinguished Lecture delivered at the 83rd Annual Meeting of the American Council on Education, Washington, D.C., February 18, 2001. Available online at http://www.ucop.edu/news/sat/speech1.html.

Beatty, A., Greenwood, M. R. C., & Linn, R. L. (1999). *Myths and Tradeoffs: The Role of Tests in Undergraduate Admissions.* Washington, D.C.: National Academy Press.

Brown, M. T., Castillo, S., & Velasco, S. (2001). *UCSB and the SAT.* Paper presented at the conference Rethinking the SAT in University Admissions, held at the University of California at Santa Barbara, November 16–17, 2001.

The College Board (2001). *What does the SAT measure and why does it matter?* NY: College Board.

Dorans, N. J. (2000). *Distinctions among classes of linkages.* College Board Research Notes RN-11. New York: College Board.

Douglass, J. A. (1997, February). *Setting the conditions of undergraduate admissions: The role of University of California faculty in policy and process.* Report to the Task Force on Governance, University of California Academic Senate. Available online at http://ishi.lib.berkeley.edu/cshe/jdouglass/pub/toc.html.

Geiser, S., & Studley, R. (2001A). *UC and the SAT: Predictive Validity and Differential Impact of the SAT I and SAT II at the University of California.* Oakland: University of California Office of the President. Available online at http://www.ucop.edu/sas/research/researchandplanning/pdf/sat_study.pdf.

Geiser, S., & Studley, R. (2001B). Research addendum: Additional findings on UC and the SAT. Oakland: University of California Office of the President. Available online at http://www.ucop.edu/news/sat/resaddendfinal.pdf.

Kowarsky, J., Clatfelter, D., & Widaman, K. (1998). *Predicting university grade-point average in a class of University of California freshmen: An assessment of the validity of A–F GPA and test scores as indicators of future academic performance.* Oakland: UC Office of the President.

Lawrence, I., Rigol, G. W., Van Essen, T., & Jackson, C. A. (2002). *A historical perspective on the SAT: 1926–2001.* College Board Research Report No. 2002–7. New York: College Board.

Lemann, Nicholas (1999). *The big test: The secret history of the American meritocracy.* New York: Farrar, Straus and Giroux.

Lindquist, E. F. (1958). The nature of the problem of improving scholarship and college entrance examinations. Paper presented at the ETS Invitational Conference on Testing Problems, November 1, 1958.

Zwick, R. (2002). *Fair game? The use of standardized admissions tests in higher education.* New York: Routledge Falmer.

Zwick, R., Brown, T., & Sklar, J. C. (2003). *California and the SAT: A reanalysis of University of California admissions data.* (Draft report), Berkeley, CA: Center for Studies in Higher Education.

UC and the SAT: Predictive Validity and Differential Impact of the SAT I and SAT II at the University of California

SAUL GEISER
ROGER E. STUDLEY

The debate over "aptitude" versus "achievement" tests in college admissions is an old one. Aptitude-type tests, exemplified by the SAT I, are intended to assess students' capacity for future learning, whereas achievement-type tests, exemplified by the SAT II subject tests, are designed to assess students' current mastery of college-preparatory subjects. As one of the few institutions in the nation that requires both the SAT I and SAT II, the University of California (UC) has an extensive database with which to assess their relative utility in predicting student success in college. This study examines the relationship between SAT scores and freshman grades based on the records of 77,893 students who entered UC between Fall 1996 and Fall 1999. The study found that (a) the SAT II achievement tests are consistently better predictors of student success at UC than the SAT I, although the incremental gain in prediction is relatively modest and there is substantial redundancy across the tests; (b) the predictive validity of the SAT II appears to be less conditioned by socioeconomic factors than is the SAT I; and (c) racial/ethnic group performance is substantially similar across the SAT I and SAT II. Contrary to the conventional wisdom, these findings suggest that the benefits of achievement tests for college admissions—greater clarity in admissions standards, closer linkage to the high-school curriculum—can be realized without any sacrifice in the capacity to predict success in college.

Calling the overemphasis on SAT scores "the educational equivalent of a nuclear arms race," University of California (UC) President Richard C. Atkinson recently proposed to abandon use of the SAT I in university admissions. The intent of Atkinson's proposal is not to eliminate standardized tests, but to change the focus of admissions testing and the kinds of tests that colleges use in selecting students: "I recommend that the University require only standardized tests that assess mastery of specific subject areas rather than undefined notions of 'aptitude' or 'intelligence'" (Atkinson, 2001). In place of tests such as the SAT I, with its historical roots in intelligence and aptitude testing, Atkinson would emphasize curriculum-based achievement tests such as the SAT II, designed to assess students' mastery of college-preparatory subjects. Because achievement tests are linked more directly to the high-school curriculum, Atkinson believes such tests provide clearer standards of what students must accomplish to be admitted to college and at the same time create incentives for educational improvement at the high-school level.

Atkinson's proposal did not come out of the blue. UC has required applicants to take both the SAT I and SAT II achievement tests since 1968; therefore, UC has considerable experience with the two tests. Two years before President Atkinson made his proposal, BOARS (Board of Admissions and Relations with Schools), the UC faculty committee charged with formulating admissions policy, voted to de-emphasize the SAT I and to increase the weight given to the SAT II in its "Eligibility Index," a formula used to identify the top 12.5% statewide pool of California high-school graduates based on their grades and standardized test scores. Subsequently, President Atkinson's speech to the American Council of Education in February 2001 prompted the growing national debate about the validity and role of the SAT in college admissions (Atkinson, 2001).

The primary rationale for using standardized tests, such as the SAT, in college admissions is to predict success in college. Quoting from a recent publication of the College Board

> The SAT has proven to be an important predictor of success in college. Its validity as a predictor of success in college has been demonstrated through hundreds of validity studies. These validity studies consistently find that high-school grades and SAT scores together are substantial and significant predictors of achievement in college. (Camara & Echternacht, 2000, p. 9).

Yet although it is true that the "predictive validity" of the SAT I has been widely studied, the same cannot be said of the SAT II achievement tests.

One reason for that neglect is that very few colleges and universities require the SAT II—UC being the largest and most notable exception. As a result, UC has an extensive database on the two tests and is uniquely positioned to assess their relative utility in predicting success in college.

What is UC's experience with the SAT I and SAT II, and what do the UC data show? This article presents systemwide data for UC's eight undergraduate campuses, examining the relationship between SAT scores and academic outcomes based on the records of almost 78,000 first-time freshmen.

The article is divided into five parts. Part I describes the study methodology. Part II examines the relative power of the SAT I and the SAT II achievement test in predicting student success at UC. These findings are important for assessing the extent to which use of achievement-type tests might diminish prediction and thereby lower the academic quality of admitted students. Part III analyzes the conditioning effects of socioeconomic status and family background on the predictive validity of SAT I and SAT II. Part IV looks at the differential impact of the tests on various racial/ethnic groups. These findings are important for assessing the extent to which use of achievement-type tests might exacerbate socioeconomic or racial/ethnic disparities in college admissions. Part V concludes with a discussion of the implications of the study findings for admissions policy.

Methodology

The study examined the relative contribution of high-school grade-point average (HSGPA), SAT I, and SAT II scores in predicting college success for a sample of 77,893 first-time freshmen who entered UC over the four-year period from Fall 1996 through Fall 1999. The only exclusions from the sample were students with missing SAT scores or high-school GPAs; students who did not complete their freshman year and/or did not have a freshman GPA recorded in the UC Corporate Student Database; freshmen at UC Santa Cruz, which did not assign conventional grades at this time; and freshmen entering UC Riverside in 1997 and 1998, during which years the campus data upload into the UC Corporate Student System had extensive missing data.

HSGPA used in this analysis is an honors-weighted GPA with additional grade-points for honors-level courses; HSGPA is uncapped and may exceed 4.0. SAT I scores used in this analysis represent a composite of students' scores on the verbal and math portions of that test, whereas the SAT II is a composite of three achievement tests that UC uses in determining students' eligibility for admission: SAT II writing, SAT II mathematics (either level IC or IIC), and an SAT II third subject test of the student's choosing. Although the mathematics Level IIC test assesses students' mastery of more advanced material than the Level IC, the tests are scaled in such a way that a student is neither advantaged or disadvantaged by choosing one exam over the other, according to the College Board, provided that the student has taken the appropriate coursework to prepare for the exam. The maximum possible composite score is 1600 on the SAT I and 2400 on the SAT II. Analysis of individual components of the SAT I and SAT II, including the SAT II third subject test, is presented later in this article.

Data on family income and parents' education are drawn from information provided by students on the UC admissions application. UC has periodically conducted analyses comparing family income data from the admissions application with that from the UC financial aid application, which is subject to audit. These analyses show that, although there are sometimes substantial differences in individual cases, in general data from the two sources are very similar.

The criterion of collegiate "success" employed here is the same as that used by the College Board in the majority of its research on the SAT, namely, freshman GPA. According to a College Board research summary

> The overwhelming majority of these studies use . . . freshman GPA as the criterion representing success in college. Freshman GPA is the most frequently used criterion because
>
> • The courses that freshmen take are more similar and less variable than at any other year in college, thus minimizing comparability issues that occur with grades;
> • Predictor and criterion data are readily available; and
> • Freshmen grade averages are highly correlated with cumulative grade averages. (Camara & Echternacht, 2000, p. 1).

Many have criticized the narrowness of freshman GPA as a measure of success in college and have urged the use of other criteria, such as college graduation rates. We are now examining the relationship between SAT scores and persistence and graduation rates at UC, and those findings will be presented in a later analysis. For purposes of this article, the analysis focuses on UC first-year GPA (UCGPA), because freshman GPA is by far the most commonly employed criterion of "success" in studies of the predictive validity of college admissions tests and because use of the SAT is most often justified on this basis.

Table 1 presents descriptive data on the main variables of the study. It provides means, standard deviations, interquartile ranges, and medians for each of the main variables considered in the analysis, including not only composite SAT I and SAT II scores, but also scores on each of the SAT I and SAT II component tests.

Table 1: Descriptive Statistics: Grades, Test Scores, and Demographic Variables for UC Sample

VARIABLE	N	MEAN	SD	25TH PERCENTILE	MEDIAN	75TH PERCENTILE
Freshman GPA	77,893	2.92	0.62	2.53	2.98	3.39
High school GPA	77,893	3.84	0.41	3.56	3.86	4.14
SAT-I Verbal	77,893	588	93	530	590	650
SAT-I Math	77,893	625	89	570	630	690
SAT-I	77,893	1213	158	1110	1220	1330
SAT-II Writing	77,893	568	97	500	570	640
SAT-II Math	77,893	608	94	540	610	680
SAT-II Third Test	77,893	612	106	530	610	690
SAT-II	77,893	1789	240	1620	1790	1960
Family income–1998 $	67,064	78,246	74,353	32,088	63,106	101,560
Parents' highest education (years)	74,450	15.9	3.2	13.0	16.0	19.0

Predictive Validity of the SAT I, and the SAT II Achievement Tests

As noted previously, the primary rationale for using standardized tests, such as the SAT, in college admissions is to predict success in college. This section examines the variance in students' UCGPA explained by each of the predictor variables and the strength of the standardized regression coefficients associated with each. Relative weights by campus and year of admission, quality of high school, and intended major are also considered.

Explained Variance in UC Freshman GPA

Table 2 shows the percentage of explained variance in UCGPA that is accounted for by HSGPA, SAT I, and SAT II composite scores. The effects of these predictor variables on UCGPA were analyzed both singly and in combination, three main conclusions can be drawn from table 2:

- First, looking at the predictor variables individually—rows 1 to 3 in the table—SAT II scores were the best single predictor of UCGPA in two of the four years studied (1998 and 1999), and also the best single predictor for the pooled, four-year data. Over the four-year period, SAT II scores accounted for the greatest percentage of variance in UCGPA, 16.0%, followed by HSGPA with 15.4%. SAT I scores ranked last, accounting for 13.3% of the variance in a single-variable prediction equation.
- Second, using the predictor variables in combination—rows 4 to 7 of table 1—the percentage of explained variance increases beyond

Table 2: Percent of Variance in UC Freshman GPA Explained by HSGPA, SAT I, and SAT II Scores by Year

PREDICTOR VARIABLES/EQUATIONS	1996	1997	1998	1999	1996–1999
(1) HSGPA	17.0%	16.7%	14.7%	12.9%	15.4%
(2) SAT I	13.8	10.8	12.2	14.2	13.3
(3) SAT II	16.4	14.4	15.6	16.4	16.0
(4) SAT I + SAT II	16.7	14.4	15.6	16.8	16.2
(5) HSGPA + SAT I	21.9	20.1	19.2	20.4	20.8
(6) HSGPA + SAT II	23.0	21.7	21.1	21.5	22.2
(7) HSGPA + SAT I + SAT II	23.2	21.7*	21.1*	21.9	22.3
SAT I increment: [(7)–(6)]	0.2%	0.0%	0.0%	0.4%	0.1%

Source: UC Corporate Student System data on first-time freshmen entering UC from Fall 1996 through Fall 1999. $N = 77,893$.
*SAT I not statistically significant in prediction equation; all other variables are statistically significant at <.01 level.

that which is possible using any one variable alone. Thus, the three predictor variables combined—HSGPA, SAT I, and SAT II (row 7)—account for 22.3% of the total variance in UCGPA over the four-year period (row 7, right-hand column).

- Third, and finally, it is evident that SAT I scores add little, if any, incremental power in predicting UC freshman grades after SAT II scores and HSGPA are taken into account. SAT II scores and HSGPA together account for 22.2% of the variance in UCGPA in the pooled, four-year data (row 6, right-hand column). Adding SAT I into the equation (row 7) improves the prediction by an increment of only 0.1% in the pooled data. Indeed, in two of the four years (1997 and 1998), SAT I scores add nothing to the percentage of variance explained.[1]

Standardized Regression Coefficients

Standardized regression coefficients, or "beta weights," provide another indication of the relative strength of different predictor variables. Table 3 displays the beta weights for HSGPA, SAT I, and SAT II scores, within a combined regression equation (UCGPA = HSGPA + SAT I + SAT II, in simplified form), for the UC sample. The pattern of beta weights shown here is similar to the pattern of explained variance shown previously. HSGPA has the most predictive weight followed closely by SAT II composite scores, while the SAT I ranks a distant third in each year and for the pooled, four-year data. In fact, in two of the four years (1997 and 1998), SAT I scores are not statistically significant predictors of UC freshman grades within a regression equation that also includes SAT II scores and HSGPA.

Table 3: Standardized Regression Coefficients for HSGPA, SAT I, and SAT II Scores by Year

	STANDARDIZED REGRESSION COEFFICIENTS			% OF VARIANCE EXPLAINED
	HSGPA	**SAT I**	**SAT II**	
1996	.29	.07	.21	23.2
1997	.30	.01*	.24	21.7
1998	.26	.02*	.26	21.1
1999	.24	.11	.22	21.9
1996–99	.27	.07	.23	22.3

Source: UC Corporate Student System data on first-time freshmen entering UC from Fall 1996 through Fall 1999. $N = 77,893$. Regression equation: UCGPA = HSGPA + SAT I + SAT II.

*Not statistically significant at <.01 level.

Table 4: Standardized Regression Coefficients for HSGPA, SAT I, and SAT II Scores by UC Campus

	STANDARDIZED REGRESSION COEFFICIENTS			% OF VARIANCE EXPLAINED
	HSGPA	SAT I	SAT II	
UC Berkeley	.21	−.02*	.27	15.5
UC Davis	.30	.04	.27	22.7
UC Irvine	.25	.09	.21	16.5
UC Los Angeles	.23	.05	.26	18.1
UC Riverside	.31	.16	.10	19.6
UC San Diego	.27	.03*	.25	16.3
UC Santa Barbara	.36	.11	.15	22.8
UC Santa Cruz[a]	n/a	n/a	n/a	n/a
UC system	.27	.07	.23	22.3

Source: UC Corporate Student System data on first-time freshmen entering UC from Fall 1996 through Fall 1999. $N = 77,893$. Excludes UC Riverside data for 1997 and 1998, due to missing data. Regression equation: UCGPA = HSGPA + SAT I + SAT II.
[a] Does not assign conventional grades.
* Not statistically significant at <.01 level.

Variation Across UC Campuses

Table 4 shows the relative weights for HSGPA, SAT I, and SAT II scores in predicting freshman GPA at each UC campus. As Table 4 makes clear, the superior predictive power of the SAT II (and HSGPA) is also evident at individual campuses. The SAT II is a consistently stronger predictor of freshman grades than the SAT I at all UC campuses except one, UC Riverside, which is the least selective campus in the UC system in terms of its admissions requirements.[2] At the most selective UC campuses—Berkeley, Los Angeles, and San Diego—the difference in beta weights between the SAT II and SAT I is largest, suggesting that the predictive superiority of the SAT II may be even greater in a more selective admissions context.

Variation by High School of Origin

Table 5 examines the predictive weights of HSGPA, SAT I, and SAT II scores controlling for students' high school of origin. One of the arguments sometimes made for the SAT I is that, insofar as it may be more "curriculum independent" than the SAT II, it might be more useful in identifying high-potential students in low-performing schools, where the curriculum tends to be weakest. Table 5 shows the standardized regression coefficients for

Table 5: Standardized Regression Coefficients for HSGPA, SAT I, and SAT II Scores by High School API Quintile

SCHOOL API QUINTILE	STANDARDIZED REGRESSION COEFFICIENTS			% OF VARIANCE EXPLAINED
	HSGPA	SAT I	SAT II	
5 (high)	.33	−.01*	.20	20.4
4	.32	.01*	.20	21.2
3	.29	.03*	.25	23.5
2	.28	.07	.22	22.3
1 (low)	.25	.12	.18	18.4
All schools	.27	.07	.23	22.3

Source: UC Corporate Student System data on first-time freshmen entering UC from Fall 1996 through Fall 1999, for whom complete API data were available. $N = 61,933$. Regression equation: UCGPA = HSGPA + SAT I + SAT II.
* Not statistically significant at <.01 level.

HSGPA and SAT scores for UC students from each API (Academic Performance Index) quintile of California high schools; the API is a measure developed by the California Department of Education to rate school performance based on the state's Standardized Testing and Reporting (STAR) system for K–12. As Table 5 demonstrates, the SAT II is a better predictor of UC freshman grades than the SAT I across all school API quintiles. Although it is true that the beta weights for the SAT I tend to be larger in lower-performing than in higher-performing schools, the SAT II is still clearly the better predictor at all levels.

Variation by Intended Major

Table 6 shows standardized regression coefficients for HSGPA, SAT I, and SAT II scores controlling for students' intended major at UC. This analysis is important to test the hypothesis that students who score highest on the SAT I tend to enter more difficult academic disciplines such as engineering, where grading standards are tougher. Such differences across disciplines might therefore mask the true predictive power of the SAT I, which would become apparent only after controlling by major.

Table 6 provides no support for the hypothesis that the SAT I is a better predictor of freshman grades than the SAT II in certain academic disciplines than others. In fact, among students intending to major in the physical sciences, mathematics, and engineering, which are among the most competitive academic disciplines at UC, SAT I scores have negative predictive

Table 6: Standardized Regression Coefficients for HSGPA, SAT I, and SAT II Scores by Intended Major

	STANDARDIZED REGRESSION COEFFICIENTS			% OF VARIANCE EXPLAINED
	HSGPA	SAT I	SAT II	
General/Undeclared	.27	.08	.22	23.9
Social Sciences/Humanities	.28	.11	.20	21.2
Biological Sciences	.31	.12	.25	29.2
Physical Sciences/Math/ Engineering	.28	−.05	.30	20.3

Source: UC Corporate Student System data on first-time freshmen entering UC from Fall 1996 through Fall 1999, for whom data on intended major were available. $N = 73,279$. Regression equation: UCGPA = HSGPA + SAT I + SAT II.

weight within a regression equation that simultaneously takes into account HSGPA and SAT II scores. Across all other major disciplinary areas as well, the SAT II is consistently the stronger predictor of student performance at UC than the SAT I.

Directions for Further Research

The previous findings make a strong presumptive, if not yet conclusive, case for the superiority of the SAT II over the SAT I in predicting students' success at UC. The analysis needs to be extended, however, in at least one other important direction: Analysis of outcome indicators other than freshmen grades, such as student persistence and graduation rates, and their relationship to SAT I versus SAT II scores. Data needed to conduct these analyses were not readily accessible at the UC system level at the time of this writing, but the data are now being developed and their analysis will be presented in a later article. Nevertheless, one conclusion that can be drawn at this time is the following: If prediction of student "success" as measured by freshman grades is the raison d'être for the use of standardized tests in college admissions, as College Board and other researchers have emphasized in the overwhelming majority of validity studies, then the SAT II is consistently superior to the SAT I on this criterion, according to the UC data. Although the gain in incremental prediction is modest and there is substantial redundancy across the tests, the predictive superiority of the SAT II achievement tests is consistently evident not only for the overall UC sample, but also by campus, academic year, quality of high school, and intended major.

Conditioning Effects of Socioeconomic and Other Variables on the Predictive Validity of the SAT I and SAT II

The next set of analyses examines the impact of socioeconomic factors on the predictive validity of the SAT I and SAT II achievement tests. In particular, we examine the impact of two indicators of socioeconomic status (SES): (a) family income, using the log of family income in constant 1998 dollars, and (b) parents' education, in years, for the student's highest-educated parent. The logarithm of family income is used here to take into account the diminishing marginal effects of income on UCGPA and other variables. That is, a $10,000 increase in income is likely to have a larger effect for a student whose family earns $35,000 annually than for a student whose family earns $135,000. The following findings are based, once again, on the pool of freshmen entering UC from Fall 1996 through Fall 1999.[3]

Table 7 compares standardized regression coefficients for HSGPA, SAT I scores, and SAT II scores with and without inclusion of SES variables in the regression analysis. That is, rows 1 through 3 of the table were derived by regressing UCGPA on HSGPA + SAT I, HSGPA + SAT II, and HSGPA + SAT I + SAT II, whereas rows 4 through 6 show the results of the same regression equations plus family income and parents' education. Note particularly the difference in beta weights between equations 3 and 6, where HSGPA, SAT I, and SAT II scores are combined within the same regression equation. After introducing socioeconomic factors into the equation, the predictive weights for both the SAT II and HSGPA are undiminished and in fact increase slightly (from .23 to .24 for the SAT II, and from .27 to .30 for HSGPA). In contrast, the predictive weight for the SAT I, which is low to begin with, falls sharply (from .07 to .02). What these data suggest is that much of the apparent relationship between the SAT I and UC freshman grades may be conditioned by socioeconomic factors, whereas the SAT II remains correlated with success at UC even after controlling for socioeconomic background.

This same conclusion is supported by the findings on explained variance in Table 7. Comparing equations 2 and 3—before SES variables are introduced in the regression analysis—the addition of SAT I scores to HSGPA and SAT II (equation 3) appears to increase the percentage of explained variance by a small but statistically significant margin over HSGPA and SAT II alone (equation 2); the percentage of explained variance increases from 22.1% to 22.3%, a gain of 0.2%. Adding SES variables into the regression analysis, the percentage of explained variance increases further to 22.8% (equation 6). Note, however, that removing SAT I scores from the regression equation (equation 5) now has no effect on explained variance, which remains at 22.8%. After controlling for socioeconomic background, in short, SAT I scores add nothing to the prediction of freshman grades beyond that which HSGPA and the SAT II already provide.

Table 7: Standardized Regression Coefficients and Percent of Variance in UC Freshman GPA Explained by HSGPA, SAT I, and SAT II Scores With and Without Consideration of Socioeconomic Status (SES)

| | STANDARDIZED REGRESSION COEFFICIENTS | | | | | % OF VARIANCE |
REGRESSION EQUATIONS	HSGPA	SAT I	SAT II	INCOME	EDUCATION	EXPLAINED
Without SES						
(1) HSGPA + SAT I	.30	.25	–	–	–	20.7
(2) HSGPA + SAT II	.28	–	.28	–	–	22.1
(3) HSGPA + SAT I + SAT II	.27	.07	.23	–	–	22.3
With SES						
(4) HSGPA + SAT I	.30	.22	–	.03	.05	21.2
(5) HSGPA + SAT II	.28	–	.25	.04	.06	22.8
(6) HSGPA + SAT I + SAT II	.28	.02	.24	.03	.06	22.8

Source: UC Corporate Student System data on first-time freshmen entering UC from Fall 1996 through Fall 1999, for whom complete data on family income and parents' education were available. $N = 66,584$.

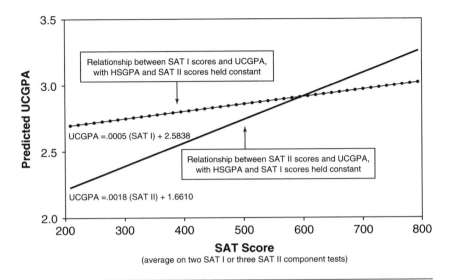

Figure 1. Relationship between SAT scores and predicted UC Freshman GPA, controlling for HSGPA and other test scores.
Source for Figures 1 through 3: UC Corporate Student System data on first-time freshmen entering UC from Fall 1996 through Fall 1999, for whom complete data on family income and parents' education were available. $N = 66,584$.

Conditional Effect Plots

The conditioning effect of socioeconomic and other variables on the predictive power of the SAT I versus SAT II, reflected in the previous regression data, is illustrated graphically in the following conditional effect plots, which show the relationship between SAT scores and UCGPA with other factors held constant. Figures 1 through 3 demonstrate that the larger the number and variety of background factors held constant, the clearer the predictive superiority of the SAT II. The conditional effect plots were developed by regressing UCGPA against the variables considered in Figures 1 through 3 and then, within the resulting regression equations, holding constant all variables except SAT I or SAT II scores at their mean values.

Figure 1 shows that, controlling only for high-school grades and other test scores, the SAT II has about three times the predictive power of the SAT I: Each 100-point increase in SAT II scores adds about .18 of a grade point to predicted freshman GPA, whereas a 100-point increase in SAT I scores adds only about .05 of a grade point.

Controlling for family income and parents' education in addition to high-school grades and other test scores, as shown in Figure 2, the SAT II has about

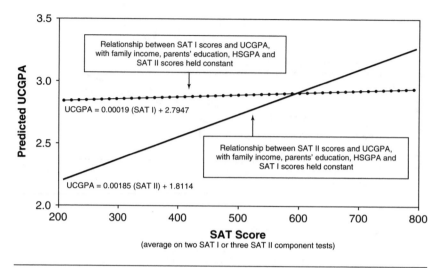

Figure 2. Relationship between SAT scores and predicted UC freshman GPA, controlling for family income, parents' education, HSGPA and other test scores.

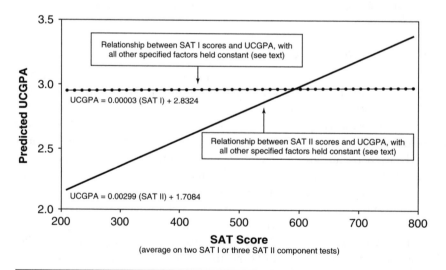

Figure 3. Relationship between SAT scores and predicted UC freshman GPA, controlling for race/ethnicity, campus and year of admission, family income, parents' education, HSGPA and other test scores.

10 times the predictive power of the SAT I: Each 100-point increase in SAT II scores adds about .19 of a grade point to predicted freshman GPA, whereas a 100-point increase in SAT I scores adds only about .019 of a grade point.

Finally, controlling for a still broader array of factors—race, ethnicity, year of admission, and UC campus of enrollment, in addition to family background, high-school grades, and other test scores, as shown in Figure 3—the SAT II retains its predictive power, but the power of the SAT I virtually disappears. Each 100-point increase in SAT II scores adds about .21 of a grade point to predicted freshman GPA, whereas a 100-point increase in SAT I scores adds only .001 of a grade point.

Directions for Further Research

If it is true that the predictive validity of the SAT II achievement tests is less affected by socioeconomic factors than the SAT I, the question arises as to why and how this occurs. One obvious hypothesis is that SES-related differences in patterns of test preparation and/or repeat testing on the SAT I and SAT II may differentially affect the predictive validity of these tests. We are now gathering data with which to examine this hypothesis, and results will be presented in a forthcoming article.

Differential Impact of the SAT I and SAT II by Race/Ethnicity

A final question that the UC data allow us to explore is the relative impact of the SAT I and SAT II on different racial and ethnic groups—a focus of much speculation following President Atkinson's proposal. In particular, speculation has focused on the role of the SAT II third subject test, which UC has long included along with SAT II writing and SAT II mathematics achievement tests in the battery of tests required of applicants. That is, all students are required to take the SAT II writing and math, but for the third subject they may select from a variety of specific achievement tests. Because about half of all Chicano/Latino students as well as almost a quarter Asian American applicants opt to take the SAT II language tests, questions have been raised about the extent to which various ethnic groups might be advantaged, or disadvantaged, if the SAT I was discontinued in favor of achievement tests such as the SAT II (Golden, 2001).

The following analyses examine, first, how well the SAT I and SAT II (including the third subject test) predict freshman grades for students from different racial/ethnic backgrounds. We then examine the relative performance of students, by race and ethnicity, on the SAT I versus SAT II achievement tests, with and without the SAT II third subject test. Finally, the analysis concludes with preliminary findings on the predictive power of the SAT II third test itself.

Table 8: Percent of Variance in UCGPA Explained by HSGPA, SAT I, and SAT II Scores by Race/Ethnicity

	HSGPA	SAT I	SAT II*	HSGPA + SAT I	HSGPA + SAT II[a]
African American	9.5%	10.0%	12.3%	15.0%	16.4%
American Indian	8.8	8.5	11.1	12.5	13.9
Asian American	15.9	12.6	16.9	20.8	23.4
Chicano/Latino	12.0	10.9	10.1	17.3	16.4
White	15.6%	10.1%	13.9%	19.1%	20.9%

Source: UC Corporate Student System data on first-time freshmen entering UC from Fall 1996 through Fall 1999. $N = 77,893$.

[a] Composite includes SAT II Writing and Mathematics plus third subject test.

Explained Variance and Over- and Underprediction by Race/Ethnicity

Table 8 shows the percentage of total variance in UCGPA that is accounted for by HSGPA, SAT I, and SAT II scores (including the third subject test) for each racial/ethnic group. Again, the data are for all freshmen entering UC between 1996 and 1999. As Table 8 demonstrates, the SAT II is a better predictor of UC freshman grades than the SAT I for all racial/ethnic groups except Chicano/Latinos, among whom the variance in freshman grades accounted for by SAT II scores (10.1%) is slightly below that for the SAT I (10.9%). The same overall pattern is evident when SAT I and SAT II scores are combined with HSGPA to predict freshman grades, as the tests are normally used in practice.

Table 9 next presents findings on over- and underprediction by racial/ethnic group. A phenomenon long noted in the research literature

Table 9: Over- and Underprediction of UCGPA by HSGPA, SAT I, and SAT II Scores by Race/Ethnicity; Difference Between Predicted and Actual UCGPA (in Grade Points)

	HSGPA	SAT I	SAT II[a]	HSGPA + SAT I	HSGPA + SAT II[a]
African American	+.10	+.06	+.02	.00	−.03
American Indian	+.02	+.06	.00	+.01	−.03
Asian American	+.07	+.07	+.07	+.08	+.08
Chicano/Latino	+.13	+.04	+.10	+.04	+.08
White	−.11	−.08	−.10	−.09	−.10

Source: UC Corporate Student System data on first-time freshmen entering UC from Fall 1996 through Fall 1999. $N = 77,893$.

[a] Composite includes SAT II Writing and Mathematics plus third subject test.

on testing, over-prediction refers to the tendency of the SAT I to predict slightly higher freshman GPAs for underrepresented students than these students actually achieve (Bridgeman, McCamley-Jenkins, & Ervin, 2000; Ramist, Lewis, & McCamley-Jenkins, 1994). Given the tendency of the SAT I to over-predict, some have raised the concern that underrepresented students might be disadvantaged if SAT I scores were eliminated in college admissions. Data for the UC sample are presented in Table 9.

Like the SAT I, the SAT II achievement tests also exhibit a slight tendency to over-predict UCGPA for minority students, and there are only minor differences between the two tests in this respect—less than one-tenth of a UC freshman grade point for any racial/ethnic group. Moreover, when SAT I and SAT II scores are used in conjunction with HSGPA to predict freshman grades, as is the normal practice in admissions, these minor differences tend to become even smaller: At most, the difference in prediction is four hundredths of a grade point, or the difference between a predicted freshman GPA of 2.50 and 2.54. These data suggest that eliminating the SAT I in UC admissions in favor of achievement tests such as the SAT II would have little effect on predicted outcomes for students from any racial/ethnic group.

Racial/Ethnic Differences in Student Performance on the SAT I and SAT II

How do UC students from different racial/ethnic groups perform on the SAT I versus SAT II? Table 10 presents mean scores and standard deviations for each racial/ethnic group on three SAT composite scales: (a) SAT I composite including math and verbal, (b) SAT II composite including writing and mathematics but not the third subject test, and (c) SAT II composite including the third subject test as well as Writing and mathematics.

As Table 10 shows, mean scores for underrepresented minority applicants—African American, American Indian, and Chicano/Latino students—fall below those for Asian American, White, and others on all three SAT composites. It is not possible to draw direct comparisons of student performance on the various SAT composites, however, because the composites have different scales and standard deviations (i.e., the maximum possible score on the SAT I composite is 1600 with a standard deviation of 200, whereas the maximum on the SAT II composite that includes the third test is 2400 with a standard deviation of 322). To facilitate comparison, Table 11 converts the data into standardized differences. That is, Table 11 shows the number of standard deviations that average test scores for each racial/ethnic group are above or below the average for all applicants on each of the three SAT composites.

Table 10: SAT I and SAT II Mean Scores and Standard Deviations by Race/Ethnicity (UC Fall 2000 Applicant Pool)

	SAT I VERBAL + MATH		SAT II WRITING + MATH		SAT II WRITING + MATH + THIRD TEST	
	M	SD	M	SD	M	SD
African American	1050	195	1041	191	1559	291
American Indian	1172	172	1144	192	1709	290
Asian American	1217	207	1208	214	1833	337
Chicano/Latino	1061	195	1051	191	1674	312
White	1228	170	1213	186	1811	285
Other/unknown	1191	194	1178	205	1765	313
All applicants	1192	200	1180	209	1785	322

Source: UC Corporate Student System data on UC freshman applicants for Fall 2000. $N = 54,146$.

Table 11: Standardized Differences[a] in Mean SAT Scores by Race/Ethnicity; Racial/Ethnic Group Means Compared to Mean for All Applicants (UC Fall 2000 Applicant Pool)

	SAT I VERBAL + MATH	SAT II WRITING + MATH	SAT II WRITING + MATH + THIRD TEST
African American	−.71	−.67	−.70
American Indian	−.10	−.17	−.24
Asian American	.12	.13	.15
Chicano/Latino	−.66	−.62	−.34
White	.18	.16	.18
Other/unknown	−.01	−.01	−.06

Source: UC Corporate Student System data on UC freshman applicants for Fall 2000. $N = 54{,}146$. Number of standard deviations that average scores for each racial/ethnic group are above (+) or below (−) the average for all applicants.
[a] Standardized difference = (ethnic group mean − mean for all applicants)/standard deviation for all applicants.

Table 11 reveals a number of interesting between-group variations in student performance on the three SAT composites. African American applicants score consistently below average on all three composites, and there is little difference in the relative performance of these students on the SAT I, the SAT II composite with writing and math only, or the SAT II composite that includes the third test. American Indian applicants also score lower than average on all of the composites but tend to perform slightly worse relative to other students on the SAT II, both with and without the third test, than on the SAT I. White applicants, on the other hand, score higher than average on all three composites and tend to score highest on the SAT I. Finally, whereas Asian American applicants score better than average and Chicano/Latino worse than average on all three SAT composites, both groups score best on the SAT II composite that includes the third subject test. The latter pattern undoubtedly reflects the influence of the language tests.

Notwithstanding these between-group differences, however, the overriding pattern that emerges from Table 11 is the striking within-group similarity in mean performance on the SAT I versus SAT II, with or without the third subject test. African American applicants, for example, average −.71 standard deviations below the mean for all applicants on the SAT I, and −.70 standard deviations below the mean on the SAT II composite including the third test. Even among Chicano/Latino applicants, for whom the standardized difference is greatest (i.e., −.66 standard deviations on the SAT I vs.

Table 12: Racial/Ethnic Composition of Top Decile of SAT I Versus SAT II Takers (Fall 2000 UC Applicant Pool)

	SAT I VERBAL + MATH	SAT II WRITING + MATH	SAT II WRITING + MATH + THIRD TEST
African American	0.7%	0.7%	0.6%
American Indian	0.3	0.3	0.2
Asian American	41.4	42.3	45.0
Chicano/Latino	2.5	2.5	3.0
White	40.6	40.2	37.4
Other/unknown	14.5	14.0	13.7
Total	100.0%	100.0%	100.0%

Source: UC Corporate Student System data on UC freshman applicants for Fall 2000.

—.34 standard deviations on the SAT II composite with third test), the difference in mean performance is relatively modest, approximately one-third of one standard deviation—or about 64 points on a 1600-point scale.

Test-score differences of this order of magnitude are too small to have any substantial effect on the demographic make-up of the UC admissions pool. To demonstrate, Table 12 compares the racial/ethnic composition of the top decile of UC applicants in Fall 2000 selected on the basis of same three SAT composites: SAT I math and verbal, SAT II with writing and math only, and SAT II with writing, math, and the third subject test. In considering the potential effects of these tests on admissions, it is important to examine not only differences in mean SAT scores among different racial/ethnic groups, but also differences at the high end of the SAT distribution, because there is an important distinction between eligibility for the UC system versus admissibility at the more selective UC campuses. Table 12 shows the demographic breakdown of the topmost portion of the UC applicant pool: As Table 12 illustrates, even among the most highly competitive applicants to UC, there are only small differences in the racial/ethnic composition of the top SAT I versus the top SAT II takers—with or without the third subject test.[4] Moreover, because actual admissions decisions are based on high-school grades and many other factors in addition to test scores, the small differences shown here, which are based solely on test scores, are likely to be muted by other factors in practice. These data suggest that eliminating the SAT I in favor of achievement tests such as the SAT II would have only a marginal effect on the demographic composition of students admitted to the University, even at the most selective UC campuses.

Experience with UC's New Eligibility Index

But perhaps the best evidence of the potential impact of the SAT I versus SAT II on different racial/ethnic groups is provided by the University's actual experience this year in implementing its new Eligibility Index, which doubles the weight given to SAT II scores (including the third subject test) over SAT I scores. The Eligibility Index is a sliding scale in which a low HSGPA can be offset by high test scores, and vice versa; the Index was originally introduced in the 1960s, and has been periodically updated to identify the top 12.5% statewide pool of California high-school graduates as mandated by the state's Master Plan for Higher Education. Table 13 compares UC's previous Eligibility Index[5] with the new Index that was used for the first time as part of the Fall 2001 admissions cycle.

Comparing the old and the new Eligibility Indexes, three differences are noteworthy. First, SAT II scores are now combined along with SAT I scores in the Index. Second, there is a minimum combined test-score requirement at every HSGPA level, not just at the lowest HSGPA levels. Third, SAT II scores (including scores on the third subject test) are given double the weight of SAT I scores in the Index calculation; BOARS's decision to double the weight

Table 13: Old UC Eligibility Index Prior to New UC Eligibility Index Introduced Fall 2001

HSGPA IN UC-REQUIRED COURSEWORK	SAT I (OR ACT EQUIVALENT MINIMUM SCORE	HSGPA IN UC-REQUIRED COURSEWORK	SAT II (OR ACT EQUIVALENT) + SAT II WEIGHTED MINIMUM SCORE*
2.82	1600	2.80–2.84	4640
2.85	1570	2.85–2.89	4384
2.90	1490	2.90–2.94	4160
2.95	1370	2.95–2.99	3984
3.00	1270	3.00–3.04	3840
3.05	1170	3.05–3.09	3720
3.10	1070	3.10–3.14	3616
3.15	960	3.15–3.19	3512
3.20	840	3.20–3.24	3408
3.25	690	3.25–3.29	3320
3.30 and above	No minimum—applicants	3.30–3.34	3248
	required to submit SAT I	3.35–3.39	3192
	and SAT II scores, but	3.40–3.44	3152
	score values do not count	3.45–3.49	3128
	toward UC eligibility	3.50 and above	3120

* Weighted test score = [SAT I composite] + [2 × (SAT II Writing + SAT II Mathematics + SAT II third subject test)].

for SAT II scores was based on UC predictive validity findings similar to those presented in this article (Kowarsky, Clatfelter, & Widaman, 1998) and advice and research provided by College Board. Note also that, because the total possible score on the SAT II with the third test is 2400, compared to 1600 on the SAT I, doubling students' SAT II scores in the eligibility calculation has had the effect of trebling the maximum total points possible on the SAT II (4800) versus the SAT I (1600) in the new Eligibility Index. Clearly the new Eligibility Index gives much greater emphasis to the SAT II, and if the SAT II does have a substantially different demographic footprint than the SAT I, then one might expect to observe this effect in UC's Fall 2001 applicant pool.

Yet the racial/ethnic distribution of students who are eligible for UC under the new Index is almost identical to the distribution produced by the old Index. Table 14 was developed by applying the old Eligibility Index to the Fall 2001 applicant pool and comparing the results with those actually achieved using the new Index. As Table 14 demonstrates, the racial/ethnic distributions are virtually the same under UC's old and new Eligibility Indices. Doubling the weight given to SAT II scores and extending test-score minima across all HSGPA levels has had almost no effect on the racial/ethnic composition of the pool of applicants eligible for UC under statewide eligibility criteria.[6]

Predictive Validity of the SAT II Third Subject Test

Finally, we present a surprising, if still preliminary, finding about the relative weight of the SAT II third subject test itself in predicting student success at

Table 14: Racial/Ethnic Distribution of UC-Eligible Students Under Old Versus New Eligibility Index (Fall 2001 UC Applicant Pool)

	OLD STATEWIDE ELIGIBILITY INDEX	NEW STATEWIDE ELIGIBILITY INDEX[a]
African American	3.1%	3.1%
American Indian	0.6	0.6
Asian American	32.9	32.7
Chicano	10.6	10.8
Latino	3.4	3.5
White	39.5	39.2
Other	1.8	1.8
Unknown	8.2	8.2
Total	100.0%	100.00%

Source: UC Corporate Student System data for UC freshman applicants for Fall 2001. $N = 58,424$.

[a] Does not include students newly eligible under UC's Top 4% by School policy.

Table 15: Contribution of SAT II Third Subject Test to Explained Variance in UC Freshman GPA

PREDICTION EQUATIONS	% OF VARIANCE EXPLAINED
(1) HSGPA	15.4
(2) HSGPA + SAT II M	18.1
(3) HSGPA + SAT II third test	19.0
(4) HSGPA + SAT II W	21.8
(5) HSGPA + SAT II WM (combined score on 2 tests)	21.5
(6) HSGPA + SAT II WM + SAT I	21.7
(7) HSGPA + SAT II WM + SAT II third test	22.2

Source: UC Corporate Student System data on first-time freshmen entering UC from Fall 1996 through Fall 1999. N = 77,893.

UC. After the SAT II writing test, the SAT II third test is the next-best predictor of the five component SAT I and SAT II tests that UC uses in admissions.

Table 15 shows the percentage of variance in UC freshman GPA explained by high-school grades, SAT I scores, and the three SAT II achievement tests required by UC: SAT II writing, SAT II mathematics, and the SAT II third subject test. The findings are again based on the pool of freshmen entering UC between 1996 and 1999.

As shown in equations 1 through 4, after taking into account students' HSGPA (equation 1), introducing the SAT II third test into the prediction equation (equation 3) adds more to the percentage of variance explained than the SAT II mathematics test (equation 2), although less than the SAT II writing (equation 4).

Equations 5 through 7 show that, after taking into account students' HSGPA and their combined score on the SAT II writing and mathematics tests (equation 5), introducing the SAT II third test into the prediction equation (equation 7) adds more to the percentage of variance explained than the SAT I (equation 6).

In sum, the analysis of explained variance indicates that the SAT third test ranks behind only HSGPA and the SAT II writing test, but ahead of the SAT II mathematics test and the SAT I, in predicting UC freshman GPA.

The predictive power of the SAT II third test is also evident in the pattern of standardized regression coefficients shown in Table 16. This table presents the beta weights for HSGPA and each of the five SAT component tests within a combined regression equation (UCGPA = HSGPA + SAT I V + SAT I M + SAT II W + SAT II M + SAT II third test). Beta weights are shown both for the overall freshman pool (right-hand column) and by intended major disciplinary area.

Table 16: Standardized Regression Coefficients[a] for HSGPA and SAT Component Tests by Intended Major

	GENERAL/ UNDECLARED	SOCIAL SCI/ HUMANITIES	BIOLOGICAL SCIENCES	PHYSICAL SCI/MATH/ ENGINEERING	OVERALL
HSGPA	.27	.28	.31	.29	.27
SAT I Verbal	.06	.10	.04	−.06	.05
SAT I Math	.02*	.00*	.07	.02*	.01*
SAT II Writing	.18	.16	.10	.10	.18
SAT II Mathematics	.02*	.05	.14	.15	.02
SAT II third test	.08	.07	.10	.12	.09

[a] Prediction equation: UCGPA = HSGPA + SAT IV + SAT IM + SAT II W + SAT II M + SAT II 3rd.
*Not statistically significant at <.01 level.

Looking first at the data for the overall freshman pool in the right-hand column of Table 16, the beta weights exhibit the same rank order among the predictor variables as observed previously in the explained-variance data in Table 15: The SAT II third test ranks behind only HSGPA and SAT II writing scores, but ahead of the SAT II mathematics test and SAT I verbal and math scores, in terms of its predictive weight.[7]

A more nuanced picture emerges when one examines the pattern of beta weights within different disciplinary areas in the body of Table 16. Although HSGPA continues to have the greatest predictive weight in all major areas, the relative weighting of the various SAT component tests varies across fields. The SAT II writing test has the greatest predictive weight among general/undeclared majors and students intending to major in the social sciences and humanities but not, as might be expected, among intended majors in the biological and physical sciences, mathematics, and engineering, for whom the SAT II mathematics test is the best predictor of freshman grades. On the other hand, the SAT I test of mathematical reasoning is among the poorer predictors in all academic disciplines, even in the physical sciences, mathematics, and engineering, where the standardized coefficient for the SAT I math test is not statistically significant within a regression equation that also includes the SAT II mathematics and other component tests.

These variations notwithstanding, the main point to draw from Table 16 is that, compared to the other SAT I and SAT II component tests, the SAT II third test is among the better predictors of student success in all major fields. Of the five component SAT tests required for UC admission, the SAT II third test ranks as the second-best predictor both among general/undeclared majors (after the SAT II writing) and among intended majors in the biological and physical sciences, mathematics, and engineering (after the SAT II mathematics), and as the third-best predictor for students planning to major in the social sciences and humanities (after the SAT II writing and the SAT I verbal).

Directions for Further Research

These findings must be regarded as preliminary, as more detailed analyses need to be conducted on the particular tests that applicants take to satisfy the third test requirement. Under UC policy, applicants may choose to submit results for any of the following SAT II achievement tests: Chinese, French, French with listening, German, German with listening, Modern Hebrew, Italian, Japanese, Korean, Latin, Spanish, Spanish with listening, U.S. history, world history, literature, ecological biology, molecular biology, chemistry, and physics. We have begun analyses of the predictive validity of each of the 19 tests, with appropriate statistical controls for major disciplinary area, race/ethnicity, SES, and, in the case of the language tests, first-language background. These analyses are essential to refine our understanding of why the SAT II third subject test has predictive value as an admissions requirement. Results will be presented in a forthcoming article.

Nevertheless, even before the results of that research are known, the fact remains that the third subject test, as an elective admissions requirement, does have evident predictive value, both overall and within every major disciplinary area. And although unexpected, this finding is perhaps not so surprising in the final analysis, given the intended purpose of the third test requirement, namely, to allow students the opportunity to demonstrate their particular areas of academic strength. That those strengths correlate with later success at the University may not be surprising at all.

Conclusions and Implications for Admissions Policy

The analyses presented here support three main conclusions

- First, the UC data indicate that students' scores on the SAT II achievement tests are consistently better predictors of freshman grades than SAT I scores. If prediction of college success as measured by freshman GPA is the standard by which admissions tests should be judged, as College Board and other researchers have emphasized in the vast majority of validity studies, then the SAT II achievement tests appear to have a clear edge over the SAT I on this criterion, according to the UC data. Although the incremental gain in prediction is relatively modest and there is substantial redundancy across the tests, the predictive superiority of the SAT II achievement tests is consistently evident not only for the overall UC sample, but also by campus, academic year, quality of high school, and intended major.
- Second, the UC data suggest that the predictive validity of the SAT II is less affected by students' socioeconomic background than the SAT I: After controlling for family income and parents' education, the predictive power of the SAT II is undiminished, whereas the relationship between the SAT I and UC freshman grades virtually disappears. These findings suggest that the predictive validity of the SAT II is less sensitive than the SAT I to socioeconomic differences.
- Third, our findings with respect to the racial/ethnic impact of the SAT I versus SAT II indicate that, in general, differences between the test are relatively minor. The SAT II is a slightly better predictor of freshman grades for most racial/ethnic groups than the SAT I, but both tests tend to "over-predict" freshman grades for minority

students to a small but measurable extent. And while there are large between-group differences in student performance on the SAT I and SAT II, the within-group differences are relatively small, both at the mean as well as at the high end of the test-score distribution. Including the third subject test within the SAT II composite does produce modest test-score improvements for Chicano/Latino and Asian American students, but the improvements are too small to have any substantial effect on the demographic composition of the UC admissions pool. In sum, these findings suggest that eliminating the SAT I in favor of achievement tests such as the SAT II would have little effect on rates of UC eligibility and admission among students from different racial/ethnic groups. UC's experience this year with its new Eligibility Index, which doubles the weight given to SAT II scores, supports this conclusion.

The choice between the SAT I and the SAT II reflects a choice between two contrasting approaches to college admissions: An approach that emphasizes prediction of students' general capacity to learn as against an approach that emphasizes demonstrated mastery of specific academic subjects required for college-level work. The first attempts to assess students' aptitude for future learning in college, whereas the second evaluates students' current level of achievement in college-preparatory subjects. It is a long-standing debate (Crouse & Trusheim, 1988; Jackson, 1980; Slack & Porter, 1980). Advocates of the SAT I argue that it taps generalized verbal and mathematical reasoning abilities needed for success in college, and that without the SAT I, admissions officers would make poorer decisions in predicting which students will succeed. Advocates of achievement tests counter that our ability to predict college outcomes is limited; even in combination with high-school grades, the SAT I accounts for only a fraction of the variance in the grades of college freshmen. They argue that, because achievement tests are linked more directly to the high-school curriculum, such tests provide clearer standards of what students must accomplish to be admitted to college and at the same time create incentives for educational improvement at the high-school level.

If the UC data add anything new to the long-standing debate over aptitude versus achievement testing, it is this: Insofar as "aptitude" or "readiness for college" refer to tested competencies that bear a demonstrable relationship to freshman grades, curriculum-based achievement tests such as the SAT II perform at least as well as the SAT I in identifying such competencies. The benefits of achievement tests for college admissions—greater clarity in admissions standards, closer linkage to the high-school curriculum—can be realized without any sacrifice in the capacity to predict success in college.

Acknowledgments

We wish to thank the following individuals for their constructive criticism of earlier drafts of this article, although we remain solely responsible for the findings and conclusions herein: Michael Brown, Michael Feuer, Ed Haertel, Dan Koretz, Bob Linn, Juliet Shaffer, Rich Shavelson, and Gregg Thomson.

This research was conducted under the joint auspices of the University of California, Office of the President and the Board of Admissions and Relations with Schools, the university-wide faculty committee responsible for UC admissions policy.

Interested readers may also contact the author for sources of additional data available on the UC Office of the President website at www.ucop.edu/sas/research at the time of publication.

Notes

Requests for reprints should be sent to Saul Geiser, University of California, Office of the President, 1111 Franklin Street, 9th floor, Oakland, CA 94607-5200.

1. The UC data were also examined carefully for range-restriction effects, and there was no evidence that range restriction had differential effects on the relative predictive validity of the SAT I and SAT II. For example, comparing the pool of admitted students with all UC applicants, the standard deviation of SAT I composite scores was 158 for admitted students and 174 for applicants, a ratio of .908, whereas the standard deviation of SAT II composite scores was 240 for admitted students and 262 for applicants, a ratio of .916.

2. Due to problems of missing data at the time of the study, results for UC Riverside shown here were based on analysis of only two years' worth of data—1996 and 1999—but excluded data for 1997 and 1998.

3. It should be noted that the pool used in the following regression analysis is somewhat smaller than that used in the preceding analyses, which were based on the set of 77,893 students entering UC between Fall 1996 and Fall 1999 for whom complete information was available on HSGPA, SAT I scores, SAT II scores, and UC freshmen GPA. The following analysis is further limited to the subset of 66,584 students from this group for whom complete information was also available on family income and parent's education. This subset of students closely resembled the larger pool with respect to demographic characteristics such as race/ethnicity.

4. Comparing the percentages in Table 11 with the *total* UC applicant pool, the racial/ethnic proportions among all UC applicants in Fall 2000 for whom SAT data were available were as follows: African American 3.6%, American Indian 0.6%, Asian American 29.3%, Chicano/Latino 12.4%, White 39.7%, Other/Unknown 14.5%.

5. For reasons of brevity, Table 13 presents a simplified depiction of the previous Eligibility Index, which established SAT I minima at each hundredth of a grade-point between 2.82 and 3.30.

6. Table 14 excludes students who did not meet statewide eligibility criteria, as determined by the Index, but who become eligible as the result of UC's new Eligibility in the Local Context (ELC) policy, which makes eligible the top 4% of students from each high school; ELC also took effect in Fall 2001.

7. In view of the predictive power of the SAT II Writing test, it is interesting to note that this test is the only one of the five SAT component tests that involves an actual performance element—writing—in addition to multiple-response items.

References

Atkinson, R. C. (2001, February). Standardized tests and access to American universities. The 2001 Robert H. Atwell Distinguished Lecture, delivered at the 83rd Annual Meeting of the American Council on Education, Washington, DC.

Bridgeman, B., McCamley-Jenkins, L., & Ervin, N. (2000). *Predictions of freshman grade-point average from the revised and recentered SAT I reasoning test* (College Board Report No. 2000–1). New York: College Entrance Examination Board.

Camara, W., & Echternacht, G. (2000). *The SAT I and high school grades: Utility in predicting success in college* (College Board Report No. RN–10). New York: College Entrance Examination Board.

Crouse, J., & Trusheim, D. (1988). *The case against the SAT.* Chicago: The University of Chicago Press.

Golden, D. (2001). Bilingual students use language to get a leg up on college admission. *Wall Street Journal,* Tuesday, June 26, 2001, p. 1.

Jackson, R. (1980). The Scholastic Aptitude Test: A response to Slack and Porter's "critical appraisal." *Harvard Educational Review, 50,* 382–391.

Kowarsky, J., Clatfelter, D., & Widaman, K. (1998). *Predicting university grade-point average in a class of University of California freshmen: An assessment of the validity of GPA and test scores as indicators of future academic performance* (Institutional research paper). Oakland, CA: University of California Office of the President.

Ramist, L., Lewis, C., & McCamley-Jenkins, L. (1994). *Student group differences in predicting college grades: Sex, language, and ethnic groups* (College Board Report No. 93–1). New York: College Entrance Examination Board.

Slack, W., & Porter, D. (1980). The Scholastic Aptitude Test: A critical appraisal. *Harvard Educational Review, 50,* 154–175.

Commentary on Part II: Changing University of California Admissions Practices: A Participant-Observer Perspective

EVA L. BAKER

In this commentary, I will try to identify the underlying conflicts between the goals and the reality of changing University of California admissions practices from the perspective of a participant observer. A contrast with the British system of university admissions will be posed, and the steps taken to change the way tests are used in the University of California system will be examined from both technical and policy perspectives.

Background in Two Settings

On the day in February 2001 that Richard C. Atkinson gave his lecture raising questions about the utility of the SAT in the admissions policy of the University of California I was in England, beginning a set of meetings intended to evaluate for the British government the quality and utility of their university admissions examinations. My thoughts, reactions, and recommendations have been naturally influenced by the juxtaposed tasks, each addressing a perceived key challenge on the path to admission to higher education and the benefits of a university degree.

Although both sets of processes, the California path and that in the United Kingdom, differ in many significant ways, they share a common goal—to assure that instruments and processes used in the admissions decision are functioning as intended, are of sufficient technical quality, and result in fair action, both in reality and as perceived by the public, students, educators, and parents.

Underneath, atop, and suffused through the narrow question of higher education admissions is the reality of educational reform that is still underway in both countries in precollegiate educational systems. Both systems have placed a priority on raising performance results and have, to varying degrees, applied different sanctions and incentives to enhance accountability. Parental choice, for example, was an attribute of both systems, using a market model to draw parents and their children to successful schools and away from schools not making progress. Although the problem as formulated in California was focused on admission to the University of California, the link between changes in that process and changes in secondary school performance was palpable.

In both settings there were concerns about the distribution of access to higher education among minority students, whose representation did not correspond to population statistics. In California, with its burgeoning numbers of Latino and Asian immigrant and first-generation families, the problem was more directly linked to the public schools and the dissatisfaction about the distribution of access. This issue rose in salience in geometric proportion to the rise in power of Latino members in the California legislature. (See, for instance www.ucaccord.org for an analysis of disparate access.) In the United Kingdom, the putative success of the reforms was changing the proportion of students (including those previously underrepresented) who were attempting and achieving success taking the "A-level" examinations and being admitted to prestigious institutions. Both those in the higher education community and media writers were concerned that the tests and therefore the "standards" had dropped, since the pass rates were improving over time.

Testing for More Than One Purpose

From a technical perspective, the question is whether a test or testing system can be designed to optimize two sets of outcomes: (1) making fair and appropriate admissions decisions, and (2) linking the university testing requirements to productive learning that could in part be undertaken in the secondary schools. The use of a testing system for multiple purposes raises the hackles of technical specialists, who rightly assert that the validity of the system is determined by how the results—for each purpose—are used. To optimize multiple uses of test results is a particularly challenging assignment. However, in the present world of policy and practice, a single examination often is used for multiple purposes. For example, in the No Child Left Behind (2002) legislation, test results are supposed to identify schools needing to make progress, help in identifying subgroups that need particular attention, guide teachers' instructional practices, and influence policy decisions about resources intended to improve performance. For the most part, these requirements have been greeted with few complaints about potential validity of the states' tests for these purposes and more concern over the details of the procedures to be used in the new policy. Nonetheless, the melding of instructional certification (the learning of specific outcomes) and the selection from a large pool of highly qualified individuals into a single system would have to overcome a series of important hurdles. Consider the following list:

1. There would need to be congruence between university entrance requirements, domains of student competency and skills, and those appropriately addressed by the secondary schools. This goal requires a procedure for determining the relationship between the sets of university and secondary-school requirements. For the most part, both sets of expectations are framed far too generally to be compared.

2. There would need to be systematic preparation in the secondary schools designed to help students achieve the standards to help them be admitted to the university. This requirement has multiple implications, the most obvious of which is the controversial proposition that admissions examinations should tap school-acquired knowledge rather than world knowledge or general ability.

3. An obvious corollary is the need to prepare practicing and novice teachers in the subject matter competency that they need to be successful. Where the interest or money will be found for that task is as yet unknown.

4. There is still a tension about the degree to which "challenging" standards must mean academically oriented standards. In other words, is all education directed toward a UC admissions profile?

5. Tests would need to be developed, preferably connected to particular courses or courses of study, so that student opportunity to learn could be monitored (see the recommendations in *Raising Standards for American Education,* National Council on Education Standards and Testing, 1992).

Technical Studies and Real Policy Change

Despite these weighty concerns, a good deal of effort was expended in an attempt to disabuse the public and higher education university faculty of the idea that the SAT represents an implacable gold standard for university admissions. The analyses conducted by Geiser & Studley (2001; see also Geiser & Studley in this volume) were designed to document the degree to which content-based tests (such as the SAT II examinations in subject matter) would serve as adequate admissions measures. The argument was almost wholly based on the idea that the SAT I and II examinations did not greatly differ in predictive validity. The analyses were conducted and reviewed with a look to who would "win" or do better and who would "lose" should the system be changed. While of doubtless great interest, such analyses assumed that behaviors, such as teaching and learning in secondary school, would remain the same under both systems. In fact, the argument made by UC president Richard C. Atkinson was that school offerings should shift (in the direction of systems such as those in England and Australia, or the International Baccalaureate Program) in such a way that admissions tests would examine students on material drawn from clearly delineated courses.

This spirit of the proposal, of course, threatened present notions of local control, both at a local board level and in terms of the "academic freedom" of teachers in the classroom. It is easy to imagine that some believe that specifying *what* students should learn is tantamount to decreeing *how* they should learn. It is true that specificity of goals and prescriptive means have become a fact of elementary school policy in California. Yet, it was clear to me, perhaps because of my knowledge of the A-level and Australian examination systems, that the goals of increased competence, equitable access, and productive effort would be best achieved by moving slowly toward a system that focused on measuring results tied to the curriculum.

There were at least three options available to California: (1) begin the design of such a system; (2) adapt the extant Golden State Examinations (course-based examinations taken for endorsed diplomas) or the emerging Standardized Testing and Reporting (STAR) examinations (state assessments); or (3) induce large-scale test producers to create the system for the state.

Criteria to be considered in making such a decision were cost, credibility among the higher education community, practicality, and the validity of the ensuing system. Let's assume all options further our opportunity to begin a new design. The key issue, then, is whether to use California-specific material as opposed to more national examinations. Using existing tests would have the advantage of allowing the reduction of the high number of required tests for students. Such tests would also reflect California curricula. This strength would also lead to a deficiency—the parochial nature of the tests and the attendant difficulties raised for out-of-state students who wish to apply to UC. In addition, questions related to cost, capacity, and cycle time need to be considered.

In considering potential vendors for a "new" or more content-focused admissions test, UC began discussions with two concerns: the College Board, which has overseen the SAT examinations, and ACT, Inc. (formerly known as the American College Testing Program), which manages the ACT college admission tests. Representatives of both organizations made presentations intended to be responsive to the spirit of the change. It was also clear that if a substantial shift occurred away from College Board products, there might well be a national trend. On the other hand, ACT, Inc. presented an approach that was very consistent with many of the requirements of a new, curriculum-focused assessment, and they showed substantial evidence of using curricula in the formulation of their current assessments. But it also rapidly became apparent that ACT, Inc. would be unlikely to compete unless there were development resources available to them.

Contrast this situation with the A-level examinations, where three different "awarding bodies" (read test companies) compete for a school's business. Schools select the courses, and perhaps determine the professional development needed for staff. Examinations are administered by different groups who are monitored by a government body, the Qualifications and Curriculum Authority (QCA; see www.qca.org.uk). QCA set criteria for syllabi and tests. The testing groups also police themselves. Students who wish to apply, for example, to a mathematics or law university program meet with the relevant officers at the university and are told what examinations are required and about what grades (A or B, usually) they would need to attain to be admissible. The examinations are administered nationwide in the early summer, and results are provided in a two-month cycle. Students matriculate the same year that they take the examinations.

There are a number of features of this system that would be difficult to translate to California. In particular, teachers are the examination readers, teachers may read papers from students in their own schools, and student papers usually receive only one reading. The questions of reliability and technical merit are less addressed, and few studies of predictive validity are routinely conducted. This approach also makes the assumption that students know the area in which they wish to specialize well before they enter the university. The result is that the entire system pushes students toward a more narrow, yet deeper, focus and places greater hurdles for them to overcome in order to rethink or change directions successfully.

The system in the United Kingdom does have characteristics that might be imported in a future reconsideration of the linkage of secondary school preparation and college admissions. For one thing, there is great care taken in selecting the questions and in identifying the framework of answers that would be acceptable when judging answers prepared by students. Those charged with the effort are individuals of great expertise, authority, and credibility among teachers and the public. Furthermore, there is some evidence that scores are rising as a function of improved performance. Imagine the problem UC would have if the pool of qualified candidates were even greater than it is now.

If the testing system at UC undergoes modification as proposed, and adds a writing test and uses subject-matter-based SATs, there is still much evaluation work to be done. First, it would be important to study whether the system yields different distributions of student performance, and how distributions change over a number of years. For instance, how do students of other language backgrounds do on the examinations? Second, it would be important to evaluate how and the extent to which schools modify their curriculum in response to UC changes, or whether organizations offering test preparation simply modify their wares. Third, it would be desirable to see whether the institution of subject matter tests, writing examinations, and so forth improves the entering capabilities of students. Will there be fewer failures on the university placement examinations in writing and mathematics? Will students be able to make more rapid progress through their academic programs and greatly reduce parental costs? Will we have happy (or at least happier) professors? Will the university ratchet up its requirements because it is dealing with better-prepared students?

Evaluation studies should be conducted of the consequences of the use of assessments, especially when different purposes are intended to be combined, granting the complexity of the political and economic settings in which education is placed. There are strong conceptual approaches available to create systems of measures that meet various needs, and simultaneously to give coherent signals to those participating in education. Atkinson started on a wise and difficult path. UC faculty and administrators should recognize that the time will come for even more change, with the continuing goals of making our educational system stronger, fairer, and more effective. So we will plan for this future now, and await the time when budget pressures subside, further technical advances are made, costs are better controlled, and education is once again strongly at the top of our public policy agenda.

Notes

This report was supported in part under the Educational Research and Development Centers Program, PR/Award Number R305B960002, as administered by the Office of Educational Research and Improvement, U.S. Department of Education, and in part by the University of California Office of the President.

The findings and opinions expressed in this report do not reflect the positions or policies of the National Institute on Student Achievement, Curriculum, and Assessment, the Office of Educational Research and Improvement, or the U.S. Department of Education; nor do they reflect the positions or policies of the University of California Office of the President.

References

Geiser, S., & Studley, R. (2001, October). *UC and the SAT: Predictive validity and differential impact of the SAT I and SAT II at the University of California.* Oakland: University of California Office of the President.

National Council on Education Standards and Testing. (1992). *Raising standards for American education. A report to Congress, the Secretary of Education, the National Education Goals Panel, and the American people.* Washington, DC: U.S. Government Printing Office.

No Child Left Behind Act of 2001, Pub. L. No. 107–110, 115 Stat. 1425 (2002).

Race, Class, and Admissions Testing: How Are Test Scores Related to Student Background and Academic Preparation?

Part III addresses the academic preparation and test performance of students from various ethnic and socioeconomic backgrounds, and also features a chapter on SAT coaching. In the first chapter of Part III, Patricia Gándara reviews the findings about the effectiveness of intervention programs intended to prepare students from underrepresented ethnic groups to attend college. "If the goal is to increase students' and parents' aspirations and knowledge about college options, to provide information about financial aid options, or to increase 'college-going' at any level, then well-implemented programs can probably claim a high degree of success," according to Gándara. The most effective programs are those that provide long-term mentors who can make cultural connections with students, rigorous high-quality instruction, a supportive peer group, and financial incentives. But Gándara cautions that college access programs have significant limitations. These efforts touch only a few students and are largely ineffective in improving academic achievement per se. Finally, the increase in college-going promoted by the programs often involves attendance at community colleges, rather than matriculation at four-year institutions. Gándara concludes by calling upon schools to incorporate "more of the successful practices of college access programs, and provide a more equitable education for all students...."

In their chapter, Amy Elizabeth Schmidt and Wayne J. Camara review evidence on the differences in academic performance among racial and ethnic groups, and discuss some of the possible reasons for these gaps. They describe the large differences between white and African-American students and between white and Hispanic students on the SAT I, the ACT, and other standardized tests. They note that disparities also exist in average scores on "performance assessments," which involve hands-on tasks, and in high school and college grades and persistence in college. Schmidt and Camara review many of the existing hypotheses about these performance differences, including inadequate academic preparation, poverty, discrimination, teacher and test administrator attitudes, and family background and parenting practices. They end by describing the initiative of the National Task Force on Minority High Achievement, which is working to improve educational outcomes for underrepresented minorities.

While the Camara and Schmidt chapter illustrates disparities in academic achievement among racial and ethnic groups, the chapter by Rebecca Zwick focuses on achievement gaps among groups that differ in terms of family income and education.[1] The association between socioeconomic factors and standardized test scores is often attributed to either the middle-class perspective that is presumed to be embedded in the tests or to the greater availability of test coaching to wealthier test takers. Zwick provides evidence that socioeconomic status influences not only admissions test scores, but performance on curriculum-based tests for which coaching is unavailable, grades, course completion patterns, and teacher evaluations. She describes some recent research by the Public Policy Institute of California showing that schools attended by low-income students are less likely to have teachers who are experienced and fully credentialed, and that these teacher characteristics are the "resource variables" that are most strongly associated with student achievement. From this perspective, the achievement disparities among income groups are not surprising. While acknowledging that the SAT may, in a sense, be a "wealth test," as some test critics claim, Zwick argues that, because of pervasive inequities in our country's education system, all traditional measures of achievement function as wealth tests.

In his chapter, Derek C. Briggs describes his research on SAT coaching, which is based on data from the National Education Longitudinal Study (NELS) of 1988. Briggs's study was unusual in that he was an employee of neither a testing company nor a test preparation company when he conducted it. He sought to investigate the effects of commercial test preparation while taking into account the fact that candidates who take tests more than once tend to improve their scores, regardless of whether they receive coaching. Briggs's analyses were also intended to adjust for the fact that test candidates who choose to get coached tend to be different in several important respects from uncoached candidates. In the NELS data, for example, coached students tended to have parents who were better educated and wealthier than those of uncoached students, and who were more likely to have prestigious occupations. The parents of coached students were also much more likely to encourage their children to take the SAT than were the parents of uncoached students. Taking these factors into account, Briggs concludes that, on average, the effect of coaching on SAT total score (math score plus verbal score) is about 30 points—"nowhere near the average gains typically promoted by commercial test preparation companies."

In his commentary, Michael E. Martinez notes the presence of two themes underlying the chapters in Part III. First, that the "achievement gap among racial/ethnic and socioeconomic groups is pervasive," and second, that the causes of the gap are complex and do not lend themselves to simple policy solutions. Martinez points out that inequality of educational opportunity "extends to the numerous and diverse aspects of experience that span the age range and involve both school and non-school settings.... It is deeply rooted socially and economically, and in the cumulative experience of the individual child." According to Martinez, remedying this situation requires the development of a better theory of preparedness for college success: "A strong theoretical understanding of what it takes to be successful in the academy could guide test construction, and could have even more important effects in the design of educational experience."

Note

1.   Michael T. Brown served as action editor for this chapter.

Equitable Access and Academic Preparation for Higher Education: Lessons Learned from College Access Programs

PATRICIA GÁNDARA

With the passage of the University of California Regents' resolution SP1 and California's Proposition 209 in California, which banned the consideration of race and ethnicity in public university admissions, there has been an increased sense of urgency about the need to better prepare underrepresented students for competitive college admissions. California schools have been in a protracted period of reform for the last two decades, and while academic achievement appears to be inching upward for all students (Chavez, 2002), the gaps between majority and some minority students remain large, and in some cases, are growing. Importantly, the differences in performance between Latino, Native American, and African-American students, on the one hand, and Asian-American and white students on the other, are significant across all quantitative measures of academic accomplishment—grade point average (GPA), test scores, and rank in class (see tables 1 and 2).

It is notable that while all students' GPAs rose during the 1980s and '90s, the increase was greater for white and Asian-American students than for Latino and black students, increasing the achievement gaps between these

Table 1: Grade Point Averages, 1983, 1986, 1990, 1996 California High School Graduates by Ethnicity

ETHNIC GROUP	1983	1986	1990	1996	GAIN 1983–96
White	2.69	2.65	2.74	2.90	.21
Asian-American	2.96	2.96	3.11	3.19	.23
Black	2.26	2.29	2.33	2.41	.15
Latino	2.42	2.44	2.44	2.55	.13

Source: California Postsecondary Education Commission, 1998

groups as measured by grades. Most observers attribute the growing gap, at least in part, to the differences in enrollment in Advanced Placement (AP) and honors courses between the groups, inasmuch as these courses confer additional grade points (Betts, Rueben, & Danenberg, 2000). A recent study by the Public Policy Institute of California showed that there is considerable disparity among schools both in A–F courses (those classes required for eligibility to the University of California, and increasingly for the California State University as well) and in AP courses. The lowest income schools offered only 52% of their classes as meeting A–F requirements, while this figure rose to 63% in the highest income schools. Similar patterns held up when the analysis was done using the percentage of nonwhite students in the school (Betts et al., 2000). Likewise, Julian Betts and colleagues found that "the median high [socioeconomic status, or SES] school has over 50 percent more AP courses than the median low-SES school" (2000, p. 72). Another disturbing finding of their analysis was that even when these courses are offered in low-income and high-minority schools, the enrollments are significantly lower than in more affluent schools. Of course, students who do not expect to go to college have little incentive to take these courses.

Whether measured by GPA, numbers of college preparatory and advanced courses taken, or rank in class, Chicano/Latinos, African Americans, and Native Americans consistently perform below the level of white and Asian peers. Concern about the slow progress that the public schools have made in preparing underrepresented students for postsecondary education has led to increased emphasis on out-of-school interventions to help ensure greater access to college for these students. Such intervention programs are known by various names—college access, academic development, pipeline or bridge programs. All share the general goal of preparing more underrepresented students for college. There are literally thousands of these programs across

Table 2: Profile of California's College-Going Students College Board Data, 1998

	BLACK (8,868)	MEXICAN-AMERICAN (18,494)	LATINO (6,606)	ASIAN-AMERICAN (29,889)	AMERICAN INDIAN (1,415)	WHITE (56,217)
% of School Population	8.7	37	4.3	11.1	.9	37.8
% of SAT I Takers	6.2	13	4.6	21	.9	39.5
Average GPA	2.86	3.08	3.09	3.36	3.12	3.33
SAT I Scores:						
Mean Verbal	433	442	450	488	489	532
Mean Math	428	452	456	550	497	540
% Who Are in the Top 10% of Class	9	14	14	23	16	24

Note: These numbers are based on unpublished data from the College Board, 1998. The first row of entries gives the representation of the group in the high school population. The second row gives the representation among those who take the SAT I. For example, black students constitute 8.7% of the high school population but only 6.2% of SAT takers; likewise, while 37% of the high school population was of Mexican origin in 1998, only 13% of SAT takers were.

the country, and many here in California (Gándara & Bial, 2001; Swail & Perna, 2002).

How Effective Are These Early Intervention Programs?

Patricia Gándara and Deborah Bial (2001) searched for published evaluations of early intervention programs in an effort to determine their effectiveness. They found that few programs were rigorously evaluated. For most programs, a simple accounting of how many students participated at any given time, and how many went on to college was all that program funders required and therefore all that program directors reported. Of course, it is not possible to establish whether a program is providing any "value added" to students beyond what they would have accomplished without the program on the basis of this kind of data. Participants may have been headed for college already, regardless of participation in the program, or they may have participated in other programs that provided the critical support or incentive. Moreover, it is not at all clear from this kind of data *how much* participation is necessary to effect the desired result.

In spite of the small pool of studies, the researchers located 13 evaluations,[1] across a variety of program types, that met reasonably rigorous evaluation standards. These studies were augmented in most cases with interviews of evaluators and program directors that helped to describe the programs in greater depth. Table 3 lists these program evaluations. Most of the programs for which evaluations were located are anchored in the high schools and serve either individual students or classroom groupings of students. The focus among these programs on individual students or individual classrooms of students means that their impact remains relatively isolated from the rest of the school. Program effects *may* carry over to other aspects of school or personal life for the students in the program, but they are unlikely to have a major impact on students in the same school who are not in the program (see, for example, Gándara, Mejorado, Molina & Gutiérrez, 1998).

Not surprisingly, the degree to which programs are effective depends to a great extent on what they set as their goals. If the goal is to increase students' and parents' aspirations and knowledge about college options, to provide information about financial aid options, or to increase college-going at any level, then well-implemented programs can probably claim a high degree of success. Good programs appear to be able to at least double the college-going rates of students in particular schools or programs (see Table 3).

Features of Effective Programs

The programs that appeared to be capable of significantly increasing college-going—however that was defined—shared a number of characteristics in

Table 3: Program Evaluations

PROGRAM	CHARACTERISTICS	OUTCOMES	EVALUATION SOURCE
1. General Electric College Bound	**Whole (high) school intervention**; 5-year grants to schools to reform themselves; program models vary, but almost all include SAT prep, tutors, summer academic enrichment, college counseling, and campus visits.	7 of 10 schools with sufficient data significantly increased college-going compared to state-wide data; effects were strongest for lowest-SES students.	Bailis, Melchior, Sokatch & Sheinberg, 1999.
2. Neighborhood Academic Initiative (NAI)	NAI targets **cohorts of** about 50 very low-income **students** with daily two-hour classes before school plus Saturdays, campus visits, college counseling, full scholarship to prestigious university.	64% persistence for six years of program; of these, about 2/3 went to four-year colleges. 96% went on to some kind of postsecondary education. Program is "Cadillac model"—expensive and labor intensive.	Tierney & Jun, 1998.
3. Upward Bound	High school program, targets **individual students** with summer bridge program, college counseling, tutoring, campus visits. Hundreds of programs, varying by site, but all have same key elements.	High attrition, some impact on college prep course taking, but no impact on GPA or college-going for sample of 67 programs. Impact greatest for males, Hispanics, whites, lowest-income students, and those who stay in the program the longest.	Myers & Schirm, 1999.

Continued

171

Table 3: *Continued*

PROGRAM	CHARACTERISTICS	OUTCOMES	EVALUATION SOURCE
4. A Better Chance (ABC)	Identifies **individual** high-potential (usually black) **students** from very low income backgrounds and places them in strong high schools or prep schools with some counseling support. Many programs around the country.	Attrition rate is not known, but among those who persisted, at least 96% went on to college; 20% go to Ivy League schools. Students reported they would recommend the program to a friend, but also report high levels of depression and isolation.	Griffin, 1990.
5. Posse	Selects **individual** low-income **students,** program extends from senior year of high school through college. Leadership and skill and team-building workshops last 32 weeks; mentors in college, full tuition scholarship.	Compared to other similar students at the same college, did no worse or no better on GPA, but had higher persistence. SAT scores were significantly lower than comparison students.	Bowman & Gordon, 1998.
6. AVID (Advancement via Individual Determination)	Targets individual **students grouped into AVID classes.** Students must be underperforming academically according to test scores. AVID focuses on study skills, rigorous classes, college counseling, campus visits, tutoring.	Attrition is not known, but AVID students attended college in higher proportions than city-wide comparisons. Greatest impact on those who stayed longer and on low-SES black and Hispanic students. Peers considered important factor.	Mehan, Villanueva, Hubbard & Lintz, 1996.
7. High School Puente	**Individual** (mostly Hispanic) **students** grouped into special English classes for two years. Emphasis on Latino literature, writing process, college counseling, and Latino mentors.	Attrition low for both participants and controls, but Puente students went to college at twice the rate of non-Puente and had better attitudes toward school. Credited counselors largely with choice to go to college.	Gándara, Mejorado, Gutiérrez, & Molina, 1998. Gándara, 2002.

172

8. College Pathways	**Classrooms of students** visited weekly or biweekly for three years of high school by program staff or volunteers. Focuses on academic support, college counseling, college campus visits. Separate mentoring program for some students.	Attrition is high after 10th grade, but those who persisted went on to college at much higher rates than others in the same district. Higher aspirations for college for all participants.	CHEPA, 1998.
9. I Have a Dream (IHAD)	Sponsors adopt a **whole class** in low-income schools. Many programs nationally that vary by site, but all must include counseling, mentoring, tutoring, and college scholarships. Students begin in elementary school and continue through high school.	IHAD students graduated from high school at double the district rate in Chicago, appeared to go on to college at three times the rate of comparisons. Trusting relationships with program staff attributed with the success; relationships appeared to work best with staff from same backgrounds as students.	Kahne & Bailey, 1997.
10. Project GRAD	**Whole school** intervention starting in the elementary school and continuing up to high school. Focus on reforming curriculum and classroom discipline for students in "at risk" schools; provides college scholarships for persisters.	Study was conducted in Houston schools. Longer term outcomes still unknown because of length of the program, but early indications were that school climate was significantly improved, student achievement somewhat improved. Student mobility (attrition) a problem.	Opuni, 1998.

Continued

Table 3: *Continued*

PROGRAM	CHARACTERISTICS	OUTCOMES	EVALUATION SOURCE
11. Florida's CROP	Individual students selected for **statewide program.** Florida counties compete for grants to participate in the College Reach Out Program. Intervention must include academic enrichment, career and personal counseling. Programs vary by site.	More CROP than non-CROP students graduated high school and went on to college. Program evaluators attribute success to three key factors: parent involvement, close tutor/teacher/ counselor relationships, and long-term consistent contact with students.	Postsecondary Education Planning Commission, 1998.
12. Indiana's ICPAC and 21st Century Scholars Program	Indiana Career and Postsecondary Advancement Center sends information about preparing for college to all 7th to 12th graders in the state; the 21st Century Program includes parent education, outreach, tutoring and mentoring for 8th graders and beyond who sign a contract. If they complete the Core 40 curriculum with a 2.0+ GPA they are guaranteed a full state scholarship.	Indiana increased students taking core college curriculum from 11% to 37%, and those graduating with honors from 5.5% to 15.3%. Increased college going by about 8%. It doubled the financial aid awards (college scholarships) over 10 years—1989 to 1999.	Gillie, 1999. Orfield & Paul, 1994.
13. Minnesota's PEOP	Postsecondary Enrollment Options Program focuses on providing opportunities for high school students to attend local colleges and gain college credit before graduating from high school.	PEOP provides the opportunity for some students to gain high school and college credit at the same time—a strategy that has been used elsewhere (e.g., New Jersey) to increase college-going. However, the program appears to benefit females and higher income students more than others.	Office of the Legislative Auditor, 1996.

174

common. Among these characteristics are:

- Providing a key person who monitors and guides the student over a long period of time. Sometimes this is a mentor, program director, faculty member, or guidance counselor. Studies, however, are not clear on which of these is most effective. Nonetheless, the personal relationship with a supportive mentor was a nearly universal element of the programs that appeared to be particularly effective at increasing college-going. The evaluation of the I Have a Dream program considered the "trusting relationship" between program coordinators and students to be the primary factor in the program's success, and the Puente program students were almost four times as likely to name their counselor as key in their decision to go to college as were non-Puente students.
- Providing high-quality instruction, either through access to the most challenging courses offered by the school ("untracking"), through special coursework that supports and augments the regular curricular offerings (tutoring and specially designed classes), or by revamping the curriculum to better address the learning needs of the students. All of the programs that were able to demonstrate effectiveness incorporated a strand of rigorous coursework, whether through summer or after-school programs, enrollment in honors courses, or in some cases, enrollment in more rigorous schools outside the students' neighborhoods. The critical importance of rigorous coursework is confirmed in a recent study by Adelman (2000). Based on an analysis of the National Education Longitudinal Study (NELS) data, Adelman concluded that students who take at least one math course beyond Algebra 2 in high school are significantly more likely to complete college than all other students, independent of race, ethnicity or socioeconomic status. In other words, taking higher-level math is a better predictor of college outcomes than parents' income or education, or students' racial/ethnic background—background factors that have long been considered the best predictors of academic performance (cf. Jencks, et al., 1972).
- Making long-term investments in students rather than implementing short-term interventions. The longer students stay in a program, the more they are reported to benefit from it. Virtually every evaluation that monitored program participation came to this same conclusion. Moreover, programs that extend over various segments of the students' schooling—across the K–12 system, or between K–12 and postsecondary education—appear to hold the greatest

promise for changing academic achievement and helping students to sustain gains over time. Numerous studies have demonstrated that program effects for "at risk" youth decline when interventions are not sustained over time (Rumberger & Larson, 1998: Currie & Thomas, 1995; Mehan, et al., 1996). Thus, Project GRAD, which extends across the K–12 continuum and is embedded in the schools, seeks to improve not just college-going, but grades and test scores as well.

- Stemming attrition from the program by finding ways to hold students in for its duration. Even the most attractive interventions, if voluntary, suffer heavy attrition unless there are structural elements that act to increase retention, like assigning students to a core class in which the program is at least partially delivered, and making it difficult for them to transfer out. Puente uses this strategy to great effect by delivering the core of the program in a two-year English course that meets both graduation and college preparatory requirements.

- Paying attention to the cultural background of students and using this as a supportive resource. Many programs report having greater success with a particular group of students, such as Latinos, African Americans, or women. For example, Upward Bound reported greater success with Hispanics, whites, and males, while AVID reported success with blacks, and the Minnesota PEOP cited female students as being greater beneficiaries of its program than male students. We suspect this effect was related, at least in part, to the background and expertise of the staff and directors, and the kinds of cultural connections they were able to make to students. It also calls into question the one-size-fits-all policy of serving all groups of students under a single program. Tierney and Jun (1998) reported that a critical element in the success of the NAI project was the cultural linkages to the students' communities, and Kahne and Bailey (1997) found that project directors who did not understand the backgrounds of students often were less successful with them.

- Providing a peer group that supports students' academic aspirations and that meets for academic as well as social and emotional support. For example Mehan et al. (1996) attributed a part of the success of AVID to the peer group from similar backgrounds formed by the program that supported each others' academic aspirations. Other programs, such as Puente, that targeted classrooms or students also reported this as an important strategy.

- Providing financial assistance and incentives. Financial assistance is important for access to academic leveling experiences—college visits and SAT preparation courses, as well as to provide the monetary support to make college a realistic possibility for some students. Scholarships *do* make the difference between going to college or not for many low-income students (Akerheilm, Berger, Hooker, & Wise, 1998; Terenzini, Cabrera, & Bernal, 2001) but financial assistance alone is not sufficient (Gladieux & Swail, 1998). The many I Have A Dream programs demonstrate this principle well. Begun in 1986 as an incentive program to provide the funds to make college possible for students in a low-income area of New York City, the IHAD Foundation operates more than 160 programs in 60 cities. However, as a result of high program attrition and limited success, the program began to incorporate other supportive services. Today the program incorporates a range of interventions including counseling and tutoring, to help students remain in school and become eligible for college. This approach has improved its college-going record.

Program Limitations

While there are wonderful successes among these programs, there are also clear limitations to what they appear to be able to produce, at least under current circumstances. Among the still unresolved problems associated with early intervention programs are the following:

Increases in College-Going Are Not the Same for All Types of Postsecondary Institutions

Some good programs are able to increase college-going rates by 100% and more, but most are nonspecific about what "going to college" means. A closer look at the data reveals that the increase in college-going usually involves attendance at community colleges and less selective four-year institutions. In other words, students who might not have otherwise gone to college at all choose to go to local community colleges, and some students who were headed for a community college are diverted to a four-year campus that is not highly selective. Moreover, programs often do not provide data on whether students enroll on the campuses full-time or part-time. In other words, it is frequently not possible to distinguish between a student who is working full-time and taking some courses part-time at a community college and a student who is a full-time college enrollee. This does not diminish the importance of the program's outcomes, but it is important to keep in mind that few students are catapulted into selective four-year colleges who were not already on track for these institutions. Unfortunately, among African-Americans, Native Americans, and Latinos, those who are already on track for selective universities represent a very small percentage of the total population of these groups.

There is a particular irony in the fact that these programs appear to promote college-going mostly at the less selective institutions. Much of the recent attention—and increased funding—toward early intervention has been spurred by the concerns over the impact of the loss of affirmative action on selective public colleges and universities. In fact, in many cases, these institutions have made major investments in the programs with the hope that they will help to diversify their student bodies. It is unlikely, however, that the impact will be very large at the more selective institutions, *at least for the short term*. More substantive change in college readiness and competitiveness will require longer term investments in these students' precollege educations.

Quantitative Measures of Academic Achievement are Largely Unaffected

The reason that few students make great leaps up into more selective colleges and universities is probably related to the fact that these programs—which largely focus on high school students—appear to be limited in the extent to which they can have an impact on students' measured academic achievement. Few programs actually use grade point averages or test scores as an outcome measure. However, among those that do, there is virtually no evidence of significant increases as a result of the programs. But why should there be? Most of these programs begin in high school, a point by which the average underrepresented student is functioning three to four years behind the average white or Asian student in tested academic ability (Puma, et al., 1997; Donahue, Voelkl, Campbell, & Mazzeo, 1999; Braswell et al., 2001). Under the best of circumstances, the gap is already too large to close very quickly. But the programs do not normally touch, in any significant way, the day-to-day schooling experience of the students. The participants continue, for the most part, to struggle in the same environment with the same courses and teachers as their peers who are not in the program. The additional years of intensive, high quality instruction with the most capable teachers that would be needed in order to close the huge achievement gap is not something that these programs can provide. Some programs, such as AVID, attempt to have participating students placed into college preparatory curricula and rigorous academic courses, but the preparation that students receive in middle school usually limits the courses to which they can gain access in high school (Paul, 2001). Perhaps tutoring helps raise some grades at the margin, but some students who are not in special programs also take advantage of tutoring services that are available, and so the differences between program participants and non-participants in controlled studies are not usually large.

Program Attrition Is High

Attrition is a very large problem for most programs. High school students have busy lives, and they tend to become busier as each year passes. Many work at part-time jobs and engage in sports and other extracurricular activities. Often, social lives take on greater importance as students move through high school. Students who are interested in going to competitive colleges are usually aware of the need to include experiences like service activities and student government in their applications, and so their schedules can be prodigious. One of the few things that can be viewed as optional for many students is a voluntary intervention program, so it is one of the first things to be abandoned when other demands get in the way. However, few programs either report or know how many students who begin their program actually remain with it for the duration.

Based on more careful examination of cohorts of students, it appears safe to estimate that between one-third and one-half of all students who begin in these programs leave the program prematurely. Nonetheless, many programs report very high percentages of participants going on to college because they only count the number of participants still present in the graduating class. Thus, a program may enroll 100 students in the 9th grade. Typically, by the 10th grade a fourth to a third have dropped out. The program adds more students at this point to bring the total back to 100. By the 11th grade another third have dropped out, and the program picks up some more students. In the 12th grade, only a fourth to a third of the original participants may still be present, but the program reports that 95% of its participants go on to college. Does it make sense to attribute the decision to go to college for the majority of these students to the effects of the program? Or, is it that students who have already made it through the high school gauntlet by other means are attracted to programs that will help them apply to college at that point? Of course, this also raises the issue of "dosage." How much exposure to a program is required in order for it to have an effect? Programs are often vague on this point, and it is not often clear how much of a program must be experienced in order for it to have an effect. Hugh Mehan and his colleagues (1996) showed that students who dropped out of the AVID program in the first year did not look different from students who did not participate in the program at all.

Programs Do Not Appear to Be Equally Successful with All Students

Because most programs are not very specific about the characteristics of their participants, it is difficult to know which kinds of students are most likely to profit from the interventions that are provided. However, the evidence suggests that programs are often more successful with one group of students than another. For example, low income Latino students may have consistently better outcomes than African-Americans, or female students may show greater gains than male students in a particular program. Based on interviews with project directors, it appears that this is related to the "culture" of the program. A program that is designed by, or heavily staffed with persons like a subset of the participants is probably better able to anticipate that group's needs and to make better personal connections with them. Whether it is possible to create a program that can serve a diverse population of students equally well, and whether programs should be tailored to particular groups are unexamined, but important, questions.

Little Attention Is Paid to the Interaction of Program Features and Students' Needs

There is little evidence in evaluations, reports, or interviews with program directors that they attempt to match different program components or features to the different academic profiles of students. It is reasonable to assume that a high-achieving student may profit from a different mix of services than a student who is struggling to keep up academically. Yet most programs appear to select a range of students without explicitly attending to the *particular* academic needs of the participants. For some programs, the mix of higher and lower achievers is an important feature of the program itself, and the assumption is that stronger students will help weaker students. However, this will not always be the case if the program is not explicit about this intent. Moreover, there is a tendency to believe that high functioning students need less attention, which is often not the case; in fact, they may be the *best* targets for programmatic efforts. The high school Puente evaluation, which analyzed outcomes by categories of participants—from high achievers to struggling achievers—found that the greatest program impact was on the highest-achieving students (Gándara, 2002).

Relatively Few Students Are Touched by These Programs

Because good, comprehensive programs are labor intensive and require frequent one-to-one contact with students, they are therefore expensive. Most programs cannot afford to enroll large numbers of students. Even given the high turnover, not many students have contact with these programs. Based on High School and Beyond data, Adelman (2000) has estimated that no more than 11.4% of African-American and 5.3% of Latino students nationwide participate, *at any level,* in such programs.

There Is a Serious Underrepresentation of Male Students in Programs

Young men are seriously underrepresented in these programs. Across all kinds of programs, only about one-third of participants are male. This is a particular concern because minority male students are overrepresented in all categories of risk, and underrepresented at almost all levels of school and college participation (Mortenson, 1999). The scarcity of young men in these programs is also especially ironic, because the aim of these programs is to level the playing field for those students who are not adequately represented among college-goers, and so minority males should be the most important target population. Programs admit to having great difficulty both attracting and retaining males, yet few systematic strategies are employed to increase the enrollment of males.

Long-Term Outcomes for Students Are Unknown

Almost nothing is known about long-term outcomes for program participants. Only one program (Posse) was found that reported systematically on students' achievement and graduation from college. This program was reasonably effective with respect to retention, but could not demonstrate any significant impact on achievement. While the most effective of these programs send more students on to college, we do not know if these students are likely to remain in college or graduate with a degree when compared to students who have not participated in an intervention program. Mehan and his colleagues tried to follow up a small cohort of graduates from the AVID program two years after enrolling in college. The investigators were able to locate and interview 46 AVID graduates in 1993, two years after finishing high school. Of these 46, 35% were enrolled in four-year colleges, 39% were enrolled in two-year colleges, and 26% were "doing other things." It was disconcerting, however, that only two (11%) of the community college students had transferred from two-year to four-year colleges at the point in which the transfer might have normally occurred, but three students (16%) who had been in four-year colleges transferred back to community colleges. The investigators concluded that "there is not much mobility from two-year to four-year colleges" (Gándara, Rumberger, Larson, & Mehan, 1998, p. 23). Mehan cautions that the small sample size precludes drawing generalizations; José Moreno (2002), however, found similar outcomes for Puente students two years after high school graduation. He interviewed 31 matched pairs of former Puente and non-Puente students, and found that while program participants continued to attend college at higher rates than nonparticipants, several program students had either changed their minds at the last minute and failed to enroll in a four-year college, or had retreated from a four-year to a two-year college. Moreno concluded that issues involving campus environment contributed to these students' dropping back or dropping out.

It may be sufficient to simply expose students to a college experience. Even if they do not persist to degree, this experience may serve them well in the future, or may increase the likelihood that their own children will attend college. However, it is important to be clear about the goals of the program, and what is counted as "success."

Programs Operate Independently of School Reform Efforts

At the same time that college access/early intervention programs are being developed and expanded across the country, virtually every state in the nation is engaged in large-scale education reform activities. Among the many reforms in which schools are engaged are various efforts to close the achievement gap between low income, minority students and all others. Inasmuch as the core of these intervention programs deals with the same issue—preparing more underrepresented students for college—it would seem to make sense that the efforts would be linked; but they are not. For the most part, these two endeavors are like trains running on parallel tracks. Clearly, there are resource issues that should be addressed but rarely are because good data on program costs are rare. We do know, however, that effective programs are labor intensive and as a result, personnel costs can be high. Better coordination between programs and schools would almost certainly yield greater cost effectiveness. Perhaps even more important, one must question how much more could be accomplished on students' behalf if these efforts were coordinated?

Quality of the Evidence

The programs included in this review represent those most rigorously evaluated that we have been able to locate. Nonetheless, there is great variability in the rigor of these studies, and in almost all cases, they could be improved considerably with a few standard modifications. It was rare to encounter an evaluation that had employed true control groups. That is, comparisons between students who had been randomly selected into the program and those who had not, or comparisons to students who had not participated in the program and who were matched with participants on significant background characteristics like socioeconomic status, race, and ability scores. To draw comparisons to "all other students nationwide" or to other students in the same school district or state ignores the fact that the program participants were normally selected into the program by some process, and were *not* like all other students.

An important way to strengthen comparisons and partially compensate for the nonequivalence of the control groups is to collect baseline data on students from the point just prior to their entry in the program and then to compare program and nonprogram students' growth over time. However, studies with baseline data on student participants were rare. It was also uncommon to find studies that had true longitudinal comparisons.

Most studies simply collected outcome data at one point in time, leaving unknown what the actual differences were in students from preprogram to postprogram.

Some programs provided information about responses to surveys conducted on selected participants (those they were able to locate and who agreed to participate, introducing substantial selection bias). It was often impossible to determine what the response rates were to these surveys, and thus to what extent they may have represented a highly skewed sample— only those individuals who were either happy enough with the program, or upset enough with it, to want to "have their say." This kind of data can serve an important purpose in understanding how students experience a program and how the program might be strengthened or improved, but it is of limited value in measuring how effective the program was compared to other kinds of interventions or no intervention at all. In the absence of some kind of comparison group of similar individuals, it is difficult to know whether people who attribute great impact to a program would have had similar outcomes without the program.

There is also a troubling lack of specificity of outcomes and measurement. For example, many programs purported to "double" college-going, but were nonspecific about what they meant by "college." Was this part-time attendance at a community college while holding a full-time job? Was it full-time attendance at a four-year college? Of course, the answer to this question has major implications for the likelihood that the students will persist in college and actually earn a college degree. It is also rare to find programs that measured anything beyond college-going, such as grade point averages, college admissions scores, or some other measure of achievement. Thus, it is not possible to know whether achievement was actually influenced, or simply matriculation in some kind of postsecondary institution. The few studies that did report such data give reason to believe that affecting achievement is a much more difficult task than affecting college-going. And, since high school achievement is a much stronger predictor of persisting in college and completing a degree than simply matriculating, this is important missing data.

Although all of these programs were geared toward increasing college-going, very few actually asked whether students continued going to college after they initially matriculated. Even first year persistence rates are rarely reported; only one program actually investigated grade point averages in college systematically.

Few programs are careful about keeping track of participant attrition. Usually the number of students who are studied for the purposes of evaluation are actually a subset of those who started the program. Seldom is it possible to discern the percentage these students represent of that initial cohort. This, of course, introduces enormous bias into the findings, since students who persist at anything, let alone a demanding and time-consuming program, are probably more likely to be successful in any undertaking than those who do not. Moreover, the failure to keep track of program attrition means that important opportunities are lost to learn more about what might help keep students in programs and on track for high school graduation and postsecondary education.

Social-science research is fraught with limitations and pitfalls, and research in schools is many times more difficult because of severe restrictions placed on researchers and the myriad problems of tracking highly mobile students who tend to change schools or leave school altogether. Nonetheless, the incorporation of a few standard methodological procedures into evaluation studies could strengthen greatly our knowledge base about how and how well these programs work.

Conclusions

It should not be surprising that college access programs appear to have little effect on academic achievement. The programs, whether community-based, school district sponsored, or partnered with higher education, tend to be peripheral to the K–12 schools. They augment and supplement what schools do, but do not fundamentally change the ways schools interact with students. Thus, successful programs work to emulate the features of good high schools and prep schools that routinely send the children of the upper middle class on to college, but they only do it for part of the day, and often outside of school time. The rest of the time, students are exposed to the same school practices that have proved to be unsuccessful for them. Thus, the good programs tend to help students maximize their assets, expand their goals, and show evidence of increasing the college-going rate for their participants, but do not appreciably alter their academic achievement. For this to happen, the schools would need to adopt many of these program practices as their own. Among those practices that evaluation data suggest schools would be wise to consider are: (1) much more extensive college counseling for all students; (2) academic supports—tutoring, coaching, enrichment activities—that allow all students to gain access to a rigorous, college preparatory curriculum; (3) development of student groups that help support academic achievement; (4) tapping community resources for student support activities; (5) providing detailed information to parents—in a language they understand—about the options for financing higher education; (6) creating smaller groupings of students (e.g., learning communities) that emulate the close personal connections created in successful college access programs so that no student falls through the cracks, and every student is known to someone in authority at the school. It is also clear that efforts to prepare students for college must begin long before high school. Unless the fundamental relationship between underrepresented students and their schools is changed, college access programs will not be able to fully equalize opportunity to learn. None of the programs we have studied has demonstrated outcomes for participants that are equal to the schooling outcomes for advantaged students in our society.

In sum, such college access programs can, and do, make a difference for some underrepresented students, and conditions in many schools would almost certainly be worse if it weren't for the presence of such programs. But they cannot change the fundamental inequities in our educational system that lead to the differences in access to higher education for the vast majority of Latinos, African-Americans, and Native Americans. Moreover, whether or not the SAT I is eliminated from admissions formulas at some colleges and universities and replaced with some other measure of academic achievement, the relative rankings of students from different racial/ethnic and socioeconomic groups will remain unaffected. Until our schools incorporate more of the successful practices of college access programs, and provide a more equitable education for all students, our ability to increase access to higher education for large numbers of underrepresented students will remain limited.

Note

1. A number of studies representing varying degrees of rigor were located for state-wide programs, however the three selected for inclusion were chosen because they represent a range of strategies used by the states and met the criterion for systematic collection of appropriate data.

References

Adelman, C. (2000). Participation in outreach programs prior to high school graduation: socio-economic status by race. Paper presented at the U.S. Department of Education ConnectED Conference, San Diego, January 10, 2000.

Akerheilm, K., Berger, J., Hooker, M., & Wise, D. (1998). *Factors related to college enrollment*. Final Report. Mathtech, Inc. Washington, D.C.: U.S. Department of Education, Office of the Undersecretary.

Bailis, L. N., Melchior, A., Sokatch, A., & Sheinberg, A. (1999). *Evaluation of the GE fund college bound program*. Waltham, MA: Center for Human Resources, Heller Graduate School, Brandeis University.

Betts, J. R., Rueben, K. S., & Danenberg, A. (2000). *Equal resources, equal outcomes? The distribution of school resources and student achievement in california*. San Francisco: Public Policy Institute of California.

Bowman, C., and Gordon, E. (1998). *An Entrepreneurial Evaluation of the Posse Program*. New Haven, CT: Yale University Press.

Braswell, J., Lutkus, A., Grigg, W., Santapau, S., Tay-Lim, B., & Johnson, M. (2001) *The nation's report card: Mathematics 2000*. Washington DC: U.S. Department of Education, National Center for Education Statistics.

California Postsecondary Education Commission (1998). *Eligibility of California's 1996 high school graduates for admission to the state's public universities.* Sacramento: CPEC.

Chaney, B., Lewis, L., & Farris, E. (1995). *Programs at higher education institutions for disadvantaged precollege students.* NCES 96–230. Washington, DC: Office of Educational Research and Improvement, US Department of Education.

Chavez, E. (2002, August 30). Schools inch up in state testing. *Sacramento Bee*, pp. A1, A25.

CHEPA (Center for Higher Education Policy Analysis) (1998). *National study of college preparation programs: Program summary: Los Angeles.* Internal document, CHEPA.

Currie, J., & Thomas, D. (1995). Does Head Start make a difference? *American Economic Review, 85*, 361–64.

Donahue, P., Voelkl, K., Campbell, J., & Mazzeo, J. (1999). *NAEP 1998 reading report card for the nation and the states.* Washington, D.C.: US Department of Education, Office of Educational Research and Improvement.

Fenske, R. H., Geranios, C. A., Keller, J. E., & Moore, D. E. (1997). *Early intervention programs: Opening the door to higher education.* ASHE-ERIC Higher Education Report vol. 25, no. 6. Washington DC: George Washington University Graduate School of Education and Human Development.

Gándara, P. (2002). A study of high school Puente: What we have learned about preparing Latino youth for postsecondary education. *Educational Policy, 16*, 474–95.

Gándara, P., and Bial, D. (2001). *Paving the way to postsecondary education: K–12 intervention programs for underrepresented youth.* Washington DC: National Center for Education Statistics.

Gándara, P., Mejorado, M., Gutiérrez, D., & Molina, M. (1998). *Final report of the high school evaluation, 1994–98.* Davis, CA: University of California.

Gándara, P., Rumberger, R., Larson, K., and Mehan, H. (1998). *Capturing Latino students in the academic pipeline.* Berkeley, CA: University of California: California Policy Research Center and Chicano/Latino Policy Project.

Gillie, S. (1999). *An extensive system for postsecondary encouragement.* Indianapolis: Indiana Career and Postsecondary Advancement Center.

Gladieux, L., & Swail, W. S. (1998). Financial aid is not enough: Improving the odds of college success. *College Board Review, 185*, 16–21.

Griffin, J. (1990). *A Better Chance, Inc. internal program review: Preliminary findings.* Submitted to De-Witt Wallace-Reader's Digest Fund. Boston: A Better Chance.

Jencks, C., Smith, M., Acland, H., Bane, M. J., Cohen, D., Gintis, H., Heynes, B., & Mickelson, R, (1972). *Inequality.* New York: Harper & Row.

Kahne, J., & Bailey, K. (1997). *The role of social capital in youth development: The case of "I Have a Dream."* Chicago: University of Illinois at Chicago College of Education.

Mehan, H., Villanueva, I., Hubbard, L., and Lintz, A. (1996). *Constructing school success: The consequences of untracking low-achieving students.* New York: Cambridge University Press.

Moreno, J. (2002). The long term outcomes of Puente. *Educational Policy, 16*, 572–87.

Mortenson, T. (1999). Where are the boys? The growing gender gap in higher education, *College Board Review, 188*, 8–17.

Myers, D., & Schirm, A. (1999). *The impacts of upward bound: final report for phase I of the national evaluation.* Submitted by Mathematica Policy Research, Inc. Washington, DC: U.S. Department of Education, Office of the Undersecretary.

Office of the Legislative Auditor (1996). *Postsecondary enrollment options program.* St. Paul, MN: State of Minnesota.

Opuni, K. (1998). *Project GRAD: Graduation Really Achieves Dreams, 1997–98: program evaluation report.* Houston: Project GRAD.

Orfield, G., and Paul, F. (1994). *High hopes, long odds: A major report on Hoosier teens and the American dream.* Indianapolis: Indiana Youth Institute.

Paul, F. (2001, September). Pathways through high school mathematics. School/University Partnerships research brief vol. 2, no. 1. Davis: University of California-Davis.

Perna, L., & Swail, W. S. (1998). Early intervention programs: How effective are they at increasing access to college? Paper presented at the annual meeting of the Association for the Study of Higher Education, Miami, November 7.

Postsecondary Education Planning Commission (1998). *Statewide evaluation of Florida's college Reach-Out Program: Annual report: 1995–96 cohort.* Tallahassee: PEPC.

Program Evaluation Division, Office of the Legislative Auditor (1996). *Postsecondary enrollment Options Program.* St. Paul: State of Minnesota.

Puma, M., Karweit, N., Price, C., Ricciuti, A., Thompson, W., & Vaden-Kiernan, M. (1997). *Prospects: Final report on student outcomes.* Washington D.C.: U.S. Department of Education, Office of the Undersecretary.

Rumberger, R., & Larson, K. (1998). Toward explaining differences in educational achievement among Mexican American language-minority students, *Sociology of Education, 7,* 68–92.

Swail, W. S., and Perna, L. (2002). Pre-college outreach programs: A national perspective. In W. Tierney and L. Hagedorn (Eds.), *Increasing access to college: Extending possibilities for all students* (pp. 15–34). Albany: State University of New York Press.

Terenzini, P., Cabrera, A., & Bernal, E. (2001). *Swimming against the tide: The poor in American higher education.* College Board. Report no. 2001-1. New York: College Board.

Tierney, W., & Jun, A. (1998). *Tracking school success: Preparing low-income urban youth for college.* Los Angeles: Center for Higher Education Policy Analysis, University of Southern California.

Tierney, W., Hagedorn, L., Jun, A., & Fogel, S. (1999). *National study of college preparation programs for the Ford Foundation: Executive summary.* Los Angeles: University of Southern California, Center for Higher Education Policy Analysis.

Group Differences in Standardized Test Scores and Other Educational Indicators

AMY ELIZABETH SCHMIDT
WAYNE J. CAMARA

Introduction

Large-scale educational assessments have been criticized for a variety of reasons over the years, and one of the most enduring and oft-repeated criticisms is that there are consistent and substantial score differences between minority and nonminority test takers (Bronner, 1997; Jencks & Phillips, 1998; Sacks, 1997). Persistent score differences among racial groups have been very troubling and have led to charges of test bias. However, it should not be surprising that, when individuals are grouped in various ways that are related to differential educational opportunities, these groups score differently on tests such as the SATI: Reasoning Test (SAT I; Widaman, 1998).

One difficulty in evaluating the issue of test bias has to do with the definition of fairness, which is sometimes thought of as lack of bias. The latest version of the *Standards for Educational and Psychological Testing* (American Educational Research Association, American Psychological Association, and National Council on Measurement in Education, 1999) notes that the term *fairness* is used in many different ways and does not have a single technical meaning. The *Standards* state, "Most testing professionals would probably agree that . . . outcome differences across groups do not in themselves indicate that a testing application is biased or unfair" (p. 75). In other words, different mean scores on a test or any other measure are not necessarily an index of bias. Other ways to examine bias include: using statistical techniques that detect bias, such as differential item functioning (DIF) on pretest items; ensuring that tests are given in a standard way to all examinees; and determining whether there is any differential predictive ability among groups. However, group differences in mean scores that persist even after good test development and administration procedures are implemented should be of concern to test sponsors, and indeed, to anyone who uses test score information. One way to begin to understand why such differences occur is to examine the extent to which these differences are reflected in other educational indicators.

Previous work by Wayne Camara and Amy Elizabeth Schmidt (1999) provide a wealth of data on the actual differences, or "gaps," found among racial groups on various measures of academic achievement and preparedness. This paper will summarize that work and extend it with a discussion of possible causes for the gaps. We will examine group differences on standardized admission tests and compare these to differences on other standardized tests as well as other measures and indicators of educational achievement, such as academic preparation, high school grades, and class rank. We will also examine differences on two types of educational outcomes: (1) educational attainment, such as college graduation, and (2) academic achievement, such as course grades and grade point average (GPA). Measures such as the SAT I, ACT, high school grades, high school rank, and the quality of high school courses completed are typically used by admission officers to predict academic performance in college. Do differences between groups on these predictors correspond to similar differences in the criteria used to determine college performance? Do group differences in predictors mirror differences in performance? If test fairness is best conceived as comparable validity for all groups, as Nancy Cole and Warren Willingham suggest (1997), then these are the key questions to ask in assessing fairness claims for tests that are designed to predict future performance.

Group Differences in Standardized Tests
Admission Tests

Table 1 illustrates the mean standardized group differences for several prominent standardized tests, such as the SAT I, ACT, Graduate Record Examinations (GRE), Graduate Management Admission Test (GMAT), Law School Admission Test (LSAT), and the Medical College Admission Test (MCAT).

Table 1: Group Means and Standardized Differences on Standardized Tests

GROUP	SAT[1] VERBAL	SAT MATH	ACT[2] COMP	ACT ENGLISH	ACT MATH	ACT READING	ACT SCIENCE	GRE[3] VERBAL	GRE QUANT	GRE ANAL	GMAT[4] TOTAL	LSAT[5]	MCAT VERBAL	MCAT[6] PHYSICAL SCIENCES	MCAT BIO SCIENCES
African American	434 (−.83)	426 (−.92)	17.1 (−.98)	16.4 (−.89)	16.9 (−.88)	17.2 (−.82)	17.3 (−.98)	391 (−.96)	416 (−.98)	423 (−1.11)	416 (−1.03)	142.7 (−1.14)	6.0 (−.96)	6.1 (−.96)	6.1 (−1.08)
Asian American	498 (−.25)	526 (−.02)	21.8 (.02)	20.5 (−.13)	23.4 (.39)	21.3 (.13)	21.6 (−.04)	487 (−.07)	598 (.46)	557 (−.06)	533 (.02)	152.7 (−.08)	7.6 (−.29)	8.9 (.21)	8.8 (.04)
Hispanic	456 (−.63)	460 (−.61)	18.9 (−.60)	17.9 (−.61)	19.0 (−.47)	19.1 (−.5)	19.1 (−.59)	438 (−.53)	482 (−.46)	485 (−.62)	492 (−.35)	145.2 (−.88)	5.9 (−1.00)	6.3 (−.88)	6.4 (−.96)
White	526	528	21.7	21.2	21.4	22.1	21.8	495	540	564	531	153.5	8.3	8.4	8.7

Note: Standardized differences are given in parentheses. They are obtained by subtracting the white mean from the group mean, and then dividing by the standard deviation for all groups combined. (All standardized differences for the white group are equal to zero by definition.)

[1] College Board (1997) SAT I Verbal and SAT I Math scores range from 200 to 800 with a standard deviation of 111 to 112.

[2] ACT Composite includes scores on Reading, Math, Science, and English Tests, and ranges from 1 to 36 with a standard deviation of 4.7 in 1997–98. Each of the four subscales also ranges from 1 to 36 with the following standard deviations in 1997–98: English (5.4), Math (5.1), Reading (6), and Science (4.6). (ACT, 1998).

[3] GRE Verbal, Quantitative, and Analytical Tests range from 200 to 800 with standard deviations of 108 (Verbal) and 127 (Quantitative and Analytical) for 1997–98. (Educational Testing Service, 1998a).

[4] GMAT Total comprises Verbal and Quantitative Test scores and ranges from 200 to 800 with a standard deviation of 112 for 1996–97. (Educational Testing Service, 1998b).

[5] LSAT scores range from 120 to 160, and the standard deviation is not available for this group. LSAT scores reported are for all students applying to law school in 1997–98. The standard deviation across all LSAT tests administered in 1998 was 9.44. (Law School Admission Council, personal communication, 1999).

[6] MCAT Verbal Reasoning, Physical Sciences, and Biological Sciences scales range from 1 to 15 with a standard deviation of 2.4. (Koenig, Sireci, & Wiley, 1998).

Examination of this table reveals that there are substantial standardized differences among groups in mean scores on standardized tests.

Standardized differences are used to compare mean test scores of groups in standard deviation units. This technique is helpful when trying to compare performance on tests with different scales. Standardized differences were computed between white students and students from each of the following subgroups: African American, Asian American, and Hispanic.[1] The white students' group mean was subtracted from each of the other groups' means and divided by the standard deviation for all test takers combined. As can be seen from table 1, the group differences appear fairly consistent across standardized admission tests, with the largest gaps between white and African-American test takers, followed by Hispanic test takers. With only two exceptions, Asian Americans' mean test performance is nearly identical to that of whites. The exceptions occur on the SAT I Verbal Test, where Asian Americans score about one-quarter standard deviation unit lower than whites, and the GRE Quantitative Test, where they exceed the performance of whites by nearly one-half a standard deviation unit. Of course, each of these tests is administered to self-selected samples that will differ on a variety of factors.

National Assessments

The National Assessment of Educational Progress (NAEP), sponsored by the U.S. Department of Education, is an assessment of a nationally representative sample of students in grades 4, 8, and 12 in a variety of content areas. Mean scores by racial group along with standardized differences were calculated from the twelfth-grade NAEP reading and math test results for several years and are presented in table 2. An examination of this table reveals that for reading, the standardized differences in NAEP scores are somewhat smaller than those found in the standardized tests involving verbal skills from table 1, while the math standardized differences in NAEP scores are somewhat larger than those found in the table 1 results involving math skills. A disturbing finding is the trend toward larger standardized differences over time in NAEP scores. Even wider disparities are found on the 1996 12th-grade NAEP science test (Bourque, Champagne, & Crissman, 1997; Reese, Miller, Mazzeo, & Dossey, 1997).

A third assessment sponsored by the federal government is the National Adult Literacy Survey (U.S. Department of Education, 1992). The 1992 assessments of prose, document, and quantitative literacy were entirely open-ended and administered to a nationally representative sample of adults 16 years of age and older. Again, these data illustrate substantial differences in average proficiency among groups, with African-American and Hispanic participants falling disproportionately at lower proficiency levels (Kirsch,

Table 2: Group Means and Standardized Differences on NAEP 12th Grade Reading and Math for Selected Years

GROUP	NAEP 12TH GRADE READING			NAEP 12TH GRADE MATH		
	1992	1994	1998	1992	1996	2000
African-	273	265	270	275	279	274
American	(−.58)	(−.65)	(−.67)	(−1.03)	(−1.06)	(−1.14)
Asian-	291	279	288	314	318	318
American	(−.16)	(−.33)	(−.24)	(.27)	(.23)	(.29)
Hispanic	280	272	276	286	289	283
	(−.42)	(−.50)	(−.53)	(−.66)	(−.73)	(−.84)
White	298	294	298	306	311	309

Note: Standardized differences are given in parentheses. They are obtained by subtracting the white mean from the group mean, and then dividing by the standard deviation for all groups combined. (All standardized differences for the white group are equal to zero by definition.)

Jungeblut, Jenkins, & Kolstad, 1993). It is important to note that these national testing programs do not rely on self-selected samples, as admission tests do, but instead use nationally representative samples.

Performance Assessments

It has been suggested that performance assessments, popularized as an important component in educational reform movements, will reduce differences among groups because they provide students with hands-on opportunities to demonstrate their knowledge and understanding of how to solve problems rather than requiring students to simply recall facts (Shavelson, Solano-Flores, & Ruiz-Primo, 1997). Proponents of these reason that such assessments should narrow gaps among groups because they are designed to allow for varying styles, with less emphasis on guessing and "test-wiseness" strategies that would penalize minority groups (Jenkins & MacDonald, 1989; Neil & Medina, 1989).

Unfortunately, few large-scale studies have examined differences among racial groups on performance assessments. Studies on performance assessments published at the beginning of the current educational reform movement mostly indicated that subgroup gaps on traditional tests remain for these assessments (Dunbar, Koretz, & Hoover, 1991; Linn, Baker, & Dunbar, 1991). The results from the NAEP math test support this contention. The NAEP math assessment administered in 1996 included a variety of question formats, favoring constructed-response and performance-assessment questions over multiple-choice questions (Braun, 1998), and yet table 2 reveals that the standardized differences during that year are quite substantial for African-American and Hispanic students.

Few additional studies have added new information to this discussion. Stephen Klein and colleagues (1997) discuss several studies that used the NAEP 4th- and 8th-grade assessments. They also reported gaps among racial groups on extended-response tasks in mathematics and in oral reading that were comparable to, or exceeded the gaps found on, multiple-choice NAEP items. These authors then examined differences among groups on hands-on performance assessments and a traditional standardized test (the Iowa Test of Basic Skills, or ITBS) administered to students in grades 5, 6, and 9 in conjunction with a field test of the California Learning Assessment System. Klein and colleagues (1997) found differences on the ITBS science subtest were almost identical to differences on the performance assessments, concluding that "differences in mean scores among racial/ethnic groups were not related to test or question type. No matter which type was used, whites had much higher means than blacks and Hispanics" (p. 95). Similar results have been found on performance assessments in mathematics (by Baxter, Shavelson, Herman, Brown, and Valdez, 1993).

Group Differences in High School Grades, Academic Preparation and College Success

High School Rank and Course Grades

While there has been increasing focus placed on the racial score gaps in tests over the past few years, there has been substantially less attention paid to performance on other educational indicators. Admission officers report that the greatest weight (i.e., 40%) is placed on high school grades for making admission decisions, with less weight placed on admission test scores (G. Black, personal communication, September 1998).

Traditional measures of academic achievement, such as grades and class rank, also show severe underrepresentation of African Americans and Hispanics among top students (National Task Force on Minority High Achievement, 1999). Table 3 illustrates these differences for the 1997 college-bound seniors who took the SAT I. Over 40% of white and Asian-American students reported having an A average in high school in 1997, compared to less than 20% of African-American and 30% of Hispanic students. The racial group disparities persist when we examine GPA and class rank. Again, according to their self-reported class rank, white and Asian-American students are twice as likely to be in the top 10% of their high school class as African Americans.

Table 3: Percentage of Students by GPA and Class Rank for Ethnic and Racial Groups

	GPA				CLASS RANK			
GROUP	A	B	C	BELOW C	90TH	80TH	60TH	BELOW 60TH
African-American	18.9	53.2	26.8	1.1	11.9	18.8	28.7	40.6
Asian-American	47.5	42.7	7.0	0.0	27.8	24.9	25.7	21.7
Hispanic	30.0	53.4	16.1	0.5	16.5	21.5	28.5	33.5
White	40.3	47.8	11.7	0.3	23.2	23.2	27.3	26.3

Source: Data are from 1997 college-bound seniors (College Board, 1997).

Academic Preparation

Student course-taking reflects both the breadth and depth of course offerings at a school and the opportunities or challenges taken by students. For example, a school's curriculum may contain mostly "basic" or "survey" courses, or it may contain a range of advanced or honors courses. Attending a school with an extensive list of courses may not be enough to assure equal access to such challenging courses. If advanced courses are not required, students may elect to take less challenging courses that require less work. Other schools may deny access to some groups of students, employing gatekeeper courses and student tracking (Finn, 1999). Research on academic preparation indicates that academic achievement is directly related to challenging course work (Adelman, 1999). Of course, high-achieving students are more likely to take challenging courses, but Clifford Adelman also found that *all* groups of students benefit from taking more rigorous courses, even after controlling for differences in socioeconomic status (SES) or prior achievement (1999). Given this finding, it is of interest to examine whether challenging courses are offered in all high schools.

Using data from the NAEP High School Transcript Study, Jeremy Finn (1999) reports that about one-third of high schools did not offer any advanced courses in science and another 28% offered advanced work only in one science subject (typically biology). Graduation requirements tend to include far fewer advanced and core academic courses than most colleges and universities hold as a minimum for admission. Less than half of U.S. high schools required three years of math, and just over one-quarter of high schools required three years of science. Students in private schools generally take more courses in core academic areas than students in public schools. Notes Finn, "Both the breadth and depth of course offerings were consistently lacking in schools located in small and rural communities [and] . . . students in high-SES schools took more courses, and more advanced courses than students attending schools in other SES categories" (1999, pp. 5–7).

Some research has attempted to account for differences in school quality in examining subgroup score differences. Klein and colleagues (1997) found that rough adjustments for school quality reduced the gap on the ITBS and performance assessments between white and African-American students by about one-quarter of a standard deviation. They note that differences in school quality and opportunities might account for much of the difference found among groups, particularly if better adjustments could be developed.

In a similar study, Schmidt (1999) found that, when controlling for parental education, family income, and course-taking patterns, the gap between mean scores for white and Hispanic test takers on the SAT I was reduced from approximately 55 points on math and 59 points on verbal to 28 points on math and 33 points on verbal. The same type of analysis reduced the white and African-American SAT I mean score gap from 93 points on math and 84 points on verbal to 65 points on math and 56 points on verbal. In other words, when minority students are compared to majority students who are most like them in terms of parental education, family income, and course-taking patterns, the gap in SAT I scores is substantially reduced. Of course, these groups may still differ in various ways that are not readily detected by using these three background variables to control for differences. Access to quality instruction; the breadth and depth of instruction; opportunity to learn; and level of educational support available in the school, home, and family may still differ among groups in ways that are largely undetected when using simple contrasts and descriptive comparisons of groups.

College Success

A metric that is commonly used to evaluate college success is freshman grade point average (FGPA), which is viewed as an important indicator for a variety of reasons. It is collected more easily than later college performance, and a review of the research indicates that the strength of the relationship between predictor variables (admission test scores and high school grade point average) and FGPA is similar to the strength of the relationship between these variables and cumulative four-year college grade point average (Burton & Ramist, 2001). Table 4 illustrates mean FGPA and high school grade point average by racial group for 46,379 students attending 55 colleges and universities (Ramist, Lewis, & McCamley-Jenkins, 1994), and reveals that mean racial group differences in FGPA are even larger than differences in high school grades. The disparity between high school and college grades is quite striking for all groups, ranging from .74 to 1.06 grade points, with the largest differences found for underrepresented minorities (African American, 1.04; Hispanic, 1.06), with somewhat smaller disparities for Asian-American (.78) and white test takers (.74). That is, Hispanics and African Americans are

Table 4: Mean High School and College GPA and Differences by Ethnicity and Race

GROUP	HIGH SCHOOL GPA	FRESHMAN GPA	DIFFERENCE
African-American	3.18	2.14	1.04
Asian-American	3.58	2.80	.78
Hispanic	3.43	2.37	1.06
White	3.40	2.66	.74

Source: Ramist, Lewis, & McCamley-Jenkins, 1994.

still likely to get lower average grades in high school and college than other groups of students; however, high school grades used alone will dispro-portionately overpredict college performance for these groups relative to Asian-American and white students.

Alternative criteria such as persistence in college and graduation also illustrate similar gaps. For example, the National Center for Education Statistics (1996) reported that 56.4% of white students seeking a bachelor's degree in 1989–90 received a degree or certificate within four years, while the figures for African-American and Hispanic students were 45.2% and 41.3%, respectively. Using the College and Beyond database of 28 selective universities, William Bowen and Derek Bok (1998) reported the following six-year graduation rates for 1989 matriculating freshmen: African American, 75%; Hispanic, 81%; Asian American, 88%; and white, 86%. Among persons 25 to 29 years of age, whites were twice as likely to have completed four or more years of college (28.1%) in 1996 than African Americans (14.6%) or Hispanics (10.0%) (U.S. Department of Commerce, 1997). In addition, several studies have demonstrated that scores on college admission tests and high school grades have a strong and practical impact on graduation rates (Adelman, 1999; Burton & Ramist, 2001; Educational Testing Service, 1998c; Manski & Wise, 1983; Widaman, 1998). Keith Widaman (1998) explains that SAT I scores have only slightly less weight in predicting graduation than high school grades within the University of California system. The actual effect of high school grades and admission tests in predicting attrition and graduation is underestimated in most such studies because a substantial proportion of students included as college dropouts are in good academic standing and either transfer to other colleges or leave for personal or financial reasons (Adelman, 1999).

Discussion and Conclusions

So far in this paper we have illustrated that racial gaps are present in a variety of educational indicators, including standardized test scores, high school and college grades, and college graduation rates. The more pressing questions to address are Why are the gaps present at all, and why do they persist? There is evidence that the gaps between white and black test takers' scores have decreased since 1965, although the rate of this decrease slowed after 1972 (Hedges & Nowell, 1998). However, as was seen from the NAEP data presented earlier, gaps in math scores, and to a lesser extent, reading scores, appear to have increased slightly since 1992.

Several theories have been offered recently for the presence of African-American–white test score gaps. Among the factors mentioned are family background and parenting practices (Phillips, Brooks-Gunn, Duncan, Klebanov & Crane, 1998), teacher's and test administrator's perceptions and expectations of students' abilities (Ferguson, 1998; Steele & Aronson, 1998), and black students' attitudes about the value of achieving at a high level in school (Cook & Ludwig, 1998). Educational leaders have also advanced possible causes for the gaps, such as the inequities minorities have suffered through inadequate academic preparation, poverty, and discrimination; years of tracking into dead-end educational programs; lack of advanced and rigorous courses in inner city schools, or lack of access to such programs when available; threadbare facilities and overcrowding; teachers in critical need of professional development; less family support and experience in higher education; and low expectations (Stewart, 1999). There have been some encouraging signs—the SAT score gap has declined somewhat for most minorities in the past 20 years, and minorities now represent a record 33% of college-bound students, up from 22% in 1987. In addition, the work of Adelman (1999) and Schmidt (1999) suggests that when minority students are given opportunities to take more rigorous courses, the test score gaps not only diminish, but more important, the outcomes, such as graduation rates, significantly improve. There is also increasing evidence that well-designed and well-implemented elementary school reform programs can help disadvantaged minority students attain high levels of achievement.

However, as Christopher Jencks and Meredith Phillips (1998) point out, much more research is needed to identify the causes of the differences that persist across test scores, grades, and educational outcomes so that real change can occur. They also warn that change will only occur with sustained effort over a period of time. Certainly, research that takes into account the context in which the student learns, including school and home characteristics, as well as individual student characteristics, such as racial group membership, is urgently needed.

In 1999, the National Task Force on Minority High Achievement offered recommendations for action in three areas in order to improve educational outcomes for underrepresented minorities: (1) expand efforts to increase the number of high-achieving underrepresented minority students in college, (2) build a sustaining minority high-achievement dimension in school reform initiatives, and (3) expand the use of supplementary educational strategies as a means of supporting high academic performance among more minority students (1999). They also support the development of "affirmative development," which they define as "an extensive array of public and private policies, actions, and investments . . . which would collectively provide many more opportunities for academic development for underrepresented minority students through the schools, colleges and universities that they attend, through their homes, and through their communities." (National Task Force on Minority High Achievement, 1999, p. 35). Clearly, this is an initiative that, like the Jencks and Phillips recommendations, will take a great deal of time, sustained energy, and considerable resources to implement.

Note

1. The authors acknowledge that the category "Hispanic" does not constitute a racial group but rather an ethnic group. A decision was made to use the term *racial group* rather than *racial/ethnic group* to enhance readability.

References

ACT (1998). *ACT Assessment results: 1998 summary report.* Iowa City, IA: ACT, Inc.

Adelman, C. (1999). *Answers in the toolbox: Academic intensity, attendance patterns, and bachelor's degree attainment.* Washington, DC: U.S. Department of Education, Office of Educational Research and Improvement.

American Association of Medical Colleges (1998). *April/august MCAT performance by sex, racial/ethnic group, age, language status, undergraduate major, and testing history.* Washington, DC: AAMC.

American Educational Research Association, American Psychological Association, & National Council on Measurement in Education (1999). *Standards for educational and psychological testing.* Washington, DC: AERA/APA/NCME.

Baxter, G. P., Shavelson, R. J., Herman, S. J., Brown, K. A., & Valdez, J. (1993). Mathematics performance assessment: Technical quality and diverse student impact. *Journal for research in mathematics education, 24(3),* 190–216.

Bourque, M. L., Champagne, A. B., & Crissman, S. (1997) *1996 science performance standards: Achievement results for the nation and states.* Washington, DC: National Assessment Governing Board.

Bowen, W. G., & Bok, D. (1998). *The shape of the river.* Princeton, NJ: Princeton University Press.

Braun, H. I. (1998). "Standardized testing in American higher education: Background, data, and options." Paper presented at the interdisciplinary workshop on skills, test scores, and inequality, Hubert H. Humphrey Institute of Public Affairs, University of Minnesota, Minneapolis.

Bronner, E. (1997, November 8). Colleges look for answers to racial gaps in testing. *New York Times,* pp. A1, A12.

Burton, N. W., & Ramist, L. (2001). *Predicting success in college: SAT studies of classes graduating since 1980.* College Board Report No. 2001-2. New York: College Board.

Camara, W. J., & Schmidt, A. E. (1999). *Group differences in standardized testing and social stratification.* College Board Report No. 99-5. New York: College Board.

Cole, N. S., & Willingham, W. W. (1997). *Gender and fair assessment.* Mahwah, NJ: Erlbaum.

College Board (1997). *1997 college-bound seniors.* New York: College Board.

Cook, P. J., & Ludwig, J. (1998). The burden of "acting white": Do black adolescents disparage academic achievement? In C. Jencks & M. Phillips (Eds.), *The black-white test score gap* (pp. 375–400). Washington, DC: Brookings Institute.

Dunbar, S. B., Koretz, D. M., & Hoover, H. D. (1991). Quality control in the development and use of performance assessments. *Applied Measurement in Education, 4(4)*, 289–303.

Educational Testing Service (1998a). *Graduate record examinations: Sex, race, ethnicity and performance on the GRE General Test 1998–99*. Princeton, NJ: Educational Testing Service.

Educational Testing Service (1998b). *Profile of Graduate Management Admission Test candidates: Five-year summary*. Princeton, NJ: Educational Testing Service.

Educational Testing Service (1998c). *B.A. attainment within five years among SAT test-takers*. Princeton, NJ: Educational Testing Service, Office of Public Leadership.

Ferguson, R. F. (1998). Teachers' perceptions and expectations and the black-white test score gap. In C. Jencks & M. Phillips (Eds.), *The black-white test score gap* (pp. 273–317). Washington, DC: Brookings Institute.

Finn, J. D. (1999). Opportunity offered—opportunity taken: Course-taking in American high schools. *ETS Policy Notes, 9(1)*. Princeton, NJ: Educational Testing Service.

Hedges, L. V., & Nowell, A. (1998). Black-white test score convergence since 1965. In C. Jencks & M. Phillips (Eds.), *The black-white test score gap* (pp. 149–181). Washington, DC: Brookings Institute.

Jencks, C., & Phillips, M. (1998). *The black-white test score gap*. Washington, DC: Brookings Institute.

Jenkins, L. B., & MacDonald, W. N. (1989). Science teaching in the spirit of science. *Issues in Science and Technology, 63*, 60–65.

Kirsch, I. S., Jungeblut, A., Jenkins, L., & Kolstad, A. (1993). *Adult literacy in America: A first look at the results of the National Adult Literacy Survey*. Washington, DC: National Center for Educational Statistics.

Klein, S. P., Josavnoic J., Stecher, B. M., McCaffrey, D., Shavelson, R. J., Haertel, E., Solano-Flores, G., & Comfort, K. (1997). Gender and racial/ethnic differences on performance assessments in science. *Educational Evaluation and Policy Analysis 19(2)*, 83–97.

Koenig, J. A., Sireci, S. G., & Wiley, A. (1998). Evaluating the predictive validity of MCAT scores across diverse applicant groups. *Academic Medicine, 73*, 1095–1106.

Linn, R. L., Baker, E. L., & Dunbar, S. B. (1991). Complex, performance-based assessment: Expectations and validity criteria. *Educational Researcher, 20(8)*, 15–21.

Manski, C. F., & Wise, D. (1983) *College choice in America*. Cambridge, MA: Harvard University Press.

National Center for Education Statistics (1996). *Digest of educational statistics*. Washington, DC: National Center for Education Statistics.

National Task Force on Minority High Achievement (1999). *Reaching the top: A report of the national task force on minority high achievement*. New York: College Board.

Neil, D. M., & Medina, N. J. (1989). Standardized testing: Harmful to educational health. *Phi Delta Kappan, 70*, 688–96.

Phillips, M., Brooks-Gunn, J., Duncan, G. L., Klebanov, P., & Crane, J. (1998). Family background, parenting practices, and the black-white test score gap. In C. Jencks & M. Phillips (Eds.), *The black-white test score gap* (pp. 103–45). Washington, DC: Brookings Institute.

Ramist, L., Lewis, C., & McCamley-Jenkins, L. (1994). *Student group differences in predicting college grades: Sex, language and ethnic groups*. College Board Report No. 93-1. New York: College Board.

Reese, C. M., Miller, K. E., Mazzeo, J., & Dossey, J. A. (1997). *NAEP 1996 mathematics report card for the nation and states: Findings from the National Assessment of Educational Progress*. Washington, DC: National Center for Educational Statistics.

Sacks, P. (1997). Standardized testing: Meritocracy's crooked yardstick. *Change*, vol. 29, pp. 25–31.

Schmidt, A. E. (1999). Explaining racial and ethnic differences in large-scale assessments. Paper presented at the annual meeting of the American Educational Research Association, Montreal, Canada, April 22, 1999.

Shavelson, R. J., Solano-Flores, G., & Ruiz-Primo, M. (1997). Toward a science performance assessment technology. *Evaluation and program planning, 21(2)*, 171–84.

Steele, C. M., & Aronson, J. (1998). Stereotype threat and the test performance of academically successful African Americans. In C. Jencks & M. Phillips (Eds.), *The black-white test score gap* (pp. 401–427). Washington, DC: Brookings Institute.

Stewart, D. S. (1999). "Standardized testing and social stratification." Invited Address at the Macalester College Forum on Higher Education, St. Paul, MN, June 22, 1999.

U.S. Department of Commerce (1997). *Educational attainment in the United States.* Current Population Reports, P-20 Series. Washington, DC: Bureau of the Census.

U.S. Department of Education (1992). *National Educational Longitudinal Survey of 1988: Follow-up of 1992: Preliminary results.* Washington, DC: National Center for Educational Statistics.

Widaman, K. F. (1998). Utility of SAT scores for the admissions process at the University of California. Testimony before the California State Senate Select Subcommittee on Higher Education Admissions and Outreach, February 5, 1998.

Is the SAT a "Wealth Test?" The Link between Educational Achievement and Socioeconomic Status

In a recent visit to the University of California, Santa Barbara, Harvard University law professor Lani Guinier drew big cheers from the students in the audience when she suggested that, in the interest of truth in advertising, the SAT should simply be called a "wealth test."[1] And Professor Guinier is certainly not alone in criticizing standardized admissions tests on the grounds that the resulting scores are related to the income and educational level of the test-taker's family. Test critic Alfie Kohn recently suggested that the verbal section of the SAT, which includes some difficult vocabulary, merely measures "the size of students' houses" (Kohn, 2001, p. B12). A University of California dean told the Los Angeles Times in 1997 that the "only thing the S.A.T. predicts well now is socioeconomic status" (Colvin, 1997, p. B2). "Call it the 'Volvo Effect,'" said journalist Peter Sacks, claiming that "one can make a good guess about a child's standardized test scores simply by looking at how many degrees her parents have and at what kind of car they drive" (1997, p. 27).

In making his case, Sacks referred to a National Center for Education Statistics study of the accomplishments of high school students. The NCES researchers computed the percentages of students who met each of several academic standards intended to resemble the admissions criteria of selective

203

Table 1: Association Between Family Income and ACT and SAT Averages

ANNUAL FAMILY INCOME	ACT COMPOSITE	SAT MATH	SAT VERBAL
Less than $20,000[a]	18.1	452	435
More than $100,000	23.4	569	557
Difference	5.3	117	122
Standard Deviation (SD) for Total Group	4.7	113	111
Standardized Difference (Ratio of Difference to SD)	1.1	1.0	1.1

Source: ACT, Inc., 2001; College Board, 2001.

[a] For the ACT, 18.1 is the average score corresponding to an income of less than $18,000 per year. For the SAT, the average scores of 452 and 435 correspond to an income of less than $20,000 per year. These values were obtained by taking weighted averages of the average scores provided for income levels of less than $10,000 per year and $10,000 to $20,000 per year, respectively.

colleges. They compared the results for students of high, medium, and low socioeconomic status (or SES), as measured by parental education, occupation, and income. Thirty-two percent of the high-SES students earned a combined SAT score (math score plus verbal score) of at least 1100, but only 9% of the low-SES group did so.

In fact, the assertion that standardized test scores are associated with socioeconomic factors has been repeatedly confirmed by researchers, including those at the College Board. According to College Board data from 2001, the average combined SAT score for college-bound seniors whose families earned less than $20,000 was 887. The SAT average increased steadily with family income, reaching 1126 for students whose families earned over $100,000 (see table 1).

Two conjectures are frequently offered as explanations for the recurrent finding that test performance is correlated with family income and education. One hypothesis is that this association stems from a (white) middle-class perspective that is presumed to be ingrained in the content of standardized admissions tests. Some SAT critics have claimed that exams that emphasized material taught in the classroom would yield smaller differences among income groups. The other prevailing theory is that the correlation occurs because the scores of test takers from wealthy families are artificially boosted by test coaching.

But do these hypotheses hold up on closer examination? What can we learn by examining student performance on tests that focus on course content, or tests for which no coaching takes place? And what about the relation between socioeconomic factors and other forms of educational achievement, such as grades and course completion? It has been all too rare for commentators to consider the use of admissions tests within this broader context. Here I examine several types of data that help to shed some light on the well-established association between test scores and family income and education.

ACT Results

The ACT, competitor to the SAT in the college admissions test market, is a multiple-choice test with four sections: English, math, reading, and science. Whereas the SAT tries to steer clear of specific course material, the content of the ACT is based on an analysis of what is taught in grades 7 through 12. The curriculum analysis focuses on the areas that correspond to the four sections of the ACT. Educators are then consulted to determine which skills they consider necessary for students in college courses.

Does this grounding in classroom learning imply that ACT performance will have a smaller relation to family income than SAT performance? Scores on the ACT composite, which combines results on the four sections, range from 1 to 36, so they are not directly comparable to SAT scores. Results for the two tests can, however, be compared in terms of standard deviation units.[2] As shown in table 1, students with a family income of less than $18,000 had an average ACT score of 18.1 in 2001, compared with an average score of 23.4 for an income over $100,000. This corresponds to a *standardized difference* of 1.1 on the ACT composite, obtained by dividing the score difference (5.3) by the standard deviation (4.7). The standardized difference between the average SAT scores for similarly defined low and high income groups in 2001 was 1.0 for the math section and 1.1 for the verbal section (see table 1). Evidently, the ACT's stronger linkage to the secondary school curriculum does not translate to smaller score gaps among income levels.

SAT II Results

While the SAT I: Reasoning Test—the test we usually call the SAT—focuses on general verbal and mathematical skills, the SAT II: Subject Tests (formerly known as the College Board Achievement Tests) are intended to assess high school students' knowledge in particular areas. Twenty-two SAT II tests are available, including those in writing, American history, math, physics, Spanish, and Chinese. Like the SAT I, the SAT II exams are primarily multiple-choice, although the writing test does include an essay.

Much attention has been focused on the SAT II since University of California president Richard C. Atkinson proposed in February 2001 that

UC eliminate the SAT I as an admissions criterion. Currently, UC applicants must take the SAT I, the SAT II math and writing tests, and a third SAT II test of their own choosing. Atkinson suggested that the SAT II tests were more appropriate for use in admissions decisions and could be relied upon until new tests could be developed that were directly tied to the college preparatory courses required of UC applicants. The SAT II, he said, "begins to approximate . . . an appropriate test for UC and other American universities since it tests students on specific subject areas that are well defined and readily described" (Atkinson, 2001).

As in the case of the ACT, it is instructive to examine whether the SAT II's links with classroom learning leads to scores that are less influenced by socioeconomic standing than scores on the SAT I. A 2001 report from the UC Office of the President (UCOP) drew just this conclusion, asserting that "SAT II achievement tests are . . . a fairer test for use in college admissions insofar as they are demonstrably less sensitive than the SAT I to differences in socioeconomic and other background factors."[3] This determination was based on an application of regression analysis, a standard statistical method used in prediction: First, the UCOP analysts constructed a regression model in which high school grade point average (HSGPA) and test scores (either the SAT I or the SAT II) were used to predict freshman grade point average at UC. Then, the analysts added two more predictors to the model: parental income and parental education. They found that when these additional predictors are included, "the predictive weights for both the SAT II and HSGPA are undiminished (and in fact increase slightly). In contrast, the weight for the SAT I . . . falls sharply." These results led the UCOP analysts to infer that "much of the apparent relationship between the SAT I and UC freshman grades is conditioned by socioeconomic factors."[4]

A limitation of these regression analyses is that they were performed on combined data for four freshman cohorts (1996–1999) and seven UC campuses. Also, in the UCOP analyses, "SAT I score" is, in fact, a composite of SAT I verbal and math scores and "SAT II score" is a composite of the SAT II math and writing tests and the SAT II "third test," which is selected by the student. The SAT II composite is of particular concern because the identity of the third test is not consistent across applicants (and is not included in the UCOP data set). To further explore the UCOP conclusions regarding socioeconomic factors, I conducted analyses within each campus and freshman cohort, with each test component considered separately. The results did not generally follow the pattern described in the UCOP report. For example, consider the standardized regression coefficients for UCSB in table 2. These coefficients correspond to regression models with and without parental income and education for the freshman cohorts entering between 1996 and 1999. At UCSB—and in general—adding parental income and

Table 2: Standardized Regression Coefficients for Prediction Models with and without Parental Income and Education (University of California, Santa Barbara)

REGRESSION MODEL:	HIGH SCHOOL GPA	SAT I VERBAL TEST	SAT I MATH TEST	SAT II WRITING TEST	SAT II MATH TEST	SAT II THIRD TEST	PARENT INCOME	PARENT EDUCATION
1996: Without Income and Education	.34	.09	.06	.13	.04	.06	X	X
1996: With Income and Education	.35	.09	.03	.13	.04	.08	.03	.05
1997: Without Income and Education	.37	.05	.04	.16	.02	.06	X	X
1997: With Income and Education	.36	.04	.02	.15	.03	.08	.02	.06
1998: Without Income and Education	.34	.06	.00	.17	.01	.07	X	X
1998: With Income and Education	.34	.05	−.02	.15	.01	.04	.04	.09
1999: Without Income and Education	.36	.11	−.01	.14	.04	.03	X	X
1999: With Income and Education	.36	.12	−.05	.11	.05	.04	.02	.06

Source: Data for four freshman cohorts and seven UC campuses was provided by special arrangement with the UC Office of the President. In the above table, sample sizes ranged from 2,221 to 3,569 for the four cohorts. For each cohort, the first line shows regression coefficients for a model that included only high school grade point average and test scores as predictors of freshman grade point average. The second line pertains to a model that included parent income and education as well.

education to the model led to slight changes in the regression coefficients for the academic predictors, as is typical when models of this kind are modified. However, the coefficients for the SAT I tests were not consistently found to be more sensitive to introduction of the socioeconomic status variables than the coefficients for the SAT II tests.[5] For example, in the 1999 data, the coefficient for the SAT I verbal test increased by .01 (from .11 to .12) when the socioeconomic variables were added, while the coefficient for the SAT II writing test decreased by .03 (from .14 to .11).

These regression analyses may seem to be a rather indirect means of examining the association between test scores and family income. And indeed, an earlier memorandum from the UC Office of the President reported a simpler result—the correlation of family income with SAT II scores (.23) and with SAT I scores (.31) (Geiser & Studley, July 11, 2001, p. 3). But like the UCOP regression results, these findings are based on test score composites. My reanalysis of the same UC data set (combined across campuses and cohorts) shows that the SAT I verbal score and SAT II writing score have nearly identical correlations with income (.31 and .30, respectively). SAT I math has a slightly larger correlation with income (.23) than does SAT II math (.19).[6] When we average just the mathematical and verbal components of each test, we find that the SAT I average and the SAT II average have quite similar correlations with income (.31 and .29, respectively). The UCOP finding that the SAT II composite has a much lower correlation with income than the SAT I composite is due to the effect of including the score on the third SAT II in the SAT II composite. This "third SAT II" score, which does not have a consistent meaning across students, has a near-zero correlation with income (.06). Analyses within campuses and cohorts produced similar patterns.[7]

California High School Exit Exam Results

In 2001, about 370,000 California 9th graders took the state's first high school exit exam. The test consists of an English language arts section, which includes an essay component, and a math section. The test is intended to cover California's curriculum standards for grades 8 to 10 in English and grades 6 to 7, plus Algebra 1, in math. (State officials acknowledge that the standards had not yet been fully implemented in 2001; for this reason, the exit exam was not mandatory.) As shown in table 3, pass rates were quite dismal overall—44% for math and 64% for language arts—despite the fact that students had to get only 55% of the test questions correct to pass the math section and 60% right to pass the language arts section. For "socioeconomically disadvantaged students"—those who participate in the federal free or reduced-price lunch program administered by the U.S. Department of Agriculture[8]—pass rates were even lower: only 45% of these students

Table 3: California High School Exit Exam Results for 2001 by Economic Groups

GROUP	APPROXIMATE SAMPLE SIZE (THOUSANDS)	PERCENTAGE OF STUDENTS PASSING
Pass Rates for Language Arts Test (Pass = 60% correct)		
Socioeconomically Disadvantaged	118	45%
Not Socioeconomically Disadvantaged	188	74%
Total	370	64%
Pass Rates for Mathematics Test (Pass = 55% correct)		
Socioeconomically Disadvantaged	116	26%
Not Socioeconomically Disadvantaged	185	54%
Total	365	44%

Source: California Department of Education, October 3, 2001. Students were considered "socioeconomically disadvantaged" if they participated in the federal free or reduced-price lunch program. Sample sizes for the two groups do not add up to the total sample sizes because economic information was unavailable for some students.

passed the language arts section and 26% passed math. By contrast, 74% of the students who were not socioeconomically disadvantaged passed language arts and 54% passed math. (Pass rates for 2002 were lower across the board, with only 40% of socioeconomically disadvantaged students passing language arts and 22% passing math. Among students who were not socioeconomically disadvantaged, 64% passed language arts and 40% passed math; see California Department of Education, 2002). Unlike admissions tests, the exit exam is intended to be entirely curriculum-based, yet scores are still heavily influenced by economic factors.

The 2000 National Assessment of Educational Progress Mathematics Results

The National Assessment of Educational Progress is a federally funded student achievement survey that was first administered more than 30 years ago. NAEP differs from college admissions testing in several fundamental ways. First, students are assessed not only at the high school level (grade 12) but also at earlier points in their schooling (grades 4 and 8). Second, NAEP is a low-stakes assessment. Every year, schools and students are chosen for participation using statistical sampling procedures. Results are reported only for the nation, for participating states, and for key demographic groups. Legislation prohibits NAEP from reporting scores at the student or school level; therefore, there is no incentive for students to be coached.[9] Finally, the content of the NAEP assessment is intended to be representative of material that is being taught in schools around the country. The objectives and test specifications for the 2000 mathematics assessment had their roots in the 1990 NAEP math framework developed by the Council of Chief State School Officers (CCSSO) under a contract with the National Assessment Governing Board, a body created by the U.S. Congress to oversee NAEP. In determining the content of the math assessment, the CCSSO examined math objectives used by states, districts, and schools around the country, consulted with leading mathematics educators, and considered the curriculum standards of the National Council of Teachers of Mathematics (Braswell et al., 2001).

One of the ways that NAEP reports results is in terms of the percentage of students attaining or exceeding three achievement levels: Basic, Proficient, and Advanced. The score ranges associated with these levels are determined through consultation with national panels of expert educators and members of the general public, under the direction of the National Assessment Governing Board. Table 4 gives the percentage of test takers in the NAEP 2001 mathematics assessment who reached or exceeded the Basic level and the percentage who reached or exceeded the Proficient level at grades 4, 8, and 12. (Only a very small percentage of students overall reached the Advanced level.) Results are shown separately for students who were or were not

Table 4: Percentage Attaining the Basic and Proficient Levels in the NAEP 2000 Mathematics Assessment for Students Who Are and Are Not Eligible for the Federal Free/Reduced-Price Lunch Program

| | ELIGIBILITY FOR FREE/REDUCED-PRICE LUNCH PROGRAM | |
	ELIGIBLE	NOT ELIGIBLE
Grade 4		
At or above Basic Level	46%	79%
At or above Proficient Level	9%	33%
Grade 8		
At or above Basic Level	43%	76%
At or above Proficient Level	10%	35%
Grade 12		
At or above Basic Level	40%	69%
At or above Proficient Level	4%	19%

Source: Braswell et al., 2001. Results are based on approximately 14,000 4th graders, 16,000 8th graders, and 13,000 12th graders.

Table 5: Percentage of Students Attaining the Basic and Proficient Levels in the NAEP 2000 Mathematics Assessment for Four Levels of Parent Education

	PARENTS' HIGHEST LEVEL OF EDUCATION			
	LESS THAN HIGH SCHOOL	GRADUATED HIGH SCHOOL	SOME POST–HIGH SCHOOL	GRADUATED COLLEGE
Grade 8				
At or above Basic Level	45%	54%	72%	77%
At or above Proficient Level	8%	16%	27%	39%
Grade 12				
At or above Basic Level	38%	51%	66%	77%
At or above Proficient Level	2%	6%	12%	27%

Source: Braswell et al., 2001. Results are based on approximately 16,000 8th graders and 13,000 12th graders.

eligible for the federal free or reduced-price lunch program. Although this is yet another assessment that is linked to classroom study, the differences between the eligibility groups is striking, with the performance of the ineligible (wealthier) students always exceeding that of the eligible students by a substantial amount. For example, at grade 4, only 46% of eligible students, compared with 79% of ineligible students, performed at or above the Basic level; only 9% of eligibles, compared with 33% of ineligibles, performed at or above the Proficient level.

Table 5 shows the impact of another socioeconomic variable—parent education—on NAEP performance for grades 8 and 12. (NAEP no longer collects data on parent education from fourth graders because research has indicated that students this young are not able to provide accurate information.) The four rightmost columns of table 5 correspond to the educational level of the student's more educated parent. Like eligibility for the federal lunch program, parent education is strongly associated with NAEP performance. At grade 8, for example, only 45% of students included in the "less than high school" category (indicating neither parent graduated from high school) attained at least the Basic level, compared with 77% of those with at least one parent who graduated from college.

Grades and Other Measures of Academic Achievement

How do socioeconomic groups compare on grades and other measures of achievement? College Board surveys indicate that average high school grades, like SAT scores, are higher for students from families with larger incomes. Table 6, which is based on 1997 data, shows that, as income increases from less than $20,000 to more than $100,000, the percentage of students with an A average increases from 30% to 46%; the percentage with a C or below decreases from 19% to 10%. SAT averages for each income level are shown as well.

Additional pertinent results come from a National Center for Education Statistics study—the same one journalist Peter Sacks used to condemn the SAT for its association with socioeconomic factors. The study did indeed reveal a relationship between socioeconomic status (SES) and SAT scores, but that is only part of the story. The NCES researchers considered five academic standards, which were intended to resemble those used by selective colleges in admissions decisions. As shown in table 7, the researchers found that, for each of five standards, the percentage of students satisfying the criterion increased with socioeconomic level. In particular, 24% of the high-SES group, compared with only 10% of the low-SES group, had high school grade point averages of at least 3.5. And 65% of the high group, compared with 40% of the low group, had completed a specified number of course credits in key areas. Students from high-SES families also received better teacher ratings and reported more extracurricular activities. Clearly, then, it's not only standardized test scores that are associated with family income.

Table 6: Average SAT Scores and Percentage of Students with High School Grade-Point Averages of "A," "B," and "C or below" for Five Levels of Combined Parental Income

	LESS THAN $20,000	$20,000– $35,000	$35,000– $60,000	$60,000– $100,000	MORE THAN $100,000
Average SAT Score					
Verbal	447	487	509	531	560
Math	461	490	511	536	572
High School GPA					
A	30%	34%	38%	41%	46%
B	51%	50%	49%	47%	45%
C or below	19%	16%	14%	12%	10%
Number of students	114,475	152,425	271,209	222,870	107,685

Source: Adapted from Camara & Schmidt, 1999, p. 9. Their analysis was based on College Board data on 1997 college-bound seniors. Percentages may not add to 100% because of rounding.

Table 7: Percentage of 1992 High School Graduates Meeting Typical Admissions Criteria for Selective Colleges, by Socioeconomic Status

	SOCIOECONOMIC STATUS		
ADMISSIONS CRITERION	HIGH	MIDDLE	LOW
SAT Total at least 1100	32%	15%	9%
High School GPA at least 3.5	24%	16%	10%
Specified course credits completed	65%	50%	40%
Teacher perceptions positive	48%	38%	36%
At least 2 extracurricular activities	72%	66%	57%
All 5 criteria met	9%	4%	2%

Source: Adapted from Owings, McMillen, & Burkett, 1995, table 1. Their analysis was based on data from the National Education Longitudinal Study of 1988: Second Follow-up, 1992. The sample consisted of 6,760 students. "Specified number of credits completed" indicates that the student had four credits in English, three in math, three in science, three in social studies, and two in foreign language. Teacher perceptions were obtained from a questionnaire.

Conclusions

So, is the SAT a wealth test? Only in the sense that every measure of previous educational achievement is a wealth test. We have seen that even for low-stakes, curriculum-based tests for which no coaching is available, student performance is very strongly associated with family income and educational level. And contrary to what is often believed, grades and course completion, like test scores, typically show substantial disparities among socioeconomic groups. This evidence fails to support the frequent claim that score gaps result mainly from the inclusion of esoteric test content that is more familiar to upper-crust test takers, or from inequalities in access to test coaching services. In fact, the studies reviewed here suggest that if we were to "disqualify" any admissions criterion related to parents' income and education, we would have to eliminate high school grades, course background, teacher ratings, and extracurricular activities along with test scores.

What's the reason for these widespread performance disparities? As Pedro Noguera and Antwi Akom recently remarked in *The Nation,* it's no surprise that poor children don't do as well academically, given that they are often "educated in schools that are woefully inadequate on most measures of quality and funding" (Noguera & Akom, 2000, p. 29). Exactly how do wealthier schools differ from those with fewer resources? The Public Policy Institute of California recently published a comprehensive study of the distribution of school resources in the state, and the impact of resources on student achievement. Achievement was measured by 1998 performance on the math and reading sections of the Stanford-9 Achievement Test. In summarizing their key findings, the study's authors, Julian Betts, Kim S. Rueben, and Anne Danenberg, noted, "By far, the most important factor related to student achievement [on the school level] . . . is our measure of SES—the percentage of students receiving free or reduced-price lunches" (2000, p. 207). They also concluded that teacher experience and credential status were the resource variables that were most strongly associated with achievement, and that "variations in teacher characteristics [were] systematically related to differences in student economic status" (205).

The researchers examined the median percentage of teachers without a full credential for each of five SES levels. A school's SES was measured by the percentage of students participating in the free or reduced-price lunch program. For the lowest-SES schools at the kindergarten to grade 6 level, the median percentage of teachers who were not fully credentialed was 22%; for grades 6–8, it was 17%, and for grades 9–12, it was 12%. At the highest-SES schools, the median percentage of teachers who were not fully credentialed was much smaller, ranging from 2% to 4% across the grade levels.[10]

The researchers also drew a significant conclusion about the state's high schools: The lower the socioeconomic level of the school, the more limited the availability of Advanced Placement courses and courses satisfying the entrance requirements for the University of California and California State University (Betts et al., 2000, p. 206).

Of course, home environments, like school environments, reflect the economic status of the student's family. A government survey found that even the likelihood that young children are read to by family members varies with family income and education (National Center for Education Statistics, 1996). It's a sad reality that inequities in educational opportunity seem to make it impossible to find a measure of academic achievement that is unrelated to family income. Because test scores, grades, and course completion all reflect past opportunities and financial resources, and therefore reveal similar patterns, it is not fruitful to seek to identify features of tests that are "responsible" for the correlation between scores and economic status. Instead, debate should focus on a broader and more important question: To what degree should college admission depend on previous academic achievement? Any measure of applicants' past academic accomplishment is, in part, a reflection of the K-12 educational system with all its flaws and imbalances, and an admissions process that focuses too heavily on previous achievement, whether test scores, grades, or course background, will perpetuate these inequities. Improving diversity is a legitimate and important goal that, in the short term, can be effectively pursued only by incorporating it explicitly in our admissions policies.

Notes

This chapter has been updated to include analyses that I performed on University of California data after the November 2001 conference at UCSB. Michael Brown served as action editor for this chapter. An earlier abbreviated version of this paper appeared in *Phi Delta Kappan*, 2002, Vol. 84, No. 4, pp. 307–11.

1. The comments were made at a lecture at the University of California, Santa Barbara, on September 29, 2000.
2. The standard deviation is a measure of the average distance between a score and the average score. The standard deviation for the total group was used to compute the standardized differences.
3. Geiser & Studley, October 29, 2001, p. 10. A version of the Geiser-Studley report appears in this volume.
4. Geiser & Studley (October 29, 2001), p. 9. All reported socioeconomic analyses by Geiser and Studley are based on the log of income, a standard transformation in economic analyses that makes the income distribution more symmetric.
5. Zwick, Brown, & Sklar, 2003, Tables 5–6. A log transformation of income was used in these analyses, as in the Geiser and Studley analyses.
6. In the University of California data unlike the national data of Tables 6 and 7, high school GPA had near-zero correlations with income. The reason for the discrepancy is not obvious.
7. For further consideration of the "third" SAT II test, see the chapters in this volume by Kobrin, Camara, and Milewski, and by Bridgeman, Burton, and Cline.
8. In educational research, eligibility for such programs is often used as an indicator of inadequate financial resources.
9. Beginning in 2002, NAEP results were reported for a limited number of large school districts. Some district-level results were reported earlier under special arrangements.
10. Betts et al., 2000, p. 265. These analyses were based on 4,574 K–6 schools, 1,106 grade 6–8 schools, and 866 grade 9–12 schools.

References

ACT, Inc. (2001). *2001 ACT national and state scores: Selections from the 2001 national score report.* Iowa City, IA: ACT, Inc. Available online at www.act.org.

Atkinson, R. (2001). *Standardized tests and access to American universities.* The 2001 Robert H. Atwell Distinguished Lecture, delivered at the 83rd Annual Meeting of the American Council on Education, Washington, DC, February 18, 2001.

Betts, J. R., Rueben, K. S., & Danenberg, A. (2000). *Equal resources, equal outcomes? The distribution of school resources and student achievement in California.* San Francisco: Public Policy Institute of California.

Braswell, J. S., Lutkus, A., Grigg, W. S., Santapau, S. L., Tay-Lim, B., & Johnson, M. (2001). *The Nation's Report Card: Mathematics 2000.* NCES publication 2001517. Washington, DC: National Center for Education Statistics.

California Department of Education. (2001, October 3). *California high school exit examination state report,* Sacramento: California Department of Education. Available online at cahsee.cde.ca.gov.

California Department of Education. (2002, October 30). *California High School Exit Exam (CAHSEE results).* Sacramento: California Department of Education. Available online at http://cahsee. cde.ca.gov.

Camara, W. J., & Schmidt, A. E. (1999). *Group differences in standardized testing and social stratification.* College Board Report 99–5. New York: College Entrance Examination Board.

College Entrance Examination Board, (2001). *2001 College-bound seniors.* New York: College Board.

Colvin, R. L. (1997). Q & A: Should UC do away with the SAT? *Los Angeles Times,* October 1, B2.

Geiser, S., & Studley, R. (July 11, 2001). *Preliminary findings on the relationship between SAT scores, socioeconomic status, and UC freshman GPA* (Memorandum). Oakland: University of California Office of the President.

Geiser, S., & Studley, R. (October 29, 2001). *UC and the SAT: Predictive validity and differential impact of the SAT I and SAT II at the University of California.* Oakland: University of California Office of the President. Available online at *www.ucop.edu.*

Kohn, A. (2001). Two cheers for an end to the SAT. *Chronicle of higher education,* March 9, p. B12.

National Center for Education Statistics (1996). *National Household Education Survey.* Retrieved from the World Wide Web at nces.ed.gov/nhes.

Noguera, P., & Akom, A. (2000). Disparities demystified. *The Nation,* June 5, p. 29.

Owings, J., McMillen, M., & Burkett, J. (1995). *Making the cut: Who meets highly selective college entrance criteria?* NCES 95–732. Washington DC: National Center for Education Statistics. Available online at www.nces.ed.gov.

Sacks, P. (1997). Standardized testing: Meritocracy's crooked yardstick. *Change, 29,* 25–31.

Zwick, R., Brown, T., & Sklar, J. C. (2003). *California and the SAT: A reanalysis of University of California admissions data.* (Draft report), Berkeley, CA: Center for Studies in Higher Education.

Evaluating SAT Coaching: Gains, Effects and Self-Selection

DEREK C. BRIGGS

Introduction

For students planning to apply to a four-year college, scores on standardized admissions tests take on a great deal of importance. It may be the quality and quantity of an applicant's high school coursework that receives the closest scrutiny at the more prestigious institutions, but these are cumulative indicators of performance. The scores from standardized admissions tests, by contrast, are the product of no more than about three hours of student effort. Such tests are blind to a student's high school record—instead, they are intended as an independent, objective measure of college readiness. For students with a strong high school record, admissions tests provide a way to confirm their standing. For students with a weaker high school record, admissions tests provide a way to raise their standing. A principal justification for the use of the SAT I in the admissions process is that the test is designed to be insensitive to the high school curriculum and to short-term test preparation.[1] If short-term preparatory activities prior to taking the SAT can have the effect of significantly boosting the scores of students above those they would have received without the preparation, the validity of the tests as indicators of college readiness might be called into question.

There is an emerging consensus that particular forms of coaching have the effect of improving student scores on the SAT. That such an effect exists is not under dispute. The actual magnitude of this effect—and whether it is worth the associated cost—remains controversial. Some private tutors claim that their tutees improve their combined verbal and math SAT scores on average by over 200 points (Schwartz, 1999). Commercial test preparation companies have in the past attributed combined verbal and math SAT score increases of 100–140 points to their programs. There are two reasons to be critical of such claims. First, any estimate of a commercial program effect must be made relative to a control group of students who did *not* prepare for the test with a commercial program. If test preparation companies or private tutors advertise only the average score gains of the students who make use of their services, the "effect" of this preparation is misleading. A second related problem is that students are not assigned randomly to test preparation conditions, but select themselves into two groups: those who are "coached" and those who are "uncoached." Because the two groups of students may differ along important characteristics related to admissions test performance, any comparison of average score gains that does not control for such differences will probably be biased.

Many researchers have considered these issues when estimating the effect of commercial test preparation programs on the SAT. A nationally representative study by Donald Powers and Donald Rock (1999) estimated a coaching effect on the math section of between 13 to 18 points, and an effect on the verbal section of 6 to 12 points. Powers and Rock concluded that the combined effect of coaching on the SAT is between 21 and 34 points. Similarly, literature reviews conducted by Samuel Messick and Ann Jungeblut (1981), Rebecca DerSimonian and Nan Laird (1983) and Betsy Jane Becker (1990) found that the typical effect of commercial preparatory courses on the SAT was between 9 and 25 points on the verbal section, and between 15 and 25 points on the math section. Given that each section of the SAT has a standard deviation of about 110 points, and a standard error of measurement of about 30 points, these effect estimates seem relatively small.

This line of research has seemingly had little impact on the public consciousness. The proportion of test takers signing on for commercial test preparation for a wide range of high-stakes standardized tests shows no signs of abating, and many companies are expanding their efforts into online test preparation. The widespread perception remains that students participating in commercial courses will improve their SAT scores dramatically, and that any such improvements are in fact attributable to enrollment in the commercial course. One explanation for this phenomenon may be a certain degree of suspicion regarding the motivations of those who have found small effects for commercial test preparation. Most researchers with access to student scores from standardized admissions tests are themselves affiliated with the companies designing the tests. Faced with conflicting messages about the effectiveness of test preparation, the public may choose to embrace the more optimistic one.

I have no affiliation with either the companies that test students or those that prepare students to be tested. My intent is to offer an independent evaluation of the effectiveness of coaching for the SAT. Using nationally representative data, I first estimate an effect for coaching by comparing the average SAT scores of coached and uncoached students. In the process I make the distinction between an average gain and an average effect. This distinction explains much of the confusion over the large coaching gains reported by commercial companies, and the relatively small effects reported by researchers. Next, I estimate coaching effects after controlling for group differences statistically, using the linear regression model. I point out the difficulty of making a causal interpretation about effect estimates in the face of student self-selection. I conclude by addressing the question of just how much of an effect should be attributed to coaching for the SAT.

The NELS Data

The analysis described here is based on data taken from the National Education Longitudinal Study of 1988 (NELS:88, hereafter referred to as NELS). The NELS database is maintained by the United States Department of Education, and contains nationally representative information on a cohort of students who were high school sophomores in 1990 and seniors in 1992. The NELS data can be used to evaluate coaching effectiveness because it contains SAT scores, information about how students prepared for the SAT, and other information about student characteristics that are potentially related to SAT performance. A nationally representative sample of nearly 15,000 students completed survey questionnaires in 1990 and 1992. When population weights are applied to the sample, these 15,000 students are representative of nearly three million students in American high schools. About half of these students took either the SAT or the ACT by the end of their senior years in high school; the other half took no admissions tests at all.

We will focus on the subsample of 3,144 students from the NELS panel sample who took both the PSAT (essentially a pretest for the SAT) and the SAT. Nationally, this subsample is representative of a little over half a million students. We need to know how these students prepared to take the SAT, and this information comes from an item in the NELS 1992 questionnaire, reproduced in Figure 1.

With the exception of studying with a book, all of the preparatory methods listed have been classified as coaching in previous studies. As a starting point, I classify students who took a course offered by a commercial test preparation service as coached (i.e., students answering question B

To prepare for the SAT and/or ACT, did you do any of the following?
A   Take a special course at your high school
B   Take a course offered by a commercial test preparation service
C   Receive private one-to-one tutoring
D   Study from test preparation books
E   Use a test preparation video tape
F   Use a test preparation computer program

Figure 1. NELS test preparation survey question.

in figure 1 with a "yes"), and students who did not take such a course as uncoached (i.e., students answering question B with a "no"). Later, I will also consider a broader definition of the coaching term that incorporates the other forms of test preparation. For now, the distinction being made is whether a test taker has received systematic instruction over a short period of time. Preparation with books, videos and computers is excluded from this coaching definition because while the instruction may be systematic, it has no time constraint. Preparation with a tutor is excluded because while it may have a time constraint, it is difficult to tell if the instruction has been systematic. This definition of the term is consistent with that used by Powers and Rock (1999) in their large scale study, and this makes any coaching effect estimated from the NELS data somewhat more comparable to their results. Also, commercial coaching is the most controversial means of test preparation because it is costly, widely available, and comes with published claims as to its efficacy. Among students in the NELS subsample who took both the PSAT and SAT, 503 (15%) indicated that they had taken a commercial course to prepare for the SAT.

Estimating a Coaching Effect by Comparing Averages

One way to estimate the effect of commercial coaching is to simply compare the average SAT scores for coached and uncoached students in the NELS subsample of 3,144 students. For the verbal section of the test (SAT-V), this difference is 23 points (470–447); for the math section of the test (SAT-M), the difference is 35 points (537–502). This simple comparison would suggest that the combined effect of coaching on the SAT is almost 60 points.

Because all the students in this subsample have also taken the PSAT, another way to estimate the effect of coaching would be to compare the relative PSAT-to-SAT score changes of coached and uncoached students.[2] This calculation is shown in table 1 and suggests that the combined coaching effect is about 39 points.

Table 1: Effects for Commercial Test Preparation

SAT PREPARATION ACTIVITY	PSAT-V	SAT-V	GAIN	EFFECT
Took Commercial Course	434	470	36	13
No Commercial Course	424	447	23	
	PSAT-M	SAT-M	Gain	Effect
Took Commercial Course	481	537	56	26
No Commercial Course	472	502	30	

N = 3,144.

There are good reasons to believe that these estimates of the combined effect are too high, as I will discuss, but for the moment we put this issue to the side. If the coaching effect is actually somewhere between 40 and 60 points, how can this be reconciled with the claims by coaching companies that gains of 100 to 140 points should be attributed to their programs?

The answer lies in the distinction between an SAT score change and a coaching effect. Figures 2 and 3 show the histograms of combined verbal and math PSAT to SAT score changes for the coached and uncoached

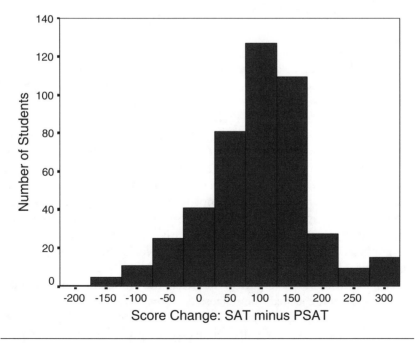

Figure 2. SAT score changes for coached students in NELS.

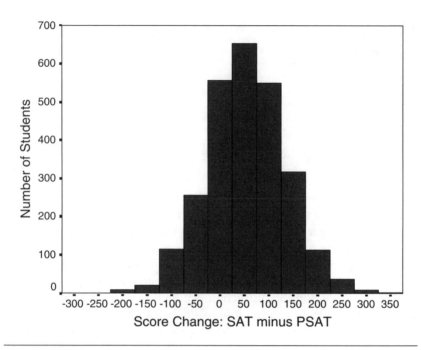

Figure 3. SAT score changes for uncoached students in NELS.

students in the NELS subsample, respectively. Figure 2 lends some support to the notion that coached students generally improve their scores by somewhere around 100 points: 53% of coached students showed gains of 100 points or more. On the other hand, figure 3 makes clear that uncoached students also tend to improve their scores significantly upon retaking the test: 30% had gains of 100 points or more. Clearly a larger proportion of coached students had big gains on the SAT than uncoached students. Part of these gains may stem from attending a coaching program, but part may just as easily stem from normal maturation or simply from taking the test more than once. The attempt to estimate an effect for coaching is the attempt to pinpoint the expected SAT score change due solely to a particular preparatory activity—in this case, enrollment in a commercial program. References to average score gains, because they do not include a control group, have an interpretation that is murky at best.

Depending upon the respective characteristics of students who have been coached and not coached, the suggested estimates for coaching effects between 40 and 60 points as presented above may still be misleading, even though they have been calculated relative to a control group. Students in the

NELS subsample have not been randomly assigned but have selected themselves into coaching programs, so there is no theoretical reason to believe that coached and uncoached groups of students are comparable. For example, if the coached students were academically stronger or more motivated than the uncoached students, then we would have expected the coached group to have done better on the SAT even if they had not received coaching. If this were the case, then estimates of coaching effects based solely on test score comparisons would be too high—in statistical jargon, the estimates would probably be "biased" upward. If, on the other hand, coached students were less motivated or academically inclined than uncoached students, then coaching effect estimates would probably be too low, or biased downward.

In many ways, coached and uncoached students are indeed quite similar on average. Contrary to the belief that there is a racial/ethnic imbalance among coached and uncoached students, the NELS data reveal no significant differences in the racial/ethnic composition of the two groups. Interestingly, there is also little to suggest that coached students as a group are academically "smarter" than uncoached students. Both groups had similar average PSAT scores, both were enrolled in college-preparatory classes during high school, and both performed about the same on standardized tests in reading and math administered as part of NELS. Finally, on average neither group seems more intrinsically motivated than the other: both report having comparable levels of self-esteem (as measured by a cluster of NELS survey items), and both report that they do about the same amount of homework per week.

There are, however, some significant differences between the two groups of students. In particular, coached students are more socioeconomically advantaged and more extrinsically motivated to take the SAT than uncoached students. Socioeconomic status (SES) is measured in the NELS database as an index value, combining information about parental education, income and occupation into a single variable. Generally, students with higher SES values come from families with parents that are better educated, wealthier and have jobs in more prestigious occupations. For the nationally representative subsample of students considered here, 72% of coached students are in the top 25% of the SES index, compared to 46% of uncoached students. With respect to variables that seem to serve as proxies for extrinsic motivation, coached students were much more likely to have been encouraged by their parents to take the SAT, and to have discussed with them their test preparation plans. Coached students are also more likely than uncoached students to have had a paid tutor that helped them with their homework during high school, and to have underachieved on the PSAT relative to their high school grade point average in math.

Given these differences between the groups, a better approach to take in estimating an effect for coaching is to compare average SAT scores while holding constant other student characteristics (e.g. SES or extrinsic motivation) that may confound the comparison. In the next section, I apply a linear regression model for this purpose.

Estimating a Coaching Effect with Linear Regression

Using linear regression, the effect of coaching can be modeled by a single equation:

$$Y = a + b_0\ COACH + b_1 X_1 + b_2 X_2 + \ldots + b_p X_p + error$$

In this equation Y denotes score values on a particular section (math or verbal) of the SAT for a given sample of test takers. The variable of interest in this equation is $COACH$, which equals 1 if a student has been coached before taking the test, and 0 otherwise. The terms "X_1" to "X_p" represent a set of variables thought to be related to performance on the SAT. They are included in the equation in order to hold constant group differences between coached and uncoached students. I refer to these as control variables. The term *error* represents the chance error that goes into each student's performance on the SAT; it is assumed to average zero across all students. The parameter a is the intercept of the equation, while the parameters b_1 to b_p indicate the association between the control variables and SAT performance. The parameter b_0 represents the effect of coaching. All parameters are estimated through linear regression by minimizing the sum over individuals of the squares of the differences,

$$Y - (\hat{a} + \hat{b}_0\ COACH + \hat{b}_1 X_1 + \hat{b}_2 X_2 + \ldots + \hat{b}_p X_p).$$

In estimating an effect of coaching on the SAT-V and SAT-M, I include 21 control variables (i.e., $p = 21$) related to demographic characteristics, academic background and student motivation. Prominent among the control variables are previous scores on both PSAT sections, the SES index variable, and high school grade point average (GPA). Given such variables, the coaching effect estimated using linear regression can be interpreted as the average SAT score change for a coached student relative to a peer with the same PSAT score, SES value, high school GPA, and so on.

Figure 4 indicates the coaching effects estimated using linear regression. The estimated effects are 11 and 19 points, respectively, on the SAT-V and SAT-M. A 95% confidence interval of 3 to 20 points for the SAT-V, and 10 to 28 points for the SAT-M, is provided around each estimate. Neither of the intervals contains the value 0, so each effect is considered statistically significant. Earlier the effect of coaching was estimated by simply taking the difference in average SAT scores for coached and uncoached students. Relative to this, controlling for the influence of other variables with linear

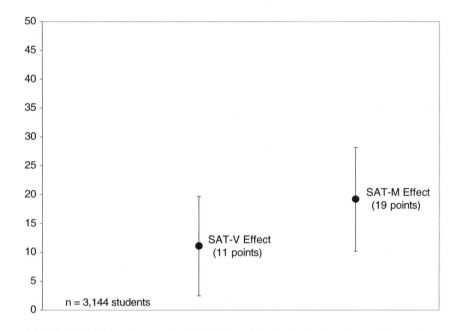

Figure 4. Estimates of coaching effects in NELS using linear regression.

regression decreases the estimated SAT-V coaching effect by 12 points, from 23 to 11, and decreases the estimated SAT-M coaching effect by 16 points, from 35 to 19.

How should these effect estimates be interpreted? We know that the average PSAT-to-SAT score gain for a coached student is about 90 points. Combining the estimated SAT-V and SAT-M effects from the linear regression model yields a total of about 30 points. It follows that one-third of the total average gain for a coached student might be reasonably attributed to having attended a commercial program; the remaining two-thirds of the score gain (60 points) might be due to other factors such as maturation, taking the test more than once, and so on.

Is Coaching More Effective for Certain Kinds of Students?

It seems reasonable to suspect that the effect of coaching might be higher or lower for certain types of students, for example, students who scored lower on the PSAT, students with better academic backgrounds, etc. To this end, I considered all possible interactions between the control variables X_1 to X_p and the variable *COACH* under the linear regression model. The results suggest that coaching may indeed be more effective for certain types of students.

For the SAT-V, there are potentially meaningful interactions between coaching and socioeconomic status, whether or not a student is Hispanic, and whether or not a student has taken an Advanced Placement (AP) course during high school. Students with high SES-index values benefit more from coaching on the SAT-V than students with low SES-index values. For example, a coached student at the high end of the SES variable would be expected to get a SAT-V effect from coaching (25 points) that is 13 points higher than the effect we would expect from a coached student somewhere in the middle of the SES variable (12 points). One explanation for this might be that high-SES students are more likely to enroll in costlier, more intensive coaching programs that are better suited to improve verbal reasoning skills. Nonetheless, the difference in estimated coaching effects for high- and low-SES students is still fairly small—roughly the equivalent of answering one more SAT-V item correctly. The linear regression model also indicates that with all else held constant, the estimated effect of coaching for Hispanic students (-18 points) is about 31 points less than that of coaching for white students (13 points), and the estimated effect for a coached student who has taken an AP course in high school (0 points) is 13 points less than the estimated effect for a coached student who has not taken an AP course (13 points). There is no obvious explanation for why coaching on the SAT-V should be less effective for Hispanic students than for white students, given that all other control variables are being held constant. This surprising finding merits further investigation. The interaction between coaching and taking an AP course suggests that the verbal reasoning strategies emphasized in coaching programs may be redundant for students who have had to prepare for the AP exam over the course of a school year.

For the SAT-M, there are interactions between coaching and school location, a student's score on the math section of the PSAT, and a student's score on the standardized math test administered as part of the NELS survey. The estimated interaction effect between coaching and school location indicates that the coaching effect for students in urban settings is about 11 points higher than the coaching effect for students in suburban settings, and about 15 points higher than the coaching effect for students in rural settings. This might be interpreted as an indication that students from schools in urban locations have access to more effective coaching programs than students in other high school settings, though again, the difference in estimated coaching effects is fairly small. Students who are above average at math, but do poorly on the PSAT-M, benefit more from coaching than students who are below average at math but do fairly well on the PSAT-M. For coached students who did very well on the NELS test (above the average score for all coached students), the estimated coaching effect is 26 points. For coached students who did more poorly on the test (below the average for all coached students), the effect is actually negative. The opposite relationship holds for coached students with respect to their prior performance on the PSAT-M. Students who did well on the PSAT-M apparently do not get the same benefit from coaching as students who did more poorly. Perhaps this latter group of students are more apt to benefit from instruction that emphasizes test-taking strategies and general "testwiseness."

A Broader Definition of Coaching

Up to this point, coaching has been defined solely as participation in a course offered by a commercial company. As we saw in figure 1, students in the NELS subsample were also asked if they had prepared for the SAT with other test preparation activities, many of which have also been classified as coaching in previous studies. Table 2 presents the percentage of students who reported that they had prepared for the SAT with each of the six possible preparatory activities. While a fairly small number of students reported having prepared for the SAT with a private tutor (7%) or video (6%), a more substantial number of students reported having taken a commercial course (15%), or a high school course (23%) or having studied with computer software (17%). More than 60% of students prepared for the test by using a book. Close to three-quarters of all students prepared for the SAT with at least one of these six activities. It is thus important to recognize that when it comes to preparing for the SAT, only a minority of students appear to do "nothing."

Coaching can be defined more broadly if we include the information about all six forms of test preparation as distinct variables in the linear regression model. Table 3 shows the estimated effects on the SAT-V and SAT-M associated with each unique form of test preparation. Preparing with a commercial course, high school course, or private tutor all have effect

Table 2: Six Forms of Preparation for the SAT

	PERCENT OF STUDENTS BY TEST PREPARATION ACTIVITY					
CATEGORY	COMMERCIAL COURSE	HIGH SCHOOL COURSE	PRIVATE TUTOR	BOOK	VIDEO	COMPUTER
0 ("no")	85	77	93	37	94	83
1 ("yes")	15	23	7	63	6	17

Note: Deletion of cases with missing data reduced the sample size from 3,144 to 3,128 students.

Table 3: Linear Regression with Broader Definition of Coaching

PREPARATORY ACTIVITY	SAT-V			SAT-M		
	EFFECT ESTIMATE	95% CONFIDENCE INTERVAL		EFFECT ESTIMATE	95% CONFIDENCE INTERVAL	
		LOWER	UPPER		LOWER	UPPER
Commercial Course	11	−1	23	20	8	32
High School Course	0	−9	9	9	0	18
Private Tutor	9	−8	25	28	10	45
Book	4	−2	10	2	−5	8
Video	3	−16	21	−4	−22	15
Computer	−9	−20	2	−7	−18	5

N = 3,128 students.

estimates that are statistically significant for the SAT-M. It appears that the single most effective way for a student to score higher on the SAT-M is by preparing with a private tutor. Of course, it is also the most expensive means of preparation, to which the fewest number of students have access.

If coaching were defined as any combination of the six possible preparatory activities, the largest coaching effect estimate is about 40 points, all else held constant, for students preparing for the SAT-M with commercial coaching and a private tutor.[3] On the SAT-V the largest estimated coaching effect is about 18 points for students preparing with a commercial course and computer software. The coaching effect does not necessarily increase with the quantity of test preparation activities. In fact, the estimated effect for a student doing all six activities (relative to a student doing no preparatory activities) is about −11 points on the SAT-V and 13 points on the SAT-M.

The Problem of Self-Selection

Should we believe the estimated effects of coaching produced by the linear regression model? One critical assumption about the model must hold: we must assume that conditional on the control variables included in the equation, the expected value of the error term across all students is zero. This is a strong assumption. In the context of coaching, we must believe that all the factors related to differences in the performance of coached and uncoached students on SAT scores have been quantified in the equation as control variables. In practice, an assumption like this will almost never be entirely met.

In this case there is some reason for optimism because the linear regression model includes control variables, (e.g. PSAT scores) that are strongly correlated to SAT performance. As a result, the variance explained by the variables in the SAT-V and SAT-M coaching regressions (R^2) is about .8, an extremely high value for social science research. With little variance in SAT scores left to predict, there is some reason to believe that the addition of omitted variables to the regression model will not dramatically change the estimated coaching effect.

An important potential source of bias in estimated coaching effects is the fact that students not only self-select whether they will be coached, but also whether they will even take the SAT. As I pointed out earlier, nearly half the students in the NELS panel sample did not take the SAT during their senior years of high school. Nonetheless, roughly 8% of these students reported that they had prepared for an admissions test by taking a commercial course, and even larger proportions reported that they had prepared with other activities. If many students decide not to take the SAT because of a negative coaching experience, leading them to believe they would perform poorly on the test, then the omission of these students might serve to bias upwards the coaching effects estimated here and in other studies.

Study Limitations

On the one hand, NELS is an ideal source of observational data for evaluating the effectiveness of coaching on standardized admissions tests. First, the data in NELS are nationally representative. Second, unlike data used in previous coaching studies, which is often exclusively student-reported, most of the NELS data on student academic performance is collected from official transcripts. There is evidence that self-reported data on student grades and test scores tend to overstate student performance (Morgan, 1989; Frucot & Cook, 1994). This criticism has been levied at the Powers and Rock study, which relied on student responses to a mailed survey for information about high school grade and course-taking patterns. Such criticism is not applicable to the NELS academic achievement and test score variables.

One limitation of this study is that the data used here are from the early 1990s, and may not reflect the state of the world more than ten years later. In addition, the NELS survey was not explicitly designed to evaluate the effectiveness of coaching on the SAT. If it had been, students would surely have been asked more detailed questions about their test-taking experiences and how they prepared for them. This is another clear limitation of this study: no information is available to shed light on the quality of test preparation activities. Since this study was first published, it has generated some responses along these lines from representatives of commercial test preparation companies. Seppy Basili, vice president for learning and assessment at Kaplan, Incorporated, was quoted in the *New York Times* as saying, "What we've seen over the past 15 years is this huge increase in weekend courses and one-day courses (Kolata, 2001, p. 16). The whole notion of grouping commercial courses with this broad brush causes a problem for us." This suggests that there are two types of commercial coaching programs offering either high- or low-quality test preparation. The proposition is that companies offering high-quality coaching for the SAT are misrepresented by the NELS data because they cannot be differentiated from companies offering low-quality coaching.

This proposition can be tested in part with the NELS data, given certain assumptions. In two different national surveys of the test preparation activities of students taking the SAT, Powers (1988; 1998) found that about 12% of all students reported that they had been coached by commercial companies. This is not far off the 15% estimate for the NELS subsample analyzed here. Of students who reported taking commercial courses in the Powers survey, 40% indicated that they had been coached specifically by one of the two largest companies offering these services: Kaplan or the Princeton Review. These percentages did not change much over the ten-year period between 1986 to 1996. It seems reasonable then to presume that about 40% of the coached students in the NELS sample were enrolled in the Kaplan or Princeton Review programs. That is, about 201 of the 503 coached students in the NELS subsample were probably coached by one of the two largest coaching companies. Both companies claim that the gains due to their coaching program are about 50 to 70 points per section. If this were true, how low would the effects for the other 302 coached students need to have been in order to arrive at the estimated SAT-V and SAT-M effects of 11 and 19 points found for the full NELS subsample?

Some quick algebra answers the question. If the SAT-V effect for just the students coached by Kaplan and the Princeton Review were actually 50 points, then to arrive at an effect estimate for all coached students of 11 points, the effect for students coached by all other programs would have to be -15 points: (i.e., solve for "Z" in $[50 \times 201 + Z \times 302])/503 = 11$). Likewise, the SAT-M effect estimate for students coached by all other programs would have to be -2 points. In other words, if the claims by Kaplan and the Princeton Review are to be believed, then the coaching effects of all other commercial companies must be *negative*—that is, students taking these courses do worse on the SAT than they would have done if they had not taken the course. Such a scenario is not impossible to imagine, but seems highly implausible.

Discussion

Does coaching have an effect on SAT performance? It seems clear that an effect does exist, but the magnitude of this effect varies somewhat as a function of the definition of coaching and the characteristics of the students. Based on the linear regression results based on the NELS data, the best guess for the effect of commercial coaching is somewhere between 3 and 20 points on the SAT-V, and between 10 and 28 points for the SAT-M. Students with high socioeconomic backgrounds who have not taken an Advanced Placement course during high school appear to benefit most from coaching on the SAT-V. Students in urban settings who are above average in math appear to benefit the most from coaching on the SAT-M. If coaching is defined more broadly as all possible combinations of six test preparation modes, the potential effect ranges from about -9 to 30 points on the SAT-V, and from about -7 to 44 points on the SAT-M. Regardless of how it is defined, coaching appears to be more effective for the SAT-M than it is for the SAT-V.

This analysis suggests rather unequivocally that the average effect of coaching is nowhere near the average gains typically promoted by commercial test preparation companies. For the average student, the combined effect of coaching is about 30 points. Whether these benefits are worth the cost—commercial programs can charge anywhere from $800 up to $3,000, while private tutors often charge as much as $450 per hour—is unclear.

From a policy standpoint, one potentially troubling finding in this study is that there seem to be a significant number of students with aspirations for a college education who select themselves out of the sample of students taking college admissions tests. Students who engage in test preparation activities but choose not to take an admission test tend to be less academically able and much less socioeconomically advantaged than their test-taking counterparts. These are not necessarily students who are unfit for college admission. Ideally, coaching should be most effective and at least readily available to these types of students, but in practice this does not seem to be the case.

It has been suggested that the benefits of coaching and private tutoring may extend beyond potential admission test score improvements by teaching students better study habits and imbuing them with greater discipline and self-confidence (Schwartz, 1999). This certainly might be the case. The data used in this analysis do not consider the potential side benefits of commercial test preparation. It is also possible that specific programs and tutors currently exist that are capable of producing higher effects than the average ones found in this study. The evidence for this however, is at best very limited, most often anecdotal, and at worst intentionally misleading.[4] In evaluating coaching claims and guarantees by commercial companies, students and parents at the very least need to ask the following question: How much better will the average student do on the SAT with company X's help than he or she would have done without it? At this point, no company can point to compelling evidence in the form of an independent, large-scale study that could give an answer to this question considerably different from the one provided here. Perhaps this suggests that the scientific burden of proof should be placed back where it belongs—on those marketing the product.

Notes

The content of this chapter is based for the most part on my doctoral dissertation, "SAT Coaching, Bias and Causal Inference," published in the fall of 2002. For a more detailed and technical presentation of the topic, the reader is encouraged to consult this manuscript, available at ProQuest (www.proquest.com) or from the author by request. An earlier version of the study, which also considered the effect of test preparation on the ACT, was published in the winter 2001 issue of *Chance* magazine (Briggs, 2001).

1. Prior to 1994, the SAT I was known simply as the SAT. The data used in this study come from before 1994, so for the sake of consistency I refer to the test generically as the SAT throughout.

2. Note that it would be preferable to have data on students who had taken the SAT twice when considering score changes. Instead, PSAT scores (also referred to as PSAT/NMSQT scores) are

used as proxies for SAT scores. This is reasonable since the PSAT is very similar in structure to the SAT, with verbal and math sections containing multiple-choice questions. The scores of students on each section of the PSAT have a very high correlation (almost .9) with their scores on the corresponding sections of the SAT. Because PSAT scores range from 20 to 80 points, previous studies have compared raw scores from the PSAT to SAT by multiplying PSAT scores by 10. The same tactic is used here.

3. When coaching is defined as the combination of different preparatory activities, the estimated effect is the sum of the individual main effects along with the corresponding interaction effect. Only the main effects are shown in table 3.

4. For an informative and entertaining look at the misleading nature of many commercial coaching claims, see Smyth, 1990.

References

Becker, B. J. (1990). "Coaching for the Scholastic Aptitude Test: Further synthesis and appraisal." *Review of Educational Research, 60(3)*, 373–417.

Briggs, D. C. (2001). "The effect of admissions test preparation: Evidence from NELS:88." *Chance, 14(1)*, 10–18.

Briggs, D. C. (2002). "SAT Coaching, Bias and Causal Inference." Ph.D. diss., University of California, Berkeley.

DerSimonian, R., and N. M. Laird (1983). "Evaluating the effect of coaching on SAT scores: A meta-analysis." *Harvard Educational Review, 53*, 1–15.

Frucot, V., and Cook, G. (1994). Further research on the accuracy of students' self-reported grade point averages, SAT scores, and course grades. *Perceptual and Motor Skills, 79*, 743–46.

Kolata, G. (2001). Admissions test courses help, but not so much, study finds. *New York Times*, March 25, p. 16.

Messick, S., and A. Jungeblut (1981). Time and method in coaching for the SAT. *Psychological Bulletin, 89*, 191–216.

Morgan, R. (1989). *Analyses of the predictive validity of the SAT and high school grades from 1976 to 1985* College Board Report 89-7. New York: College Board.

Powers, D. E. (1988). *Preparing for the SAT: A survey of programs and resources*. Princeton, NJ: Educational Testing Service.

Powers, D. E. (1998). *Preparing for the SAT I: Reasoning Test—An update*. New York: College Board.

Powers, D. E., and D. A. Rock (1999). "Effects of Coaching on SAT I: Reasoning Test Scores." *Journal of Educational Measurement, 36(2)*, 93–118.

Schwartz, T. (1999). The test under stress. *New York Times*, January 10, sec. 6, p. 30.

Smyth, F. L. (1990). "SAT Coaching: What really happens and how we are led to expect more." *Journal of College Admissions, 129*, 7–17.

Commentary on Part III: Differential Achievement: Seeking Causes, Cures, and Construct Validity

MICHAEL E. MARTINEZ

The four chapters in this section document the pervasiveness of the achievement gap, especially its manifestations in college matriculation, success, and graduation. The papers explore possible causes of the gap, and consider what can be done to combat longstanding disparities among population groups identified by race and ethnicity. All four papers implicitly reject simplistic arguments that find obvious villains and straightforward prescriptions. They scrutinize the proposal that academic aptitude, as indexed by the SAT I, directly reinforces (if not causes) differential achievement, and that if academic aptitude were replaced with something else, then significant strides could be made toward parity in college success and other outcomes of interest. Collectively, the authors dismiss this thesis and, instead, implicitly advance two major themes: (1) the achievement gap among racial/ethnic and socioeconomic groups is pervasive over many cognitive outcomes, including academic achievement; and (2) the achievement gap is complexly determined and does not admit to simple policy solutions; instead, its causes reflect disparities in the quality of school experiences, as well as differences in experience in nonschool environments. My commentary on the four papers will follow a two-part organization based on these two themes. The conclusion I derive is that our models for understanding and predicting academic success are weak, and this weakness bears directly on the construct validity of admissions testing instruments. Moreover, improved understanding of the psychological construct of academic readiness can elevate the predictive power of measures as well as inform the design of experience to promote readiness.

The Achievement Gap Is Pervasive

The paper by Rebecca Zwick, "Is the SAT a Wealth Test?" asks whether the SAT I is a protector of socioeconomic privilege in college admissions. If the SAT is a wealth test, then if it were dismantled, the college admissions process would be fairer and yield more equitable outcomes. The existence of a strong statistical relationship between the SAT I and family wealth gives the argument some credibility and is one rationale for shifting University of California admissions criteria toward achievement testing in academic subjects. A shift to achievement measures makes sense if subject-matter achievement is less a proxy for wealth than are general academic aptitudes. The trouble with this argument, as Zwick shows, is that school achievement is as highly correlated with socioeconomic status (SES) as are more general aptitude constructs. Both the aptitude-oriented SAT I and the achievement-based SAT II writing and math tests are associated with family wealth to about the same degree. Zwick's analysis shows that introducing SES-related variables into a regression equation to predict UC freshman grade point average affects the coefficients of the SAT I and SAT II in similar ways.

Zwick shows that not only the SAT II, but also many important measures of academic achievement, are about as strongly correlated with SES variables as are the SAT I and SAT II. Student achievement indices—such as the ACT Composite, the California High School Exit Exam, the NAEP Mathematics Assessment, and high school grades—are all substantially linked to SES. The obvious conclusion is that to look to school achievement variables in the hope that they will be uncontaminated by variation in family wealth is wrongheaded. Stated another way, academic achievement is every bit as enmeshed in robust differential outcomes as are the typical "culprit" variables, including SES and general academic aptitude. These correlations are most directly interpreted as yet another manifestation of the nefarious and multifarious achievement gap. Accordingly, achievement measures are not a promising basis on which to promote more equitable college admissions outcomes.

Amy Elizabeth Schmidt and Wayne Camara, and to a degree Patricia Gándara, build largely the same case as does Zwick. Schmidt and Camara present data that testify to substantial racial/ethnic group differences on academic admissions tests, such as the SAT and the ACT, on high school and college grades, and on standardized measures of school achievement, such as the NAEP mathematics assessment. Large group differences also appear on college persistence and graduation rates. The authors show that group gaps are not static over decades. Differences in achievement between racial/ethnic groups have decreased overall since the mid-1960s, although those gaps appear to have widened somewhat starting about 1992. Even the recent regressive trend is not uniform across indicators, however: Minority students now constitute a larger portion of college-bound students (33%) than anytime in the past.

In a way, it is too bad that the SAT I is not the obvious and exclusive villain. If it were, then conceptualizing the sources of and solutions to the achievement gap would be straightforward. Zwick's conclusion: "It's a sad reality that inequities in educational opportunity seem to make it impossible to find a measure of academic achievement that is unrelated to family income or ethnic background." This conclusion should not squelch discussion of the relative merits of achievement or ability testing, nor should it exonerate large-scale tests of possible unfairness or bias. But the conclusion does direct attention to larger, more pervasive, and more complex causes of differential achievement. This leads to the second major strand of thought in this collection of papers.

The Underlying Causes of Differential Achievement Are Complex

None of the papers' authors accepts a simple explanation or easy solution to the problem of differential academic outcomes—in particular, to differential outcomes in college admissions and success. The authors recognize that if the underlying causes of inequality are complex, then necessarily so must be the solutions. One direction to look for possible causes is toward systematic differences in the quality of schooling. Another possible source is unequal access to admissions-test coaching. Still, the authors know that differences in quality of schooling or access to test preparation do not exhaust the possible sources of inequality. Rather, inequality extends to the numerous and diverse aspects of experience that span the age range and involve both school and nonschool settings. Inequality is everywhere and always. It is deeply rooted socially and economically, and in the cumulative experience of the individual child.

Differential Quality of Schooling

Three of the papers—those of Zwick, Camara and Schmidt, and Gándara—direct some blame for inequality of college-going outcomes toward inequitable variation in the quality of precollege education. Straightforward manifestations of inequality are differences in the quality of teachers and in courses offered at the high school level. Zwick shows, for example, that poorer schools are much more likely than are wealthy schools to have noncredentialed and less-experienced teachers. Teachers matter; so do courses. Gándara points to substantial discrepancies among high schools in terms of course offerings, particularly courses that are required for UC admissions. As Gándara indicates, the opportunity to take rigorous coursework reduces gaps in achievement. Schmidt and Camara also acknowledge that group differences are traceable, in part, to disparate course-taking patterns. Differences in the quality of school experience are surely important in accounting for differential achievement by race and subculture.

Other Experiential Factors

Schmidt and Camara show that group differences are related to parental education and family income. They also note that this is not a complete explanation: Controlling for these variables reduces, but does not eliminate, racial/ethnic group differences. The authors cite other differences in typical experience that are likely to underlie differential achievement outcomes but are harder to measure. These factors include depth of instruction and level of support in the school and at home. Zwick also points to typical differences in home environments related to family wealth. For example, middle-class parents are more likely to read to their children than are poorer parents (see Hart & Risley, 1995). If differential achievement reflects differences in experience broadly conceived, then elucidating those differences in the daily, proximal experience of the child must be a long-term project for the education research community. There is hardly a more compelling research question.

Programs Designed to Boost College Success

If extracurricular experience can help to explain inequality, it also holds promise to correct it. In that vein, Gándara's paper appraises the effectiveness of programs designed to increase underrepresented students' matriculation into, and success in, college. In surveying programs designed to increase minority participation in higher education, Gándara finds that the best interventions can actually double college-going rates. The most effective programs tend to have certain key features. These include a mentoring aspect, high-quality instruction linked to challenging courses, long-term investments (including financial investments) in students, and efforts to stem attrition from programs. Gándara notes, however, that although such programs can increase rates of college going, rarely do they affect rates of matriculation into *selective* four-year institutions to any significant degree.

Neither are these programs particularly effective at actually closing the gap in academic achievement per se, between program participants and white or Asian-American students. Program attrition is also a problem. Yet another difficulty is that such programs are not particularly good at reaching male minority students—whom Gándara calls "the most important target population" because they are most poorly represented in postsecondary education.

Gándara recognizes that efforts to prepare students for college must begin "long before they begin high school." Accordingly, she is not optimistic that removal of the SAT I from the college admissions process would redress inequities in college admissions. Such differences are the result, she maintains, of fundamental inequities in our educational system. Any efficacious reversal of inequities will likely involve smartly conceived interventions along a broad front. In the long run, Schmidt and Camara advocate a policy of "affirmative development" that recognizes the importance of long-term preparation in multiple contexts: school, home, and community.

Coaching for Admissions Tests

The paper by Derek Briggs addresses whether differential racial/ethnic and socioeconomic representation in selective colleges is significantly an expression of unequal access to coaching for admissions tests. Briggs examines specifically the effects of coaching on the SAT I. At issue here is not whether coaching has an effect on scores—it does. What is contentious is the typical size of the coaching effect. Naturally, providers of coaching services claim large effects. Tutors, for example, sometimes claim improvements of 200 points or more on the combined SAT. Commercial test preparation companies claim benefits of 100 points or more. At first glance, these claims seem to be consistent with available data: gains of 100 to 150 points are in fact not uncommon for coached students. In his paper, Briggs marshals evidence that challenges the validity of these prima facie conclusions.

Crucial to Briggs's argument is that *uncoached* students also make gains on the SAT, although smaller ones than do coached students. Gains for uncoached students average about 50 points. The question is, What part of SAT gains is attributable to coaching, and what portion results from other factors, such as maturation or practice? Briggs tries to answer this using regression analysis to cut through the jungle of confounds.

Briggs employs the National Educational Longitudinal Study (NELS) database, which includes both Preliminary SAT/National Merit Scholarship Qualifying Test (PSAT/NMSQT) scores and SAT scores, as well as data on whether students received some form of coaching. Briggs transformed PSAT/NMSQT scores so that they are on the same scale as the SAT (mean = 500; sd = 100 for each test; therefore, a combined mean of 1000). Briggs then subtracted the rescaled PSAT/NMSQT score from the SAT to produce an index of change. For coached students, the distribution of score change (SAT minus PSAT/NMSQT) is concentrated between −150 and +300, with an average gain of 100 points. Are coaching services responsible for these gains? No, not entirely, because both coached and uncoached students typically make gains. When these two groups are contrasted, Briggs finds a coaching benefit of only 13 points on the SAT-V (verbal) and 26 points on the SAT-M (mathematical), for a total effect of 39 points. Moreover, because coached and uncoached students are "self-selected" and therefore not strictly comparable, it is possible that the background characteristics of the coached students—such as stronger motivation or greater family wealth—might have led to higher scores even if the students had not received coaching. Coached and uncoached students are similar on certain background variables (e.g., PSAT/NMSQT scores, race/ethnicity), but not all. Notably, coached students are higher in SES, on average.

Using regression analysis to control 21 background variables, Briggs attempted to make a fair estimate of a coaching effect. Briggs's expressed goal was to estimate an average effect for a coached student "relative to a peer with the same PSAT score, SES value, high school GPA, etc." Controlling for background variables, Briggs found a modest effect of 11 points and 19 points for the SAT-V and the SAT-M, respectively, with total effect of about 30 points. Along with this overall effect, Briggs identified some interactions that complicate the picture. For example, the coaching effect on the SAT-V for high-SES students is about 25 points, much higher than the average adjusted effect of 11 points. Briggs notes one possible explanation—that high-SES students might be in a position to purchase more intensive preparation programs, which are more effective in boosting verbal scores. There is also a significant interaction between school location (urban, suburban, rural) and the effect of coaching on the SAT-M. Urban students benefit most, rural students least. Another finding that complicates the picture is a puzzling result for Hispanic students. Briggs found a coaching effect of −18 points on the SAT-V. How does one account for significantly negative effects of coaching on scores?

Briggs's analysis is illuminating and rightly makes the reader skeptical about the vaunted claims of coaching services. However, even the modest adjusted effect of coaching on the SAT composite, 30 points, may be important for some students. For students on the threshold of admissibility to the University of California, 30 points would amount to a boost of about 3 percentile points—not much, but possibly enough to tip the balance toward a favorable result. The exceptions or qualifications to the general pattern of modest positive effects for coaching on the SAT are also germane to whether coaching makes a difference on admissions decisions. For high-SES and urban students, for example, the expected effect of coaching is higher than the average effect of 30 points.

How do these findings, along with what is known about the cost of coaching for college admissions tests, bear on questions of equity? The cost of coaching services is obviously relevant. Some forms of coaching— commercial courses and tutoring especially—are expensive. An expenditure of many hundreds of dollars is absolutely prohibitive for some families and trivial for others. As for the effectiveness of coaching in boosting SAT scores, it is true the Briggs's regression analyses lead to the conclusion that it is unrealistic to expect coaching to have very large effects. On the other hand, the expected modest benefits of coaching might make a difference to the admissibility of some students, perhaps especially to high-SES students. That possibility, combined with the high cost of some forms of coaching, does present enduring concerns about equity.

Conclusions

In the polemic attendant to educational inequality, castigations of the SAT I and other general aptitude measures might amount to no more than benignly misguided stone throwing. More seriously, though, they direct attention away from the substantive causes of inequality and hamper progress toward finding solutions. One question that might help us find more adequate answers is, What factors in the total experience of the child are educative in terms of enhancing learning outcomes? Relevant factors must include school quality and home environment, but each of these, too, is complex. School factors can include, for example, the quality of teachers and teaching, access to resources such as books and information technology devices, a peer culture that values academic achievement, and physical and emotional safety.

In my view, Zwick's attention to differences in quality of school and home experience are warranted because they believably account for inequities. Significant home factors might include the presence of books, the depth and frequency of intellectually stimulating conversations, positive beliefs and aspirations about what is achievable academically, and parental or sibling support on homework or long-term projects. Early experience is also likely to be crucial. Even prenatally, optimal nutrition, protection from toxins (e.g., alcohol, nicotine, drugs) and disease, and access to medical care are also possibly key factors. Differences among students in more proximal experience are deeply connected to economic inequalities that are, in turn, associated with social policy and law. To make progress in addressing one of society's most pernicious problems, easy answers must be rejected not only by scholars accustomed to the complexity of causation in the social reality, but also in messages sent to the broader public. It must be widely understood that the inequality that is manifest in academic and social outcomes can be explained adequately only by recognizing a multitude of causes reflecting pervasive inequality of experience. Only a sustained inquiry will reveal it, and only a battery of honed corrective efforts will cure it.

These conclusions all connect to the psychometric consideration of construct validity. Our coarse theories of preparedness for college success now include a rather basic distinction between ability (aptitude) and achievement, but it should widen to consider diverse aspects of readiness for college, both cognitive and noncognitive. I refer to a sense of aptitude that embraces personal qualities that are not strictly intellective, but that also includes components of emotion, volition, values, habits, and beliefs, among others (Snow, 1989). A complete theory requires an understanding of the relevant repertoire of dispositions that make for success in admission to college, and success in the university and beyond.

To be clear: readiness to succeed in the university is not yet understood, a fact acknowledged by Schmidt and Camara. We might have limited success in predicting important outcomes (e.g., freshman grade point average) by rough-and-ready empiricism, but our theory is poor. To make larger gains we need to peel back the identity of the intended construct (Cronbach & Meehl, 1955). Explication of a fuller construct would have value not only for providing assurance of test quality, it could also guide the design of education of a far more effective and fair sort than we now have. A strong theoretical understanding of what it takes to be successful in the academy could guide test construction, and could have even more important effects in the design of educational experience. Validity research is research that can inform education practice powerfully, not simply assure consumers that tests have passable technical quality (Messick, 1988).

Notwithstanding decades of research on admissions testing, explication of the full construct of college readiness has barely begun. Full construct explication will require effort over decades and is likely never to be achieved fully. The problem is to understand what personal qualities make for academic success and how those can be cultivated. The concern here is larger than the short term, but important, policy dilemmas involving the SAT I and SAT II. The larger and more difficult problem is one whose solution will depend on reconceptualizing the entire enterprise of academic readiness and the meaning of education. It will involve sustained inquiry into what qualities, cognitive and otherwise, constitute preparedness for success in the academy, on the job, and in life—and the range of experiences that produce those qualities.

References

Cronbach, L. J., & Meehl, P. E. (1955). Construct validity in psychological tests. *Psychological Bulletin, 52*, 281–302.

Hart, B., & Risley, T. R. (1995). *Meaningful differences in the everyday experience of young American children.* Baltimore: Brookes.

Messick, S. (1988). *Testing to facilitate, not just to forecast success: Implications of new developments in measurement and cognitive science for the admissions process.* Paper presented at the annual meeting of the Graduate Management Admissions Council, San Francisco.

Snow, R. E. (1989). Toward assessment of cognitive and conative structures in learning. *Educational Researcher, 18(9)*, 8–14.

The Predictive Value of Admissions Tests: How Well Do Tests Predict Academic Success for Students from a Variety of Backgrounds?

Part IV includes research contributions concerning the predictive effectiveness of admissions tests, as well as chapters about alternatives to current admissions procedures. The final paper presents the position of an opponent of standardized testing.

The first two chapters of part IV, contributed by researchers from the College Board and Educational Testing Service, respectively, report on studies that compare the effects of using the SAT I: Reasoning Test and the SAT II: Subject Tests as admissions criteria. While the SAT I is a test of verbal and mathematical reasoning abilities, the SAT II exams, which are available in 22 subjects, measure knowledge in specific areas, including writing, math, science, and foreign languages. Using data from California and from the nation as a whole, Jennifer L. Kobrin, Wayne J. Camara, and Glenn B. Milewski show that in terms of the scores they obtain, "Hispanics benefit the most from the SAT II. . . ." Hispanic applicants who take a language test perform especially well. The authors also consider the effectiveness of the SAT I and the SAT II in predicting freshman college grade point average (GPA). They show that the "SAT II tests have marginally greater predictive validity for predicting first-year college GPA than the SAT I for ethnic groups other than American Indian and black." They also conclude that, in data from four University of California campuses, "the predictive validity of the

SAT II for Hispanic students is lower than that for any of the other racial/ethnic groups."

In their chapter, Brent Bridgeman, Nancy Burton, and Frederick Cline examine the impact of substituting SAT II tests for the SAT I on the ethnic composition and freshman grades of the entering class. In their study, students at ten colleges were treated as though they were applicants in order to simulate the effects of various admissions criteria. The top two-thirds of "applicants" at each college were selected using a composite that included high school GPA along with either scores on the SAT I verbal and math tests or the average score on the SAT II tests taken by the candidates. The authors found that, for 86% of "applicants," the selection decision was the same under the two admissions strategies, and that the two models were equally likely to produce successful students (defined as those with freshman GPAs of at least 2.5). Application of the SAT II model, however, led to the selection of a notably higher proportion of Mexican-American and other Latino students, and a slightly lower proportion of white and Asian-American students. Among Mexican-American and other Latino students who took the SAT II Spanish test, the admissions model based on the SAT II led to the selection of almost twice as many students as the rule using the SAT I. However, those selected with the SAT I criterion were more likely to earn a freshman GPA of at least 2.5. The authors note that, because "language tests taken by native speakers . . . reflect a different kind of achievement than mastery of school-based subjects, some have argued that language tests . . . give an unfair advantage to the native speakers of the foreign languages. . . . However, a counterargument suggests that the supposed advantage may only partially compensate for . . . the disadvantages that nonnative speakers of English have on . . . other subject tests. . . ." Also, the authors point out, foreign language skills might be valued in their own right, regardless of where they were learned or whether they predict freshman grades.

John W. Young's chapter is a review of 25 years of research on the ways in which the predictive effectiveness of the SAT varies among racial groups, and between men and women. Young reports that in general, both SAT scores and high school GPA are more highly correlated with freshman GPA for Asian-American and white students than for African-American and Hispanic students. Young suggests that traditional admissions measures and college grades may more accurately reflect the capabilities of some ethnic groups than of others. Young also reports on the phenomena known in the literature as overprediction and underprediction. When regression analysis, a standard statistical procedure, is applied to a particular entering class to determine how well admissions test scores and high school GPA predict freshman college GPA, certain patterns of systematic errors in prediction are sometimes found. For some student groups, the regression equation tends to predict higher freshman GPAs than are actually earned; for other groups, the reverse is true. Young notes that a recurrent finding is the overprediction of freshman GPA for African-American and Hispanic students: the actual grades for these students are lower than the predicted grades. Young notes that one explanation for this finding is that "some students may face extraordinary difficulties in acclimating to the college environment, resulting in lower earned grades than would be expected."

Comparison of prediction results for men and women has shown that, except in the most selective institutions, both test scores and high school grades are more highly correlated with freshman GPA for women than for men. In general, however, these traditional admissions measures tend to underpredict the grades of college women, though this is less so at selective institutions. Young points out that this pattern of results is likely to be a result of greater stringency in grading in the sciences than in other fields: "Since women are more likely to choose courses and majors in the humanities and social sciences and men are more likely to choose courses and majors in the natural sciences and engineering, the net effect of these choices is to raise women's grades and to lower men's grades."

Young makes several recommendations for admissions policy. Because evidence "demonstrates that the traditional admissions predictors ... are less informative and less accurate regarding first-year college grades for African-American and Hispanic students than for Asian-American and white students, it would appear that these students can benefit from a more holistic admissions process such as the comprehensive review of applicants recently implemented by the University of California." Because "the grades of men in college depend less on prior academic credentials than is true for women," he makes a similar recommendation for men. Finally, Young calls for additional research on the underprediction of college grades for women.

The chapter by Julie Noble is unique among the contributions to this book in that it pertains to the ACT rather than to the SAT. The purpose of her study, which was based on over 400,000 ACT test takers, was "to investigate differential prediction *and* the differential effects on African-American, Hispanic, and white students of using ACT Composite scores, high school averages, or both for making non-race-based admissions decisions." (The ACT Composite score is the sum of the scores on the four sections of the ACT: English, mathematics, reading, and science reasoning.) Logistic regression, a statistical method used to predict binary outcomes, was used to estimate the probability of obtaining a freshman GPA of 2.5 or higher, using either ACT scores, high school GPA, or both. (As in the Bridgeman et al. study, students achieving a GPA of at least 2.5 were considered "successful.") Noble then estimated, for each ethnic group, the admission rate and the percentage of decisions that were accurate in determining whether the student would be successful.

Noble found that whether admissions decisions were based on high school grades, ACT scores, or both, fewer African-American and Hispanic "applicants" than whites were selected. Also, among those selected for admission, Hispanic and African-American students had lower ACT scores and high school grades than white students. Finally, "for a given ACT Composite score or high school average, African-American students typically had a lower probability for obtaining a 2.5 or higher GPA, relative to Caucasian-American students. . . ." The same pattern held for Hispanic students relative to white students, though the discrepancies were not as large. Interestingly, Noble also found that ACT scores and high school grades were more accurate predictors of the attainment of a freshman GPA of at least 2.5 for African Americans than for white students. The accuracy for Hispanics, however, was lower than that for whites.

Noble concludes that "postsecondary institutions are in a quandary. Diversity . . . is an important part of their mission, but in order to achieve it, institutions might rely less on standardized test scores for college admissions. In so doing, they would admit students who may be less well prepared academically to do college-level work."

In his chapter, Roger E. Studley proposes a method for admitting a socioeconomically and ethnically diverse student population without explicitly considering race. In Studley's conceptualization, a college applicant's academic achievement is influenced by two sets of factors—the student's underlying ability and motivation and economic and social circumstances. A student's *potential* achievement is the maximum achievement he could attain if circumstances were optimal. Studley explores the possibility of admitting students based on their estimated potential achievement rather than their realized achievement. To do so, he conducts analyses intended to adjust SAT scores and high school GPA for the effects of "circumstance," as measured by family income, education, and language characteristics; home zip code; and high school attended. These adjustments have the effect of reducing performance disparities among ethnic groups. Studley then simulates the effects of an admissions model based on the adjusted versions of SAT scores and high school GPAs, called the "underlying ability" policy, and compares it to a model based on a traditional SAT-GPA index, and a third "affirmative action" model that selects those who rank most highly on the traditional achievement index within their own ethnic groups. The "underlying ability" policy was found to select an entering class whose income distribution was nearly identical to that of the California high school population. In addition, black and Hispanic students were better represented than in the actual group of students admitted to the University of California. The average SAT score for those admitted under the "underlying ability" policy was essentially the same as the average for the actual UC admits, and the average high school GPA was slightly higher. Studley concludes that "an admissions policy that systematically accounts for circumstance holds promise as a feasible, fair, and effective remedy for socioeconomic and ethnic disparity in college admissions."

In the book's final chapter, Christina Perez, a testing reform advocate at the National Center for Fair and Open Testing (FairTest), addresses the possibility of eliminating admissions tests entirely. "Why any test at all?" she asks. As she points out, "[p]ublic debate has largely focused on the question of *which* admission tests to use rather then *whether or not* any exam is needed." Noting that "nearly 400 colleges and universities [have eliminated] test score requirements for a substantial number of their applicants," Perez argues that the SAT has weak predictive power, "offers little information on long-term success in college. . . . does not accurately reflect the capabilities of females, students of color, and older applicants," and can hinder educational equity. Furthermore, she notes, the effects of test coaching can exacerbate the score gaps among socioeconomic groups. She points out that high school grades are ordinarily found to be stronger predictors of freshman GPA than are test scores, and also remarks on the utility of the rigor of the high school curriculum, class rank, interviews, personal essays, extracurricular activities, and socioeconomic background as admissions criteria. Perez concludes by asserting that the "broader goal of higher education—to provide opportunities to students from diverse backgrounds—is severely truncated by the employment of test scores." "Shifts in admissions policies from one test score requirement to another," she says, "will simply uphold the faulty paradigm that test scores equal merit. . . ."

Robert L. Linn opens his commentary on part IV by remarking that "[l]iterally thousands of analyses involving millions of students have been conducted by ACT, Inc. and the College Board, using tests and high school grades as predictors of success at individual colleges and universities." But, Linn points out, the political climate in which these studies are to be interpreted has changed as a result of two major developments: the elimination by some states of affirmative action policies in college admissions and the broader legal challenges to these programs, and UC President Richard C. Atkinson's proposal that the SAT I be phased out as an admissions criterion. Linn notes that Perez and Studley offer different approaches to addressing today's admissions challenges. Although "Perez claims that holistic evaluations of student records without test scores work well to achieve diversity regardless of the size or selectivity of the institution," he says, "she does not present evidence to support this claim. . . . Nor is it clear that such an approach avoids the introduction of subjective biases . . . or that it leads to the selection of underrepresented minority students who are best prepared to be academically successful." Linn labels Studley's statistical approach for achieving diversity without explicitly considering race as "quite promising and worthy of serious consideration." The chapters in this section, Linn concludes, "present a number of important findings and perspectives on the prediction of success in college for students from a variety of backgrounds."

The Utility of the SAT I and SAT II for Admissions Decisions in California and the Nation

JENNIFER L. KOBRIN
WAYNE J. CAMARA
GLENN B. MILEWSKI

Introduction

The validity of the SAT I for predicting college performance has been widely studied (see, e.g., Bridgeman, McCamley-Jenkins, & Ervin, 2000; and Ramist, Lewis, & McCamley-Jenkins, 1994). A recent meta-analysis of approximately 3,000 studies of the predictive validity of the SAT I involving over one million students found that this test is a valid predictor of performance early in college, with multiple correlations of the SAT I Verbal and Math Composite with freshman college grade point average (FGPA) ranging from .44 to .62 (Hezlett et al., 2001). This same study found that the SAT I is also a valid predictor of academic performance later in college (e.g., graduation, cumulative grade point average) with multiple correlations ranging from the mid-30s to the mid-40s.

While the SAT I has been the focus of thousands of validity studies, the SAT II Subject Tests (hereinafter referred to as the SAT II) have not enjoyed this same amount of attention. Approximately 60 institutions of higher education require the SAT II for admissions in addition to the SAT I. About 100 additional institutions highly recommend the SAT II for admissions or placement of incoming students. The majority of these institutions are competitive institutions, and therefore students taking the SAT II tests are typically more able (e.g., they have better high school grades, take more rigorous high school courses, and have higher SAT I scores and higher freshmen grades) than the average student completing the SAT I. The largest institution using the SAT II is the University of California (UC), which currently requires all applicants to submit three SAT II scores, including the Writing test, a math test (Math IC or IIC), and a third test of the applicant's choice.

The SAT I is a three-hour test that measures verbal and mathematical reasoning abilities that students develop over time, both in and out of school. The test's content and format reflect accepted educational standards and practices, which emphasize critical thinking and problem-solving skills that are essential for college-level work. The SAT II tests are one-hour tests designed to measure knowledge in specific subject areas and the student's ability to apply that knowledge. There are 22 SAT II tests that cover English, history/social studies, mathematics, science, and foreign languages. These tests are independent of particular textbooks or methods of instruction, but the content evolves to reflect current trends in high school curricula.

In the year 2000, the most popular SAT II test, the Writing Test, was taken by 217,179 college-bound seniors, while as few as 465 students took the Italian-language SAT II test. During that same year, more than four times as many students (1,072,577) took the SAT I (The College Board, 2000). The SAT I and SAT II tests are reported on the same score scale so that scores on the tests may be compared. In 2000, the mean SAT I score was 505 for the Verbal Test and 514 for the Math Test. Because a smaller and more able group of students take the SAT II tests, the means on these tests are higher than the SAT I, ranging from 576 (Writing) to 745 (Chinese Listening) in the year 2000.

A recent report by Leonard Ramist, Charles Lewis, and Laura McCamley-Jenkins (2001) examined the predictive validity of 14 of the SAT II tests in predicting college grades alone and in combination with high school grade point average (HSGPA) and SAT I for entering freshmen at 39 colleges. The authors used multiple regression analysis, the most common method for studying predictive validity. The results indicated that HSGPA was a better predictor of FGPA, while the SAT I was a better predictor of individual college course grades. The correlations of SAT I Verbal and Math, the average of SAT II tests taken, and HSGPA with FGPA were generally higher for female students than for male. Among the ethnic groups, white and Asian-American students had higher correlations and American Indian students had lower correlations. Among the three main predictors (HSGPA, SAT I and SAT II average), HSGPA had the highest correlation for American Indian, Hispanic, and white students, and the SAT II average had the highest correlation for Asian and African-American students.

Ramist, Lewis, and McCamley-Jenkins (2001) also examined the predictive validity of the SAT II and the over- and underprediction of FGPA by subgroups, including those of gender, language, and ethnicity. Overprediction means that a group's average predicted FGPA, based on an overall regression equation, is greater than its average actual FGPA, and underprediction means that a group's average predicted FGPA is lower than its average actual FGPA. Using the average SAT II score as the predictor of FGPA, female students were slightly underpredicted ($-.05$) and male students were slightly overpredicted (.06). Underprediction occurred for Asian Americans ($-.05$) and whites ($-.02$), while overprediction occurred for American Indians (.23), African Americans (.26), and Hispanics (.23). However, these findings differed, sometimes substantially, across the different SAT II tests.

The Predictive Validity of SAT I versus SAT II

A question frequently asked is whether the SAT I and SAT II provide similar predictive information; that is, do the two tests contribute uniquely to the prediction of college achievement? This question has been addressed to some degree, but there is a need for additional research. Saul Geiser and Roger Studley (2001) analyzed the relative contribution of HSGPA, SAT I, and SAT II scores for predicting college success for freshmen who entered the University of California from fall 1996 to fall 1999. They found that SAT II scores were the single best predictor of FGPA, and that SAT I scores added little to the prediction once SAT II scores and HSGPA were already considered.

Geiser and Studley combined three SAT II scores into a single composite variable that weights each SAT II test equally. While applicants to UC are all required to submit scores from the SAT II Writing test, they may choose to submit scores from either of the two SAT II Math tests (Math IC or Math IIC), and any third SAT II test. The two SAT II Math Tests differ in content coverage and test difficulty (Math IIC is more difficult than Math IC). Among other SAT II tests that may be submitted as the third test,[1] differences in subject, content, test-taking populations, and difficulty are even more substantial. Ramist, Lewis, and McCamley-Jenkins (2001) reported correlations of each individual SAT II test with FGPA ranging from .17 (German or Spanish) to .58 (Math IIC or Chemistry), showing that the predictive effectiveness of the various SAT II tests varies greatly, with some of the language tests showing the least predictive validity. The

SAT II tests also differ in incremental validity (the degree to which including the test improves predictive power, after SAT I and HSGPA have already been considered). These differences may appear across cohorts of students with different backgrounds (e.g., different ethnicity/race, socioeconomic status). When student choice is involved in selecting tasks within a test or among available tests, differences between students or groups of students may be due not only to differences in achievement, but to the ability to accurately select among tasks or tests on which one is most likely to succeed.

Geiser and Studley (2001) reported only the uncorrected correlations between individual tests or composite tests (e.g., SAT I Verbal and Math, or three SAT II tests) with FGPA.[2] However, Ramist, Lewis, and McCamley-Jenkins (2001), who did provide corrected correlations, reached similar conclusions. They found that the SAT I added little to the prediction of FGPA when HSGPA and the SAT II were used, and that the SAT II added little to the prediction once HSGPA and the SAT I were already considered. The incremental validity of the SAT II over HSGPA was similar to that of the SAT I over HSGPA (the increase in the multiple correlation was .09 versus .08).

In a similar study, Brent Bridgeman, Nancy Burton, and Frederick Cline (2001; see also their chapter in this volume) compared the predictive efficacy of SAT I and SAT II. They noted that the SAT II increment over HSGPA is slightly larger than the increment from the SAT I because it is the composite of three distinct tests while SAT I is the composite of only two tests. Using the same data employed in the present study from four UC institutions, they compared regression results from three SAT II tests to the two SAT I tests and the third SAT II test. They reported that with just two SAT II tests in the model (in addition to HSGPA), "predictions are virtually the same whether the two tests are SAT I Verbal and Math or SAT II Writing and Math (the R-squares are .236 and .237 respectively). The increment for the third test is also essentially the same (.007 and .008 respectively)" (2001, p. 4). They also found similar results for six non-UC campuses and concluded that from a purely predictive perspective, SAT I Verbal and Math scores are about as effective as SAT II Writing and Math scores, and including a third SAT II test is responsible for the slight increase in prediction obtained when the SAT II composite is used.

In their study, Bridgeman, Burton, and Cline conducted a simulation to determine what would happen if SAT II composite scores were used in place of SAT I to make college selection decisions. While success rates in terms of freshman grade point average were virtually identical whether SAT I or SAT II scores were used, slightly more Latino students were selected with the model that used SAT II scores in place of SAT I scores.

The Relationship of Socioeconomic Status to SAT I and SAT II Scores

Critics of the SAT I often claim that students' socioeconomic status (SES) determines their performance on the test. Researchers studying the validity of the SAT I and SAT II for predicting college performance have also examined the relationship of socioeconomic status to these admission tests. Geiser and Studley (2001) conducted multiple regression analyses using HSGPA, SAT I and SAT II scores, and socioeconomic variables (family income and parents' education) as predictors of FGPA. They found that SAT I scores were more sensitive to students' socioeconomic status than were SAT II scores, and that after controlling for socioeconomic status, the power of the SAT I to predict FGPA at the University of California was diminished, while the predictive power of the SAT II remained strong.

Bridgeman (personal communication, October 15, 2001) replicated the Geiser and Studley (2001) analyses and conducted additional analyses to determine the relationship of family income and parental education to various composites of SAT I and SAT II scores. The sample for these analyses consisted of California students who took the SAT I and either two SAT II tests (Writing and Math) or three SAT II tests (Writing, Math, and a varying third test). Table 1 shows that there are indeed slightly stronger relationships between family income and parental education with SAT I scores than between either of these two demographic variables and the SAT II composites. However, the overall correlation between the SAT II composite and socioeconomic factors differs greatly depending on the third SAT II test.

For students taking only the SAT II Writing and Math tests, the correlations of both family income and parental education with the SAT I and

Table 1: Selected Correlation Coefficients for Socioeconomic Variables and SAT I and SAT II Scores in California

SAT II TESTS TAKEN	FAMILY INCOME			PARENTAL EDUCATION		
	N	SAT I	SAT II	N	SAT I	SAT II
Writing and Math	47,646	.38	.35	54,626	.43	.40
Writing, Math, and Biology	2,430	.25	.21	2,849	.28	.27
Writing, Math, and U.S. History	15,915	.31	.27	18,277	.35	.33
Writing, Math, and Spanish	7,129	.55	.30	7,977	.58	.31
Writing, Math, and Physics	4,094	.30	.24	4,900	.34	.31
Writing, Math, and Chemistry	7,622	.36	.31	8,825	.39	.36

Source: B. Bridgeman, personal communication, October 15, 2001. Based on all students attending UC in 2001 who took the SAT I and two or three SAT II tests, including Writing and Math.

SAT II tests are similar. Yet, for those students taking the SAT II Spanish test as their third test, the correlations between the demographic variables and the SAT I are substantially higher than the correlation of these variables and the SAT II. For example, the correlations for Mexican-American students on the SAT II Spanish with Listening Test and parental education and family income are −.28 and −.27, respectively, indicating that students from less educated and less affluent families actually perform better on this test, a pattern that is not repeated with any nonlanguage SAT II tests. The correlations between parental education and family income are generally substantially lower for all ethnic groups on the language tests than they are on other SAT II tests.

Rebecca Zwick, Terran Brown and Jeffrey Sklar (2003; see also Zwick in this volume) also replicated the Geiser and Studley analyses but examined each UC campus and cohort separately, as well as each SAT I and SAT II test separately. They found that the SAT I tests were not consistently more sensitive to SES variables than the SAT II tests. Therefore, the choice of the third SAT II test used has a substantial effect in the magnitude of any correlations between SAT II composite test score and parental education and family income. Comparing correlations between SAT I and SAT II on socioeconomic factors can be very misleading unless they take into account the choice of the third SAT II test.

The Current Study

In response to the University of California's proposal in 2001 to stop using the SAT I for admission, there has been renewed interest in the utility of the SAT II in college admissions. The purpose of the current study was to comprehensively examine the relative utility and predictive validity of the SAT I and SAT II for various subgroups both in California and the nation. There is a special focus on California because this state has a very large population of nonnative English speaking students applying to college, and this state is the largest user of the SAT II in college admissions, thus providing a wealth of SAT II data.

Methods

Two data sets were used in this study. The first data set (Data Set 1) included SAT I scores, SAT II scores, and Student Descriptive Questionnaire (SDQ) data for all college-bound students in the nation in the year 2000. The second data set (Data Set 2) included SAT I scores, SAT II scores, SDQ data, and FGPA, collected in 1995 from 23 universities and colleges participating in the first comprehensive validity study after the revision of the SAT I in the mid-1990s (Bridgeman, McCamley-Jenkins, & Ervin, 2000). Data Set 1 was used to examine descriptive statistics for the SAT I and SAT II, and Data Set 2 was used to examine the relationship between the SAT I, SAT II, HSGPA and FGPA.

The remainder of this chapter presents the following analyses: (1) an investigation of racial/ethnic group differences (sometimes called test impact) in SAT I and SAT II scores (Data Set 1); (2) a comparison of performance on the SAT I and SAT II for students taking both tests (Data Set 1); and (3) an investigation of the predictive validity of the SAT I, SAT II, and HSGPA, the over- and underprediction of FGPA, and the incremental validity of the SAT I and SAT II over HSGPA by racial/ethnic group (Data Set 2). Additional analyses and results are reported in Kobrin, Camara, and Milewski (2002).

Results

Test Impact. The first set of analyses was performed to determine the extent of test impact by ethnic group using various combinations of SAT I and SAT II scores. Test impact is defined as "a measure of relative standing in a group expressed in standard deviation units" (Vogt, 1999, p. 276). Table 2 presents the standardized mean differences (the raw mean difference divided by the standard deviation of the total group[3]) for each group in the nation and in California. Standardized differences allow comparison across different groups that have different standard deviations. A negative value indicates that the group as a whole performed worse than the total group and a positive value indicates that the group as a whole did better than the total group.

The impact for American Indian and black students in California is greater on the SAT II composite than on the SAT I composite. In other words, these student groups obtain lower scores relative to the total group on the SAT II than on the SAT I. The impact on the SAT I is smaller for American Indian, Asian-American, and black students in California than in the nation. Asian-American students perform the best of all ethnic groups on SAT I Math, and white students perform best on SAT II Writing. For most groups, the impact is reduced or remains the same as the difficulty of the test increases. This is shown by comparing the impact for SAT I Math with SAT II Math IC and IIC. For Hispanic students, however, the negative impact increases as the difficulty of the test increases. In California, using both SAT I and SAT II scores rather than using SAT II scores alone reduces the negative impact for all groups except for Hispanics. Hispanic students benefit the most from the SAT II composite. The least impact for this group occurs with the use of the SAT II composite alone (i.e., SAT II Writing + SAT II Math IC or IIC + highest third SAT II).

Table 3 shows the SAT I means and standard deviations of Verbal and Math and the SAT II means for Writing, Math IC or IIC, and highest third SAT II score for each racial/ethnic group in the nation and in California. The means reported in these tables are the grand means, which are computed by

Table 2: SAT I and SAT II Standardized Differences in the Nation and California

NATION

ETHNIC GROUP	SAT I VERBAL	SAT I MATH	SAT I V + M	SAT II WRITING	SAT II MATH IC	SAT II MATH IIC	SAT II W + (M IC OR M IIC) + HIGHEST THIRD	SAT I + SAT II W + (SAT II M IC OR M IIC) + HIGHEST THIRD
American Indian	-.23	-.30	-.29	-.26	-.26	-.35	-.37	-.33
Asian	-.07	.45	.20	-.25	.19	.21	0	-.03
Black	-.67	-.79	-.79	-.56	-.71	-.75	-.74	-.74
Hispanic	-.46	-.48	-.51	-.62	-.68	-.60	-.47	-.64
White	.19	.13	.18	.22	.13	.00	.14	.17

CALIFORNIA

ETHNIC GROUP	SAT I VERBAL	SAT I MATH	SAT I V + M	SAT II WRITING	SAT II MATH IC	SAT II MATH IIC	SAT II W + (M IC OR M IIC) + HIGHEST THIRD	SAT I + SAT II W + (SAT II M IC OR M IIC) + HIGHEST THIRD
American Indian	-.09	-.21	-.16	-.14	-.15	-.41	-.29	-.24
Asian	-.08	.30	.12	-.16	.22	.16	.04	.03
Black	-.56	-.76	-.72	-.50	-.76	-.74	-.80	-.78
Hispanic	-.46	-.54	-.54	-.50	-.61	-.75	-.33	-.49
White	.34	.23	.31	.35	.17	.05	.17	.22

Note: Based on all college-bound seniors taking the SAT I and/or the SAT II in 2000. Source: College Board, 2000. Highest third is the highest SAT II score other than Writing or Math.

Table 3: Mean SAT I and SAT II Composite for Students Taking Both Tests in the Nation and California in 2000

NATION

ETHNIC GROUP	SAT I MEAN*			SAT II MEAN**			SAT II MEAN W/ LANGUAGE TEST			SAT II MEAN W/O LANGUAGE TEST		
	N	MEAN	SD	N	MEAN	SD	N	MEAN	SD	N	MEAN	SD
American Indian	714	590	86	714	578	87	76	593	75	638	576	88
Asian	34,738	608	95	34,738	608	96	7,853	631	83	26,885	602	98
Black	6,784	555	91	6,784	544	88	931	554	86	5,853	542	88
Hispanic	13,010	540	98	13,010	566	82	6,359	577	72	6,651	556	90
White	87,928	634	74	87,928	621	80	10,618	620	80	77,310	621	80
Other	7,779	608	89	7,779	603	91	1,005	607	87	6,774	603	91
Total	150,953	615	88	150,953	609	88	26,842	610	83	124,111	609	89

CALIFORNIA

ETHNIC GROUP	SAT I MEAN*			SAT II MEAN**			SAT II MEAN W/ LANGUAGE TEST			SAT II MEAN W/O LANGUAGE TEST		
	N	MEAN	SD	N	MEAN	SD	N	MEAN	SD	N	MEAN	SD
American Indian	345	560	85	345	549	81	32	575	82	313	546	81
Asian	17,940	575	96	17,940	578	96	4,893	618	83	13,047	563	96
Black	2,187	508	92	2,187	503	84	257	524	85	1,930	501	83
Hispanic	8,336	509	91	8,336	545	76	4,449	560	66	3,887	528	82
White	23,000	600	77	23,000	589	83	2,312	602	85	20,688	588	83
Other	3,575	580	90	3,575	574	91	470	580	89	3,105	574	91
Total	55,383	573	93	55,383	574	89	12,413	591	83	42,970	569	91

Note: Based on all college-bound seniors taking the SAT I and three or more SAT II tests in 2000.

Source: College Board, 2000.

*SAT I Mean is the average of SAT I Verbal and SAT I Math.

**SAT II Mean is the average of SAT II Writing, the higher of SAT II Math IC or Math IIC, and the highest third SAT II score (computed for only those students with three or more SAT II scores).

averaging the individual tests or subtests for each student, summing across students, and computing a grand mean for all students on the SAT 200–800 scale. For example, if a student got a 560 on the SAT I Verbal and a 600 on the SAT I Math, the mean for that student would be (560 + 600) / 2 = 580. Similarly, if a student got a 600 on the SAT II Writing, a 510 on the SAT II Math (either IC or IIC) and a 630 on the third SAT II, the mean would be (600 + 510 + 630) / 3 = 580. In this way, mean scores on two SAT I tests can be compared to means across three SAT II tests. The last two columns of the tables show the SAT II means and standard deviations when the third test is a language test and when the third test is not a language test.

In the nation, white, black, and American Indian students tend to score higher on the SAT I than on the SAT II. Asian-American students score the same on both tests, and Hispanic students score higher on the SAT II than on the SAT I. When the third SAT II test is a language test, all groups except white, black, and "other" score higher on the SAT II than on the SAT I. On the other hand, when the third SAT II test is not a language test, all groups except for Hispanics score higher on the SAT I. In California, all groups except white and "other" score significantly higher on the SAT II when the third test is a language test. When the third test is not a language test, black students score about the same on the SAT I and SAT II; American Indian, Asian-American and white students score higher on the SAT I, and Hispanic students still score higher on the SAT II.

These results show that Hispanics benefit the most from the SAT II, regardless of whether they take a language test. However, those who take an SAT II language test obtain higher SAT II composite scores than those who take another SAT II as their third test. Among Hispanic students taking the SAT I and three SAT II tests, 49% in the nation and 53% in California took a language test. This is compared to only 18% of students in the nation and 22% in California from all ethnic groups combined.

The Predictive Validity of the SAT I and SAT II.   Perhaps the most frequently asked question regarding the SAT II is, Is the SAT II a valid measure for predicting college performance? Other questions regarding the predictive validity of the SAT II include, Can the SAT II be used without the SAT I in admissions without losing a substantial amount of predictive power? and Are there differences in the predictive validity of the SAT II across racial and ethnic groups? In order to address these questions, single and multiple correlations of HSGPA, SAT I (Verbal and Math Tests), two SAT II tests (Writing and Math IC or Math IIC), and three SAT II tests (Writing, Math IC or Math IIC, and a third test) with FGPA were calculated using Data Set 2. A subset of these data from four UC institutions was used to compute correlations for California. There were 20,417 students in Data Set 2, and

10,281 students in the UC sample; thus approximately half of the data set consisted of UC students.

Kobrin, Camara, and Milewski (2002) presented analyses comparing characteristics of Data Set 2 with the 1995 population of college-bound seniors taking the SAT I and three SAT II tests. The samples used to examine predictive validity in this study are very similar to the 1995 populations in terms of gender. However, the samples comprise a larger percentage of Asian-American students and fewer black, Hispanic, and white students; a larger percentage of permanent residents or refugees and a smaller percentage of citizens from other countries; and a smaller percentage of students who speak English as a first language. Finally, the samples have higher mean SAT scores (except for SAT II Math IIC which is similar to the population mean) and a higher mean HSGPA. These differences should be taken into account when interpreting and generalizing the results that follow.

Tables 4 and 5 show the correlations between HSGPA, SAT I, three SAT II tests, and FGPA across different racial and ethnic groups in the nation (based on data from 23 institutions) and in California (based on data from four UC institutions). These correlations constitute coefficients of predictive validity and are labeled as such in the following discussion. The tables allow for comparisons of the predictive validity of HSGPA, SAT I and SAT II, considered separately and in combination. The correlations were adjusted for restriction in range using either the univariate or multivariate Pearson-Lawley correction formula (Dunbar & Linn, 1991; Gulliksen, 1950). The validity coefficients were also corrected for shrinkage, employing the formula used by Ramist, Lewis and McCamley-Jenkins (2001).[4]

When comparing the predictive validity of HSGPA, SAT I (Verbal and Math Tests combined), and SAT II (Writing, Math, and a third test combined), the results revealed that the three SAT II tests combined provides the best prediction of FGPA for students from all ethnic groups except for American Indians and blacks (see rows 1, 7, and 9 in table 4). For American Indian students, HSGPA has the highest validity coefficient; for black students, the validity coefficients for HSGPA and the three SAT II tests are equal. A comparison of the predictive validity of the SAT II composite with only the Writing and Math Tests (see row 8 in table 4) with the SAT II composite including the third test shows that the addition of the third test increases the predictive validity for all ethnic groups except for American Indian.

When HSGPA is used in combination with either the SAT I or SAT II to predict FGPA (see rows 12 and 14 in table 4), the SAT II and HSGPA combination provides a slightly stronger prediction than the SAT I and HSGPA combination for each ethnic group except for American Indian and Black. However, when two SAT II tests are considered (row 13 in table 4), the SAT I and HSGPA provide equal or stronger prediction of FGPA for all groups except for Hispanic.

Table 4: Predictive Effectiveness by Student Ethnic Group for 23 Institutions* in 1995

	ETHNIC GROUP					
FGPA CORRELATIONS	AMERICAN INDIAN	ASIAN-AMERICAN	BLACK	HISPANIC	WHITE	OTHER
1. HSGPA						
Uncorrected	0.37	0.34	0.35	0.27	0.33	0.27
Corrected for range restriction	0.40	0.41	0.35	0.30	0.40	0.32
Corrected for range restriction and shrinkage	0.39	0.41	0.35	0.30	0.40	0.32
2. SAT I: Verbal						
Uncorrected	0.27	0.34	0.29	0.27	0.30	0.29
Corrected for range restriction	0.33	0.34	0.32	0.30	0.37	0.33
Corrected for range restriction and shrinkage	0.32	0.34	0.32	0.30	0.37	0.33
3. SAT I: Math						
Uncorrected	0.11	0.36	0.26	0.22	0.26	0.29
Corrected for range restriction	0.14	0.39	0.27	0.24	0.31	0.34
Corrected for range restriction and shrinkage	0.11	0.39	0.27	0.24	0.31	0.34
4. SAT II: Writing						
Uncorrected	0.30	0.35	0.30	0.28	0.31	0.30
Corrected for range restriction	0.33	0.35	0.32	0.33	0.35	0.33
Corrected for range restriction and shrinkage	0.32	0.35	0.32	0.33	0.35	0.33
5. SAT II: Math						
Uncorrected	0.17	0.38	0.25	0.23	0.28	0.32
Corrected for range restriction	0.21	0.43	0.27	0.26	0.33	0.37
Corrected for range restriction and shrinkage	0.19	0.43	0.27	0.26	0.33	0.37

6. SAT II: Third Test					
Uncorrected	0.19	0.38	0.27	0.11	0.35
Corrected for range restriction	0.22	0.38	0.30	0.11	0.38
Corrected for range restriction and shrinkage	0.20	0.38	0.30	0.11	0.38
7. SAT I: Combined					
Uncorrected	0.28	0.40	0.31	0.28	0.33
Corrected for range restriction	0.34	0.44	0.34	0.31	0.38
Corrected for range restriction and shrinkage	0.32	0.44	0.34	0.31	0.38
8. SAT II: Writing & Math					
Uncorrected	0.30	0.43	0.32	0.30	0.36
Corrected for range restriction	0.34	0.46	0.34	0.36	0.40
Corrected for range restriction and shrinkage	0.32	0.46	0.34	0.36	0.40
9. SAT II: Writing, Math, & Third Test					
Uncorrected	0.30	0.45	0.33	0.31	0.39
Corrected for range restriction	0.34	0.48	0.36	0.39	0.43
Corrected for range restriction and shrinkage	0.31	0.48	0.35	0.39	0.43
10. SAT I: Combined and SAT II: Writing & Math					
Uncorrected	0.33	0.43	0.33	0.31	0.36
Corrected for range restriction	0.39	0.47	0.35	0.37	0.41
Corrected for range restriction and shrinkage	0.35	0.47	0.34	0.37	0.41

Continued

Table 4: *Continued*

| | ETHNIC GROUP | | | | | |
FGPA CORRELATIONS	AMERICAN INDIAN	ASIAN-AMERICAN	BLACK	HISPANIC	WHITE	OTHER
11. SAT I: Combined, and SAT II: Writing, Math, & Third Test						
Uncorrected	0.33	0.45	0.34	0.32	0.37	0.39
Corrected for range restriction	0.41	0.48	0.36	0.40	0.43	0.43
Corrected for range restriction and shrinkage	0.37	0.48	0.35	0.39	0.43	0.42
12. HSGPA and SAT I: Combined						
Uncorrected	0.45	0.47	0.41	0.35	0.40	0.38
Corrected for range restriction	0.53	0.55	0.44	0.42	0.50	0.46
Corrected for range restriction and shrinkage	0.51	0.55	0.44	0.42	0.50	0.46
13. HSGPA and SAT II: Writing and Math						
Uncorrected	0.43	0.48	0.41	0.36	0.42	0.39
Corrected for range restriction	0.50	0.55	0.42	0.43	0.50	0.46
Corrected for range restriction and shrinkage	0.48	0.55	0.42	0.43	0.50	0.46
14. HSGPA, and SAT II: Writing, Math, & Third Test						
Uncorrected	0.43	0.50	0.41	0.36	0.43	0.42
Corrected for range restriction	0.50	0.56	0.43	0.46	0.51	0.47
Corrected for range restriction and shrinkage	0.48	0.56	0.42	0.46	0.51	0.47

15. HSGPA, SAT I: Combined, and SAT II: Writing & Math

Uncorrected	0.46	0.48	0.42	0.37	0.42	0.40
Corrected for range restriction	0.53	0.56	0.44	0.44	0.51	0.47
Corrected for range restriction and shrinkage	0.50	0.56	0.43	0.44	0.51	0.47

16. HSGPA, SAT I: Combined, and SAT II: Writing, Math, & Third Test

Uncorrected	0.46	0.50	0.42	0.37	0.43	0.42
Corrected for range restriction	0.56	0.56	0.44	0.46	0.52	0.47
Corrected for range restriction and shrinkage	0.53	0.56	0.43	0.45	0.52	0.46

Source: The data presented in this table are based on students entering college in 1995 (see Bridgeman, McCamley-Jenkins & Ervin, 2000.)
*Institutions include Barnard College, Bowdoin College, Clemson University, Colby College, Georgia Institute of Technology, Harvard University, Northwestern University, Pennsylvania State University, Prairie View A & M University, Southwest Texas State University, St. Edwards University, SUNY-Stony Brook, New York University, UC Davis, UCLA, UC Irvine, UC San Diego, University of Connecticut, University of North Carolina–Chapel Hill, University of Texas-Austin, Vanderbilt University, Washington State University, and Young Harris College.

Note: The range restriction corrections for single predictors used the standard deviations based on all college-bound students in 1995. One overall standard deviation was used for all ethnic groups.

Table 5: Predictive Effectiveness by Student Ethnic Group for Four UC Institutions* in 1995

FGPA CORRELATIONS	ETHNIC GROUP						
	AMERICAN INDIAN	ASIAN-AMERICAN	BLACK	HISPANIC	WHITE	OTHER	
1. HSGPA							
Uncorrected	0.45	0.31	0.42	0.22	0.29	0.27	
Corrected for range restriction	0.47	0.33	0.47	0.25	0.31	0.31	
Corrected for range restriction and shrinkage	0.46	0.33	0.47	0.25	0.31	0.31	
2. SAT I: Verbal							
Uncorrected	0.24	0.30	0.25	0.23	0.31	0.29	
Corrected for range restriction	0.26	0.36	0.30	0.28	0.32	0.35	
Corrected for range restriction and shrinkage	0.24	0.36	0.30	0.28	0.32	0.35	
3. SAT I: Math							
Uncorrected	0.27	0.33	0.29	0.19	0.27	0.27	
Corrected for range restriction	0.28	0.33	0.34	0.23	0.25	0.28	
Corrected for range restriction and shrinkage	0.26	0.33	0.34	0.23	0.25	0.28	
4. SAT II: Writing							
Uncorrected	0.26	0.33	0.31	0.24	0.32	0.32	
Corrected for range restriction	0.27	0.40	0.37	0.31	0.34	0.38	
Corrected for range restriction and shrinkage	0.25	0.40	0.37	0.31	0.34	0.38	

5. SAT II: Math						
Uncorrected	0.36	0.35	0.30	0.21	0.27	0.29
Corrected for range restriction	0.37	0.36	0.33	0.25	0.25	0.29
Corrected for range restriction and shrinkage	0.36	0.36	0.33	0.25	0.25	0.29
6. SAT II: Third Test						
Uncorrected	0.24	0.35	0.27	0.08	0.25	0.36
Corrected for range restriction	0.25	0.36	0.31	0.08	0.26	0.37
Corrected for range restriction and shrinkage	0.23	0.36	0.31	0.07	0.26	0.37
7. SAT I: Combined						
Uncorrected	0.30	0.38	0.32	0.24	0.33	0.33
Corrected for range restriction	0.33	0.39	0.34	0.26	0.38	0.37
Corrected for range restriction and shrinkage	0.30	0.39	0.33	0.26	0.38	0.37
8. SAT II: Writing & Math						
Uncorrected	0.38	0.41	0.37	0.27	0.36	0.37
Corrected for range restriction	0.41	0.44	0.42	0.33	0.41	0.42
Corrected for range restriction and shrinkage	0.39	0.44	0.41	0.33	0.41	0.42
9. SAT II: Writing, Math, & Third Test						
Uncorrected	0.38	0.44	0.38	0.28	0.37	0.40
Corrected for range restriction	0.41	0.46	0.43	0.36	0.43	0.44
Corrected for range restriction and shrinkage	0.37	0.46	0.42	0.36	0.43	0.43

Continued

Table 5: *Continued*

FGPA CORRELATIONS	ETHNIC GROUP					
	AMERICAN INDIAN	ASIAN-AMERICAN	BLACK	HISPANIC	WHITE	OTHER
10. SAT I: Combined, and SAT II: Writing & Math						
Uncorrected	0.39	0.42	0.37	0.28	0.37	0.37
Corrected for range restriction	0.43	0.45	0.46	0.33	0.43	0.42
Corrected for range restriction and shrinkage	0.38	0.45	0.45	0.32	0.43	0.41
11. SAT I: Combined, and SAT II: Writing, Math, & Third Test						
Uncorrected	0.39	0.44	0.38	0.29	0.38	0.40
Corrected for range restriction	0.42	0.46	0.43	0.36	0.44	0.44
Corrected for range restriction and shrinkage	0.36	0.46	0.41	0.35	0.44	0.43
12. HSGPA and SAT I: Combined						
Uncorrected	0.50	0.45	0.49	0.31	0.41	0.39
Corrected for range restriction	0.55	0.49	0.51	0.35	0.48	0.45
Corrected for range restriction and shrinkage	0.53	0.49	0.50	0.35	0.48	0.45
13. HSGPA and SAT II: Writing & Math						
Uncorrected	0.50	0.47	0.50	0.32	0.42	0.40
Corrected for range restriction	0.51	0.51	0.53	0.38	0.49	0.46
Corrected for range restriction and shrinkage	0.48	0.51	0.52	0.38	0.49	0.46
14. HSGPA and SAT II: Writing, Math, & Third Test						
Uncorrected	0.50	0.49	0.51	0.32	0.43	0.44
Corrected for range restriction	0.51	0.53	0.54	0.40	0.50	0.48
Corrected for range restriction and shrinkage	0.47	0.53	0.53	0.39	0.50	0.47

15. HSGPA, SAT I: Combined, and SAT II: Writing & Math						
Uncorrected	0.52	0.47	0.50	0.32	0.43	0.41
Corrected for range restriction	0.55	0.52	0.54	0.39	0.51	0.48
Corrected for range restriction and shrinkage	0.51	0.52	0.53	0.38	0.51	0.47
16. HSGPA, SAT I: Combined, and SAT II: Writing, Math, & Third Test						
Uncorrected	0.52	0.49	0.51	0.33	0.43	0.44
Corrected for range restriction	0.55	0.53	0.54	0.41	0.51	0.48
Corrected for range restriction and shrinkage	0.50	0.53	0.53	0.40	0.51	0.47

Source: The data presented in this table are based on students entering college in 1995 (see Bridgeman, McCamley-Jenkins & Ervin, 2000).

*Institutions include UC Davis, UC Irvine, UCLA, and UC San Diego.

Note: The range restriction corrections used the standard deviations based on students attending the University of California who took both the SAT I and the SAT II test in 1995. Separate standard deviations were used for each ethnic group.

Surprisingly, the multiple correlation between HSGPA, SAT I, three SAT II tests and FGPA does not provide the highest validity coefficient across all ethnic groups (see rows 15 and 16 in table 4). When uncorrected coefficients are used, it must be true that the more tests or variables used in prediction, the higher the validity coefficient. Yet this was not always found to be the case when corrections were applied. For example, the predictive validity of HSGPA combined with SAT I and three SAT II tests for Asian-American students is just as large as the predictive validity of HSGPA and three SAT II tests. This unexpected pattern also occurred with other ethnic groups. Sometimes, the combination of HSGPA with the SAT I provided a higher validity coefficient than when the SAT II was added as a third predictor, and sometimes the combination of HSGPA with the SAT II provided a higher validity coefficient than when the SAT I was added.

Table 4 also provides information on the extent of improvement in predictive validity offered by the SAT I over and above that offered by the SAT II and HSGPA (by comparing the coefficients in rows 13 or 14 with those in row 16). Similarly, the data allow an examination of the extent of improvement offered by the SAT II over and above that provided by the SAT I and HSGPA (by comparing the coefficients in row 12 with those in rows 15 or 16). For this sample of college students, adding the SAT I to HSGPA and three SAT II tests increased the corrected validity coefficient for American Indian, African-American, and white students. The corrected validity coefficient did not change, however, for Asian students, and decreased by .01 for Hispanic and "other" students.[5] When only two SAT II tests were used as predictors along with HSGPA, the SAT I added between .01 to .05 to the corrected validity coefficient for all ethnic groups except for students in the "other" ethnic category.

The SAT II composite contributed to the prediction of FGPA over the use of HSGPA and the SAT I for all but two ethnic groups. For African-American students, adding the SAT II decreased the (corrected) predictive validity by .01, and for "other" students, the SAT II did not increase the validity coefficient. When only two SAT II tests were considered with HSGPA and the SAT I, the validity coefficient increased by .01 to .02 for Asian-American, Hispanic, white, and "other" students, but decreased by .01 for American Indian and African-American students.

For the most part, the same patterns found in the validity coefficients for the 23 institutions are found for the four California institutions, as shown in table 5. For example, when considering HSGPA, SAT I and SAT II separately, three SAT II tests provided the best prediction of FGPA for UC students from all ethnic groups except American Indian and African-American. HSGPA had the highest separate validity coefficient for American Indian and black students. The SAT I had the second largest validity coefficient for

Asian-American, Hispanic, white and "other" students, while the SAT II (three tests) had the second highest validity coefficient for American Indian and black students.

When multiple predictors were considered, HSGPA and the SAT II (either two tests or three tests) had higher validity coefficients with FGPA than HSGPA and the SAT I for all ethnic groups except American Indian. As found for the 23 institutions, the use of all three predictors (HSGPA, SAT I, and SAT II) did not increase the predictive validity over the use of two predictors for students from some ethnic groups. For example, the addition of the three SAT II tests to HSGPA and the SAT I actually decreased the corrected validity coefficient for American Indian students. However, when the SAT I was added to HSGPA and three SAT II tests, the validity coefficients increased or remained unchanged for all ethnic groups.

Tables 4 and 5 also allow comparison of single subtests, although such an analysis is typically not very informative since no college or university uses a single test (e.g., SAT I Verbal or SAT I Math, or only one SAT II test) in admissions. Still there may be some curiosity about comparisons of the predictive validity of single components of tests. When the predictive validity of the SAT I Verbal and SAT II Writing Tests were compared for the 23 institutions (see rows 2 and 4 in table 4), the SAT I Verbal Test had validity coefficients that were greater than or equal to those for the SAT II Writing Test for American Indian, black, white, and "other" ethnic group students. The SAT II Writing Test had greater predictive validity for Asian-American and Hispanic students. In contrast to the national sample, for students at UC the SAT II Writing Test had a higher validity coefficient than the SAT I Verbal Test for all ethnic groups (see table 5). In both samples of institutions, the SAT II Math Test had greater or equal predictive validity than the SAT I Math Test for students from all ethnic groups, with the exception of black students in the UC sample.

If one rank orders all six single predictors by their corrected correlations, there are substantial differences in relative predictive validity among these measures for the various ethnic groups. For the 23 institutions, HSGPA is the best predictor of FGPA for American Indian, black, and white students. For Asian-American students, the SAT II Math test is the best predictor; for Hispanic students, the SAT II Writing test is the best predictor; and for "other" students, the third SAT II test is the best predictor of FGPA. The SAT I Verbal Test is the second-best predictor for all groups except for Asian-American and "other" students. The SAT I Math Test, the SAT II Math Test, and the third SAT II test generally rank fourth, fifth, or sixth among the six single predictors for most groups. A very different pattern emerges for the four UC institutions. HSGPA is the best single predictor for only American Indian and black students, while the SAT II Writing Test is the best predictor for Asian-American, Hispanic, white, and "other" students. The SAT I Verbal Test is the second best predictor for Hispanic and white students and is tied with the SAT II Math Test and the third SAT II test as the second best predictor for Asian-American students. The SAT I and SAT II Math Tests rank either third, fourth, or fifth for many student groups. The third SAT II ranks fourth, fifth, or sixth for four of the ethnic groups, but ranks second for Asian-American and "other" students.

In summary, the combination of HSGPA, SAT I, and SAT II provided the largest validity coefficients for most ethnic groups. The predictive validity using all three measures was usually higher across ethnic groups than the predictive validity using only two measures—HSGPA and the composite of three SAT II tests. These results suggest that the SAT I offers an important increase in predictive validity over and above HSGPA and three SAT II tests. Differences in validity coefficients across ethnic groups were found when different sets of predictor variables were used, but these differences were slight overall. One instance where there was a difference in validity coefficients across ethnic groups was when the third SAT II test was considered separately. In this instance, Hispanic students had a substantially lower validity coefficient than the other ethnic groups. This may be due to the fact that Hispanic students tend to choose a Spanish language exam as their third SAT II test. If an Hispanic student does very well on the Spanish-language SAT II test primarily because Spanish is his native language, performance on the exam may not be strongly linked to success in college.

At this point, the three questions presented at the outset of this section can be addressed. First, it seems that the SAT II tests can be considered valid measures for predicting college performance. Second, since the SAT I adds to the validity coefficients for HSGPA and three SAT II tests for most ethnic groups, this suggests that it is better from a purely predictive validity standpoint to consider all three of these measures when making admissions decisions, although in some cases a second test may not have a practical effect in admissions. Third, there are differences between validity coefficients for the SAT II across ethnic groups. Most notable is the fact that validity coefficients for American Indian and Hispanic students are lower than those for Asian-American, black, white and "other" students. Finally, choice of the third SAT II test introduces additional complexities and can have significant impact on subgroup differences in comparing test composites.

Table 6 shows the over- and underprediction of FGPA based on various combinations of predictors (SAT I, SAT II, and HSGPA), both in the nation and at the four UC institutions. These data suggest little difference among combinations of predictors—the one consistent finding appears to be that SAT II and HSGPA produce a slightly greater overprediction for Hispanic students and SAT I and HSGPA result in a slightly greater

Table 6: Over- and Underprediction of FGPA for Students in the Nation* and California**

ETHNIC GROUP	NATION						CALIFORNIA					
	SAT I + HSGPA		SAT II + HSGPA		SAT I + SAT II + HSGPA		SAT I + HSGPA		SAT II + HSGPA		SAT I + SAT II + HSGPA	
	N	MEAN	N	MEAN	N	MEAN	N	MEAN	N	MEAN	N	MEAN
American Indian	131	0.15	131	0.12	131	0.12	90	0.14	90	0.08	90	0.09
Female	76	0.07	76	0.04	76	0.04	54	0.06	54	0.02	54	0.02
Male	55	0.28	55	0.23	55	0.24	36	0.25	36	0.18	36	0.20
Asian	5,849	0.02	5,792	0.01	5,792	0.01	4,158	0.04	4,129	0.03	4,129	0.02
Female	3,106	−0.03	3,081	−0.03	3,081	−0.03	2,222	−0.02	2,209	−0.02	2,209	−0.03
Male	2,743	0.07	2,711	0.06	2,711	0.06	1,936	0.10	1,920	0.09	1,920	0.08
Black	715	0.05	701	0.04	701	0.04	300	−0.02	298	−0.03	298	−0.04
Female	470	−0.01	464	−0.02	464	−0.02	200	−0.08	199	−0.08	199	−0.09
Male	245	0.16	237	0.14	237	0.14	100	0.09	99	0.07	99	0.07
Hispanic	1,027	0.11	1,017	0.15	1,017	0.14	835	0.09	831	0.14	831	0.12
Female	581	0.04	577	0.10	577	0.08	493	0.03	490	0.10	490	0.07
Male	446	0.20	440	0.22	440	0.21	342	0.18	341	0.21	341	0.19
White	10,296	−0.02	10,199	−0.03	10,199	−0.02	3,703	−0.03	3,696	−0.03	3,696	−0.03
Female	5,451	−0.09	5,411	−0.08	5,411	−0.08	2,028	−0.10	2,026	−0.09	2,026	−0.09
Male	4,845	0.05	4,788	0.04	4,788	0.05	1,675	0.05	1,670	0.04	1,670	0.04
Other	837	−0.04	830	−0.04	830	−0.04	550	−0.04	547	−0.04	547	−0.05
Female	444	−0.12	439	−0.11	439	−0.11	278	−0.11	275	−0.11	275	−0.12
Male	393	0.04	391	0.04	391	0.04	272	0.03	272	0.03	272	0.03

Source: The College Board.

*Institutions include Barnard College, Bowdoin College, Clemson University, Colby College, Georgia Institute of Technology, Harvard University, New York University, Northwestern University, Pennsylvania State University, Prairie View A & M University, Southwest Texas State University, St. Edwards University, SUNY Stony Brook, UC Davis, UC Irvine, UCLA, UC San Diego, University of Connecticut, University of North Carolina-Chapel Hill, University of Texas-Austin, Vanderbilt University, Washington State University, and Young Harris College.

**Institutions include UC Davis, UCLA, UC Irvine, and UC San Diego.

overprediction for African Americans and American Indians. Kobrin, Camara, and Milewski (2002) present tables showing the over- and underprediction for each measure separately. Consistent with other research, results showed that HSGPA and all tests are more likely to overpredict college performance for males than females irrespective of ethnicity. Overprediction is the greatest for Hispanic students, especially on the third SAT II test. This overprediction is reduced when multiple measures are combined (e.g., SAT I + HSGPA).

Conclusions

This study examined the relative utility and predictive validity of the SAT I and SAT II for various subgroups in both California and the nation. The effect of eliminating the SAT I on the test impact and on the over- and underprediction of various gender and racial/ethnic subgroups was examined. The following salient findings emerged from the study:

- The impact (i.e., difference between the mean score for each racial/ethnic group and the mean score for all students) for both the SAT I and SAT II is generally greatest for African-American students. If the SAT II (Writing, Math, and a third test) was to be used without the SAT I, the negative impact would be reduced only for Hispanic students in this sample. The positive impact would decrease slightly for white students and the negative impact would increase slightly for American Indian students. There would be no difference for Asian-American or black students.
- Absolute score differences in composite means between SAT I and SAT II are quite small for all groups. On average, white, American Indian and African-American students score slightly higher on SAT I than SAT II, Hispanic students score higher on three SAT II tests than on the SAT I and there is no difference among Asian-American students. However, performance on SAT II tests is better among California students than is found nationally. In California the SAT I advantage for whites and African Americans is reduced, and Hispanics and Asian Americans score higher on SAT II tests. When the third SAT II test taken is not a language test, Hispanic students still score comparably higher on the SAT II tests, while this is not the case for other groups.
- The SAT II tests have marginally greater predictive validity for predicting first-year college GPA than the SAT I for ethnic groups other than American Indian and black, both in a larger sample of institutions across the nation and in four University of California

institutions. Similarly, the combination of HSGPA and three SAT II tests has slightly greater predictive validity than the combination of HSGPA and the SAT I for all ethnic groups except American Indians and Blacks, though Bridgeman, Burton, and Cline (2001) show that this may be attributed to comparing three SAT II tests to two SAT I tests. The SAT I had a positive incremental validity over HSGPA and the SAT II tests for three out of the six ethnic groups, and the SAT II tests added to the predictive validity of HSGPA and the SAT I for all ethnic groups in the nation except black and "other."

- In the UC sample, the predictive validity of the SAT II for Hispanic students is lower than that for any of the other racial/ethnic groups. Furthermore, the third SAT II test has very low predictive validity for Hispanic students in both the national and California samples. Similarly, HSGPA and SAT I had lower validity coefficients than found for most other ethnic groups in both samples. In the national sample, when SAT I, SAT II and HSGPA were used, the predictive validity for Hispanic students was comparable to that found for other ethnic groups. However, that was not the case at the four UC institutions where multiple predictors still resulted in lower validities for Hispanics than other ethnic groups.

- When the SAT II (Writing, Math, and a third test) is used to predict first-year college GPA, Hispanic students are overpredicted to a greater extent than when the SAT I is used as a predictor. The pattern of prediction remains similar for other ethnic groups, regardless of whether the SAT I or the SAT II are used.

- Results of predictive validity studies show some differences across the national and UC samples in this study, and results also differ as a function of the degree of restriction of range in the sample and choice of the third SAT II test. Institutions interested in comparing the utility of the SAT I and SAT II should conduct their own validity studies and should be extremely cautious in generalizing results from this study or any other study to their institution.

Notes

1. The SAT II Subject Tests accepted by UC include: Writing, English Literature, U.S. History, World History, Math Level IC, Math Level IIC, Biology E/M, Chemistry, Physics, Chinese, French, French with Listening, German, German with Listening, Japanese, Korean, Latin, Modern Hebrew, Spanish, and Spanish with Listening.

2. A statistical formula to correct for restriction in range is sometimes applied because the range of test scores for students in the sample is narrower than the range of scores typically found in the population. This restriction in range is known to underestimate the true validity of the predictors and the statistical correction may provide a more accurate estimate (Nunnally, 1978).

3. The standardized differences for the nation in table 2 are computed using the standard deviation for all college-bound seniors in the nation in 2000. The standardized differences for California are computed using the standard deviation for all college-bound seniors in California in 2000.
4. A statistical correction for shrinkage is applied because it is likely that the validity coefficients in the current study would not be as large if a different student sample was used.
5. "Other students" refer to those who did not indicate their ethnic group, or whose ethnic group did not fit into any of the categories provided.

References

Bridgeman, B., Burton, N., & Cline. F. (2001). *Substituting SAT II: Subject tests for Sat I: Reasoning Test: Impact on admitted class composition and quality.* College Board Report No. 2001-3. New York: College Entrance Examination Board.

Bridgeman, B., McCamley-Jenkins, L., & Ervin, N. (2000). *Predictions of freshman grade point average from the revised and recentered SAT I: Reasoning test.* College Board Report No. 2000-1. New York: College Entrance Examination Board.

Camara, W., & Echternacht, G. (2000). *The SAT I and high school grades: Utility in predicting success in college.* Research Note RN-10. New York: College Entrance Examination Board.

College Board (2000). *College bound seniors: A profile of SAT program test takers.* New York: College Entrance Examination Board.

Dunbar, S. B., & Linn, R. L. (1991). Range restriction adjustments in the prediction of military job performance. In A. K. Wigdor and B. F. Green (Eds.). *Performance assessment for the workplace,* vol. 2 (pp. 127–57). Washington DC: National Academy Press.

Geiser, S., & Studley, R. (2001). *Relative contribution of high school grades, SAT I and SAT II scores in predicting success at UC: Preliminary findings.* Unpublished manuscript.

Gulliksen, H. (1950). *Theory of mental tests.* New York: John Wiley and Sons.

Hezlett, S. A., Kuncel, N. R., Vey, M., Ahart, A. M., Ones, D. S., Campbell, J. P., & Camara, W. J. (2001). The effectiveness of the SAT in predicting success early and late in college: A comprehensive meta-analysis. Paper presented at the annual meeting of the National Council of Measurement in Education, Seattle.

Kobrin, J. L., Camara, W. J., & Milewski, G. B. (2002). *The utility of the SAT I and SAT II for admissions decisions in California and the nation.* College Board Report No. 2002-6. New York: College Entrance Examination Board.

Nunnally, J. C. (1978). *Psychometric theory.* New York: McGraw-Hill.

Ramist, L., Lewis, C., & McCamley-Jenkins, L. (2001). *Using achievement tests/SAT II Subject tests to demonstrate achievement and predict college grades: Sex, language, ethnic, and parental education groups.* College Board Research Report No. 2001-5. New York: College Entrance Examination Board.

Ramist, L., Lewis, C., & McCamley-Jenkins, L. (1994). *Student group differences in predicting college grades: Sex, language and ethnic groups.* College Board Report No. 93-1. New York: College Entrance Examination Board.

Vogt, P. W. (1999). *Dictionary of statistics and methodology: A nontechnical guide for the social sciences,* 2nd ed. Thousand Oaks, CA: Sage.

Zwick, R., Brown, T., & Sklar, J. C. (2003). *California and the SAT: A reanalysis of University of California admissions data.* (Draft report), Berkeley, CA: Center for Studies in Higher Education.

Replacing Reasoning Tests with Achievement Tests in University Admissions: Does It Make a Difference?

BRENT BRIDGEMAN
NANCY BURTON
FREDERICK CLINE

The SAT I: Reasoning Tests are measures of "verbal and mathematical reasoning abilities, which develop over time" (College Board, 1999a, p. 3). The SAT II: Subject Tests "measure your knowledge and skills in particular subjects and your ability to apply that knowledge" (College Board, 1999b, p. 3). Richard C. Atkinson, the president of the University of California, emphasized this difference in proposing to eliminate the SAT I as an admissions requirement to the University of California system and instead to rely more heavily on the SAT II tests (Atkinson, 2001). In his speech to the American Council on Education, Atkinson argued, "The problem is not the use of standardized tests to assess knowledge in well-defined subject areas. The problem is tests that do not have a demonstrable relationship to the student's program of study—a problem that is amplified when the tests are assumed to measure innate ability." As noted above, the College Board states that the SAT I measures reasoning abilities that develop over time, not innate abilities; nevertheless, Atkinson's comments indicate that the perception of an innate ability test remains. Atkinson's view of the SAT II tests was quite different. He argued, "The SAT II begins to approximate what I judge to be an appropriate test for the University's admissions process. It tests students on specific subjects that are well defined and readily described."

In terms of their overall ability to predict first year grades, the SAT I and SAT II tests may be nearly identical. Using data from 22 highly selective colleges that used the SAT and College Board Achievement Tests (predecessors to the SAT I and SAT II), Crouse and Trusheim (1988) found essentially no difference in the ability of these two types of test to predict freshman grade point average (FGPA). This conclusion of no difference held whether the tests were used by themselves or combined with high school grades. They suggest that factors other than the ability to predict FGPA may then enter into decisions of which type of test should be used. One of these factors could be the ethnic and gender composition of the selected class; two tests that are equally good at identifying students who can succeed in college may nevertheless select somewhat different groups of students.

One argument for using achievement tests rather than general developed ability tests is the simple assertion that general tests are biased and unfair (McClelland, 1973; see Barrett and Depinet, 1991, for a critical assessment of McClelland's assertions and McClelland, 1994, for his response to Barrett and Depinet). Because of their closer link to school subjects, though not to a particular well-specified curriculum, SAT II tests may be seen as inherently less vulnerable to complaints of test bias. Poor performance on SAT II: Chemistry, for example, is more likely to be attributed to the quality of the chemistry instruction in the school or the student's work in chemistry class rather than test bias. A different argument suggests that even tests that are not a direct measure of the curriculum will influence instruction and thus should contain content that is worth being taught (Linn, 1994; Messick, 1989; Resnick & Resnick, 1992; Shepard, 1992, 1997).

Colleges in the University of California system now weight SAT II more heavily than SAT I for determining the pool of students who will be eligible for admission. Under current policy for the test score component of the UC Eligibility Index, the two SAT I Tests (Verbal and Math) are summed and added to the sum of three SAT II tests (Writing, Math IC or Math IIC, and a third test of the student's choice). Each test is scored on a 200–800 scale, so SAT I contributes a maximum of 1600 points and SAT II contributes a maximum of 2400 points (Geiser & Studley, 2001). Some have proposed simply substituting SAT II for SAT I (e.g., Crouse & Trusheim, 1988; Atkinson, 2001). Such a substitution could impact not only the quality of the class selected, but also its gender and ethnic composition.

We decided to investigate the consequences of substituting SAT II tests for the SAT I in the selection of a freshman class. These consequences have clear implications for the University of California system or any other colleges that may be contemplating a change to increased emphasis on achievement testing. Because the database used included first-year grades, we could model not only the composition of the selected class, but also its academic success, at least to the extent that success can be defined by grades. This modeling was necessarily limited to the data available, namely test scores and grades. We do not intend to suggest that these indicators are or should be the only factors considered in making admissions decisions. Nevertheless, as long as test scores remain as one of the important considerations in selective admissions, any differences produced by the tests in the nature and composition of the students admitted are relevant.

Where We Got the Data

The data that we evaluated came from a database of 23 colleges that was assembled for an SAT I validity study which compared the predictive validity of the old SAT to the new SAT I (Bridgeman, McCamley-Jenkins, & Ervin, 2000). This database contains SAT I and SAT II scores and responses from a questionnaire that students complete when they register to take the SAT; the questionnaire asks students about their high school grade point average, ethnic identification, best language (English, English and another, or another), parental education, family income, and intended college major. In addition, the database contains the FGPA. Students in the database were freshmen in 1995, so scores were available for relatively recent versions of the SAT II tests, including Writing and Math IIC (advanced math that requires calculator use).

From this database of admitted and enrolled students, we selected only colleges in which at least 80% of the freshman class had taken SAT II: Writing plus at least one other SAT II: Subject Test. Most students took three SAT II tests: Writing, Math, and a variety of different tests for the third test. At the campuses studied, students who took SAT II tests were the rule and not the exception. The 10 colleges included in the final sample were: Barnard College, Bowdoin College, Colby College, Harvard University, Northwestern University, four campuses of the University of California (Davis, Irvine, Los Angeles, and San Diego), and Vanderbilt University. Mean SAT I: Verbal scores in these colleges ranged from 524 to 731 and mean SAT I: Math scores ranged from 574 to 726; in all but two of the colleges, mean Verbal and Math scores were above 600. The study sample contained 500 African-American, 4,725 Asian-American, 923 Mexican-American, 542 other Latino, and 6,086 white students. There were 6,264 male and 7,610 female students.

Using Achievement Tests or Reasoning Tests to Decide Who Gets "Admitted"

Freshmen at each of the 10 colleges who had scores on SAT II: Writing and at least one other SAT II test were treated as if they formed an applicant pool for an even more selective institution. At each college, two-thirds of the "applicant pool" was "selected" based on various score composites. (A second set of analyses that "selected" the top third produced similar conclusions and will not be discussed here.) Because any realistic selection scenario would include the high school grade point average (H), we decided to include H in each composite even though this would have the effect of muting the differences between selections made by alternative models. The self-reported H scores in this select sample had a narrow range with no student reporting an average lower than C. Ninety-two percent of the students reported grade averages in one of the four highest categories (B+ through A+). These grades were placed on an SAT-like scale by setting a C to 400 and proceeding in 50-point increments to 750 for an A+, producing a scale with a mean of 669 and a standard deviation of 61. In each model, the composite score was formed by equally weighting each test score and giving H nominally equal weight with the combined test scores (e.g., if there were two SAT I scores [verbal and mathematical] and one SAT II score, these scores would be summed and H would be multiplied by three and added to the total). The technique of using data on enrolled students to model the results of employing different admission strategies has been used for many years (see, for example, Kane, 1998; Wightman, 1997; Willingham and Breland, 1982; and Wing and Wallach, 1971).

The following composites were evaluated:

- H+ the sum of the two SAT I reasoning tests (R)-HR
- H+ Achievement (Subject) Test Average-HA
- H+ Achievement Test Average excluding language tests-HAxL

The average that excluded language tests was included in the analyses because of the possibly unique role that language tests could play; most subject tests are measures of school learning, but when language tests are taken by native speakers of those languages, they measure primarily out-of-school learning.

Are Students Admitted with Achievement Tests More Successful in College than Students Admitted with Reasoning Tests?

Students selected by one of the new composites with SAT II scores were compared to students selected by the traditional HR index. We defined successful students as those who attained an FGPA of at least 2.5. (We also investigated a first-year GPA of 2.0 or better as the criterion, but the overall success rate was 87%, allowing for little variation among the different selection methods. Even with the 2.5 criterion, the overall success rate was 80%.) The percentage of successful students selected was compared for four groups: (1) students selected by both the new composite and traditional index; (2) students rejected by both methods; (3) students selected by the new but rejected by the traditional; and (4) students selected by the traditional but rejected by the new.

The selection decision was the same under both models (HR and HA) for 86% of the students. Thus, the vast majority of students should not care whether reasoning or achievement scores are used; admissions decisions would be identical. In the group accepted by both models, 87% of the students were successful (FGPA average above 2.5), while in the group rejected by both models only 67% were successful. This result suggests that valid selections were made even though the initial selection pools were already quite restricted because they consisted of only students who had already been admitted to and enrolled in selective colleges.

Students who were accepted by the model that used reasoning scores (HR) and rejected by the model that used achievement scores (HA) were compared to students accepted by HA and rejected by HR. Both groups were equally successful, with 77% of the former group and 75% of the latter group classified as successful. A complementary analysis that focused on grade point averages (GPAs) rather than percentage of successful students reached the same conclusion; there were no statistically significant differences in the GPAs of students that were accepted by one method and rejected by the other. With first-year grades as the criterion, there is no reason to favor either SAT I or SAT II in making selection decisions. The same was true for the comparison that excluded language tests from the Subject Test average.

Who Gets Selected If Achievement Tests Replace Reasoning Tests?

Although the overall success of students selected using SAT I is comparable to the success of students selected using SAT II, there might still be differences in the ethnic or gender composition of groups selected by the different criteria.

Gender Differences. Using HR, 63.4% of the women in the applicant pool would be selected. Using HA instead, 64.7% of the women in the pool would be selected. Looking at these numbers from a different perspective, the selected pool would be 52.4% female with HR and 53.4% female with HA.

Ethnic Differences. As indicated in figure 1, more substantial differences were evident in the ethnic group comparison of HR selections with HA selections. This figure also includes selections that combined H with the average of the non-language subject tests (HAxL). In particular, the proportion of Mexican-American and other Latino students selected would increase if HA were used in place of HR. Because we were keeping the size of the

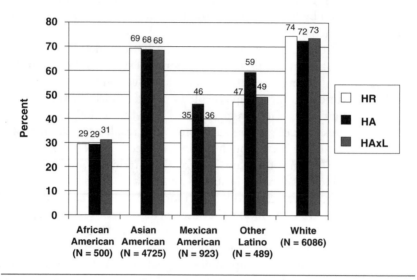

Figure 1. Percentage of each group selected by HR, HA, and HAxL.

admitted class fixed, at least one of the other groups had to show a reduction in this zero-sum game. Numerically, the loss of white and Asian-American students balanced the gains of Mexican-American and other Latino students, although the percentage loss in each of these groups was small because of the relatively large numbers of white and Asian-American students in the sample. The percentage of the eligible African-American group that was selected was virtually identical for the HA and HR models. Selection with an achievement test average that excluded language tests (HaxL) resulted in a slight increase in the number of underrepresented minorities selected relative to HR selection.

Language Differences. Figure 2 divides the Asian-American, Mexican-American, and other Latino groups by the language categories that students selected when they completed the questionnaire. Students who responded "English and another" or "Another" to the question on best language were classified in the "English as a second language" (ESL) category while the remaining students were in the "English as best language" (EBL) category. For the Asian-American ESL students, HA selection resulted in only a slight increase over HR selection, but in both Latino ESL groups, almost twice as many students were admitted with HA as with HR. The minimal impact on Asian Americans compared to the Latino groups may be explained by differential test-taking patterns; over 40% of the students in the Latino groups took an SAT II Spanish test, but only 8% of the Asian Americans

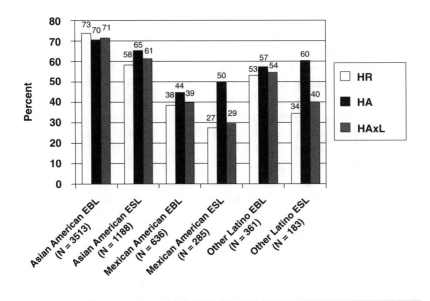

Figure 2. Percentage of each ethnic/ESL subgroup selected by HR, HA, and HAxL.

took an Asian language test. Excluding the language tests from the subject test average resulted in selections that were more similar to HR.

Is the Glass Half Empty or Half Full?

A very different picture emerges if we focus on the percentage of the selected population that fell into each of the ethnic/ESL categories rather than the percentage of the ethnic/ESL group that was selected. There were 468 Latino ESL students (combining Mexican American and other Latino) in the eligible pool of 13,874 students. Using HR, 139 Latino ESL students would be selected, so 1.50% of the selected students would be Latino/ESL. Using HA, 2.72% of the selected students would be Latino/ESL. The proportion of Latino/ESL students increases by about one percentage point, which may seem like a trivial difference. From the perspective of a professor looking out on a class of 100 students, this difference would be hardly noticeable—just one additional Latino/ESL student with the HA policy. But consider this policy change from the perspective of a group meeting of all the Latino/ESL students in the pool. They know that under the HR policy, about 29.7% of their group would be going to college. If the policy shifted to HA, then 53.8% of their group would be college bound. The change that caused a yawn in the faculty club might cause a celebration in the Latino/ESL student association.

Selections among Latino Students Who Took the Spanish Subject Test

The impact of including or excluding the language tests is somewhat muted because only 43% of the Mexican-American students and 51% of the other Latino students took a Spanish subject test. In order to gauge the impact of the language test on the likelihood of selection, we examined the sample of Mexican-American and other Latino students who had taken one of the Spanish tests (Spanish with and without a listening component). In both groups almost twice as many students were selected with the index including the subject-test average (HA) as by the index that used SAT I scores (HR). Excluding the Spanish test from the subject-test average markedly reduced the number of students selected from these groups almost to the level selected by HR. Recall that roughly half of the weight in the prediction equation is on the high school average and, because most students take three subject tests, the Spanish test is approximately one-third of the subject test weight (or one-sixth of the total weight); given this relatively small weight, the effect of including or excluding the Spanish test is indeed dramatic. Test means show the reasons for this relative advantage. In the combined Hispanic group, the mean score on the Spanish tests (combining the tests with and without listening) was 147 points higher than the mean score on SAT I: Verbal (666 vs. 519; standard deviations of 90 and 91 respectively); in the white sample, the mean score on the Spanish tests was 85 points lower than the mean score on SAT I: Verbal (556 vs. 641; standard deviations of 89 and 77 respectively).

We next determined how successful these students were, defining success as achieving a first-year GPA of 2.5 or better, and again using the sample of students who had taken one of the Spanish subject tests. For the sample of Mexican-American students, including those who were not selected with any of the indices, 59% were successful by this criterion. In the other Latino sample, the overall success rate was 69% for the 2.5 or better criterion. As indicated in figure 3, the students selected by HR were most successful on a percentage basis; 79% of the Mexican-American students selected by HR were successful, compared to 66% for HA. For the other Latino students, 84% selected by HR were successful, compared to 76% for HA.

Should We Maximize the Percentage or Number of Successful Latino Students?

If maximizing the percentage of successful students in the Latino groups is the goal, selections should be based on HR. However, recall that many more Latino students were selected with HA than with HR. If emphasis is placed on the number of successful students selected from the subgroup instead of on the percentage of students in the selected subgroup who are

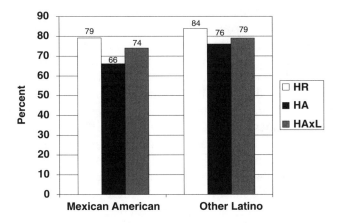

Figure 3. For students who took a Spanish subject test, percentage of selected students in each group who were successful (GPA 2.5 or higher).

successful, a different conclusion is reached. As indicated in figure 4, the number of successful Hispanic students was greatest for selections based on the index that used the average of the subject tests, including the Spanish subject test. If admitting the maximum number of potentially successful Hispanic students is the goal, selections should be based on HA.

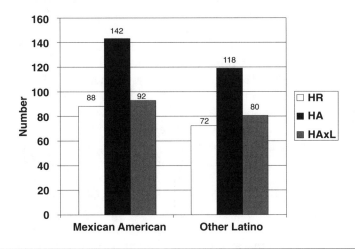

Figure 4. For students who took a Spanish subject test, number of students in each group who were successful (GPA 2.5 or higher).

Conclusion and Implications

The implications of substituting SAT II tests for SAT I tests in admissions fall into three general areas: immediate effects on institutions, effects on the overall fairness of admission policies, and wider effects on pre-college instruction. The predicted immediate effects on institutions are relatively small: overall, there would be almost a 90% overlap in the classes selected, and the selected students would be equally successful under either model. Part of the reason for this substantial overlap is that the distinction between reasoning and achievement tests is itself largely illusory. Reasoning tests require knowledge of vocabulary, reading skills, and mathematical operations that are taught in schools. Quality achievement tests reflect curriculum standards that emphasize reasoning over mere memorization of facts.

If SAT II tests were substituted for SAT I tests, the characteristics of the admitted classes would be virtually identical with one important exception. A larger number of Latino students would be admitted if the Spanish test were among the subject tests permitted. From the perspective of the institution, this difference might be hardly noticeable; the percentage of the class that was Latino would probably not change by more than a percentage point or two. However, from the perspective of the Latino applicants, the change would be more dramatic, noticeably increasing their likelihood of admission. Because language tests taken by native speakers of those languages reflect a different kind of achievement than mastery of school-based subjects, some have argued that language tests should be excluded from any composite SAT II score because they give an unfair advantage to the native speakers of the foreign languages. However, a counterargument suggests that the supposed advantage may only partially compensate for some of the disadvantages that nonnative speakers of English have on all of the other subject tests that require a good working knowledge of English. Also, skill in a language might be valued in its own right, whether those language skills were learned at home or in the classroom, and whether the language skills predicted freshman grades or not.

All of the institutions in the current sample were at least moderately selective, and most were highly selective. They should not be considered as representative of all American universities. Further study is needed before generalizations to less selective institutions and more diverse applicant pools can be made.

In general, considering each SAT II score separately rather than creating an SAT II composite can lead to a much fuller understanding of the unique strengths of each student. No matter what kind of scaling is done, it is nonsensical to assert that a 600 in Chemistry means the same thing as a 600 in Writing and a 600 in Spanish or that a student with a 750 in Physics would respond the same in all courses as a student with a 750 in U.S. History. Instead of using a composite of all SAT II scores, test scores considered individually should take their proper place among all of the evidence that is reviewed in making admissions decisions.

As noted by William Bowen and Derek Bok (1998), "Talk of basing admissions decisions strictly on test scores and grades assumes a model of admissions radically different from the one that exists today" (p. 29). This study cannot predict the effect of substituting the SAT II for the SAT I in institutions that do a comprehensive review of the admission folder, including subjective information such as letters of recommendation and personal statements as well as objective information on individual test scores and grades in specific courses. Nevertheless, it is important to understand the characteristics of more mechanistic composites if they are used to define a qualified pool of students (e.g., the Eligibility Index at the University of California).

Finally, one can ask what the effect of substituting the SAT II for the SAT I might have on instruction. Currently, with the SAT I as the major high-stakes admission test, there is a considerable amount of commercial test preparation that tends to concentrate on superficial aspects of the test and test-taking tricks. Requiring subject tests for admission could lead students to seek more legitimate instruction in the specific subject fields, but it remains to be seen whether these hopes actually would be realized.

Note

The authors gratefully acknowledge the financial support of the College Board. The College Board encourages researchers to freely express their professional judgment, so the views and opinions expressed do not necessarily represent official College Board position or policy. This paper was modified from a manuscript entitled "Substituting SAT II Subject Tests for SAT I: Reasoning Tests: Impact on Admitted Class Composition and Quality" that was published in 2003 in the journal *Research in Higher Education*, vol. *44(1)*, 83–98.

References

Atkinson, R. C. (2001). Standardized tests and access to American universities, The 2001 Robert H. Atwell Distinguished Lecture delivered at the 83rd Annual Meeting of the American Council on Education, Washington, D.C., February 18, 2001. Available online at http://www.ucop.edu/news/sat/speech.html.

Barrett, G. V., & Depinet, R. L. (1991). A reconsideration of testing for competence rather than for intelligence. *American Psychologist, 46,* 1012–24.

Bowen, W. G., & Bok, D. (1998). *The shape of the river: Long-term consequences of considering race in college and university admissions.* Princeton, NJ: Princeton University Press.

Bridgeman, B., McCamley-Jenkins, L., & Ervin, N. (2000). *Predictions of freshman grade point average from the revised and recentered SAT I: Reasoning Test.* College Board Report No. 2000–1. New York: College Entrance Examination Board.

College Board (1999a). *Taking the SAT I: Reasoning Test.* New York: College Entrance Examination Board.

College Board (1999b). *Taking the SAT II: Subject Tests.* New York: College Entrance Examination Board.

College Board (2001). *What does the SAT measure and why does it matter?* New York: College Entrance Examination Board.

Crouse, J., & Trusheim, D. (1988). *The case against the SAT.* Chicago: University of Chicago Press.

Geiser, S., & Studley, R. (2001). *UC and the SAT: Predictive validity and differential impact of the SAT I and SAT II at the University of California.* Oakland: University of California Office of the President. Available online at http://www.ucop.edu/sas/research/researchandplanning/pdf/sat_study.pdf.

Kane, T. J. (1998). Racial and ethnic preferences in college admissions. In C. Jencks and M. Phillips, Eds., *The black-white test score gap.* Washington, DC: Brookings Institution.

Linn, R. L. (1994). Performance assessment: Policy promises and technical measurement standards. *Educational Researcher, 23(9),* 4–14.

McClelland, D. C. (1973). Testing for competence rather than for "intelligence." *American Psychologist, 28,* 1–14.

McClelland, D. C. (1994). The knowledge-testing-educational complex strikes back. *American Psychologist, 49,* 66–69.

Messick, S. (1989). Validity. In R. L. Linn (Ed.), *Educational measurement,* 3rd ed. (pp. 13–103). New York: American Council on Education/Macmillan.

Resnick, L. B., & Resnick, D. P. (1992). Assessing the thinking curriculum: New tools for educational reform. In B. R. Gifford & M. C. O'Connor (Eds.), *Changing assessments: Alternative views of aptitude, achievement and instruction* (pp. 37–75). Boston: Kluwer Academic.

Shepard, L. A. (1992). Commentary: What policy makers who mandate tests should know about the new psychology of intellectual ability and learning. In B. R. Gifford & M. C. O'Connor (Eds.), *Changing assessments: Alternative views of aptitude, achievement and instruction* (pp. 301–28). Boston: Kluwer Academic.

Shepard, L. A. (1997). The centrality of test use and consequences for test validity. *Educational Measurement: Issues and Practice, 16(2),* 5–8, 13, 24.

Wightman, L. F. (1997). The threat to diversity in legal education: An empirical analysis of the consequences of abandoning race as a factor in law school admission decisions. *New York University Law Review, 72(1),* 1–53.

Willingham, W. W., & Breland, H. M. (1982). *Personal qualities and college admissions.* New York: College Entrance Examination Board.

Wing, C. W., & Wallach, M. A. (1971). *College admissions and the psychology of talent.* New York: Holt, Rinehart and Winston.

Differential Validity and Prediction: Race and Sex Differences in College Admissions Testing

JOHN W. YOUNG

Introduction

During the past four decades, as access to higher education has increased for virtually all segments of American society, the demographic composition of the pool of examinees taking college admissions tests has changed markedly. In particular, during this period, the test-taking population has become increasingly diverse and is now more representative of American society as a whole. As diversity increases, so do questions about the tests that are used in college admissions. Specifically, are these tests equally valid for all subgroups of test takers? Studies about test validity for different populations of examinees fall under the general topics known as differential validity and differential prediction. Historically, test-taker subgroups classified by race and sex have been the ones most studied since these groups are of greatest interest for educational, political, and social reasons, and because they are the groups most easily identified. The first studies of race and sex differences in college admissions testing date back more than 30 years (Cleary, 1968; Linn, 1973). Although other demographic characteristics, such as family socioeconomic status and students' English proficiency, are of wide interest, few studies of differential validity and prediction using these variables have been conducted to date. The studies by Leonard Ramist, Charles Lewis, and Laura McCamley-Jenkins (1994, 2001) are two of the few studies that examined student language proficiency and parental education for group differences in validity and prediction. Previously, summaries of the research findings in differential validity and prediction have been written by Hunter Breland (1979), Robert Linn (1982), and Richard Durán (1983).

In educational measurement, the most common statistical approach for validating an admissions test is to estimate validity coefficients and regression equations. Validity coefficients are the correlation coefficients between a predictor variable (such as a test score) and a criterion (such as a grade point average, or GPA). Most validity studies in college admissions examine the correlation between the predictors available at the time of application (high school GPA and test scores, such as the SAT) and freshman college GPA. A regression equation uses one or more predictors to forecast the value of a criterion. Regression equations are used to determine how accurately (as measured by the multiple correlation coefficient) the predictors can forecast the criterion and to estimate the value of the criterion for an individual based on his or her scores on the predictors. In the college admissions process, validity coefficients provide a measure of the utility of an admissions test while regression equations provide a measure of the accuracy in predicting students' college grades.

Differential validity and differential prediction refer to two related but not identical problems. Differential validity refers to differences in the magnitude of the correlation coefficients for different groups of test takers, while differential prediction refers to differences in the best-fitting regression equations. Differences in regression equations are measured as differences in the slopes, intercepts, or standard errors of estimate. In validity studies based on two or more groups, differential validity can and does occur independently of differential prediction. Of the two issues, differential prediction is the more crucial because differences in prediction have a more direct bearing on considerations of fairness in admissions and selection than do differences in correlation (Linn, 1982). In addition to questions of a technical nature, differential validity and prediction as topics of research are important because they have relevance for the issues of test bias and fair test use. Differential validity and prediction are problems distinct from differences in the average test score for various demographic groups. For example, it has been reported that the mean scores on the SAT have differed for men and women as well as for different race groups for a number of years. Studies of differential validity and prediction do not investigate differences in the averages, but rather of the differences in the correlations and predictions of test scores with college grades for different groups of test takers.

The most widely used test for college admissions, historically and at present, is the SAT. The SAT was first administered in 1926 and is currently taken by well over one million students annually. In 1964, the College Board in conjunction with Educational Testing Service instituted the Validity Study Service (VSS) to assist colleges and universities in conducting their own institutional validity studies on the effectiveness of SAT scores and high school grades in predicting first-year college grades. In 1997, the Admitted Class Evaluation Service replaced the Validity Study Service. Over the years, the results from thousands of studies conducted through these two services have provided a rich source of information about differential validity and prediction. The work of independent researchers has also added to our knowledge in this area. Because the volume of differential validity and prediction studies is large for the SAT but not for any other admissions test, summaries of the findings on this topic are possible only for the SAT. Additional information on differential validity and prediction can be found in the comprehensive review and technical analysis of race and sex differences in college admissions testing by John W. Young (2001). In this report, Young reviewed all of the published studies of differential validity and prediction for a 25-year period starting in 1974, and found 29 studies of race differences and 37 studies of sex differences.

Race Differences in Validity and Prediction

In studies of race differences in validity and prediction, white students are used as the reference group to which minority students are compared. The minority groups that have been studied include African Americans, Asian Americans, Hispanics, and Native Americans. (Note that the term *Hispanic* refers to ethnicity rather than to race, but Hispanic students are treated as a separate category in most studies.) In addition, there have been one or two studies that have examined subcategories of Asian Americans (e.g., Chinese or Japanese) and Hispanics (e.g., Mexicans or Puerto Ricans), but due to sample size considerations, most studies report results only for the larger race classifications. Also, due to their low numbers at most schools, Native Americans have been studied only when students from this racial group have been combined across institutions. Of these race groups, more studies have included African-American students than any other group.

With regard to differential validity, there are distinct general patterns to the coefficients, by race groups, that are reported in validity studies. In general, the values of the validity coefficients for SAT scores and high school GPA in predicting freshman college GPA (FGPA) are higher for Asian-American and white students than for African-American and Hispanic students. That is, the traditional academic measures used in college admissions (SAT scores and high school GPA) are generally better correlated with grades in the first year of college for Asian Americans and whites than for the other two race

Table 1: Summary of the Averages of Validity Coefficients for Predicting FGPA Based on Morgan, 1990.

	AFRICAN AMERICANS	ASIAN AMERICANS	HISPANICS	WHITES	FEMALES	MALES
HS GPA	.28	.36	.35	.45	.45	.41
SAT V	.25	.22	.25	.33	.37	.30
SAT M	.25	.34	.21	.32	.39	.34
SAT V, SAT M	.32	.38	.29	.38	.44	.38
SAT V, SAT M, HS GPA	.40	.48	.43	.52	.54	.50

groups (Young, 2001). Rick Morgan (1990) reported similar findings in his study of over 275,000 students enrolled at almost 200 colleges and universities that participated in VSS in 1978, 1981, or 1985. Means for the validity coefficients for the four race groups in Morgan's study, weighted by sample size and averaged over the three years, are shown in table 1. For the correlation of high school GPA with FGPA, white students had the highest average, followed by Asian Americans and Hispanics. African Americans had a substantially lower value. For SAT Verbal (SAT V) scores, whites had the highest average correlation with FGPA while the three minority groups had similar lower values. With SAT Mathematical (SAT M), Asian Americans and whites had significantly higher averages than was found for African Americans and Hispanics. For the multiple correlation of the two SAT scores (SAT Multiple) with FGPA, Asian-American and white students had the highest averages, which were larger than the comparable values for African Americans and Hispanics. Finally, for the combination of the three traditional predictors (high school GPA, SAT V, and SAT M), the multiple correlations with FGPA were highest for white and Asian-American students and lowest for Hispanics and African Americans. Across a wide variety of institutions, one can conclude that it is usually the case that SAT scores and high school grades have a stronger association with first-year college grades for Asian-American and white students than for African-American and Hispanic students.

The causes of these race differences in the magnitude of the correlations with FGPA are not well established. A number of plausible explanations exist that are consistent with the results we observe: (1) the traditional admissions measures more accurately capture the academic skills and abilities that relate to college grades for Asian-American and white students than for African-American and Hispanic students; (2) college grades do not reflect the academic achievement as accurately for African Americans and Hispanics as for the other two racial groups; and (3) some unknown factors serve to diminish the relationship between the admissions variables and college GPA for African-American and Hispanic students but not for the other two groups. These factors may be personal, institutional, or a combination of the two, but the net effect is to weaken the association between the predictors and the grade criterion. At present, the studies in the differential validity literature do not provide sufficient details that could allow one to accept or refute any of these explanations. One or more of these explanations may hold true at a particular institution, and the implications for admissions practice will vary depending on which explanation seems most plausible.

With regard to differential prediction, the research design used to determine whether group differences exist is more complex than simply comparing correlation coefficients. Typically, a regression equation is computed for a yearly cohort of students at an institution using the traditional admissions predictors (sometimes supplemented with variables of particular interest to the institution) and the criterion of FGPA. For each student, the predicted FGPA from this equation is compared to the actual FGPA earned, and a residual error value is calculated. This residual is positive if the student has a higher actual FGPA than the predicted FGPA and is negative if the actual FGPA is less than the predicted FGPA. The term used to describe the first situation is called underprediction, while in the second situation it is known as overprediction. When these residuals are averaged for all of the students in a particular racial group, any substantial degree of misprediction (either in the form of underprediction or overprediction) is of interest since this indicates that the relationship between the predictors and criterion for these students differs from that of the majority, which at most institutions consists of white students. Since white students are used as the reference group in studies of differential prediction, the residuals for the white group are usually not of interest; rather the residual values for the minority students are the focus of most studies. An alternative design, infrequently used, is to compute the regression equation for white students only and then apply the resulting formula to the other groups. This has the general effect of magnifying the values of the residuals (without changing the sign of the residual) since this approach does not include minority students in computing the original regression equation.

Young (2001) reported that the greatest degree of misprediction occurred for African Americans with an average overprediction of −.11 (on a four-point GPA scale) based on a total of 11 studies. That is, on average, African-American students earned somewhat lower FGPAs (by .11, on average) than was predicted from their SAT scores and high school GPAs. In the eight differential prediction studies that included Hispanic students, the average overprediction value was −.08. For both of these race groups, the traditional admissions measures actually overestimated the grades these students earned in their first year of college. Another way to think of these results is to consider two students, one who is white and the other African American or Hispanic, with identical SAT scores and high school GPAs. If both of these students enrolled at the same college or university, then on average, the FGPA of the white student will be slightly higher than that of the African-American or Hispanic student. The findings from the seven studies with Asian Americans were not as clear with the degree of misprediction being generally smaller than for African Americans or Hispanics. Some of the studies found overprediction of Asian-American students' FGPA, however, while other studies resulted in underprediction. In addition, studies that have addressed the misprediction problem by adjusting FGPA based on the relative difficulty of the courses in which a student enrolled found that the FGPAs of Asian-American students tended to be underpredicted while the overprediction problem for African-American and Hispanic students was not substantially altered (Young, 1991a).

Similar results of differential prediction by race were found in a study of 38 colleges and universities by Ramist, Lewis, and McCamley-Jenkins (1994). They reported that using SAT scores and high school GPA to forecast FGPA yielded an average overprediction of −.24 for Native Americans, −.16 for African Americans, and −.13 for Hispanics. Since Ramist, Lewis, and McCamley-Jenkins were able to pool students from all 38 institutions, their study included 184 Native Americans, which represented the largest sample of this race group used in any study of differential validity and prediction. In addition, in this study, they reported an average underprediction of +.04 for Asian-American students. They also predicted grades in individual first-year college courses and found similar misprediction results for the four race groups as when FGPA was used as the criterion. The pattern of overprediction in certain kinds of courses for the underrepresented minority groups is especially troubling as the grades that students earn in first-year courses often have a large influence on their ultimate choice of majors and careers. In particular, as reported by Ramist, Lewis, and McCamley-Jenkins (1994), the lower-than-predicted grades earned by Native American and African-American students in mathematics and science courses may deter these students from majoring in these fields and steer them away from careers that required training and skills in these disciplines. The severe underrepresentation of racial minority professionals in the physical sciences and in mathematics may have its roots in the grades received by some students in their first-year college courses.

Why race differences exist in the prediction of FGPA and course grades in college has not been definitively explained. As with differential validity, several plausible explanations are possible that are consistent with the results from numerous studies: (1) The traditional admissions measures may tend to overestimate the academic skills of African-American and Hispanic students with regard to college level work. (2) College grades do not reflect the academic performance of African Americans and Hispanics as accurately as is true of the other two racial groups. (3) Some unknown factors impact the college GPA for African-American and Hispanic students in a negative way but do not affect the other two groups. As with differential validity, these factors may be personal, institutional, or interactional in nature, but the net effect is to alter the relationship between the predictors and the grade criterion for African-American and Hispanic students so that it bears a different relationship than for Asian-American and white students. A study by John Young and Sheridan Koplow (1997) at a large public university in the northeastern U.S. found that adding a measure of academic adjustment to the three traditional admissions predictors reduced the degree of overprediction of the cumulative GPA for African-American and Hispanic students. This study supports the premise that some students may face extraordinary difficulties in acclimating to the college environment, resulting in lower earned grades than would be expected.

Sex Differences in Validity and Prediction

In studies of sex differences in validity and prediction, male students are universally regarded as the reference group. In contrast to studies of race differences, sex differences are easier to describe and understand since there are only two groups under consideration. With regard to differential validity, Young (2001) reported that the magnitude of the validity coefficients for the traditional preadmissions measures, singly and in combination, were higher for women than for men. This finding holds true for most schools except for the most selective institutions (usually defined as those institutions with the highest average SAT scores for their entering classes). In these selective schools, the correlations of the predictors with FGPA for men are as high as for women and sometimes higher (Elliott & Strenta, 1988; Young, 1991b). One hypothesis for this finding is that at the most selective institutions, men are better engaged in the role of being students, so that the traditional preadmissions measures are as effective in assessing their academic skills and achievement as for their female counterparts.

The findings reported by Morgan (1990) in his study of almost 200 colleges and universities that participated in VSS in 1978, 1981, or 1985 are consistent with those reported by Young (2001). Means for males and females on various combinations of the validity coefficients, based on the results in Morgan's study, are shown in table 1. On average, the correlation of each of the three predictors with FGPA is higher for women than for men, with SAT V being substantially higher. The multiple correlation for the two SAT scores as well as for all three predictors in combination is also higher for women than for men. This indicates that the association between the predictors and FGPA is stronger for female students than for male students, so that the traditional preadmissions predictors are more informative with respect to forecasting the college grades of women than of men. One result of the higher correlations for women that could affect college admissions decisions is that, on average, the margin of error in predicting the grades of women is smaller than for men.

In terms of differential prediction, the main finding reported by Young (2001), based on 21 studies reviewed, is one of underprediction for women's college grades. From these studies, a total of 17 prediction values for women were reported, with an average underprediction value of +.06 (on a 4-point grade scale). As is the case with differential validity, the findings from the most selective institutions appear to be somewhat different from that found at less selective institutions. Four studies of students enrolled at highly selective institutions, Dartmouth University (Elliott & Strenta, 1988), the University of California, Berkeley (Leonard & Jiang, 1999), the eight undergraduate campuses of the University of California (Sue & Abe, 1988), and Stanford University (Young, 1991b), found, on average, slightly less underprediction of women's grades (with a mean value of +.04 for these studies). Similarly, at the most selective of the 38 colleges in the study by Ramist, Lewis, and McCamley-Jenkins (1994), no underprediction for female students on average, was found. In comparison to the typical overprediction values reported for African-American and Hispanic students, the amount of misprediction for women is not as large. Bear in mind, however, that at most institutions and on a national level, women constitute the majority of students enrolled in college. Thus, because the underprediction of women's grades affects a much larger percentage of the college population, the net impact of the differential prediction by sex has a much greater overall effect than the overprediction problem for minority students.

A number of possible explanations have been put forth in attempting to understand the pervasive underprediction of women's grades in college. Some of these theories are based on the use of standardized tests such as the SAT: the inclusion of multiple-choice items in a timed format; the role assigned to females in test questions; and the presence of a penalty for guessing have all been hypothesized as factors that artificially depress the scores of female test takers. However, the most plausible explanation to date of the underprediction problem is found in studies of sex differences in the courses that men and women take in college. Numerous studies have found that instructors and departments within an institution vary widely in the average grades assigned and in the grades assigned for the same level of student achievement (Strenta & Elliott, 1987; Willingham, 1985; Young, 1990). Typically, course grades awarded by humanities and social sciences departments are higher than those in the natural sciences and engineering. This finding is true in a wide variety of colleges and universities in spite of the fact that students enrolled in natural science and engineering courses generally have higher SAT scores and high school GPA than students enrolled in humanities and social science courses. Because men and women generally differ in the courses in which they enroll, primarily because of the requirements for different majors, the courses that make up FGPA and cumulative GPA differ by sex. Since women are more likely to choose courses and majors in the humanities and social sciences and men are more likely to choose courses and majors in the natural sciences and engineering, the net effect of these choices is to raise women's grades and to lower men's grades. Thus, the underprediction problem associated with women's college grades appears more likely to be caused by the use of a criterion measure with inconsistent definition from student to student than by inherent gender bias associated with the SAT. An analysis by Warren Willingham (1990) of the decline in validity coefficients for the SAT during a ten-year period beginning in the mid-1970s reached a similar conclusion in that the weakening psychometric properties of the FGPA (i.e., its lower internal consistency because of greater variation in students' choice of courses) was the most likely explanation for the decline.

Differential prediction studies that have applied statistical adjustment or scaling methods to college grades have confirmed that the underprediction problem results from sex differences in the courses taken by students and in differences in the grade distribution of courses and departments (Elliott & Strenta, 1988; Ramist, Lewis, & McCamley-Jenkins, 1994; Young, 1991b). Young (1993) reviewed and summarized grade adjustment methods and their impact when used in differential prediction studies. The findings from these studies showed that the use of an adjusted GPA as the criterion substantially reduced, and sometimes eliminated, the underprediction problem. This was true for samples of students where underprediction was found using the FGPA or cumulative GPA calculated using the standard methods at most institutions. As further evidence of the difficulties in interpreting differential prediction findings when a composite measure such as FGPA is used, a study by Robert McCornack and Mary McLeod (1988) found that in 88 large introductory college courses at San Diego State University, underprediction of women's course grades was the exception rather than the rule. In the few courses where gender-related prediction bias was found, it most often involved overprediction (not underprediction) for women in courses where men earned a higher average grade. This is the opposite of the differential prediction bias against female students usually found when predicting FGPA.

Implications for College Admissions

During the past three decades, some consensus has emerged based on the findings regarding race and sex differences in validity and prediction. For African-American and Hispanic students, the correlations of SAT scores and high school GPA with FGPA are not as strong as for Asian-American and white students. Furthermore, the traditional academic predictors tend to overestimate the FGPA of African-American and Hispanic students; their actual first-year college grades are generally lower than those forecasted from these measures. Given these two sets of findings, one could argue that for African-American and Hispanic students, less weight should be given to SAT scores and high school GPA in admissions decisions than is used for Asian Americans and whites, and that other indicators of academic abilities and skills that can provide useful information should be identified. In addition, the overprediction problem may be reduced or eliminated through the use of measures that can reliably assess significant nonacademic characteristics that influence students' first-year grades.

Because the evidence from the differential validity and prediction litera-ture demonstrates that the traditional admissions predictors of high school grades and SAT scores are less informative and less accurate regarding first-year college grades for African-American and Hispanic students than for Asian-American and white students, it would appear that these students can benefit from a more holistic admissions process such as the comprehensive review of applicants recently implemented by the University of California. Although a policy of comprehensive review for all applicants is more com-plex and costly than one of selecting students on the basis of the traditional admissions variables only, the findings from the differential validity and prediction studies indicate that the simpler approach does not work as ef-fectively for students of certain racial backgrounds. Documented evidence of academic achievement and accomplishments that is not normally captured by the traditional admissions measures may provide useful supplemental information on the likelihood of success in college for African-American and Hispanic students. For example, Willingham's (1985) study of nine pri-vate liberal arts colleges found that a measure of productive follow-through based on high school accomplishments was predictive of success at the end of four years in college beyond what was already known from test scores and grades.

With regard to sex differences in validity and prediction, there appear to be two key issues that are important to consider in the college admissions process. The first is the commonly observed underprediction of women's grades when the criterion of FGPA is used. Based on studies of adjusted GPAs and of individual course grades, there is sufficient evidence to conclude that the most plausible explanation for the overprediction problem is sex differences in course selection. However, this is still an issue that should be further monitored. Although these differences in the choice of courses in college explain much of the underprediction problem, they do not always completely eliminate the prediction bias. In addition, as the variability across students in the courses they take continues to increase (Willingham, 1990), the overprediction problem may worsen with each succeeding cohort of entering students. In particular, at large universities where students have the greatest flexibility in choosing courses, these institutions should investigate how large the problem of grade underprediction for women actually is (apart from differences in course selection) and determine whether underprediction is increasing with each new class. If the underprediction problem appears to be a persistent and worsening one, then one implication for admissions is that some preference should be given to female applicants since, on average, their college grades will turn out to be better than those of male applicants with identical academic credentials.

The second issue that results from sex differences in validity and prediction is due to the generally lower correlations of the traditional admissions predictors for men as compared to women. This problem is similar to that observed for African-American and Hispanic students who have lower correlations than those for their Asian-American and white counterparts. In considering male applicants, the same recommendation for admissions practices would be given: other indicators of academic abilities and skills, beyond test scores and grades, that can provide useful information should be identified. Except at the most selective institutions in the country, it is generally the case that the grades of men in college depend less on prior academic credentials than is true for women. By implication, then, other factors play important roles in the grades that men earn so that identifying and assessing these other factors will lead to an improved admissions process.

Summary

For more than 30 years, the exploration of group differences in performance on college admissions tests such as the SAT has been an active field of research. More specifically, race and sex differences in the validity and predictive accuracy of college admissions tests have been studied intensely, both to understand the technical issues involved and also to grasp the potential implications of these differences for college admissions policies and practices. Notable differences in the validity and predictive accuracy of SAT scores and high school grades by race and sex have been substantiated through numerous studies: The correlations of these traditional admissions measures with FGPA are higher for women, Asian Americans, and white students, and lower for men, African Americans, and Hispanics. Furthermore, these admissions variables often overpredict the grades of African-American and Hispanic students and may underpredict those of women, although this latter finding is less consistent. Given these findings, which have been consistently observed at a wide variety of institutions, current admissions policies may need to be reconsidered with respect to the data on academic qualifications that is available on applicants. Other measures that can supplement the traditional admissions measures by providing useful information for forecasting students' achievement in college would serve to eliminate some of the inequities that are unavoidable under current admissions practices at many institutions.

References

Breland, H. M. (1979). *Population validity and college entrance measures.* Research Monograph No. 8. New York: College Board.

Cleary, T. A. (1968). Test bias: Prediction of grades for Negro and white students in integrated colleges. *Journal of Educational Measurement, 5,* 115–24.

Durán, R. P. (1983). *Hispanics' education and background: Predictors of college achievement.* New York: College Board.

Elliott, R., & Strenta, A. C. (1988). Effects of improving the reliability of the GPA on prediction generally and on comparative predictions for gender and race particularly. *Journal of Educational Measurement, 25,* 333–47.

Leonard, D. K., & Jiang, J. (1999). Gender bias and the college predictions of the SATs: A cry of despair. *Research in Higher Education, 40,* 375–407.

Linn, R. L. (1973). Fair test use in selection. *Review of Educational Research, 43,* 139–61.

Linn, R. L. (1982). Ability testing: Individual differences, prediction and differential prediction. In R. L. Linn (Ed.), *Ability testing: Uses, consequences, and controversies.* Washington, DC: National Academy Press.

McCornack, R. L., & McLeod, M. M. (1988). Gender bias in the prediction of college course performance. *Journal of Educational Measurement, 25,* 321–31.

Morgan, R. (1990). Analyses of predictive validity within student categorizations. In W. W. Willingham, C. Lewis, R. Morgan, & L. Ramist (Eds.), *Predicting college grades: An analysis of institutional trends over two decades* (pp. 225–38). Princeton, NJ: Educational Testing Service.

Ramist, L., Lewis, C., & McCamley-Jenkins, L. (1994). *Student group differences in predicting college grades: Sex, language, and ethnic groups.* College Board Report No. 93-1. New York: College Board.

Ramist, L., Lewis, C., & McCamley-Jenkins, L. (2001). *Using achievement tests/SAT-II Subject Tests to demonstrate achievement and predict college grades: Sex, language, ethnic, and parental education groups.* College Board Research Report No. 2001-5. New York: College Board.

Strenta, A. C., & Elliott, R. (1987). Differential grading standards revisited. *Journal of Educational Measurement, 24,* 281–91.

Sue, S., & Abe, J. (1988). *Predictors of academic achievement among Asian American and white students.* Research Report No. 88–11. New York: College Board.

Willingham, W. W. (1985). *Success in college.* New York: College Board.

Willingham, W. W. (1990). Conclusions and implications. In W. W. Willingham, C. Lewis, R. Morgan, & L. Ramist (Eds.), *Predicting college grades: An analysis of institutional trends over two decades* (pp. 85–99). Princeton, NJ: Educational Testing Service.

Young, J. W. (1990). Adjusting the cumulative GPA using item response theory. *Journal of Educational Measurement, 27,* 175–86.

Young, J. W. (1991a). Improving the prediction of college performance of ethnic minorities using the IRT-based GPA. *Applied Measurement in Education, 4,* 229–39.

Young, J. W. (1991b). Gender bias in predicting college academic performance: A new approach using Item Response Theory. *Journal of Educational Measurement, 28,* 37–47.

Young, J. W. (1993). Grade adjustment methods. *Review of Educational Research, 63,* 151–65.

Young, J. W. (2001). *Differential validity, differential prediction, and college admission testing: A comprehensive review and analysis.* College Board Research Report No. 2001-6. New York: College Board.

Young, J. W., & Koplow, S. L. (1997). The validity of two questionnaires for predicting minority students' college grades. *Journal of General Education, 46,* 45–55.

The Effects of Using ACT Composite Scores and High School Averages on College Admissions Decisions for Ethnic Groups

JULIE NOBLE

With the elimination of racial preference in admissions policies in Texas, Florida, California, and Washington, and the legal challenge to the University of Michigan for its uses of racial preferences in college admissions, many other institutions are considering eliminating race-based admissions policies (Orfield & Miller, 1998; Schmidt, 1998; 1999). Some institutions are basing their admissions policies primarily on high school rank or grades, with test scores and other information as secondary sources. Other institutions have reduced the use of standardized tests, but have not eliminated them entirely. Most are maintaining their current practices, but with great concern about the future of their admissions policies, particularly if their policies consider ethnicity.

Some people believe that standardized college admissions tests are "biased" or unfair, because African-American and Hispanic students typically score lower on them than do white or Asian-American students (e.g., Cloud, 1997; Cortez, 1997; Cross & Slater, 1997; Hebel, 1999; St. John, Simmons, & Musoba, 1999; Marklein, 2000). What appears to be forgotten, however, is that African-American and Hispanic students typically score lower on most achievement measures used for admissions, including high school

303

average. Using almost any measure of academic achievement for college admissions will therefore result in a smaller proportion of African-American and Hispanic students being admitted, relative to white and Asian-American students (D'Souza, 1995; Orfield & Miller, 1998; Zwick, 1999).

The issue of test score "bias" in college admissions has been extensively researched from the perspective of success in college. When the relationships among college grades, test scores, and high school averages differ among various population subgroups of students, using a prediction equation developed from the total group of students may result in systematic over- or underprediction for different subgroups (i.e., differential prediction). In other words, students' actual freshman grade point averages (GPAs) are higher or lower than their predicted GPAs (see Young & Kobrin, 2001, and the chapter by Young in this volume). Prior research on differential prediction using admissions test scores (typically ACT Assessment or SAT scores) and high school averages as predictors (e.g., Donlon, 1984; Linn, 1982; Pennock-Román, 1988; 1990; Sawyer, 1985) has shown that the first-year GPAs for African-American and Hispanic students with given test scores are lower than the GPAs of white students with the same scores. In addition, African-American students tend to have lower college English or algebra grades than white students with the same high school English or mathematics grades (Noble, Crouse, & Schulz; 1996; J. Crouse, personal communication, 9/19/00). The differences in college outcomes between African-American and white students with the same high school grades were larger than the corresponding differences based on students with the same ACT scores.

Some people believe that by reducing or eliminating the use of standardized tests and reverting to measures such as high school rank or grade average, the resulting proportions of ethnic minorities admitted might approach the proportions achieved using race-based admissions policies (which may or may not be optimal, depending on the goals of the institution). But at what cost? Because of large disparities between schools in their grading practices and the rigor of their courses, a high-ranking or high-GPA student from one school could differ substantially from a high-ranking or high-GPA student from another institution in preparedness for college-level work. Even within schools, students' high school ranks or grade averages do not necessarily reflect the rigor of the courses they take. The potential result is that students who appear to be prepared for college, but who are actually underprepared, could have much lower chances of achieving good college grades and persisting to graduation. Conversely, students from high-quality schools with lower high school ranks or grade averages who are actually prepared for college are less likely to be admitted (D'Souza, 1995; Krauthammer, 1998; Orfield & Miller, 1998; Selingo, 2000; Stewart, 1998). Though these outcomes have been noted in California and Florida (e.g., Selingo, 2000), the

University of Texas-Austin (Lavergne & Walker, 2001), unlike other Texas institutions, has had nearly the same percentage of minority students enroll in recent years as they had prior to ending affirmative action programs in 1996. However, minority enrollments at the university are still below the levels of enrollment achieved prior to the 1996 *Hopwood v. Texas* decision.

Consider the purposes and uses of tests and their utility relative to other achievement measures (e.g., high school average). The ACT Assessment measures academic skills and knowledge that are taught in typical college-preparatory curricula in high school, and is intended to facilitate both college admissions and course placement decisions. If ACT scores are valid for their intended uses, students taking rigorous college preparatory course work in high school will obtain higher ACT scores than those who do not, and students with higher ACT scores will be more successful their first year in college than students with lower test scores. Standardized admissions tests like the ACT Assessment will reflect differences in the educational preparation of high school students, in particular the courses they take, the grades they earn, their high school ranking, and the quality of the education they receive (Zwick, 1999).

Prior research on admissions test scores has focused primarily on the issue of differential prediction. Moreover, few studies have examined other differential *effects* (e.g., the percentage of students who would be admitted) of using admissions test scores or high school average for college admissions. The purpose of this study, therefore, was to investigate differential prediction *and* the differential effects on African-American, Hispanic, and white students of using ACT Composite scores, high school averages, or both for making non-race-based admissions decisions. Differential prediction, prediction accuracy, and percentage admitted were compared across subgroups and predictor variables. (In addition, this study investigated the relative contribution of other student information to the improvement of admission rates for African-American and Hispanic students. For brevity, results of the second analysis are not reported here, but may be obtained from the author.)

Data for the Study

The data for this study consisted of the background characteristics, high school grades, ACT scores, and college grades for 219,954 first-year students from 311 colleges. In addition, 728,957 nonenrolled students had requested that their ACT scores be sent to at least one of the 311 institutions, but they did not enroll in that institution. These students, plus those who actually enrolled in an institution and completed their first year, constituted the applicant pool for that institution.

The applicant pools for the institutions in this study approximate actual applicant pools, but are not true applicant pools. Students may send their ACT scores to any number of institutions, but actually apply to only a subset of them. Conversely, some students may apply to some institutions without submitting official ACT score reports. Future research based on actual application and enrollment information will help identify the effects of approximating the applicant pools used in this study.

The ACT Assessment consists of four academic tests (in English, mathematics, reading, and science), a student profile section, an interest inventory, and the course grade information section, which requests information about students' grades in 30 specific high school courses. Students receive scores on each of the four academic tests, as well as a composite score. Test scores are reported on a scale of 1 to 36.

The applicant pool for each institution was limited to students with ACT Composite scores and high school averages (and first-year GPAs, for enrolled students). A minimum sample size of 40 enrolled students per ethnic group was used to help ensure accurate and stable predictions. Of the original files, 71 institutions (comprising 94,786 enrolled students and 325,821 nonenrolled students) had at least 40 enrolled white and 40 enrolled African-American students. In addition, 30 institutions (comprising 66,479 enrolled students and 209,761 nonenrolled students) had at least 40 enrolled white and 40 enrolled Hispanic students. (The Hispanic group included Mexican-American, Chicano, Puerto Rican, Cuban, and other Hispanic students.) All students had taken the ACT Assessment within two years of enrolling in college, and all students at each institution who met the criteria for inclusion were included, regardless of ethnicity.

The institutions used in this study were primarily from southern, south central, and Midwestern states, and do not represent postsecondary institutions nationally. They also varied in admissions selectivity, though the majority (60%) had traditional (top 50% of the high school graduating class) or selective (top 25% of the high school graduating class) admissions policies.

Method for the Study
Analyses were carried out separately for the African-American/white sample and for the Hispanic/white sample. The same analyses were conducted for both samples.

Descriptive Statistics
For each ethnic group and for the total group, mean ACT Composite scores, high school averages, and first-year GPAs (enrolled students only) were computed by institution. Descriptive statistics for each institution were

calculated for students who completed the first year of college (enrolled students), as well as for the entire applicant pool (enrolled and nonenrolled students combined). These statistics were then summarized across institutions for the total group of students and for each ethnic group using median, minimum, and maximum values.

Regression Models

Admissions decisions are usually made based on multiple variables and multiple cutoffs or cutoff ranges. ACT does not advocate making admissions decisions solely based on a single cutoff or a single measure; the use of single cutoffs in this paper is a mathematical simplification. The methods used here, such as those used with the joint ACT and high school average model may be generalized to multiple measures.

Probabilities of obtaining a GPA of 2.5 or higher were estimated by ethnic group and institution using three logistic regression models: one that used ACT composite only as a predictor, one that used high school average only, and one that used both (the joint predictor model). The regression weights from these models were then used to estimate probabilities of success for all students in the applicant pool, by ethnic group. These probabilities were summarized across institutions by model and ethnic group using median, minimum, and maximum values.

Logistic regression allows college admissions officials to evaluate predictor variables relative to a specific outcome threshold (e.g., first-year GPA of 2.0 or higher). It provides estimated probabilities of success, relative to the threshold, given specific values of the predictor variable(s). This approach also provides decision accuracy rates (percentages of correct decisions) for the applicant pool—the students about whom admissions decisions are to be made (see, e.g., Sawyer, 1996).

Similarly, ACT Composite, high school average, and joint predictor logistic regression models were developed for all students, by institution. The total group included all students from each institution with an ACT Composite score and high school average, regardless of ethnicity. The regression weights were then used to estimate probabilities of success for all students in the applicant pool. Then, optimal ACT Composite score and high school average cutoffs were identified (referred to here as total-group optimal cutoffs). These cutoffs were then used to show the effect of using non-race-based admissions criteria on African-American, Hispanic, and white students.

Optimal cutoffs correspond to a .50 probability of success for a given predictor or set of predictors, and maximize the estimated percentage of correct admission decisions (see Sawyer, 1996). It should be noted, however, that optimal cutoffs as defined here reflect specific statistical properties, and do not consider other factors that might be of interest to postsecondary institutions (e.g., some institutions may weigh admissions decisions differently).

For example, correctly admitting successful students (true positives) might be a higher priority than correctly excluding unsuccessful students (true negatives).

Using the probabilities of success estimated using within-ethnic group regression models and the total-group optimal cutoffs, the following statistics were estimated for each model using the applicant pool for each institution:

- the percentage of students who would be admitted (admission rate)
- the percentage of correct admission decisions (accuracy rate)
- the increase in the percentage of correct admission decisions over admitting all applicants (increase in accuracy rate)

Correct admission decisions include students who would be admitted who were successful and students who would not be admitted who would have not been successful, had they been admitted (Sawyer, 1996).

A success criterion of a 2.5 or higher GPA was selected based on statistical and practical considerations. Possibly due to student attrition or grade inflation, a relatively small proportion of students achieve GPAs of less than 2.0 at many institutions (e.g., the national average first-year GPA for enrolled freshmen was 3.23; (see ACT, Inc., 1998). In order to achieve reasonable predictions of first-year GPA, there must be a sufficient number of students with GPAs above and below a given GPA threshold. For these samples, few African-American students had GPAs above 3.0 and few Hispanic students and white students had GPAs below 2.0. Moreover, for some institutions and predictor variables, probabilities of success either all exceeded .50 or were all less than .50. In addition, some institutions showed negative predictor-GPA relationships, often due to restriction of range in either the predictor or in GPAs, or to GPAs that measured factors other than educational achievement (e.g., attendance, effort, participation). All institutions where these situations occurred were eliminated from the logistic regression analyses. A "2.5 or higher" success definition was therefore selected to maximize the number of institutions in both samples for which models could be developed. The final samples upon which all results were based consisted of 262,553 students from 43 institutions for the African-American/white sample and 174,890 students from 25 institutions for the Hispanic/white sample.

Results

Descriptive Statistics

African-American/White Students. The descriptive statistics are summarized in table 1. For both enrolled students and the applicant pool, median, minimum, and maximum (across institutions) numbers of students, mean ACT Composite score, mean high school averages, and mean first-year GPA

Table 1: Means and Standard Deviations of ACT Composite Scores, High School Averages, and First-Year GPAs, Across Institutions, of White and African-American Students, by Applicant/Enrollment Status (43 institutions)

APPLICANT/ ENROLLMENT STATUS	ETHNIC GROUP	N		ACT COMPOSITE SCORE				HIGH SCHOOL AVERAGE				FIRST-YEAR GPA			
				MEAN		SD		MEAN		SD		MEAN		SD	
		MED	MIN/ MAX	MED	MIN/ MAX	MED	MIN/ MAX	MED	MIN/ MAX	MED	MIN/ MAX	MED	MIN/ MAX	MED	MIN/ MAX
Enrolled students	Total group[1]	1,228	188/3,793	21.3	17.4/24.2	3.90	3.28/4.38	3.15	2.66/3.49	.57	.42/.69	2.47	2.09/2.90	.93	.69/1.39
	White	1,111	89/3,474	21.6	18.9/24.5	3.77	3.20/4.29	3.16	2.79/3.52	.56	.41/.70	2.54	2.19/3.16	.93	.68/1.39
	African-Am.	129	47/941	17.8	14.9/20.7	3.10	2.25/4.13	2.93	2.50/3.30	.52	.41/.65	2.06	1.58/2.66	.89	.67/1.28
Applicant pool[2]	Total group	5,076	517/18,301	20.3	17.3/22.7	4.03	3.49/4.46	3.06	2.65/3.29	.59	.50/.64				
	White	4,192	301/16,931	20.9	18.5/22.9	3.93	3.50/4.33	3.09	2.73/3.31	.58	.49/.65				
	African-Am.	620	84/1,724	17.1	14.9/18.6	3.30	2.23/4.02	2.80	2.53/3.07	.56	.48/.65				

[1]The total group included all students from each institution with an ACT Composite score and high school average, regardless of ethnicity.
[2]The applicant pool includes both enrolled and nonenrolled students.

Notes:
N = Number of students
SD = Standard deviation
Med = Median value across institutions
Min = Minimum value across institutions
Max = Maximum value across institutions

(enrolled students only) are reported for the total group and for each ethnic group.

In general, enrolled students had higher ACT Composite scores and slightly better high school averages than did the entire applicant pool (median mean ACT Composite = 21.3 vs. 20.3; median mean high school average = 3.15 vs. 3.06). As one would expect, median standard deviations for the enrolled students were somewhat smaller than those for the entire applicant pool (ACT median SD = 3.90 vs. 4.03; high school average median SD = .57 vs. .59).

For both enrolled students as well as the entire applicant pool, African-American students typically had lower mean ACT Composite scores and high school averages than did white students. African-American students also had lower mean first-year GPAs than did white students (median mean GPA = 2.54 vs. 2.06). Moreover, African-American students tended to vary less in their ACT Composite scores and high school averages than did white students, as shown by the median standard deviations for both groups.

Hispanic/White Students.   The descriptive statistics are summarized in table 2. For both enrolled students and the entire applicant pool, median, minimum, and maximum (across institutions) numbers of students, mean ACT Composite score, mean high school averages, and mean first-year GPA (enrolled students only) are reported for the total group and for each ethnic group.

In general, enrolled students had higher ACT Composite scores and somewhat higher high school averages than did the entire applicant pool (ACT median mean = 21.8 vs. 20.1; high school average median mean = 3.28 vs. 3.14). The median ACT Composite standard deviation was slightly higher for the applicant pool than for enrolled students, however (ACT median SD = 3.98 vs. 3.75).

For both the enrolled group and the applicant pool, Hispanic students typically had lower mean ACT Composite scores and high school averages than did white students. Hispanic students also typically had lower mean first-year GPAs than did white students (median mean GPA = 2.66 vs. 2.43).

Success Predictions

African-American/White Students.   Probabilities of a GPA of 2.5 were estimated for each ethnic group using ACT Composite score or high school average, by institution, and then summarized across institutions using median values. The median probabilities were then plotted for both ethnic groups, as shown in figure 1. The results showed that for a given ACT Composite score or high school average, African-American students typically had a

Table 2: Means and Standard Deviations of ACT Composite Scores, High School Averages, and First-Year GPAs, Across Institutions, of White and Hispanic Students, by Applicant/Enrollment Status (25 institutions)

APPLICANT/ ENROLLMENT STATUS	ETHNIC GROUP	N		ACT COMPOSITE SCORE				HIGH SCHOOL AVERAGE				FIRST-YEAR GPA			
				MEAN		SD		MEAN		SD		MEAN		SD	
		MED	MIN/ MAX	MED	MIN/ MAX	MED	MIN/ MAX	MED	MIN/ MAX	MED	MIN/ MAX	MED	MIN/ MAX	MED	MIN/ MAX
Enrolled students	Total group[1]	1,153	193/3,556	21.8	17.2/26.8	3.75	3.18/4.58	3.28	2.69/3.75	.50	.29/.62	2.66	2.02/3.21	.89	.64/1.06
	White	944	53/3,474	22.1	18.9/26.9	3.73	3.21/4.52	3.28	2.70/3.76	.50	.28/.61	2.66	2.19/3.21	.90	.63/1.11
	Hispanic	76	41/1,156	20.1	15.7/23.9	3.67	2.39/4.59	3.18	2.54/3.55	.51	.39/.70	2.43	2.01/2.90	.94	.62/1.22
Applicant pool[2]	Total group	6,099	619/17,247	21.1	16.7/23.9	3.98	3.23/4.48	3.14	2.68/3.54	.54	.44/.63				
	White	5,223	155/16,931	21.4	18.5/24.0	3.97	3.50/4.45	3.18	2.68/3.55	.53	.44/.63				
	Hispanic	340	82/2,829	19.2	15.9/22.2	3.79	2.59/4.63	3.05	2.60/3.45	.55	.45/.68				

[1]The total group included all students from each institution with ACT Composite scores and high school averages, regardless of ethnicity.
[2]The applicant pool includes both enrolled and nonenrolled students.

Notes:
  N = Number of students
  SD = Standard deviation
  Med = Median value across institutions
  Min = Minimum value across institutions
  Max = Maximum value across institutions

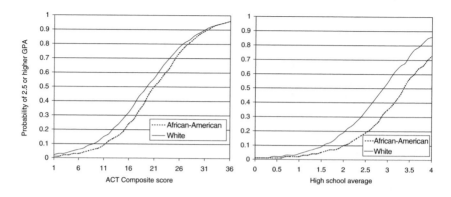

Figure 1. Median within-ethnic group probabilities of 2.5 or higher first-year GPA, using ACT Composite score or high school average (white and African-American students).

lower probability of obtaining a 2.5 or higher GPA, relative to white students with the same score or high school average.

The largest differences in median probabilities of success between African-American and white students, based on ACT Composite score, occurred for scores between 10 and 25. For these scores, differences in median probabilities of success between these two groups ranged from .05 to .10, with African-American students having the lower median probabilities.

In comparison, differences in median probabilities of success between African-American and white students, based on high school average, were generally larger than those based on ACT Composite score. At a high school average of 1.5, the difference between ethnic groups in median probability was .05, and increased to .22 at a high school average of 3.5. The between-groups difference in median probability at a high school average of 4.0 was .13.

The logistic regression statistics in table 3 reflect the effect of imposing the total-group optimal cutoff for each institution on each ethnic group. The statistics were estimated by applying the total-group optimal cutoffs to the within-ethnic group estimated probabilities of success described earlier. The results were then summarized across institutions using median, minimum, and maximum values. This approach illustrates the effects of using a common selection rule for the applicant pool based on total-group optimal ACT Composite scores and high school average.

Median probabilities of success for African-American students corresponding to the total-group optimal cutoff were lower than were those for white students for all three predictor models. The difference in median probability was the largest for high school average (.35 vs. .52, respectively) and

Table 3: Within-Group Regression Statistics, Across Institutions, for African-American and White Students, Using Total-Group Optimal Cutoffs

PREDICTOR VARIABLE	GROUP	PROBABILITY OF SUCCESS AT TOTAL-GROUP CUTOFF		ESTIMATED ACCURACY RATE		ESTIMATED INCREASE IN ACCURACY RATE		% ADMITTED	
		MED.	MIN./MAX.	MED.	MIN./MAX.	MED.	MIN./MAX.	MED.	MIN./MAX.
ACT Composite	White	.55	.49/.68	.66	.60/.84	.09	–.00/.33	56	31/93
	African-American	.45	.29/.68	.71	.58/.82	.41	.08/.62	18	15/70
HS average	White	.52	.50/.61	.70	.62/.83	.12	–.00/.30	59	37/96
	African-American	.35	.17/.49	.69	.59/.80	.37	.00/.57	37	14/96
ACT Comp. & HS average	White	.49	.43/.59	.71	.63/.83	.14	.01/.36	55	36/89
	African-American	.37	.14/.57	.74	.65/.86	.45	.10/.65	24	7/67

the smallest for ACT Composite (.45 vs. .55, respectively). In contrast, median accuracy rates were somewhat higher, and median increases in accuracy rate much higher, for African-American students than for white students for the ACT Composite and joint models.

In general, a smaller percentage of African-American students than white students would be admitted under a total-group cutoff, using any of the three models. For the high school average model, the median percentages of students who would be admitted were 37% and 59% for African-American and white students, respectively. For the ACT Composite model, the median percentages of students who would be admitted were 18% and 56%, respectively. For the joint model, the median percentages of students who would be admitted were 24% and 55%, respectively.

Hispanic/White Students. Probabilities of a GPA of 2.5 were estimated for each ethnic group using ACT Composite score or high school average, by institution, and then summarized across institutions using median values. The median probabilities were then plotted for both ethnic groups, as shown in figure 2. The results showed that for a given ACT Composite score or high school average, Hispanic students typically had a slightly lower probability of obtaining a 2.5 or higher GPA, relative to white students with the same score or high school average.

Differences in median probability of success between Hispanic and white students, based on ACT Composite score, were small, with differences not exceeding .04 (see figure 2). In comparison, differences in median probability between Hispanic and white students, based on high school average, were larger: From high school averages of 2.5 to 4.0, differences in median probability ranged from .06 to .10. For both models, differences in median

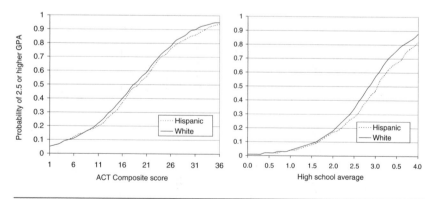

Figure 2. Median within-ethnic group probabilities of 2.5 or higher first-year GPA, using ACT Composite score or high school average (White and Hispanic students).

probabilities were smaller for this sample than for the African-American/ white sample.

Table 4 includes the ACT Composite score, high school average, and joint ACT Composite/high school average models, reflecting the effect of imposing the optimal total-group cutoff for each institution on Hispanic and white applicants. The results are summarized across institutions.

As shown in table 4, the differences between ethnic groups in median probabilities of success associated with the total-group optimal cutoffs were smallest for the ACT Composite model (.52 vs. .48) and largest for the high school average model (.51 vs. .42). The joint model did not reduce the difference between groups in the median probability of success found for the high school average model. For all three models, however, median accuracy rates were lower for Hispanic students than for white students. In contrast, median increases in accuracy rates were higher for Hispanic students than for white students for all three models (difference in medians of .03 to .11). Differences between groups in the median percentage of students who would be admitted ranged from 9% to 20%, with the high school average model having the smaller difference and the ACT Composite model having the larger difference. The joint model slightly increased the difference in median percentage over that found for the high school average model.

Conclusions

The African-American and Hispanic students in this study had lower average high school grade averages and ACT Composite scores than did the white students. These students also had lower first-year college GPAs than white students. As a result, if admission decisions were based on test scores or high school grade averages, and if ethnicity were not considered, a smaller percentage of African-American students and Hispanic students than white students would be admitted to college. *This result is true of both test scores and high school grade averages.*

African-American or Hispanic students with a given ACT Composite score or high school average have slightly lower college GPAs than white students with the same score or average. Therefore, in order to achieve the same average college performance across these ethnic groups, admissions criteria would need to be *more* restrictive for these groups than for white students. In particular, high school averages were found to result in lower probabilities of success for ethnic minority students than for white students; ethnic differences in typical probabilities using the ACT Composite score were much smaller. Therefore, by not using standardized test scores with other information for college admissions, institutions run the risk of admitting

Table 4: Within-Group Regression Statistics, Across Institutions, for Hispanic and White Students Using Total-Group Optimal Cutoffs (25 institutions)

PREDICTOR	GROUP	PROBABILITY OF SUCCESS AT TOTAL-GROUP CUTOFF		ESTIMATED ACCURACY RATE		ESTIMATED INCREASE IN ACCURACY RATE		% ADMITTED	
		MED.	MIN./MAX.	MED.	MIN./MAX.	MED.	MIN./MAX.	MED.	MIN./MAX.
ACT Comp.	White	.52	.48/.56	.67	.59/.84	.04	–.00/.23	77	31/100
	Hispanic	.48	.20/.64	.63	.53/.75	.07	–.00/.43	57	8/98
HS average	White	.51	.50/.70	.70	.62/.83	.09	–.00/.26	68	24/96
	Hispanic	.42	.27/.60	.66	.56/.79	.15	.01/.42	59	16/97
ACT Comp. & HS average	White	.50	.28/.58	.72	.64/.84	.12	.01/.29	67	31/97
	Hispanic	.41	.12/.60	.68	.59/.83	.21	.02/.47	55	14/90

African-American and Hispanic students who are underprepared for college-level work. These findings are corroborated in other research on differential prediction and admissions test scores (J. Crouse, personal communication, 9/19/00; Noble, Crouse, & Schulz, 1996; Pennock-Román, 1988; 1990; Sawyer, 1985).

The results of this study showed that ACT Composite scores or high school grade average were more accurate predictors of the probability of obtaining a first-year GPA of 2.5 or higher for African-American students than for white students. In contrast, prior research has shown less prediction accuracy for African-American students than for white students, based on test scores alone or joint use of test scores and high school grades (ACT, Inc., 1997, pp. 58–59; Maxey & Sawyer, 1981). However, both of the prior studies were based on restricted samples of enrolled students; the samples could have been affected by differential admissions practices across ethnic groups. In contrast, though the regression coefficients used here were based on restricted samples of students, the validity statistics take into account the expected outcomes for students in the applicant pool. Walter Houston (1993) showed that conditional probabilities of success could be estimated with reasonable accuracy if the sample restriction is 25% or less. Jeff Schiel (1998) showed that conditional probabilities of success can be accurately estimated when greater restriction is present if outcome information is available for some low-scoring students (e.g., some students scoring below the admissions cutoff were admitted and had first-year GPAs).

Both test score and high school average were less accurate predictors for Hispanic students than for white students. This finding is consistent with prior research (Maxey & Sawyer, 1981; Pennock-Román, 1988). Maria Pennock-Román (1990) found inconsistent results, which she attributed to range restriction in the data. She also found high school average to be a less accurate predictor of college GPA than test scores for some institutions, but found the opposite for other institutions.

It should be noted that the results of this study are not representative of institutions nationwide, and are limited to the 2.5-or-higher GPA success criterion. In addition, due to the limited number of institutions and to the limited sample sizes within institutions, gender and ethnicity could not be studied jointly. Prior research (e.g., Bridgeman, McCamley-Jenkins, & Ervin, 2000; Young & Kobrin, 2001) suggests that differential prediction of first-year GPA is affected by both ethnicity and gender.

Implications

Postsecondary institutions are in a quandary. Diversity in student populations is an important part of their mission, but in order to achieve it, institutions might rely less on standardized test scores for college admissions. In so doing, they would admit students who may be less well prepared academically to do college-level work. By admitting students who are underprepared, institutions will need to provide supplemental programs (e.g., remedial instruction) to support these students, in order for them to have a successful college experience. Moreover, using alternative measures to standardized test scores and high school grades (e.g., high school rank) does not appear to be achieving the equivalent of race-based admissions in California and Florida (Cohen, 1998; McWhorter, 2001). The percentages of African-American and Hispanic students admitted to college remain below the percentages achieved before the laws changed.

The use of both standardized test scores and high school grades in college admissions increases the likelihood of students' academic success and persistence in college. Moreover, it increases the likelihood that institutions will maintain campus diversity beyond the freshman year.

References

ACT, Inc. (1997). *ACT Assessment technical manual.* Iowa City, IA: ACT, Inc.

ACT, Inc. (1998). *College student profiles.* Iowa City, IA: ACT, Inc.

Bridgeman, B., McCamley-Jenkins, L., & Ervin, N. (2000). *Predictions of freshman grade point average from the revised and recentered SAT I: Reasoning Test.* College Board Research Report No. 2000-1. New York: College Entrance Examination Board.

Cloud, J. (1997, November 10). What does SAT stand for? *Time,* pp. 54–55.

Cohen, A. (1998, April 20). Back to square one. *Time,* pp. 30–31.

Cortez, A. (1997, February). Criteria for diversity: THECB's advisory committee suggests new criteria. *IDRA Newsletter,* pp. 3–5.

Cross, T., & Slater, R. B. (1997). Why the end of affirmative action would exclude all but a very few blacks from America's leading universities and graduate schools. *Journal of Blacks in Higher Education, 17,* pp. 8–17.

Donlon, T. F. (1984). *The college board technical handbook for the Scholastic Aptitude Test and Achievement Tests.* New York: College Entrance Examination Board.

D'Souza, D. (1995, September 15). The failure of "cruel compassion." *Chronicle of Higher Education,* pp. B1–2.

Hebel, S. (1999, February 12). Minority students sue Berkeley, charging bias in admissions. *Chronicle of Higher Education,* pp. A37.

Houston, W. M. (1993). Accuracy of validity indices for course placement systems. Paper presented at the Annual Meeting of the American Educational Research Association, Atlanta, Georgia.

Krauthammer, C. (1998, April 20). Lies, damn lies, and racial statistics. *Time,* pp. 32.

Lavergne, G. M., & Walker, B. (2001). Academic performance and persistence of top 10% and non-top 10% students: Academic years 1996–2000. HB588 Report No. 4. Available online at http://www.utexas.edu/student/research/reports/admissions/HB588-Report4.pdf.

Linn, R. L. (1982). Ability testing: Individual differences, prediction, and differential prediction. In A. K. Wigdor & W. R. Garner (Eds.), *Ability testing: Uses, consequences, and controversies; part 2* (pp. 335–388). Washington, DC: National Academy Press.

Marklein, M. B. (2000, August 30). GPA jumps to head of class. *USA Today,* p 10D.

Maxey, E. J., & Sawyer, R. L. (1981). *Predictive validity of the ACT Assessment for Afro-American/Black, Mexican-American/Chicano, and Caucasian-American/White students.* ACT Research Bulletin # 81-1. Iowa City, IA: ACT, Inc.

McWhorter, J. H. (2001, March 9). Eliminating the SAT could derail the progress of minority students. *Chronicle of Higher Education,* p. B11.

Noble, J. P., Crouse, J., & Schulz, E. M. (1996). *Differential prediction/impact in course placement for ethnic and gender groups*. (ACT Research Report #96-8). Iowa City, IA: ACT, Inc.

Orfield, G., & Miller, E. (1998). *Chilling admissions: The affirmative action crisis and the search for alternatives*. Cambridge, MA: Harvard Education Publishing.

Pennock-Román, M. (1988). *The status of research on the Scholastic Aptitude Test (SAT) and Hispanic students in postsecondary education*. ETS Research Report No. 88-36. Princeton, NJ: Educational Testing Service.

Pennock-Román, M. (1990). *Test validity and language background*. New York: The College Board.

Sawyer, R. L. (1985). *Using demographic information in predicting college freshman grades*. ACT Research Report #87. Iowa City, Iowa: ACT, Inc.

Sawyer, R. L. (1996). Decision theory models for validating course placement tests. *Journal of Educational Measurement, 33*, 271–90.

Sawyer, R. L., Laing, J., & Houston, W. M. (1988). *Accuracy of self-reported high school courses and grades of college-bound students*. ACT Research Report No. 88-1. Iowa City, IA: ACT, Inc.

Schiel, J. (1998). *Estimating conditional probabilities of success and other course placement validity statistics under soft truncation*. ACT Research Report No. 98–2. Iowa City, IA: ACT, Inc.

Schmidt, P. (1998, October 30). U. of Michigan prepares to defend admissions policy in court. *Chronicle of Higher Education*, pp. A32–34.

Schmidt, P. (1999, September 3). Minority students win right to intervene in lawsuit attacking affirmative action. *Chronicle of Higher Education*, pp. A68.

Selingo, J. (2000, June 2). What states aren't saying about the 'X-Percent Solution.' *Chronicle of Higher Education*, pp. A31–33.

Stewart, D. M. (1998, January 30). Why Hispanic students need to take the SAT. *Chronicle of Higher Education*, pp. A48.

St. John, E. P., Simmons, A. B. & Musoba, G. D. (1999, October). Merit-aware admissions in public universities: Increasing diversity. *Policy Bulletin*, No. PB-25. Indiana Education Policy Center, pp. 1–8.

Young, J. & Kobrin, J. L. (2001). *Differential validity, differential prediction, and college admission testing: A comprehensive review and analysis*. College Board Research Report No. 2001-6. New York: College Entrance Examination Board.

Zwick, R. (1999). Backdoor affirmative action. *Education Week*, pp. 56, 35.

Inequality, Student Achievement, and College Admissions: A Remedy for Underrepresentation

ROGER E. STUDLEY

Introduction

Consider two applicants to a selective college. The first applicant graduated with a 3.7 grade point average from a high school that typically sends few students to college; her parents are poor, neither of them has a college degree, and they live in a neighborhood with low property values and high unemployment. Suppose that the average SAT I score for an applicant from these circumstances is 900, but this applicant scored 1190. The second applicant graduated with a 3.7 grade-point average from a high school where college-going is the norm; his parents are wealthy, they both have advanced degrees, and they live in a neighborhood with high property values and low unemployment. Suppose the average SAT I score for an applicant from these circumstances is 1200, but this applicant scored 1290. If the college must choose between these students, should it select the more advantaged student who scored 90 points better than expected? Or should it select the disadvantaged student who, despite scoring 100 points lower, surpassed expectations by 290 points, more than three times the margin achieved by her peer? This paper presents a method for deciding—that is, for taking account of socioeconomic inequality and its role in precollege achievement.

Socioeconomic disparities in admissions have been well documented. In a national sample of selective colleges and universities, William Bowen and Derek Bok (1998) found that white students from disadvantaged socioeconomic backgrounds were represented at less than 10% of their proportion in the national population; Black students were represented at less than one-third of theirs. Socioeconomically disadvantaged students are also underrepresented, though less so, at the University of California (UC), one of the nation's largest public university systems.

Ethnic disparities have long been recognized as well. In 1998, for example, black and Hispanic students were admitted, across all eight undergraduate UC campuses, at about 40% of their proportion in the population of high school graduates. At UC-Berkeley, the system's most selective campus, these ethnic groups fared even worse: black and Hispanic students were admitted, respectively, at 37% and 27% of their proportion among high school graduates.[1] Such ethnic and socioeconomic outcomes reflect differences across groups in measures of academic performance. National data have consistently shown that students from low-income, black, or Hispanic families score substantially lower, on average, on the SAT I examination than do students from high-income, white, and Asian-American families (see, e.g., College Board, 2002).

Colleges have several options for dealing with these disparities. They can ignore them, choosing to admit students with the best precollege credentials, irrespective of socioeconomic or ethnic background. Alternatively, they can give preferential treatment to students from underrepresented ethnic groups. Such "affirmative action" policies have proven controversial and divisive, however, not only because they apply different criteria to different students, but because they do so on the basis of a characteristic that many people perceive, correctly or incorrectly, as irrelevant to students' educational opportunities. In California, this controversy led the UC Regents to pass Resolution SP-1, which prohibited ethnically based affirmative action in UC admissions.[2]

SP-1 had a large impact. Between 1995 and 2000, while the UC system experienced a 19% increase in the total number of admitted students, the number of admitted black, Hispanic, and Native American students declined by 1%. At UC's most selective campuses, the effect was even larger. While UC-Berkeley, for example, admitted 5% fewer total students in 2000 than in 1995, it admitted 42% fewer minority students. Furthermore, these declines occurred at the same time as Hispanics were the fastest growing ethnic group among California high school graduates.

A third option for addressing inequality is for colleges to directly consider socioeconomic circumstance when making admissions decisions. Under such a policy, a student's performance would be evaluated relative to his or her educational opportunities. Indeed, in the UC case, SP-1 contained a mandate for the university to consider "individuals who, despite having suffered disadvantage economically or in terms of their social environment...have nonetheless demonstrated sufficient character and determination in overcoming obstacles to warrant confidence that the applicant can pursue a course of study to successful completion" (The Regents of the University of California, 1995).

Just as affirmative action reduces ethnic inequality in college admission, a policy that considers circumstance would, by design, reduce socioeconomic inequality. Theoretically, since underrepresented minority groups tend to be relatively disadvantaged socioeconomically, such a policy should also reduce ethnic inequality. The empirical research presented in this paper supports this conjecture: a policy that systematically accounts for the effects of socioeconomic circumstance can substantially increase minority representation as well.

This approach and conclusion differ from those in the existing literature. Thomas Kane (1998) argues that since low-income white students outnumber low-income minority students, particularly among those with the strongest academic credentials, an admissions policy granting preference to low-income students would do little to reduce ethnic underrepresentation. Bowen and Bok (1998) reiterate this claim and supplement it with an analysis based on an admittedly crude measure of socioeconomic status. Neither of these studies, however, consider more comprehensive or refined measures of circumstance, and both presume that colleges would rely on simple policies that reserve places for students who fall below a socioeconomic threshold.

Many colleges and universities already consider socioeconomic factors when making admissions decisions. Typically, colleges either instruct application readers to evaluate each candidate with respect to his or her circumstance, or they establish scoring systems and award extra points to applicants who have faced socioeconomic or educational disadvantage. They do not, however, typically base their consideration of circumstance on any measure of its effect on student achievement.

A more sophisticated policy—the one examined in this paper—would be to control statistically for the effect of circumstance on precollege achievement. Anthony Carnevale and Elhum Haghighat (1998) explore a version of this approach and find that it would not significantly affect ethnic representation. There are, however, some limitations to their study. First of all, the authors use only a simple indicator to identify "strivers": they are students who outperformed circumstance-based predictions of their SAT I scores by 100 or more points. More important, the authors restrict consideration to students who score between 1000 and 1200 on the SAT I. This precludes, for example, comparing a disadvantaged student scoring 1190 to a more privileged student scoring 1290. Furthermore, within any score range, white and Asian-American students score higher, on average, than black and Hispanic students. Therefore, although the strivers pool had ethnic proportions similar to the pool of all students in the 1000–1200 band, the standard admissions procedure—selecting students above a cutoff score within this band—would have produced a less representative ethnic distribution. In a more recent and comprehensive report (although one that does not pursue this statistical methodology), Carnevale again concludes that socioeconomic preferences are not an effective substitute for affirmative action (Carnevale & Rose, 2003).

The research in this paper suggests otherwise. The second section presents a brief look at a conceptual model that explains how controlling for the effects of socioeconomic circumstance can yield a highly capable and ethnically and socioeconomically representative pool of admitted students. In the third section, California data are used to estimate empirically the effect of circumstance on pre-college achievement. In the fourth section, the empirical estimates are used to construct measures of achievement that account for circumstance. These measures are then used to simulate UC admissions under a policy that considers achievement in the context of circumstance. The final section presents a discussion and conclusions.

Conceptual Framework

Before examining data, it is useful to establish a conceptual framework for discussing economic and social circumstance, student achievement, and college admissions policy.[3]

Student Ability, Achievement, and Circumstance

In general, a student's realized academic achievement at the point of application to college is influenced by two sets of factors from the precollege years. The first set, the student's underlying ability, is broadly construed to include all factors—such as native intelligence, effort, and motivation—that the student brings to the determination of precollege achievement. The second set, referred to as the student's circumstance, constitutes the student's economic and social environment during the precollege years and includes such factors as family income, parents' education, school quality, and neighborhood characteristics (average education, average income, employment rate, etc.). Circumstance, as conceived here, does not include ethnicity, which is assumed to be unrelated to student achievement. Better circumstance leads to higher pre-college achievement, as does higher ability.

Distinct from a student's realized achievement is his *potential* achievement at the time of application to college—the hypothetical maximum achievement, for a student with given ability, under optimal precollege circumstances. For a student with such circumstances (well-educated parents, high quality schooling, etc.), realized and potential achievement will be equal; for a student with poor circumstances, realized achievement will be lower than potential achievement. Potential achievement is related only to underlying ability; it is independent of circumstance.

It is worth emphasizing that, throughout this exposition, the word *ability* refers not only to native intelligence but also to motivation and effort; it is meant to convey characteristics that might be considered internal to the student. In contrast, the word *circumstance* is used to denote characteristics external to the student: his or her opportunities or socioeconomic environment. Realized achievement, therefore, is the product of a student's intelligence, drive, and opportunities. Potential achievement depends on intelligence and drive but not opportunities. A lazy student might have the same native intelligence as his hardworking peer, but, as defined here, he will have lower underlying ability and lower potential achievement.

The ultimate level of student achievement at the point of college graduation is determined by the combination of realized precollege achievement and underlying ability. Consider, for example, two students with identical realized achievement, one of whom has higher ability but poorer circumstance than the other. The higher ability student might be expected to have higher achievement upon college graduation. He might also be expected to have higher achievement upon graduation than a third student with similar ability but lower precollege achievement. Thus, both realized achievement and underlying ability influence ultimate achievement. Since potential achievement is related only to ability, we can also conceive of ultimate achievement as determined by both realized and potential precollege achievement.

College Admissions Policies

Potential admissions policies, and the objectives that might generate them, include:

1. **Choose students with the highest level of realized achievement.** In practice, a college would implement this policy by admitting students based only on high school grades and test scores (and possibly additional indicators of achievement). College officials would use this criterion if (A) they believe students with the highest realized achievement are the most deserving of admission, (B) they desire the best possible realized achievement profile for their admitted class, or (C) they wish to select students according to underlying ability but do not have sufficient information to determine it.

2. **Choose students with the highest level of realized achievement within each ethnic group, and impose a desired ethnic distribution across groups.** This is ethnicity-based affirmative action, and it requires a different minimum achievement level for each ethnic group. College officials would choose this policy if (A) they care about both realized achievement and proportional representation across ethnic groups, or (B) they care about underlying ability, or achievement in the context of circumstance, and rely on ethnicity as a proxy for circumstance.

3. **Choose students with the highest level of underlying ability or potential achievement.** Under this policy, a college selects those students who *would have had* the highest level of precollege achievement given adequate resources, and it determines this by considering realized achievement within the context in which this achievement occurred. College officials would follow this policy if (A) they believe students with the highest underlying ability (inclusive of motivation and effort) are the most deserving of admission, or (B) they wish to "level the playing field"—that is, to require higher achievement from students who had better circumstances.

4. **Choose students who will attain the highest level of achievement upon college graduation.** This policy is based on predicted student outcomes, where predictions are based on realized precollege achievement and circumstance. College officials might choose this policy if (A) they believe students expected to have the highest final achievement are the most deserving of admission, or (B) they desire the best possible profile of student achievement upon graduation.

Policy Implications

A college's admissions policy affects the distribution of characteristics—such as ability, circumstance, and ethnicity—in its pool of admitted students. In order to examine how these characteristics would be distributed under the various policy alternatives, we make the following assumptions:

- students from minority ethnic groups are more likely to come from disadvantaged circumstances than are nonminority students.
- underlying ability is distributed equally across minority and nonminority groups
- underlying ability and circumstance are not correlated

Under policy 1, since circumstance has a direct impact on realized precollege achievement, students from disadvantaged backgrounds are less likely to be admitted to college than their more advantaged peers. Consequently, since minority groups tend to have poorer circumstances, they will be underrepresented in the pool of admitted students relative to their proportion in the college-age population. Minority underrepresentation would be remedied by policy 2, though within ethnic groups, disadvantaged students would still be less likely to be admitted to college. Under both of these policies, some students denied admission would have higher underlying ability levels than others who would be admitted.

To the extent it can be implemented—that is, to the extent a student's underlying ability or potential precollege achievement can be determined—policy 3 would select not those students with the highest absolute level of realized achievement, but those who have the highest realized achievement within their particular economic and social context. Under this policy, since we assume ability is equally distributed across population groups, minority students would be proportionately represented in the pool of admitted students. Similarly, since the admissions criterion under policy 3 is independent of circumstance, disadvantaged students would also be proportionately represented.[4] Furthermore, although some denied students would have higher realized achievement than some admitted students, all population groups are treated equally, and all admitted students would have higher underlying ability than those denied admission.

To analyze policy 4, which admits students on the basis of predicted future achievement, it is useful to consider two extreme cases. First of all, suppose college attendance allows students to remedy fully a gap in achievement—that is, to "catch up" with their more advantaged but similar ability peers. In this case, policy 4 would effectively admit students according to their underlying ability and would, therefore, have the same outcomes as policy 3. Secondly, suppose gaps in achievement are persistent and cannot be narrowed by college attendance. In this case policy 4 would effectively admit students according to realized pre-college achievement and would yield the same outcomes as policy 1. If reality lies somewhere between these two cases, or if the amount that an achievement gap can be overcome differs across students, then the outcomes of policy 4 would lie somewhere between those of policies 1 and 3.

This conceptual framework raises several empirical questions. First of all, given measures of realized precollege achievement and circumstance, how can we construct measures of underlying ability (or potential precollege achievement)? That is, how can we take account of the circumstance in which achievement occurred? Second, does the evidence suggest that an admissions policy that relies on these measures would yield the outcomes indicated by the conceptual analysis? Subsequent sections of this paper address these issues in turn.

The Effect of Circumstance on Achievement

In this section I focus on the question, What is the empirical relationship between a student's precollege achievement and the circumstances or context in which this achievement was realized? With an estimate of this relationship, I will be able to isolate the part of measured achievement that is not correlated with circumstance and use it as an indicator of underlying ability. As mentioned earlier, the notion of ability used here is broadly construed to include such factors as native intelligence, effort, and motivation—that is, any factor other than socioeconomic circumstance, whether chosen or predetermined, that the student brings to the determination of precollege achievement.

Data and Methodology

To measure precollege achievement, I use two standard academic indicators: (1) the sum of SAT I Verbal and Math examination scores [SAT], and (2) high school grade point average (GPA). To measure circumstance, I use a comprehensive set of indicators that consists of family characteristics, neighborhood of residence (defined by zip code), and high school attended. The available variables for family characteristics are income, both parents' educational attainment, and whether English is the student's first language. These data come from the College Board and constitute the 1998 cohort of college-bound seniors from California public high schools for whom we have complete data on SAT, GPA, and demographic variables. (GPA and demographic data are self-reported.) Some descriptive statistics on these 86,514 students are presented in the first column, and in the source note, of table 2.

Circumstance is a predictor of precollege achievement, and this relationship can be estimated using statistical regression techniques. When a specific set of circumstances is "plugged in," the regression model yields an estimate of the expected achievement of a student facing those circumstances. By applying the model to the circumstances faced by each student, it is possible to predict achievement for each student, where the predictions are based solely on circumstance.

Such predictions will explain only part of the variation in measured achievement across students—the part that correlates with circumstance. The remaining variation can be used to measure underlying ability (inclusive of motivation and effort). A student who outperforms a circumstance-based prediction can be considered a relatively high-ability student; one who underperforms can be considered a relatively low-ability student. Therefore, as measures of underlying ability or potential achievement, it is possible to use the differences between realized achievement and circumstance-based predictions of achievement:

[SAT Residual] = [Actual SAT] − [Predicted SAT (based on circumstance)]
[GPA Residual] = [Actual GPA] − [Predicted GPA (based on circumstance)]

These statistics, which will be used later to simulate admissions under policy 3, can be interpreted as measuring "achievement in context"—that is, achievement relative to what would be expected for a typical student facing the same circumstance.[5]

Results

Table 1 presents two sets of regression models, the first of which predicts SAT and the second of which predicts GPA. In order to account for variation in grading standards across schools, all the GPA models include indicators (i.e. "dummy variables") for high school attended. In addition to estimating the relationship between socioeconomic circumstance and achievement, we are interested in the degree to which circumstance accounts for observed differences in achievement across ethnic groups. As a benchmark, therefore, the first model from each set in table 1 predicts achievement based on ethnicity alone; the estimated parameters are average differences in mean SAT (on a scale of 400 to 1600) or mean GPA (on a scale of 0.0 to 4.3) between the indicated ethnic group and white students. Hispanic students, for example, score 181 points lower on the SAT I than white students, on average, when not controlling for other factors. Model II, for both the SAT and GPA cases, adds family characteristics, such as family income and parents' education. Model III adds neighborhood indicators, as well as school indicators in the SAT case. Model IV removes ethnicity from consideration and thus predicts achievement based on family, neighborhood, and school circumstance alone. In all models, family income has thirteen categories ranging from "below $10,000" (the reference category) to "above $100,000." Parents' education has ten categories for each parent, ranging from "missing" (presumed absent) to "completed graduate or professional school." (The reference category is "grade school for both parents.") Observations with both parents missing have been discarded. Only a few of the individual parameter estimates for the income and education variables are presented.

Perhaps the most striking result from table 1 is the degree to which SAT variation across ethnicity is reduced upon accounting for family, neighborhood, and school circumstance. As variables are added to the model, the estimated deficit for black students drops 45%, from 217 to 118 points, a decline of nearly half the standard deviation in SAT scores (213 points) in the sample population. The estimated Hispanic deficit decreases even more,

Table 1: Regression Models for the Prediction of Precollege Achievement

DEPENDENT VARIABLE	SAT I: VERBAL + MATH				HIGH SCHOOL GPA			
	I	II	III	IV	I	II	III	IV
MODEL	ETHNICITY ONLY	MODEL I + FAMILY CHARACTERISTICS	MODEL II + INDICATORS FOR NEIGHBORHOOD AND SCHOOL	MODEL III WITH ETHNICITY OMITTED	ETHNICITY (INCLUDES SCHOOL INDICATORS)	MODEL I + FAMILY CHARACTERISTICS	MODEL II + INDICATORS FOR NEIGHBORHOOD	MODEL III WITH ETHNICITY OMITTED
Explained Variance (R^2)	0.142	0.269	0.343	0.322	0.095	0.120	0.135	0.113
Parameter Estimates								
Intercept	1073	855	908	894	3.49	3.31	3.59	3.54
Family Income (vs. <$10K) (13 categories, 4 shown)								
$15,000–$20,000	—	46	38	35	—	0.02	0.02	0.01
$30,000–$35,000	—	70	52	51	—	0.03	0.02	0.02
$60,000–$70,000	—	87	65	69	—	0.05	0.04	0.05
$100,000 and Above	—	129	87	92	—	0.07	0.06	0.08

Parents' Educ. (vs. Grade School) (99 combinations, 3 shown)								
High School Graduate (Both)	—	55	29	37	—	0.04	0.03	0.06
Bachelor's Degree (Both)	—	153	104	122	—	0.22	0.21	0.27
Graduate Degree (Both)	—	206	146	160	—	0.31	0.29	0.34
First Language (vs. English)								
English and Another	—	−9	−14	−1**	—	0.04	0.04	0.08
Another	—	−8	−15	4*	—	0.14	0.14	0.19
Ethnicity (vs. White)								
Asian-American	−35	21	22	—	0.10	0.07	0.08	—
Black	−217	−155	−118	—	−0.41	−0.36	−0.35	—
Hispanic	−181	−73	−46	—	−0.19	−0.15	−0.15	—
Other	−40	−13	−9	—	−0.03	−0.04	−0.04	—

All models are based on 86,514 college-bound high school seniors from California public schools, 1998. SAT I Verbal plus Math score is on a 400–1600 scale. GPA is on a 0.0 to 4.3 scale. "Asian-American" includes Filipino and Pacific Islander. The comparison category for each group of variables is noted in parentheses. (For example, ethnicity parameters should be interpreted as average differences between the indicated groups and white students.) F-tests indicate significance of school and neighborhood indicators (not reported in the table) at the 1% confidence level. All parameter estimates are significant at the 1% confidence level except: *significant at 5%; **not significant at 5%.

from 181 to 46 points, or 75%. For Asian-American students, when circumstance is taken into account an apparent SAT score deficit is revealed to be an advantage (i.e., Asian-American students score higher than white students who have similar circumstances), although the absolute magnitude of the change is much smaller than it is for blacks or Hispanics. These results suggest that a college might remedy ethnic underrepresentation by taking account of the relationship between circumstance and precollege achievement.

In general, SAT scores are related to circumstance. As measured by the squared multiple correlation (R^2 statistic), the model with ethnicity and family characteristics captures 27% of test score variation, and the fully specified model containing neighborhood and school indicators captures 34%. Removing ethnicity from the model reduces its fit by only 2 percentage points. Both income and parents' education correlate positively with SAT. Students from families with incomes above $100,000, for example, are expected to score 49 points higher than those from families with incomes between $15,000 and $20,000 (model III). Similarly, a positive relationship between parents' education and SAT scores is clearly evident from table 1. Furthermore, not having English as a first language has a slightly negative relationship to SAT. Overall, there is strong evidence of the impact of circumstance on SAT.

The estimated relationship between GPA and circumstance is qualitatively similar to, though weaker than, the relationship between SAT and circumstance. Across all models, income—while positively correlated with GPA—never accounts for more than 0.08 grade points of variation. For comparison, the standard deviation of GPA in the sample is 0.63 grade points. Parents' education, however, is more strongly related to GPA. On average, students whose parents both have bachelor's degrees have GPAs 0.21 points (one third of a standard deviation) higher than do those whose parents have only a grade school education (model III); if both parents have graduate degrees, the advantage rises to 0.29 points. Finally, and unexpectedly, having a first language other than English correlates strongly and positively with GPA, perhaps indicating greater than average ambition among the children of immigrants.

The amount of ethnic disparity accounted for by circumstance also appears smaller for the GPA models than for the SAT models. Adding family and neighborhood variables to the model reduces the estimated average GPA deficit for blacks and Hispanics by only 17% and 23%, respectively, as compared with 45% and 75% for the SAT models. This is not because the GPA models are less useful in explaining the disparity; rather, it is because there is less disparity to explain. (In part this is because, unlike the "ethnicity only" SAT model, the benchmark GPA model already includes school indicators to control for differences in grading standards across schools). In terms of standard deviations, when not controlling for circumstance, the ethnic differences in SAT scores are much larger than those for GPA: the Hispanic SAT deficit, for example, is 0.85 standard deviations ($^{181}/_{213}$), while the Hispanic GPA deficit is 0.30 standard deviations ($^{0.19}/_{0.63}$). Adding circumstance variables to the models reduces these deficits to 0.22 and 0.23 standard deviations, respectively.

Simulation of Alternative Admissions Policies
Methodology
For the purpose of simulating admissions policies, the two measures of each student's realized precollege academic achievement can be combined into a single achievement index that gives them roughly equal weight:

$$[\text{Achievement Index}] = 2.5 \times [\text{SAT}] + 1000 \times [\text{GPA}]$$

Colleges routinely calculate this type of statistic for use in admissions decisions. In a similar spirit, we can create an index of underlying ability, or achievement in context, by combining the two measures constructed from circumstance-based predictions of achievement[6]:

$$[\text{Ability Index}] = 2.5 \times [\text{SAT Residual}] + 1000 \times [\text{GPA Residual}]$$

The residuals used in the ability index are calculated from the model IV equations, which use the full set of circumstance variables, but exclude ethnicity, to construct predictions of SAT and GPA. The achievement and ability indices are used to simulate admissions under alternative policies, as follows:

- **Policy 1—Admissions Based on Precollege Achievement:** Of the population of 86,514 seniors from California public high schools in 1998 for whom we had complete data, this policy admits the 33,566 who rank highest according to their achievement index (33,566 is the number of students from this population who were actually admitted to a University of California campus).
- **Policy 2—Affirmative Action:** This policy admits the students who rank highest, within their own ethnic group, according to their achievement index, and it maintains proportional representation across ethnic groups. Twenty-one percent of the 86,514 high school students, for example, are Hispanic: this policy admits the 7,039 (21% of 33,566) Hispanic students who rank highest according to their achievement index.

• **Policy 3—Admissions Based on Ability, Potential Achievement, or Achievement in the Context of Circumstance:** This policy admits the 33,566 students who rank highest according to their ability index.

Policy 4, admissions based on predictions of achievement during college, is not simulated in this paper and will be the topic of future work.

To interpret the following simulation results, a brief explanation of University of California admissions is required. The UC system has eight undergraduate campuses. In order to attend *any* campus, a student must meet a set of minimum eligibility requirements regarding course pattern, GPA, and admissions test scores. All eligible students are guaranteed admission to a UC campus, although not necessarily to the campus of their choice. Individual campuses select their students, using a broad range of criteria, from the pool of eligible applicants. Prior to 1998, when the consideration of ethnicity in UC admissions was abolished, UC implemented affirmative action in two ways: campuses could consider ethnicity when selecting from among eligible applicants, and each campus was allowed to "admit by exception" up to 4% of its class from underrepresented minority students who did not meet UC's eligibility requirements.[7]

The simulations of UC admissions described above, therefore, are more analogous to systemwide eligibility than to campus selection: the students who were admitted to any UC campus are, in general, those who met the systemwide eligibility requirements.[8] UC's specific eligibility rules are not incorporated into the simulation of alternate policies, however, since the available data do not include sufficient information on course patterns and grades. The simulations are therefore simplifications of the actual UC admission process, which incorporates more factors into admissions decisions. Nonetheless, the outcome of the actual UC admissions process serves as a natural benchmark for evaluating simulation results.

Results

Table 2 contrasts income and ethnic characteristics and achievement measures for the 1998 population of 86,514 college-bound high school seniors, the 33,566 of these students admitted to UC that year, and the pools of 33,566 students that would be admitted under each of the three simulations. Regarding family income, policy 3—which admits students based on a measure of their underlying ability (or achievement in the context of circumstance)—produces an income distribution nearly identical to that in the population of high school seniors and much closer to it than does actual admissions or the other simulated policies. Compared to actual 1998 admissions, for example, policy 3 admits 20% more students from families with annual incomes below $25,000 and 23% fewer from families with incomes above $70,000. Mean family income under policy 3 is similar to that for the high school pool, and substantially lower than that for actual admissions or either of the alternative policies, including affirmative action. These results, displayed graphically in the two left panels of figure 1, strongly support the income-related conclusions from the conceptual discussion in the second section of this chapter.

Though less definitively, the results regarding ethnicity also support the conceptual analysis, as is evident from the two right panels in figure 1 (which display "Ethnicity" rows from table 2). Compared to actual UC admissions, policy 3 would yield more proportionate representation for both Hispanic and black students—groups typically underrepresented in college admissions. Under policy 3, Hispanics would constitute 17.3% of the pool of admitted students, a proportion equal to 82% of their proportion in the high school population; under actual admissions they were represented at 71% of their proportion in this population. Similarly, although blacks would be represented at less than 60% of their proportion in the high school population under policy 3, they would be an 18% larger group than under the status quo. Fewer Asian-American students would be admitted under policy 3 than in actual admissions, though this means that they too would be more proportionately represented. Furthermore, under policy 3, Hispanics and blacks would be represented in proportions similar to those that existed in 1995, prior to the abolition of affirmative action. At that time, Hispanics constituted 16.5% of admitted students and blacks 4.6%; in simulations of policy 3 they constitute 17.3% and 4.2%, respectively.

The actual UC admissions process, however, is more complicated, and relies on more factors, than the simulated admissions policies. Therefore, to more directly compare the ethnic distributions from admissions based on realized achievement versus admissions based on underlying ability, we can compare the simulation outcomes for policies 1 and 3. Under policy 1, the Hispanic and black proportions in the pool of admitted students would be 11.4% and 2.3%. Under policy 3, these proportions would rise to 17.3% and 4.0%—increases of 52% and 74%, respectively. All else equal, therefore, admissions based on a measure of underlying ability can substantially increase ethnic representation over admissions based on a measure of realized achievement.[9]

These ethnic outcomes are remarkable because policy 3 omits all consideration of ethnicity: it is a factor neither in the selection criterion—which is constructed from the prediction equations that omit ethnicity (model IV)—nor in the criterion's design. (In contrast, one could design a policy that attempts to attain, through the consideration of circumstance, a target ethnic distribution.[10]) Policy 3 is deliberately intended only to address

Table 2: Admissions Simulations

	COLLEGE-BOUND HIGH SCHOOL SENIORS	ACTUAL UC ADMISSIONS (SYSTEMWIDE)	ADMISSIONS SIMULATION CRITERION		
			1 PRECOLLEGE ACHIEVEMENT	2 AFFIRMATIVE ACTION	3 UNDERLYING ABILITY
Family Income			Percent of Students in Income Category		
Below $25,000	27.8	22.5	18.5	21.6	27.1
$25,000–$70,000	45.7	43.2	46.1	45.7	45.5
Above $70,000	26.5	34.3	35.4	32.6	27.4
Ethnicity			Percent of Students in Ethnic Category		
White	41.0	40.2	49.9	41.0	42.8
Asian	24.3	34.4	29.1	24.3	28.9
Black	7.0	3.4	2.3	7.0	4.0
Hispanic	21.0	14.9	11.4	21.0	17.3
Other	6.8	7.1	7.3	6.8	6.9
		Means Within the High School Population or Admitted Class			
Income	$51,333	$58,515	$60,584	$57,614	$52,129
SAT I: Verbal + Math	1009	1156	1191	1173	1158
High School GPA	3.29	3.70	3.85	3.83	3.83

Source: Data are from the College Board and the University of California and include 86,514 college-bound high school seniors from California public schools in 1998 for whom all data were available. (GPA and demographic variables are self-reported.) For this population, the standard deviations of income, SAT scores, and GPA are, respectively, $35,685, 213, and 0.63. The number of students from this population that was admitted to UC, and the number admitted under each admissions simulation, is 33,566. The ethnic distribution of admitted students in the affirmative action simulation is constrained to be identical to the ethnic distribution in the population of college-bound seniors.

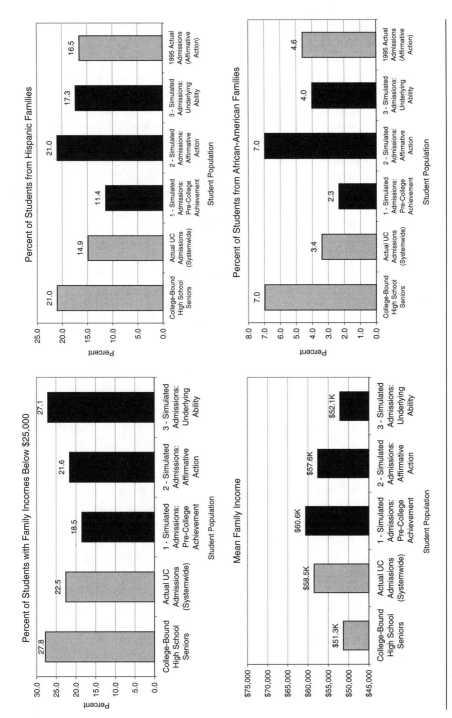

Figure 1. Admissions simulations selected demographic characteristics.

unequal circumstance. Doing so, however, helps to remedy ethnic inequality as well.

Table 2 also presents means for the measures of precollege achievement: SAT and GPA. Policy 3, which has income and ethnic distributions more closely representative of the high school population than does actual admissions, also has higher grades and higher test scores. This counterintuitive result occurs because some students with very high grades and test scores did not apply to UC and because some students admitted under policy 3 may not have met UC's course pattern requirement.[11] Perhaps more important, therefore, is a comparison of achievement measures across the three simulated policies. Mean SAT score for admissions based on underlying ability is 31 points lower than for admissions based on realized achievement and 15 points lower than under affirmative action; mean GPA is nearly identical across the three simulations. These differences in measured achievement are small, and they exist because policy 3 explicitly considers the context in which achievement occurs. Furthermore, by design, students admitted under policy 3 would have a higher underlying ability, as measured by SAT and GPA residuals, than students admitted under the alternative policies.

Discussion and Conclusions

Many, if not most, selective colleges and universities consider student circumstance when making admissions decisions. Most, if not all, however, do so in an ad hoc way, either based on a subjective assessment of a student's application or by some type of arbitrarily determined preferential treatment of students from disadvantaged backgrounds. In contrast, the analyses presented here demonstrate how a systematic, objective, and thorough consideration of circumstance might be used to "level the socioeconomic playing field" in college admissions. By using statistical estimates of the relationship between achievement and circumstance, we can construct an index of achievement that accounts for the role of circumstance. This index can be interpreted as a measure of underlying ability (broadly construed to include effort, motivation, etc.), potential precollege achievement, or realized achievement in the context of circumstance. Admissions simulations based on this index demonstrate that the systematic consideration of circumstance can redress socioeconomic inequality in college admissions while maintaining academic standards.

Systematically accounting for socioeconomic inequality would also help to reduce ethnic disparities. As table 1 shows, much of the ethnic differences in SAT I scores, and some of the ethnic differences in high school GPA, can be attributed to the fact that Hispanic and black students tend to have less advantaged circumstances than white students. A simulation of systemwide 1998 UC admissions, using a criterion that accounts for circumstance, yields an ethnic distribution that (1) rivals what UC attained in 1995 under affirmative action, (2) is more representative than the distribution attained in actual 1998 admissions, and (3) is much more representative than a simulation using a criterion that doesn't account for circumstance.

While ethnic disparities were reduced by a consideration of circumstance, they were not eliminated. One explanation may be that, despite the robust set of variables in the data, circumstance remains inadequately characterized. Just as ethnic differences in SAT I scores were reduced by the inclusion of family characteristics and then further reduced by the inclusion of school and neighborhood indicators, a more refined set of characteristics might reduce the remaining differences still further. Another potential explanation is different cultural experiences across ethnic groups—whether internally perpetuated, as argued by John McWhorter (2000), or socially imposed, as Glenn Loury (2002) and Patricia Williams (1998) contend. Either explanation—inadequate data on circumstance or dissimilar cultural experiences—suggests that the explicit consideration of ethnicity in admissions may be warranted. That is, in addition to family, school, and neighborhood characteristics, ethnicity may be a valid descriptor of circumstance. Indeed, unreported policy 3 simulations that include ethnicity as a variable in SAT and GPA predictions (that is, simulations based on predictions from model III rather than model IV) yield ethnic distributions that are more representative of the high school population than the reported policy 3 simulations that omit ethnicity. The income distributions and mean SAT and GPA, however, remain nearly identical with those from the reported simulations.[12]

To implement policy 3, a college would need to collect information on student circumstance and use the apparatus developed herein to construct measures of achievement that account for circumstance. Most colleges already collect the necessary information, and, once set up, the statistical apparatus would be straightforward to maintain. Colleges, including individual UC campuses, could introduce the GPA and SAT residuals into their existing admissions frameworks, whether they rely exclusively on quantitative information or whether they subjectively evaluate some or all of their applicants. Alternatively, colleges could use these residuals to systematize the contextual evaluation of applicants, allowing them to devote more personnel to subjectively evaluating borderline cases. In all cases, regardless of the admissions process a college uses, these statistics would provide decision makers with information not currently at their disposal: a measure of each applicant's underlying ability or achievement in the context of circumstance.

At the UC systemwide level, SAT and GPA residuals could be used to admit by exception promising students who wouldn't otherwise be eligible for UC. Alternatively, eligibility rules could be redesigned using required minimum SAT and GPA residuals—that is, minimum levels of achievement in context.[13] This is unlikely, however, because it is more complicated than current eligibility rules, hence less transparent to students and parents. It could also be misinterpreted as altering test scores and grades, rather than correctly interpreted as incorporating scores and grades into measures of achievement that account for circumstance.

Such misinterpretation is one of the main criticisms of the systematic consideration of circumstance in admissions. In 1999 the Educational Testing Service (ETS), which develops the SAT examinations for the College Board, considered providing colleges with "a richer context for [test] scores" for those applicants whose SAT scores fall into the range of 1000 to 1190 (ETS, 1999). The proposal, based on the aforementioned research by Carnevale and Haghighat (1998), was to designate as "strivers" the students in this range who scored at least 200 points higher than predicted. It was criticized in the *Wall Street Journal* (Marcus, 1999) and other media outlets because it was perceived as altering test scores and because one version of the proposal would have included ethnic background in determining which students were strivers. In short order, the College Board announced that it would not support the endeavor, and ETS withdrew the idea from consideration.

ETS may have been wise to backpedal from controversy, but it was not altering scores and was, in fact, advocating a practice in which colleges have long engaged: evaluating achievement in light of individual circumstance. What is unique about both the "strivers" approach and the approach explored in this paper is that they propose methods of *systematically* accounting for circumstance, and of doing so according to its actual effect on precollege achievement. As demonstrated above, both conceptually and empirically, a systematic consideration of circumstance (policy 3) is quite different from affirmative action (policy 2): the former treats all ethnic groups equally, selects students with the highest underlying ability, and would admit a significantly different group of students than would an affirmative action policy. Test scores would not be altered and would continue to serve as measures of realized achievement; GPA and SAT residuals would, in contrast, provide measures of achievement in context. Critics of the "strivers" proposal might have more readily received these distinctions if the entity making the proposal had not been the same one that develops the SAT, or if ETS had been more assertive in making its case.

Another concern about the systematic consideration of circumstance is that it might encourage students to falsely report their circumstance. Currently, however, many colleges rely on self-reported contextual information to subjectively evaluate applicants. Verification procedures, coupled with penalties for falsification, have proven to be an effective deterrent to misreporting.[14] If a college simply constructed a measure of achievement in context from the information it currently collects, the incentive for dishonesty would not necessarily increase. If it did, perhaps due to greater public awareness of the role of circumstance in admissions decisions, verification processes could be strengthened. Students who chose not to report circumstance would be treated the same as students from relatively advantaged backgrounds.

Perhaps the most significant critique of considering circumstance is that students from disadvantaged backgrounds may be academically unprepared for college despite having excelled relative to their socioeconomic peers. This topic is worthy of further study: What are the respective contributions of underlying ability and realized achievement to college success? Can disadvantaged students catch up to their more advantaged peers? How large of an educational disadvantage can be overcome? Despite these unresolved questions, however, selective colleges typically get many more qualified applicants than they can accommodate, and it is reasonable to suspect that high-ability candidates who would be excluded under a policy that emphasizes realized achievement would nonetheless be likely to succeed at these institutions. There would certainly be no harm in complementing subjective appraisals of students' chances for success with a statistical measure of their underlying ability. For students whose preparation is deemed insufficient, academic remediation—whether pre- or postmatriculation—could be required as an alternative to denial of admission.[15] Furthermore, retention efforts and academic counseling would likely be most successful when targeted to this group of high-ability students.

In summary, the mission of a selective university, and indeed the mandate from the University of California Regents, is to offer a rigorous and enlightening education to the most motivated and capable students. Economic and social circumstance often stand as barriers to this mission, limiting access to disadvantaged students and, as a consequence, diminishing the educational experience for an entire student body. The present research demonstrates that an admissions policy that systematically accounts for circumstance holds promise as a feasible, fair, and effective remedy for socioeconomic and ethnic disparity in college admissions.

Notes

The author wishes to thank Alan Auerbach, Saul Geiser, John Quigley, David Stern, Rebecca Zwick, and two anonymous referees for their suggestions and insight. Support from the UC Office of the President and the Center for Studies in Higher Education at UC Berkeley is gratefully acknowledged. The ideas expressed herein are those of the author and do not represent policies of the University of California.

1. Author's calculations based on students graduating from California public high schools in 1998. Data come from the California Basic Educational Data System (CBEDS) and the University of California.
2. In order to combat the perception that UC did not welcome minority students, the UC Regents rescinded Resolution SP-1 in 2001. From a policy perspective, however, the rescission

was moot because in 1996 a prohibition against affirmative action, Proposition 209, was approved by voters and incorporated into California's state constitution.

3. A formal model that builds upon this conceptual framework, and in which student behavior, college admissions policy, and their implications are derived from objectives and constraints, will be presented in a forthcoming paper.

4. The proportional representation of disadvantaged students relies, in part, on the assumption that underlying ability and circumstance are not correlated. If instead these factors are positively correlated—as might be the case if high ability parents tend both to produce children of high ability and to provide them with better circumstances—then policy 3 would produce an admitted class in which disadvantaged students were underrepresented relative to their proportion in the college-age population but still less so than they would be under policies 1 and 2.

5. It is not being claimed that the SAT and GPA residuals are perfect measures of underlying ability or achievement in context. As with actual SAT and GPA, some of the variation in the residuals is due to random error, and any systematic bias in actual SAT and GPA would occur in the residuals as well. The distinction between the actual and residual measures is simply that the latter remove the effect of circumstance. This parallels the conceptual model, where realized achievement depends on circumstance but underlying ability and potential achievement do not.

6. The presented formula has been simplified for exposition. In practice, in order to keep the same balance between SAT and GPA in the achievement and ability indices, the overall SAT and GPA means are added to the respective residuals before the ability index is constructed.

7. UC's implementation of affirmative action thus differed from the affirmative action policy simulated in this paper. The former had constraints on the number of applicants for whom ethnicity could be considered and did not require specific ethnic proportions in the pool of admitted students.

8. The group of admitted students may contain some who were "admitted by exception" (for reasons other than ethnic diversity) and thus technically ineligible for UC, although in 1998 this constituted only one percent of all admitted students. The group of admitted students does not include the small minority of eligible students who did not apply to UC. Similarly, the available data do not include private school, home-schooled, or out-of-state students; these students are therefore not accounted for in the policy simulations.

9. Furthermore, this comparison of otherwise identical policies suggests that substituting measures of underlying ability for measures of realized achievement in the actual admissions process might yield a greater increase in ethnic representation over actual admissions than was obtained by the policy 3 simulation.

10. Peter Pashley and Andrea Thornton (2002) develop a procedure for admitting a law school class under just such a policy, using an optimization technique that constrains the pool of admitted students to have a specific demographic profile and, subject to this constraint, selects the pool with the highest combination of grades and test scores. Without using ethnicity as an explicit criterion (although they do consider the ethnic distributions of the applicant's area of residence and undergraduate school), they can prescribe other demographic criteria in a manner that yields a desired ethnic distribution.

11. More than two-thirds of the students admitted under the policy 3, however, were in fact admitted to UC and are thus known to have met the course pattern requirement. The displacement policy 3 would cause to actual admissions, in this simulation, is 10,592 out of 33,566 (32%).

12. In the policy 3 simulations that include ethnicity as a component of circumstance, Hispanic representation is 19.8%, black representation is 6.6%, mean family income is $52,179, mean SAT is 1155, and mean GPA is 3.82.

13. Yet another option would be for UC to abandon the "eligibility" aspect of its admissions policy altogether. UC could still set minimum requirements, but satisfying these requirements would not necessarily guarantee admission to a UC campus. Campuses would then be free to admit more high-ability students from disadvantaged circumstances.

14. See, e.g., University of California, 2002, pp. 19–21.

15. This philosophy underlies a recent UC initiative called the Dual Admissions Program (DAP). Under this program, students whose grades in a college preparatory curriculum rank them in the top 12.5%, but below the top 4%, of their high school class will be admitted to a specific UC

campus, regardless of their admissions test scores, provided they first successfully complete a transfer program at a two-year state college.

References

Bowen, W. G., & Bok, D. (1998). *The shape of the river: Long-term consequences of considering race in college and university admissions.* Princeton, NJ: Princeton University Press.

Carnevale, A. P., & Haghighat, Elhum (1998). Selecting the strivers: A report on the preliminary results of the ETS "Educational Strivers" study. In D. Bakst (Ed.), *Hopwood, Bakke, and beyond: Diversity on our nation's campuses* (pp. 122–28). Washington, DC: American Association of Collegiate Registrars and Admissions Officers.

Carnevale, A. P., & Rose, S. J. (2003). *Socioeconomic status, race/ethnicity, and selective college admissions.* New York: Century Foundation.

College Board (2002 and prior years). *College-bound seniors: A profile of SAT program test takers.* New York: College Board.

Educational Testing Service (1999, September 1). ETS issues clarification on "strivers" research study. Press Release. Princeton: Educational Testing Service.

Kane, Thomas J. (1998). Racial and ethnic preferences in college admissions. In C. Jencks & M. Phillips (Eds.), *The black-white test score gap* (pp. 431–456). Washington, DC: Brookings Institution.

Loury, G. C. (2002). *The anatomy of racial inequality.* Cambridge, MA: Harvard University Press.

Marcus, A. D. (1999, Aug. 31). New weights can alter SAT scores: Family is factor in determining who's a "striver." *Wall Street Journal,* pp. B1, B8.

McWhorter, J. H. (2000). *Losing the race: Self-sabotage in black america.* New York: Free Press.

Pashley, P. J., & Thornton, A. E. (1999). Crafting an incoming law school class: Preliminary results. Newtown, PA: Law School Admission Council.

Regents of the University of California (1995). Regents' Policy Ensuring Equal Treatment—Admissions (SP-1, approved July 20, 1995). Oakland, CA.

University of California (2002). *First-year implementation of comprehensive review in freshman admissions: A progress report from the Board of Admissions and Relations with Schools.* Oakland: University of California.

Williams, P. J. (1998). *Seeing a color-blind future: The paradox of race.* New York: Noonday Press.

Reassessing College Admissions: Examining Tests and Admitting Alternatives

CHRISTINA PEREZ

With college admissions tests—and the SAT I in particular—coming under increasing scrutiny, many are wondering what other alternatives exist. Public debate has largely focused on the question of *which* admission tests to use rather than *whether or not* any exam is needed. The justifications for utilizing test scores in college admission include a need to whittle down large applicant pools, concern about academic standards, and placing value on having an external measure with which to gauge high school grades. These considerations have become more complicated in the past several years as a higher volume of applications and better-prepared candidates has made admission to many colleges and universities more competitive. Although such arguments are grounded in real concerns, the benefits of using test scores do not outweigh the drawbacks. Relying on SAT I and ACT scores costs students a great deal of time and money, produces unnecessary anxiety, and diverts attention away from more worthwhile academic pursuits. While using test scores may seem like an efficient and objective way to sift through large applicant pools, it leads universities to overlook many talented candidates. These concerns are among the many that have led nearly 400 colleges and universities to eliminate test score requirements for a substantial number of their applicants.[1]

Institutional Research Points to the SAT's Weak Predictive Power

A common way to gauge the usefulness of various admissions criteria is to look at their ability to predict freshman grade point average (FGPA). Since students at many colleges take a similar course load during their freshman year and receive a wider range of grades, looking at FGPA is favored as a way to reduce the influence of outside variables in distorting statistical findings.

According to their manufacturers, the SAT and the ACT are designed primarily to predict first-year college grades. The ACT has also been validated as a course placement tool. They are not designed to predict grades beyond the freshman year, graduation rates, or pursuit of a graduate degree. However, technical manuals published by the College Board and ACT, Inc. indicate that class rank and high school grade point average (HSGPA) are both better predictors of first-year college performance than either the SAT I or ACT (College Board 1999; ACT, Inc., 1998).

Validity research at individual institutions illustrates the weak predictive ability of the SAT I. At California State University's Hayward campus, researchers Sheila Cowen and Sandra Fiori (1991) studied nearly 1,000 students—one-quarter of whom were considered "slower progressors" at greater risk for academic failure—as the students advanced through their freshman year. High school grades proved to be the best prediction instrument, explaining 18% of the variation in freshman grades. Combining SAT I scores with HSGPA inched this figure up to 23% for all students, but added virtually nothing to the analysis of slower progressing students.

Bates College, which chose to make all test scores optional in 1990, first conducted several studies from 1985 to 1989 when just the SAT I was optional in order to determine the most powerful variables for predicting success at the college. One study showed that students' assessment of their "energy and initiative" as reported in a self-evaluation added more to the ability to predict performance at Bates than did either math or verbal SAT I scores (Hiss, Woodcock, & McGrath, 1984, p. 12).

During the five-year study period in the late 1980s, all applicants to Bates were still required to submit three SAT II tests (at that time called achievement tests). While SAT II scores were a slightly better predictor than the SAT I, neither could explain more than 13% of the variation in freshman grades. As a result, in 1990 the faculty voted to make all standardized tests completely optional. In a 1997 interview, then admissions director (and now vice president) William Hiss told *U.S. News and World Report* that for a quarter to a third of Bates students, the SAT I is "not predictive and, in some cases, is what a statistician would call a false negative. That is, in fact the test seems to suggest the student cannot do good work when in fact they can. They come to Bates, they make the dean's list, they graduate Phi Beta Kappa, having come with modest SATs" (Hiss, 1998).

A number of other studies have found noncognitive indicators to be stronger predictors than test scores. In a two-year study of freshmen entering the University of Maryland-College Park, Terence Tracey and William Sedlacek tested the predictive validity of a noncognitive questionnaire (NCQ) for white and African-American students. The eight components of the NCQ—self-confidence, realistic self-appraisal, community service, long range goals, leadership, support for academic plans, academic familiarity, and understanding racism—proved to be better predictors of both FGPA and eighth semester academic progress than SAT I scores (Tracey & Sedlacek, 1985).

The SAT Offers Little Information on Long-Term Success in College

In addition to considering how well various admissions criteria predict first-year college grades, looking at cumulative college GPA and graduation rates provides an important barometer of long-term performance. In *The Case against the SAT*, James Crouse and Dale Trusheim (1998) demonstrate the SAT I's contribution to predicting these outcomes accurately. Data they analyzed demonstrated that using high school record alone to predict who would complete a bachelor's degree resulted in "correct" admissions decisions (meaning students earned satisfactory freshmen grades and eventually graduated) 73.4% of the time, while using the SAT I and high school GPA forecast "correct" admissions in 72.2% of the cases.

Drawing from a national database of nearly 10,000 students, one study sponsored by the U.S. Department of Education considered the value of high school grades/class rank, test scores, and rigor of courses in predicting attainment of a bachelor's degree. One major finding from the study was that rigor of high school curriculum offered a higher correlation with bachelor's degree attainment (.54) than either SAT I scores (.48) or class rank/GPA (.44). Significantly, high school curriculum was an even stronger predictor for African-American and Latino students than for students overall, indicating a need for employing broader admissions criteria than just a test score/HSGPA index when trying to forecast the college performance of underrepresented minorities. Researcher Clifford Adelman concluded, "[T]he intensity and quality of curriculum is a cumulative investment of years of effort by schools, teachers, and students, and provides momentum into higher education and beyond. It obviously pays off. The effects of grades and tests diminish in time, but the stuff of learning does not go away" (Adelman, 1999).

One study, at the University of Pennsylvania, looked at the power of high school class rank, SAT I scores, and SAT II scores in predicting cumulative college GPA. Researchers found that the SAT I was by far the weakest predictor in analyzing differences between students, explaining only 4% of the variation in college grades, while SAT II scores accounted for 6.8% of the variation in academic performance. By far the most useful tool proved to be high school class rank, which predicted more than twice as much as SAT I scores by forecasting 9.3% of the variation in cumulative GPAs. Combining SAT I scores and class rank inched this figure up to 11.3%, still leaving almost 90% of the variation in grades unexplained (Baron & Norman, 1992).

Another study of 10,000 students at 11 selective public and private institutions of higher education found that a 100-point increase in SAT I combined scores, holding race, gender, and field of study constant, led to a .10 point gain in college GPA (Vars & Bowen, 1998). This offered about the same predictive value as looking at whether an applicant's father had a graduate degree or her mother had completed college. While large test score increases led to only minute gains in the college academic performance of students, the gap between a 1000 and a 1100 combined SAT I score could mean the difference between an admissions acceptance or rejection. Such small gains in college GPA for a relatively large jump in SAT I scores demonstrate why the benefits of using college admissions tests do not outweigh the costs.

The SAT Does Not Accurately Reflect the Capabilities of Women, Students of Color, and Older Applicants

When looking at the ability of the SAT exams in predicting academic success in college, it is important to note that the accuracy of test scores as predictors varies across population groups. The poor predictive ability of test scores becomes particularly apparent when considering the college performance of women. While test-maker research boasts that the SAT I is a more accurate predictor of college performance for women than for men, digging beneath this rhetoric reveals that the test actually underpredicts the performance of women in college while overpredicting that of men (College Board, 1999, p. 39). Despite the fact that they receive better grades in high school and college in comparable classes, women receive lower scores on the SAT I, ACT, and most of the SAT II: Subject Tests. This remains true even when course taking patterns and course difficulty are accounted for (Gross, 1988; Leonard & Jiang, 1999; Wainer & Steinberg, 1992). Test makers have been unable to adequately account for this discrepancy, but independent research shows that the timed, multiple-choice format of the exams (Kessel & Linn, 1996), the roles of women in test questions (Rosser, 1992), and the penalty for guessing (Linn, DeBenedictis, Delucchi, Harris, & Stage, 1987) may play a role in artificially depressing females' test scores.

The SAT I is also an inaccurate predictor of college success for bilingual students. For students whose best language isn't English, test-maker research shows the SAT I (and high school GPA) underpredicts their future college performance (Ramist, Lewis, & McCamley-Jenkins, 2001, p. 4). Even among students whose best language is English, test scores underestimate college potential. One study at the University of Miami compared native Spanish speaking Latinos and non-Latino white students. Though both groups earned equivalent college grades, the Latino students received average combined SAT I scores that were 91 points lower than their non-Latino white peers (Pearson, 1993). This gap existed despite the fact that 89% of the Latino students reported English as their best language and the vast majority were U.S.-educated from second grade on. Moreover, since the family income levels and educational backgrounds for both groups of students were very similar, the study concluded that the test score gap was attributable merely to being bilingual and not to differences in academic preparation or potential.

Extensive research compiled by William Bowen and Derek Bok in *The Shape of the River* highlights the SAT I's questionable predictive power for African-American students. The ability of SAT I scores to predict freshman grades, undergraduate class rank, college graduation rates, and attainment of a graduate degree is weaker for African-American students than for whites, with test scores overpredicting the college performance of African Americans. While Bowen and Bok did find that SAT I scores loosely correlated with undergraduate GPA, the magnitude of the effect was small: an additional 100 points in combined SAT I scores was associated with a gain of only 5 percentile points in class rank for African-American students (for all students, the gain hovered just under 6 percentile points; see Bowen & Bok, 1998, pp. 74–75). Such a weak relationship between test scores and class rank calls into question the usefulness of using the SAT I to assess not just African-American students but also students from all racial/ethnic groups.

The SAT I also does a poor job of forecasting the future college performance of older students. Research shows that the test's predictive power is lower for "nontraditional" students who may be out of practice taking timed, multiple-choice exams (Moffat, 1993). For this reason, many colleges and universities do not require applicants who have been out of high school for five years or more, or those over age 25, to submit test scores.

Heavy Reliance on SAT Scores Hinders Educational Equity

Another central reason why many institutions drop SAT and ACT requirements stems from a concern about the impact test scores have on the diversity of their applicant pool and student body. Due to the longstanding race and family income gaps in test scores, a heavy reliance on the exams frequently leads to a student body that is disproportionately white and affluent. After dropping test score requirements, many colleges see a rise in the number of low-income students and people of color, often also accompanied by an increase in academic quality. Several examples illustrate this point.

In *The Case against the SAT*, Crouse and Trusheim (1988) compared two admissions strategies, one using just high school record and the other using high school record and SAT I scores. More than 90% of the admissions decisions were the same under both strategies. However, for the 10% of the applicant pool in which the two strategies led to different admissions decisions, the SAT-based strategy led to a far greater number of rejections of academically qualified African-American and low-income applicants.

In Texas, implementation of the "Top 10%" Law—in which high school seniors in the top tenth of their graduating class are automatically admitted to the University of Texas (UT) campus of their choice regardless of test scores—has helped restore racial diversity at UT-Austin after enrollments by African-American and Latino students plummeted in the wake of the *Hopwood v. Texas* ruling banning affirmative action. Writing in the *Houston Chronicle*, Larry Faulkner, president of the state's flagship campus, explained that the Top 10% Law has "enabled us to diversify enrollment at UT Austin with talented students who succeed" (2001, p. 1).

At Bates College, applications and enrollments of students of color more than doubled during the first five years of going SAT I optional, with these students electing to withhold scores at a significantly higher rate (41%) than the class as a whole (22%). The next two years showed a further broadening of the applicant pool, with a higher number of women, Maine students, and students of color opting not to submit test scores. Academic quality also remained high during this time: while "nonsubmitters" averaged 160 points lower on the SAT I, their FGPA was only .05 points lower than that of "submitters" (Hiss, 1990).

The Impact of Coaching on SAT Scores Widens the Gap between Students

The impact of test-preparation coaching in boosting students' SAT I scores provides another central argument behind the movement to drop test score requirements. In recent years the College Board has backed away from its claim that the SAT I is not coachable, and now sells its own test prep materials. While debate still rages about exactly how much coaching can boost students' scores, there is no doubt that for some test takers the gains are substantial. A number of published studies have concluded that good coaching courses can raise a student's SAT I scores by 100 points or more (Zuman, 1987; National Education Association, 1980; Hopmeier, 1984). These courses, which can cost $800 or more, skew scores in favor of higher-income test takers who already tend to do well on the exam. Because college admissions officials do not know who has been coached and who has not, they cannot fairly compare two applicants' scores. State University of New York-Stony Brook president Shirley Strum Kenny articulated this concern in a letter to the *New York Times*, noting, "The SAT I often rewards test-taking ability more than the ability to do college work. Prominent schools too often 'teach to the test,' and children of parents who can afford coaching buy an unfair advantage. When sixth graders are doing practice problems for the test, something has gone woefully awry" (2001).

Why Any Test at All?

Colleges and universities that have dropped or sharply restricted the use of the SAT I and ACT are widely pleased with the results. Regardless of size or selectivity, these institutions have seen substantial benefits, including increased student diversity, more and better-prepared applicants, and positive reactions from alumni, students, guidance counselors, and the public. Test-optional colleges and universities have not experienced particular difficulties recruiting and selecting their entering classes.

Without the SAT I or ACT, how can colleges and universities select a talented pool of applicants? Many test-score-optional schools evaluate students through a more "holistic" lens, reviewing high school grades, class rank, interviews, extracurricular activities, and rigor of high school classes. Some schools even consider teacher-graded written papers or portfolios, as these provide a way to evaluate the grading standards at a particular high school and answer the concerns raised by testing proponents about the need to have an external or "objective" tool in the admissions process.

Considering an applicant holistically is an approach that works well for large public universities such as UT-Austin. Approximately one-half of the incoming freshman class is filled through the "Top 10%" law. For the rest of its 19,000 applicants, UT considers 19 other items as part of the application. Some of these criteria include academic record in high school; socioeconomic background; if the applicant would be the first generation in a family to attend college; bilingualism; involvement in community activities; commitment to a particular field of study; the applicant's admissions interview; performance on standardized tests as compared with students from similar backgrounds; and a personal essay.

The compilation of this information allows admissions officers to gain a picture of applicants that moves beyond the more traditional numerical index of grades and test scores utilized by many public universities. UT-Austin president Faulkner counters critics' claims that percentage admissions programs exclude students who were "better qualified" on the basis of test scores, noting "top-10-percent students at every level of the SAT-I earn grade point averages that exceed those of non-top-10-percent students, having SAT-I scores that are 200 to 300 points higher" (Faulkner, 2001, p. 1).

Several other public university systems admit a substantial number of students without regard to SAT I or ACT scores when applicants meet certain GPA or class rank requirements. These include the University of Alaska, the California State University system, the University of Minnesota, Montana State University, the Florida State University system, and the University of Wisconsin.

Test-score-optional policies are also a success at smaller, liberal arts colleges. Mount Holyoke College, a selective women's college in Massachusetts, made test scores optional for all applicants in 2001. Data on the first year of enrollees under this policy showed that the high school GPA, class rank, and rigor of courses for test-score "submitters" versus "nonsubmitters" were comparable (Mount Holyoke College, 2001). The change in policy was a welcome one for students of color, who constituted 30% of the applicant pool and 22% of all admitted students, up from 18% the previous year (Constantine, 2001).

Since deciding in 1991 to admit students in the top 10% of their high school class without regard to test scores, Franklin and Marshall College in Lancaster, Pennsylvania, has made a commitment to the thoughtful and individual screening of applicants, using tools more appropriate to their needs than the SAT I. The college requires two graded writing assignments from those who choose not to submit test scores: "We will be looking at a student's command of the language, ability to communicate, and willingness to probe"[2] (Van Buskirk, 1991).

At Wheaton College in Norton, Massachusetts, test scores have been an optional part of the admissions process since 1991. Since that time, the number of applicants has more than quadrupled, with a concomitant rise in the average high school GPA of applicants from 3.2 to 3.5 (Geller, 2002). Racial diversity also increased, with the percentage of minority freshmen nearly doubling over the ten-year period (College Board, 1989, 2000). Committed to comprehensively evaluating students' academic skills, Wheaton requires all applicants to submit a graded, research-based or analytical writing sample and two academic letters of recommendation.

The admissions process at Bates College relies on high school record, essays, recommendations, personal interviews, and student interests in evaluating students. In particular, the Bates staff values the personal interview, noting that "the College remains committed to the personal interview as part of its evaluation, and Bates is bucking a noticeable trend at other similar colleges away from doing personal interviews" (Hiss, 1990, p. 17).

In a recent essay in *The Chronicle of Higher Education*, William Hiss, Vice President for External and Alumni Affairs at Bates College, sounded a

challenge to all institutions—large and small, private and public—to drop
test score requirements:

> Observers often contend that even if optional testing works for Bates, it can't
> be used at a big university with tens of thousands of application... With all due
> respect, that argument is nonsense. Many large universities with tens of thou-
> sands of applicants... read applications carefully and give weight to multiple
> layers of demonstrated talents... [I]nstitutions and states should consider the
> costs of running a reasonably well-staffed admissions office versus the costs of
> throwing away a decent percentage of a college's or state's pool of talent (Hiss,
> 2001, p. B10)

The SAT's weak predictive power, its negative effects on educational equity, and its susceptibility to coaching will not substantially change with
the introduction of a revised exam in 2005. The flaws in the "old" and
"new" SAT should all lead educators to one conclusion—test score requirements can and should be dropped at both large public universities and
small private colleges. The broader goal of higher education—to provide
opportunities to students from diverse backgrounds—is severely truncated
by the employment of test scores. The debate about which test score(s)
to require doesn't acknowledge the larger issue present in reassessing college admissions practices—all current standardized admissions exams act as
gatekeepers for many otherwise talented students. Until university officials
and test makers are willing to confront this fact, shifts in admissions policies
from one test score requirement to another will simply uphold the faulty
paradigm that test scores equal merit and will maintain the narrow pipeline
through which traditionally underrepresented groups struggle to pass.

Notes

This paper was based in part on Rooney C., and Schaeffer, B. (1998). *Test scores do not equal merit:
Enhancing equity and excellence in college admissions by deemphasizing SAT and ACT results.*
Cambridge, MA: National Center for Fair and Open Testing, 1998.

1. See http://www.fairtest.org/univ/optional.htm.
2. Peter Van Buskirk, acting director of Admissions, Franklin and Marshall College, telephone
   interview, July 1991.

References

ACT, Inc. (1998). ACT prediction research summary tables. Iowa City, IA: ACT, Inc.

Adelman, C. (1999). *Answers in the tool box: Academic intensity, attendance patterns, and bachelor's
degree attainment.* Washington, DC: U.S. Department of Education.

Baron, J., & Norman, M. F. (1992). SATs, achievement tests, and high school class rank as predictors
of college performance. *Educational and Psychology Measurement, 52,* pp. 1047–55.

Bowen, W. G., & Bok, D. (1998). *The shape of the river: Long-term consequences of considering race
in college and university admissions.* Princeton, NJ: Princeton University Press.

College Board (1989). *The college handbook 1989–90.* New York: College Board.

College Board (1999). *Counselor's handbook for SAT program 1999–2000.* New York: College Board.

College Board (2000). *The college handbook 2001.* New York: College Board.

Constantine, S. (2001, June 7). Mount Holyoke confident of admissions policy. *Springfield (MA) Union News,* p. B06.

Cowen, S., & Fiori, S. (1991). Appropriateness of the SAT in selecting students for admissions to California State University, Hayward. ERIC document no. 343 934. Paper presented at the annual meeting of the California Educational Research Association, San Diego, November 14–15, 1991.

Crouse, J., & Trusheim, D. (1998). *The case against the SAT.* Chicago: University of Chicago Press.

Faulkner, L. (2001, October 29). By any measure, "top 10 percent" working for UT. *Houston Chronicle,* p. 1.

Geller, M. (2002). Testing requirements aren't what they used to be. Paper presented at a meeting of the New England Association for College Admission Counseling, Fairfield University, Fairfield, CT, May 2002.

Gross, S. (1998, July). *Participation of women and minorities in mathematics.* Department of Educational Accountability, Montgomery County (Maryland) Public Schools.

Hiss, W. E. (1988). Interview with William Hiss. *U.S. News and World Report Online,* http://www.usnews.com/usnews/edu/college/cobates.htm.

Hiss, W. (1990, September). Optional SATs: Six years later. *Bates: The Alumni Magazine.* pp. 15–19.

Hiss, W. (2001, October 26). Optional SATs at Bates: 17 years and not counting. *Chronicle of Higher Education,* p. B10.

Hiss, W. E., Woodcock, E., & McGrath, A. (1984, summer). (At least) twenty questions: Academic criteria, personal qualities, and college admissions. *Journal of College Admissions,* p. 12.

Hopmeier, G. (1984). SAT scores improve 94 points. *Electronic Education, 4(1),* 13–14.

Kenny, S. S. (2001, March 21). SATs have outgrown their usefulness. *New York Times.*

Kessel, C., & Linn, M. (1987). Grades or scores: Predicting future college mathematics performance. *Educational Measurement: Issues and Practice, 15(4),* pp. 10–14.

Leonard, D., & Jiang, J. (1999). Gender bias and the college predictions of the SATs: A Cry of despair. *Research in Higher Education, 40(3),* pp. 375–407.

Linn, M. C., DeBenedictis, T., Delucchi, K., Harris, A., & Stage, E. (1987). Gender differences in national assessment of educational progress science items: What does "don't know" really mean? *Journal of Research in Science Teaching, 24(3),* pp. 267–278.

Moffatt, G. K. (1993). The validity of the SAT as a predictor of grade point average for nontraditional students, paper presented at the annual meeting of the Eastern Educational Research Association, Clearwater Beach, FL.

Mount Holyoke College (2001, November). SAT optional: How are we doing? Available online at http://www.mtholyoke.edu/offices/comm/sat/satupdate111401.shtml. National Education Association (1980). *Measurement and testing: An NEA perspective.* Washington, DC: National Education Association.

Pearson, B. (1993). Predictive validity of the Scholastic Aptitude Test (SAT) for Hispanic bilingual students. *Hispanic Journal of Behavioral Sciences, 15,* pp. 342–55.

Ramist, L., Lewis, C., & McCamley-Jenkins, L. (2001). *Using achievement tests/SAT II: Subject tests to demonstrate achievement and predict college grades: Sex, language, ethnic, and parental education groups.* New York: College Board.

Rosser, P. (1992). *Sex-bais in college admissions tests: Why women lose out,* 4th ed. Cambridge, MA: National Center for Fair and Open Testing.

Tracey, T., & Sedlacek, W. (1985). The relationship of noncognitive variables to academic success: A longitudinal comparison by race. *Journal of College Student Personnel, 26,* pp. 405–10.

Vars, F., & Bowen, W. (1988). Scholastic Aptitude Test scores, race, and academic performance in selective colleges and universities. In C. Jencks and M. Phillips (Eds.), *The black-white test score gap* (pp. 457–79). Washington, DC: Brookings Institute.

Wainer, H., & Steinberg, L. S. (1992). Sex differences in performance on the mathematics section of the Scholastic Aptitude Test: A bidirectional validity study. *Harvard Educational Review, 62(3),* pp. 323–336.

Zuman, J. (1987). The effectiveness of special preparation for the SAT: An evaluation of a commercial coaching school. Ph.D. diss., Graduate School of Education, Harvard University.

Commentary on Part IV: Predicting Student Performance in College

ROBERT L. LINN

It is difficult to imagine a topic that has been the focus of more empirical research than the prediction of student performance in college. Literally thousands of analyses involving millions of students have been conducted by ACT, Inc. and the College Board, using tests and high school grades as predictors of success at individual colleges and universities. The most common measure of success in these studies has been freshman grade point average, but a number of other criterion measures have also been used, including, but not limited to, grades in individual courses, four-year cumulative grade point average, graduation, and ratings by faculty. For the past three decades many of the studies of the predictive value of tests have compared the validities and prediction equations obtained for subgroups of students defined by gender, race/ethnicity and disability status.

Although a great deal is already known about the degree to which tests predict academic success of students from different backgrounds, both the context in which these results are to be interpreted and the implications of the results for making college admissions decisions have changed. Two major changes in context that stimulated the research reported in this part of the volume are (1) the elimination in California, Florida, Texas, and Washington state of affirmative action admissions policies that explicitly take race or ethnic status into account, as well as the legal challenges to these policies in Michigan, and (2) the proposal put forward by the president of the University of California system, Richard C. Atkinson (2001) that the SAT I be phased out and be replaced by the SAT II.

As William Bowen and Derek Bok (1998) have clearly articulated, there are many perceived benefits to having a diverse student body and it is not surprising that most universities have had diversity as one of their goals for their admissions policies. The most direct, but controversial way of achieving a diverse student body is to have a race-sensitive affirmative action admissions process. With the elimination of race-sensitive admissions processes, universities are faced with a challenge if they want to achieve diversity while still giving preference to the students who are best prepared to pursue college work. The chapters here by Christina Perez and Roger Studley address this challenge most directly and propose quite different solutions. The Perez solution is simply to eliminate tests from consideration in admissions. This approach has found favor in institutions such as Bates College. Perez claims that holistic evaluations of student records without test scores work well to achieve diversity regardless of the size or selectivity of the institution. She does not present evidence to support this claim, however. Nor is it clear that such an approach avoids the introduction of subjective biases in admissions decisions or that it leads to the selection of underrepresented minority students who are best prepared to be academically successful.

Studley's approach is quite different from the one suggested by Perez. He responded directly to the charge in the University of California Regents' resolution that consideration be given to individuals who are economically or socially disadvantaged but have outperformed the expectations of their backgrounds. Studley demonstrates that by using what amounts to a statistical adjustment of test scores and high school grades for socioeconomic status, neighborhood, and school while ignoring race/ethnicity, a freshman class could be selected that has approximately the same degree of racial/ethnic diversity that was achieved in the past using a race-sensitive affirmative action approach. Studley acknowledges that there may be some practical difficulties in implementing his approach and there would be a need to assure that applicants would not provide misleading background information that would be used in the adjustments. Nonetheless, the approach appears quite promising and worthy of serious consideration along with other alternatives to achieving diversity without explicit consideration of race/ethnicity.

John Young reviews analyses of differential validity and differential prediction as a function of gender and race/ethnicity. He notes that validities tend to be somewhat lower for men than for women and that college grades tend to be underpredicted for women and overpredicted for men. He also reports slightly lower validities for African-American and Hispanic students than for white and Asian-American students and the now familiar finding that college grades of African-American and Hispanic students tend to be slightly overpredicted. Young suggests that the lower validities for African-American and Hispanic students than for white students might be used as a reason to give less weight to test scores for African-American and Hispanic students than for white students. It should be noted, however, that the slightly lower validity finding is not universal. Other meta-analyses have found that validities are as high or even higher for African-American and Hispanic students than they are for white students (e.g., Bridgeman, McCamley-Jenkins, & Ervin, 2001). It is also the case that the use of a single prediction equation for all students has a slight benefit built into it already to the degree that the grades are overpredicted for African-American and Hispanic students.

The chapters by Jennifer Kobrin, Wayne Camara, and Glenn Milewski and Brent Bridgeman, Nancy Burton, and Fredrick Cline provide explicit comparisons of the predictive value of the SAT I and the SAT II. Although Kobrin and colleagues found that the prediction of freshman grades was slightly better with the combination of high school grades and the SAT II than with high school grades and the SAT I, the difference is trivial. If one is to choose between the two tests, or for that matter, among the SAT I, the SAT II and the ACT, the justification would be better made on grounds other than predictive accuracy. It is clear from the Bridgeman, Burton and Cline results that for the substantial majority of students, the same admission decision would be made using high school grades together with either the SAT I or the SAT II. Bridgeman and colleagues also found that the proportion of students achieving a grade point average of 2.5 or above would not be altered by the choice of the test to combine with high school grades. Moreover, the choice between the SAT I and the SAT II has very little impact on the percentage of accepted students who are African-American or Hispanic. The difference in percentages is so small that it would not be noticed by a casual inspection of the makeup of the classes. On the other hand, Bridgeman and colleagues are correct to point out that from the perspective of Hispanic ESL (English as a second language) students, the likelihood of being selected if the SAT II were used is noticeably higher than it would be if the SAT I were used.

Julie Noble's chapter is the only one in the set that focuses on the use of the ACT for African-American, Hispanic, and white students. In addition to investigating the differential prediction, Noble studied the differential effects as judged by the percentage of students in each group who would be admitted according to a specified admissions rule (i.e., the probability of obtaining a grade point average of at least 2.5 is greater than a fixed value). Consistent with the common overprediction finding for African-American and Hispanic students, Noble displays logistic regression results that show the probability of obtaining a GPA of 2.5 or higher is greater throughout the range of predictor scores for white students than for African-American or Hispanic students. This finding holds using either the ACT alone, high school grades alone, or the two together. The comparisons of the logistic regression results are a useful way to look at the implications of differential prediction.

Collectively, the chapters in this part of the volume present a number of important findings and perspectives on the prediction of success in college for students from a variety of backgrounds. Most of the results are consistent with previously reported research and thus reconfirm earlier findings. An exception is the finding in the Studley chapter that by taking into account socioeconomic status together with neighborhood and school, the use of test and high school grade residual scores can accomplish much of what is achieved by race-sensitive affirmative action. This result deserves further consideration.

References

Atkinson, R. C. (2001). Standardized tests and access to American Universities. The 2001 Robert H. Atwell Distinguished Lecture, delivered at the 83rd Annual Meeting of the American Council on Education, Washington, DC, February 18, 2001.

Bowen, W. G., & Bok, D. (1998). *The shape of the river: Long-term consequences of considering race in college and university admissions.* Princeton, NJ: Princeton University Press.

Bridgeman, B., McCamley-Jenkins, L., & Ervin, N. (2001). *Predictions of freshman grade-point average from the revised and recentered SAT I: Reasoning Test.* Research Report No. 2001.1. New York: College Board.

Author Index

Subject Index

Academic achievement, 167–170, 176, 178, 184–185, 235–237, 239, 241, 248
achievement tests. *See* ACT, Advanced Placement Tests, California High School Exit Exam, Iowa Tests of Educational Development, National Assessment of Educational Progress, SAT II Subject Tests
aptitude versus achievement test distinction, xiii, 7–8, 12–13, 14, 15–22, 35, 37, 41–54, 97, 104, 109, 112, 114–118, 125–151, 277–287, 324–326
See also under Ethnic group differences, Gender group differences, Socioeconomic group differences
ACT, xiii, 25–32, 107, 191, 204–205, 304–317
as a measure of achievement, 11, 25–27, 47–49, 107, 204–205
history, xii-xiii, 109–111
predictive validity of, 28, 306–317, 247–248, 357–358
See also under Ethnic group differences, Gender group differences, Socioeconomic group differences

Advanced Placement Tests, 11, 12, 94
Affirmative action, ix–x, 13, 16, 178, 303, 317–318, 322–324, 326, 333–334, 336–337, 339, 341–342n.2, 342n.7, 355–356
socioeconomically-based, 321–341
African Americans, 38, 49–50, 140–146, 167–169, 176–177, 191–198, 245–248, 257–260, 266–275, 282, 291–296, 298–300, 303–304, 306–317, 322, 324, 329, 332, 335–336, 338, 342n.12
See also Ethnic group differences
American College Testing Program. *See* ACT
American Indians. *See* Native Americans
Aptitude
aptitude versus achievement test controversy. *See under* Academic achievement
crystallized versus fluid abilities, 47–54
Asian Americans, 49–50, 140–146, 151, 167–169, 191–197, 246–247, 257–260, 266–275, 282–283, 291–296, 298–300, 303–304, 322, 324, 332, 335–336
See also Ethnic group differences